Diagnosis and Correction of Reading Difficulties

Barbara E. R. Swaby

Allyn and Bacon

Boston   London   Sydney   Toronto

Copyright © 1989 by Allyn and Bacon
A Division of Simon & Schuster
160 Gould Street
Needham Heights, MA 02194

Series Editor: Sean W. Wakely
Production Coordinator: Annette Joseph
Editorial-Production Service: The Book Department
Cover Administrator: Linda K. Dickinson
Cover Designer: Christy Rosso

Library of Congress Cataloging-in-Publication Data

Swaby, Barbara E. R.
   Diagnosis and correction of reading
difficulties.

   Bibliography: p.
   Includes indexes.
   1. Reading disability.   2. Reading–
Remedial teaching.   I. Title.
LB1050.5.S92   1989   428.4'2   88-34397
ISBN 0-205-11848-8

Printed in the United States of America

10 9 8 7 6 5 4 3 2 1   94 93 92 91 90 89

Photo Credits
Ulrike Welsch: 3, 56, 129, 165, 232, 326, 384
Erika Stone: 17, 80, 112, 144, 301, 344
Susan Van Etten: 184, 262

To my parents,
Herbert and Gwendolyn Swaby,
and my son, David

Overview

Contents

PART TWO   CORRECTION   127

Preface

The acquisition of reading may be considered one of the most valuable gifts society can give to its children. Indeed, reading is such an important tool that it is a mistake to think of it as a skill; rather, it is a means of achieving success in our society and an essential extension of literacy. As critical as reading is, however, an estimated 40 million Americans are functionally illiterate, and an additional 1.3 million young people join the ranks of the functionally illiterate each year. Obviously, despite valiant efforts of committed teachers to articulate reading curricula accurately and precisely, many of our nation's children have lost the right to literacy.

This text is built on the premise that there are two broad categories of learners: inductive or traditional learners and noninductive or nontraditional learners. Inductive learners are those who, based on their learning rates, learning styles, sensory strengths, concepts, content and vocabulary knowledge, ability to learn in a variety of ways, and ability to process information from the parts to the whole, often find success and ease in learning to read from traditional reading curricula. It is my contention that these learners succeed because they possess the prerequisites demanded by traditional reading programs. Noninductive learners are those who, based on their learning rates, learning styles, sensory profiles, concepts, content and vocabulary knowledge, and concept dependence, find it extremely difficult to learn to read from traditional reading curricula. They find it difficult because they lack the prerequisites demanded by their reading programs. Children succeed or fail in reading programs because they possess or lack the prerequisites for success established within the pedagogy of those programs. This premise guides the entire content of my text.

Because I believe that learning to read is prerequisite based, I view curriculum-focused instruction as ultimately responsible for the reading failure of many children. Every program requires certain prerequisites for success. Strict adherence to programs means that children who do not have the necessary prerequisites will most likely fail. The second major premise of this book, then, is that in order to prevent or to remediate failure, all reading curricula must be modified to meet the needs of children. For all children, but particularly for children who have failed in traditional reading systems, success depends on the willingness and ability of teachers to modify material according to the observed strengths and needs of children. I place major emphasis on the daily observation of children and the continual changing of materials and instruction based on observed needs.

The text has two major divisions: diagnosis and correction. The first five chapters discuss both formal and informal diagnosis. Continuous observation is emphasized. Teachers are encouraged to be cautious in the use and interpretation of formal measures. Chapters 6–15 focus on a wide variety of corrective measures. The text adheres to psycholinguistic theory, which places primary emphasis on the importance of prior knowledge in reading. This theory views reading as an active, information-seeking activity in which a reader brings to bear prior knowledge and links that knowledge with all incoming information. Interactive teaching is therefore vital. All discussion of remediation relies on the psycholinguistic framework.

My priority during preparation has been the merging of theory and teaching practice. The text provides clear, practical, and realistic research-based information, and uses a myriad of instruction-based illustrations and case studies.

The text is written for prospective and practicing teachers. It is extremely readable, and gives preservice teachers an accurate and clear view of classroom reality. It describes practices that are research based and student focused. For inservice teachers, the text provides a vehicle for analyzing and monitoring current instructional practices. The text presents a wide range of instructional options and gives teachers permission to teach children rather than curricula.

The book includes a chapter on a comparatively new topic, neurolinguistic programming. For the past three years, I have been utilizing neurolinguistic strategies in our reading clinics at the University of Colorado, with dramatic results. I believe that the content will greatly assist teachers.

A number of people were instrumental in providing me with valuable assistance. I would like to thank Mylan Jaixen, whose support of my work encouraged me to submit my manuscript to Allyn and Bacon. I would also like to acknowledge the editorial staff of Allyn and Bacon, particularly Sean Wakely, who offered capable leadership. I sincerely thank my reviewers, who provided valuable and constructive guidance: Nancy Clements, Ball State University; Roger DeSanti, University of New Orleans; and Norman Koch, Western Oregon State College.

My thanks also to my typist, Kris Fisher, who spent many hours typing, retyping, and revising my text. Finally, my sincere appreciation to my dear son, David, who patiently and generously fended for himself for hundreds of hours as I prepared this manuscript.

B.S.

PART ONE

DIAGNOSIS

1 A Definition of Diagnosis

FOCUS
QUESTIONS
1. How is diagnosis defined in this chapter?
2. What are the basic elements of diagnosis?
3. How does the definition of diagnosis affect instruction?
4. What is the role of instructional modification in diagnostic teaching?
5. Why is the concept of change important in diagnosis?
6. What is the difference between formal and informal diagnosis?

Children can learn to read. It is a psychological imperative that those involved in teaching children and others to read believe this. Learning to read is a comparatively easy task. You know this if you have had an opportunity to observe a young child develop reading at home prior to formal reading instruction. There seems to be a natural progression in learning to read at home. First, the children are frequently read to by parents, siblings, or other more mature readers (Dunn 1981; Taylor 1983). The children often have a favorite book or set of books that they insist on hearing repeatedly, sometimes to the annoyance of those who read to them. The children hear, observe, internalize, and respond emotionally to oral and written language. Second, they begin to memorize segments of or entire favorite selections. As they are read to, they "read along" with their parents on the segments they know. They develop a sense of involvement and of anticipation. They know what events to expect and begin to develop a natural sense of order. Notice, for example, how difficult it is to fool them. Try skipping a segment or paraphrasing in order to finish the story more quickly. They call you on it every time—and correct you as well. They have a clear, emerging sense of prediction. Third, children begin to "read" independently. They might pick up a book and read to themselves, paraphrasing the segments they do not know verbatim, and repeating the segments they have memorized. Fourth, children become curious about individual words. They continually ask, What does this word spell? Where is the word ____? What is this word? What does this word say? They slowly begin to learn individual words. This process allows them to begin building a strong sight vocabulary—something which is essential to success in reading. Fifth, children begin abstracting letter-sound relationships. They use this knowledge in concert with their strong sense of context (Ehri and Wilce 1985). Finally, children read material independently. Notice the progression: reading *to* children, reading *with* children, and reading *by* children. This process of developing "into" reading does not seem to be related to intellectual giftedness (Cassidy and Vukelich 1980). Children differing greatly in intellectual capability go through this process all the time. We can make important observations as we see this process develop easily and naturally in many young children.

1. They learn by choosing their own sensory strengths. If they are strong auditorily, they tend to learn the symbol-sound system quickly and also to develop phonic abilities easily. If they are strong visually, they tend to depend on their ability to learn sight vocabulary quickly. It is easier for them to choose their area of strength because the whole of reading is presented to them, and in processing this whole they naturally gravitate toward their specific areas of strength. They are successful because they build on their strengths.

2. They first internalize what reading is; then they take steps toward decoding (Harste et al. 1982). They know that reading makes sense and should make sense. They anticipate meaning and make meaningful predictions. They expect to be entertained, amused, or informed by print. They expect their guesses about words to make sense and to fit the contexts in which they occur. Children seem to approach the task of reading with a high degree of meaning anticipation. They also have a certainty that they "can" indeed read. Reading is a surmountable task, something that can and does happen for them.

Therefore, learning to read is not difficult. Why, then, do so many children in school fail to learn to read? Why do so many children exposed to years of teaching and remediation still fail? One of the reasons is the confusion many teachers have between teaching a program, a set of materials, or a series, and teaching children to read (Smith 1971). Understanding the difference is vital to understanding the nature of reading failure and of remediation. If the major thrust is on teaching a program, then the focus becomes getting the material completed regardless of the needs, strengths, motivations, and learning characteristics of children. In this case, strategies and methods of reading instruction provided in the material are presented, repeated, and drilled, despite the failure of many children to learn, comprehend, and retain. Instructional options are rarely based on children's needs. Persistent failure or very slow growth often results. The children eventually dislike reading and divest themselves of any interaction with print.

If, on the other hand, the major thrust is on teaching a child, then the focus is on the child. The question How does this child best learn? becomes dominant. The child's basic strengths and weaknesses are assessed. The material and its demands are assessed. The teacher attempts to find the strategies that will allow the child to learn to read. On the basic assumption that the child can learn, the teacher explores instructional options suited to the child's needs.

The two points of view result in different instructional and remedial approaches, as the following examples show.

THE PROGRAM-CENTERED VIEW

Mr. Walker teaches second grade. He has a low reading group that hasn't shown much progress for four months. The basal reader adopted by his school presents a strong phonic program. The students in his low group are still in the first grade reader. They move very slowly through the basal. Their major problem seems to be the workbook; they still can't "get" symbol-sound relationships. They tend to go through the teaching, reteaching cycle a few times for each skill before they can pass the assessment test. Because they move so slowly, the students have acquired a limited sight vocabulary. They lose interest quickly and seem unmotivated during reading. Mr. Walker spends hours each week drilling the children on the skills. However, even when they successfully complete a skill lesson in the workbook, they seem unable to transfer that skill to actual reading. Because they learn skills so slowly, the entire reading period is often nearly over before they finish their skill work. They spend a minimum of the reading period actually reading from the text. Mr. Walker greatly empathizes with this group. He feels frustrated and wishes the students would learn the material more quickly. He sees continual drills as the only alternative, and hopes for a breakthrough.

THE CHILD-CENTERED VIEW

Ms. Bell is a second grade teacher. She has a low reading group that began the second grade reading in the first grade primer. After a month of instruction in her heavily phonic-oriented basal reader, Ms. Bell noticed that the low group was moving very slowly, making hardly any progress at all. At that time, Ms. Bell decided to take a closer look at the children in the group. All children were not learning, remembering, and internalizing phonic skills. They all had difficulty with auditory discrimination and blending. They tended to learn sight vocabulary such as *in, on, for, the,* and *them* very slowly. However, they easily learned such words as *house, alligator, school,* and *hamburger.* Ms. Bell decided to make some changes in her reading program.

1. Each child kept a word bank of favorite words and reviewed the words daily.
2. On the front of each word card was the "easy to learn" favorite word, e.g., *house.* On the back was the same word with one or two "hard to learn" words arranged in a phrase, e.g., *in the house.* Children practiced the words and phrases daily.
3. Each day before the children began reading, Ms. Bell introduced four or five new vocabulary items from the story. Children reviewed the words daily and used them in their spare time to play word games.
4. Ms. Bell continued to emphasize the basal reader, but illus-

trated isolated phonic skills presented in the workbook by showing how each skill was used in the reading selections.

5. Ms. Bell made a conscious effort to have the low group read from the book for at least half of the reading period each day. She felt that the children should be immersed in print as much as possible.

After making these changes, Ms. Bell began to see marked improvement in the children's reading. They were improving in decoding, word recognition, and comprehension. They also had positive attitudes and were motivated toward reading.

The first teacher taught a program and did it well. However, children who could not learn in that way did not learn. The second teacher also taught a program, but her focus was on children. She assessed the children's strengths and weaknesses, built on the strengths, and remediated the weaknesses. This ability to modify programs based on the needs of children seems to be the most central issue in the successful remediation of reading difficulties.

One reason the child-centered teacher was more effective was her internalization of the basic elements of diagnostic remediation. She practiced diagnostic instruction—instruction based on the diagnosis of children's strengths and weaknesses.

BASIC ELEMENTS OF DIAGNOSIS

Diagnosis is often presented as a dual concept including both formal and informal assessment (see Figure 1.1). Formal assessment refers to the administration of standardized instruments focusing on a variety of reading skills and yielding scores used to assess general and specific reading performance. Informal diagnosis refers to continuous teacher-directed

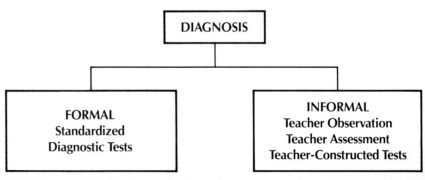

FIGURE 1.1   The Dual Nature of Diagnosis

analysis of students' reading behavior based on their actual reading performance.

Formal and informal diagnosis will be discussed in detail in Chapters 3 and 4. There are, however, basic elements which form the foundation of any diagnosis, whether formal or informal. In order to become maximally effective in diagnosing students' needs, you need to ask: What is my focus? What process does diagnosis follow? In order to begin answering these two important questions, you need to know the basic elements of diagnosis.

Diagnosis can be conceptualized as a four-sided model (see Figure 1.2). As the model suggests, in both formal and informal diagnosis equal weight is placed on four dimensions—analysis, measurement, evaluation, and change.

Analysis refers to the continuous and careful observation of a range of student behaviors to identify areas of strength and need in relation to reading performance. The following example demonstrates a practical application of the concept of analysis.

CLASSROOM APPLICATION

I teach third grade. My student of focus is John, a nine-year-old boy reading from the beginning second grade reader. My analysis of John involves answering general and specific questions about his performance.

General Analysis

- What is John's general attitude toward reading?
- What parts of reading does he enjoy? dislike?
- What are John's general areas of strength? (E.g., he knows the initial consonant sounds, and he performs well on literal comprehension.)
- What are John's general areas of weakness? (E.g., he blends sounds poorly and miscalls vowel sounds.)
- What motivates John to read? (E.g., he likes self-competition, timed readings, free time, and particular reading topics.)

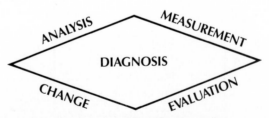

FIGURE 1.2   Four Dimensions of Diagnosis

Specific Analysis

- What are John's specific areas of strength in phonics? (E.g., John knows all of the consonants and consonant blends except *x, w, h, br, tr, fr,* and *sp.*)
- What are John's specific areas of need in word recognition? (E.g., John is weak on such structure words as *them, enough,* and *though.*)
- What are John's areas of strength and weakness in comprehension? (E.g., John responds correctly to most literal questions, but not to inferences, generalizations, predictions, etc.)
- Are there any noticeable physical problems? (E.g., John leans forward when he reads and has difficulty hearing differences and similarities among words.)

Thorough analysis provides the information needed for measurement. Measurement refers to the administration of a test—formal or informal—in order to obtain a score or set of scores related to student performance. Measurement relates to analysis in that a test is often given because certain characteristics or behaviors have been noted. Giving a test because you have observed or analyzed something important is certainly more useful than giving a test simply because it is "that time of year" or because it is expected in a job.

CLASSROOM APPLICATION

1. My analysis of John noted that he has difficulty hearing differences and similarities among words. I chose to administer an auditory discrimination test to determine the extent of the problem.
2. My analysis showed a weakness in vowels. I chose to administer a self-made test of long and short vowel recognition and production.
3. In order to assess John's vocabulary performance, I will make a record of his word recognition errors for three or four days.

The information gained both from analysis and from measurements needs to be analyzed and evaluated to determine patterns of strengths and needs.

Evaluation refers to the careful examination of the measurement scores to identify specific skill strengths, skill weaknesses, and patterns or trends in errors.

CLASSROOM APPLICATION

1. The auditory discrimination test shows that John does not hear differences and similarities between words. This is particularly difficult when the contrast is at the end or in the middle (e.g., *pat* and *pam* or *pat* and *pet*). I knew then that phonics was going to be extremely difficult for him. In addition to providing practice in discrimination,

I may need to emphasize sight vocabulary until his phonic skills begin to develop more fully.

2. John does not recognize any short vowel sounds. Considering his auditory discrimination problems, I'm certainly not surprised. He can't distinguish the differences among the sounds.

3. John's word recognition errors show that he has difficulty with such structure words as *them*, *through*, *how*, and *must*. He rarely misses content words that have been pre-taught in a group. He uses context fairly well.

Evaluation helps identify the way instruction must be modified in order to establish growth.

Change refers to the modification of instructional strategies to bring about positive changes in students' reading. If a child is not successful in reading, instruction might need to change in order for performance to improve. If you change the way you teach the child and if you change the tasks the child must practice, then the child's performance will probably also change. Notice that change goes in both directions.

CLASSROOM APPLICATION

1. Since John has great difficulty distinguishing differences in the middle and at the end of words, he needs practice in this skill. For two to five minutes a day, then, I might play the "same-different" game with John. I could assign a student from the high or average reading group or from a higher grade level to do this. At the same time, I will present phonic information through word patterns, e.g., *at*, *pat*, *hat*, *rat*, *sat*. He will also be exposed to whole reading tasks emphasizing comprehension. In this way, John will be progressing in reading while he is being remediated in phonics.

2. In order to help John remember the vowel sounds, I will use the "magic picture" technique. Each week we will focus on one vowel. John will tell me his favorite word beginning with each vowel. Picture dictionaries will provide ideas. John will learn to look at the letter, e.g., *e*, and to recall his picture for *e*, e.g., elephant. This will help him to retrieve the isolated sound /e/.

3. John will begin to keep a word bank. The bank will be filled with note cards. The front of each card will present an "easy to learn" word (e.g., *table*). The back will show a phrase incorporating "hard to learn" words (e.g., *on the table*). John will review these cards daily. Sight vocabulary will be emphasized.

4. As John reads daily, I will encourage him to use his fairly well developed skills in the use of context to assist him in recognizing words more quickly.

These four concepts form the basic elements of diagnosis: *analysis of reading behavior*, *measurement of reading ability and skills*, *evaluation* of reading performance, and *change* of teaching strategies and children's reading profile. Notice the difficulty of divorcing diagnosis from remediation. It is pointless to diagnose if remedial steps are not taken. Similarly, remediation is pointless if diagnostic steps have not been taken.

DEVELOPING A DIAGNOSTIC ATTITUDE

Internalization of the basic elements of diagnosis allows you, as a teacher, to develop an appropriate attitude toward instruction—a diagnostic attitude. Effective diagnosis and remediation depend on this attitude. Effective diagnosis is not a "thing" that one does; rather, it is what one "is" as a teacher. A diagnostic attitude is like the skill that a good detective strives to develop: looking for all possible clues enabling you to solve a puzzle successfully. A child with a reading problem is comparable to a puzzle. The child should be able to make progress in reading. The child can learn.

Reading problems have no simple answers. On the contrary, many children have complex reading problems requiring careful and competent instruction. Many such problems cannot be "fixed" quickly and simply. Not all children will be able to read on grade level and to perform at average expected levels. All children, however, can progress in reading, at least from point A to point B. Teachers should expect progress from children and should arrange instruction to facilitate progress. If appropriate progress is not taking place, something has gone wrong—the puzzle needs to be solved. Clues for solving the puzzle have three sources: the child, the material being taught, and the instructional methods being used to teach the child. The purpose of this text is to assist you in gathering diagnostic information and in choosing strategies that will help solve reading difficulties. The following list identifies the most important clues and their sources.

Factors within the Child

Interest and motivation
History of reading success and failure
Constitutional abilities (e.g., auditory, visual, intellectual, memory, attention)
Emotional level (e.g., tension, fear, frustration, embarrassment)
Vocabulary strength and weakness (e.g., sight and meaning)
Phonic strength and weakness (e.g., consonants, vowels, segmentation, blending, rules, use of phonics)
Comprehension ability (e.g., literal comprehension, inferential thinking, prediction, problem solving, creative thinking, ability to visualize)

Factors in the Material

Vocabulary demands (e.g., sight vocabulary, meaning vocabulary, phonic analysis necessary for decoding)

Conceptual demands (e.g., experiences necessary for comprehension, thinking skills necessary for understanding)

Concentration demands (e.g., length of passage)

Structural demands (e.g., syntactic complexity, syntactic clarity)

Factors within Instruction

Strategies that work for individual children, small groups, and large groups

Strategies that do not work for individual children, small groups, and large groups

Strategies that work with specific content

Strategies that do not work with specific content

Notice that these factors relate directly to the elements of diagnosis discussed earlier in the chapter. Analysis of children's performance, of the material, and of the instructional strategies gives you the necessary clues. Based on the clues you find, you measure performance for specific data. The data allow you to evaluate strengths and needs, to evaluate text demands, and to choose instructional strategies that will cause positive changes in students.

A WORKING DEFINITION OF DIAGNOSIS

The essence of diagnosis can be expressed in the following working definition:

Diagnosis is an ongoing procedure that involves continuous analysis of students' behavior, measurement of samples of that behavior, careful evaluation of the measurement results, and change of instructional strategies that results in positive changes in the students' behavior.

This definition contains six important concepts.

1. *Ongoing Procedure.* In order to be effective, diagnosis must be a continuous procedure. Teachers often tend to equate diagnosis with the use of formal standardized tests. Although formal testing is a part of diagnosis, the concept of diagnosis is much broader (Harris and Sipay 1980, Ekwall and Shanker 1983). Diagnosis is an ongoing procedure. Children's total behavior provides vital information that can be used to diagnose strengths and weaknesses.

2. *Continuous Analysis.* Each reading session is an opportunity to gather clues vital to the diagnosis of needs and the remediation of difficulties. Throughout each reading period you should listen to children read and observe their reading behavior. You might focus on children's attitudes toward reading, the language clues they use or ignore, the integration of skills in actual reading, and other reading behaviors.

3. *Sample Measurement.* Once you have identified an area of concern, you might create an informal assessment tool or use a preconstructed test to measure more accurately children's needs. Remember that most tests assess only a sample of the particular skill or of the student's knowledge base. Make an effort to test as large a sample of skills as possible to gain an accurate measure of what children know and need.

4. *Evaluation of Results.* Using the sample measurement, analyze the results carefully to ascertain specific skill strengths, specific error patterns, and the seriousness or urgency of specific problems.

5. *Change in Instructional Strategies.* If children have failed in one instructional setting, the failure must be due at least in part to the instructional strategies used. For successful remediation, the instructional strategies used in the past should be at least partially changed. Modify your presentation of material to better meet children's needs. Remember that it is your analysis of how children best learn that helps you choose the appropriate instructional strategies.

6. *Change in Student's Behavior.* When instruction is appropriately changed, the child's behavior will change and the pattern of failure will become a pattern of greater success. It is unrealistic to believe that all children will learn to read on grade level. The major goal for all children is individual growth, not equal levels of performance.

This definition of diagnosis has clear, direct implications for classroom instruction, as the following example shows.

CLASSROOM APPLICATION

Eian is a seven-year-old boy in the first semester of first grade. He repeated his kindergarten year because he showed no progress in reading readiness. Eian's emotional and developmental levels are appropriate for kindergarten. He likes first grade, interacts well with other children, follows directions, and is willing to work. His math performance is appropriate. Ms. Payne is his first grade teacher.

Ongoing Procedure

During the first month of first grade, Ms. Payne noted that Eian still had difficulty instantly recognizing several letters and letter sounds. It was generally difficult for him to identify beginning sounds, to rhyme, and to blend isolated sounds into whole words.

Continuous Analysis

Once actual reading instruction began, Ms. Payne noted that Eian experienced great difficulty learning letter sounds and used little or no phonic knowledge to guess at words. For example, Eian would see the word *will* and say *go*, or would see the word *the* and say *she*. However, Eian easily recognized his name in print, and knew the words *school*, *McDonald's*, and *elephant* by memory. Eian enjoyed listening to stories. He was able to discuss them fully when asked to do so. In addition, during reading sessions, he would answer questions based on the oral reading of other children. Eian started out with great zest for learning, but after the first month of school he became more quiet, withdrawn, and anxious to avoid reading.

Sample Measurement

After the first month of phonic instruction following the basal reader format, Eian continued to fail. At this point, Ms. Payne decided that she would test Eian informally. She constructed the following simple tests:

- Naming the letters of the alphabet
- Producing letter sounds
- Auditory discrimination
  For this test, she used pairs of words such as *hat/hate, rat/rate, bed/bad, press/dress, fed/led, mitt/met.* She said each pair to Eian and asked him to indicate whether the words were the same or different.

- Auditory segmentation and blending
  For this test, she segmented such words as *hat* (/h/ /a/ /t/) and *stop* /st/ /o/ /p/), and asked Eian to blend the sounds into whole words.
- Visual form memory
  For this test, she taught Eian five meaningful words by sight: *dog, boy, cat, girl,* and *chair.*

Evaluation of Results

The results showed that:

- Eian knew twenty letter names.
- Eian knew the sounds represented by the letters *b, d, f, g, c, k, m, n, p, r,* and *s.*
- Eian's auditory discrimination was weak, particularly for the vowel sounds.
- Eian could not blend any segmented words.
- Eian learned four out of five sight words and retained them over an instructional session.

From these results Ms. Payne concluded that Eian had underdeveloped auditory skills, but good visual skills. She realized that she was using a strongly phonic-based reading program, and since phonics demands strong auditory abilities, she knew that Eian would not be successful unless she made some instructional adjustments.

Change in Instructional Strategies

Ms. Payne made necessary modifications in her reading program. Eian continued to receive instruction and practice in letters and letter sounds. However, he also received strong sight vocabulary instruction. Sight words were always highly meaningful. When high-frequency structure words were introduced, they were always paired with meaningful content words. Once a week Ms. Payne taught a language experience lesson to Eian's reading group, and after the lesson each child received a copy of the story to take home and practice. In addition, once a week Ms. Payne read a short, simple, highly predictable print book to the entire class. She read it two or three times and encouraged the children to "read along" using the strongly predictable pattern. At the end of the session, Ms. Payne encouraged Eian to use that book in the daily free reading session. She asked Eian to choose from the story two words that he wanted to learn. He added these to his word collection for daily review.

Change in Student Behavior

Eian is now in the fourth month of first grade. He still does not know all of the letter sounds, particularly the vowel sounds. He still has great difficulty with auditory segmentation and blending. Eian is reading well in his reading group, however, and is developing a very strong sight vocabulary, which enables him to read many easy books. He loves to read, and once in a while he correctly sounds out a word and grins widely at his success. In her treatment of Eian, Ms. Payne has followed the definition of diagnosis.

The definition of diagnosis is practical. It can be translated directly into classroom realities. Internalizing and practicing the procedure leads you to behave in ways that are necessary to diagnostic teaching.

SUMMARY   Many teachers think of diagnosis as something that happens a few times a year when they administer mandatory standardized tests. Although formal testing is a significant part of diagnosis, the most essential part happens on a daily basis. Most daily diagnosis is made not with tests, but with teachers' observations—the careful use of eyes, ears, and sensibilities. Diagnosis begins with analysis and ends with change in the total learning environment. Practice leads to diagnostic teaching in which the focus is on helping each child learn in a way that is most successful for the child.

R · E · F · E · R · E · N · C · E · S

Cassidy, J., and Carol Vukelich. "Do the gifted read early?" *The Reading Teacher* 33 (February 1980): 578–582.

Dunn, N. E. "Children's achievement at school-entry age as a function of mothers' and fathers' teaching sets." *Elementary School Journal* 81 (1981): 244–253.

Ehri, L. C., and L. S. Wilce. "Movement into reading: Is the first stage of printed word learning visual or phonetic?" *Reading Research Quarterly* 20 (1985): 163–179.

Ekwall, E. E., and J. L. Shanker. *Diagnosis and Remediation of the Disabled Reader*, 2nd ed. Boston: Allyn and Bacon, 1983.

Harris, A. J., and E. R. Sipay. *How to Increase Reading Ability*, 7th ed. New York: Longman, 1980.

Harste, J. C., C. L. Burke, and V. A. Woodward. "Children's Language and World: Initial Encounters with Print." In J. Langer and M. Trika Smith–Burke, eds. *Reader Meets Author: Bridging The Gap.* Newark, DE: International Reading Association, 1982.

Smith, F. *Understanding Reading.* New York: Holt, Rinehart and Winston, 1971.

Taylor, D. *Family Literacy: Young Children Learning to Read and Write.* Exeter, NH: Heinemann, 1983.

2 Correlates of Reading Failure

FOCUS
QUESTIONS

1. What are the major causes of reading failure?
2. What instructional behaviors contribute to failure in reading?
3. What emotional factors contribute to reading success?
4. How does oral language development relate to reading development?
5. Why is it important that teachers understand reasons for reading failure?

Failure in reading is a complex issue often affected by several factors. This chapter focuses on a variety of correlates of reading disabilities. Correlates are factors that relate to reading failure. Remember that a correlate is not necessarily a cause of failure, but merely a related factor. The exact cause of a child's reading failure is very difficult to pinpoint. If you know what factors might contribute to reading disability, however, you will be able to observe and analyze children's behavior critically and to take steps to prevent or remediate some of the existing problems.

A child's learning is affected by five major factors: constitutional, intellectual, environmental, emotional, and educational (see Figure 2.1). These five factors can have both positive and negative effects on reading development. A discussion of each factor follows, including its relation to reading development, how you can alert yourself to observe its effects in children, and what steps you can take for its remediation, prevention, or compensation.

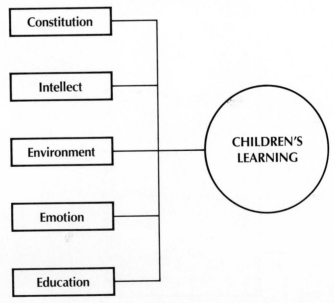

FIGURE 2.1 Five Factors Affecting Children's Learning

CONSTITUTIONAL FACTORS

Constitutional factors stem from the physiological functioning of children. They include visual, auditory, language, and neurological factors. (See Figure 2.2.)

Visual Factors

Reading is a visual act. You will see later that reading is considerably more than a visual act, and that success in reading depends to a large degree on the use of nonvisual information. However, for most sighted individuals, vision is an important factor in successful reading (Gillet and Temple 1986, Zintz and Maggart 1986). Research on the relationship between vision and reading disability shows varying conclusions. In general, however, experts agree that although poor visual skills may correlate with reading disability, it is not appropriate to view poor visual skills as predictive of reading failure (Strang 1968, Ekwall and Shanker 1983). Though many children who are reading disabled have visual problems, many children with similar problems are successful readers. According to Strang (1968), some individuals with certain visual defects can succeed in reading, while others with minimal visual defects may be severely retarded in reading.

One important implication of this information is that teachers need to be alert to visual problems in all children, whether or not they are reading disabled. The two main types of visual problems are visual acuity and visual discrimination.

Visual Acuity.   Visual refers to the sharpness or keenness of vision. You have probably heard the term "20/20 vision," which is the ability to see visual arrays that the average person with good acuity can see at 20 feet (e.g., on the Snellen Chart). If you had 20/40 vision, this would mean that you can see at 20 feet what most people can see at 40 feet. Corrective lenses would probably be needed. Several vision conditions can result in inappropriate visual acuity, making reading difficult or impeding read-

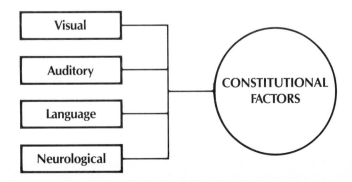

FIGURE 2.2   Constitutional Factors Affecting Reading Failure

ing progress. The most common acuity conditions affecting reading performance include:

Amblyopia	Often called "lazy eye," vision in one eye dims. Over time, information in this "lazy eye" is not interpreted by the brain, and the eye ceases to function, although no clear structural cause is found.
Astigmatism	Blurring or distortion of vision at both far and near points.
Aniseikonia	Blurring of vision caused by differences in the size or shape of the image in each eye.
Hyperopia	Farsightedness. Distortion of vision at near distances though objects at far distances are seen clearly.
Myopia	Nearsightedness. Distortion of vision at far distances though objects at near distances are seen clearly.
Strabismus	Inability to focus both eyes on the same object at the same time.

A teacher is not expected to be able to diagnose these vision problems. This is the job of a vision specialist. As a teacher, however, you have the best opportunity to observe indicators of vision problems early, because you work with children for an extended time as they perform close visual tasks in a variety of situations. Therefore, you can be alert for the important symptoms of visual acuity problems (Spache 1981, Wilson 1981). Symptoms include the child's behavior, complaints from the child, and the appearance of the child's eyes.

Symptoms of Visual Problems

The Child's Behavior

- Rubs eyes frequently
- Distorts facial expression while reading
- Loses place frequently while reading
- Loses place frequently while copying
- Holds book too close or too far away while reading
- Strains to see the chalkboard
- Quickly becomes tired during sustained work
- Squints excessively

Complaints from the Child

- Dizziness during sustained visual work
- Blurred or distorted vision
- Burning sensation in eyes
- Headaches or nausea during sustained visual work
- Print moving

Appearance of the Child's Eyes

- Redness
- Exessive watering
- Frequent styes
- Excessive mucous discharge
- Swelling of eyelids

Part of diagnostic teaching is the ongoing informal observation of children. Observation allows you to note any persisting symptoms and to inform school administrators and parents immediately. If you have a question about a child's vision, find out the child's perception of what happens while reading. Many children have a good idea of their own reading behaviors, but often do not know that what they are experiencing is atypical. Asking them clarifying questions can sometimes save a great deal of time and effort, as the following case study shows.

CASE STUDY

Some time ago, I had the pleasure of working with a remarkable young boy. He was then nine years old and in third grade. His mother brought him to me because he was experiencing severe difficulties in reading. He had been analyzed by many doctors, including neurologists and psychiatrists, and had been diagnosed as severely dyslexic. He read randomly at best, making little sense, although once in a while he would read a sentence correctly. As he read, I watched his body movements and eye movements. His body was completely rigid; it seemed that he was attempting to hold his breath as he read. He was panicking. Watching his eyes, I noticed that they would move along a line briefly, and then suddenly "drop" to several lines below. The eyes would then skip upward several times until they rested on the original line. I then understood why he read in such a random manner, and why teachers doubted his intelligence. I asked him, "Tell me what happens when you read?"

He answered, "I begin to read, and I am going along the line. Then all of a sudden, I don't know how it happens, but I find myself at the bottom of the page. Then I panic and get embarrassed and try to find my place, so I read all these words, and by the time I find my line, the teacher calls on someone else to read."

I was impressed with the accuracy of his answer. "I believe that if you use a marker it will help a lot," I said.

"It does, but I lost my marker, and my teacher said I'm too old to use one anyway." I asked him why he had never told anyone about his experience. He looked at me innocently. "Nobody asked me," he said.

With the use of a marker, rebuilding of confidence, and remediation in missed skills, he became a fine reader.

Do not underestimate the ability of children to tell you what they know of their abilities and behaviors. Important questions to ask include:

What happens when you read?
How do your eyes feel when you read?
Does the print move around when you read?
Do you find it hard to keep your place when you read?
Is it easier to read with a marker?
Do the words on the page ever look fuzzy?
Is it ever hard to see the words on the page?

Remember also that your most important diagnostic tools are your eyes, your ears, and your sensitivity. As children read, use these tools to gain vital information.

Visual Screening for Children. Some schools provide visual screening, which can be valuable in identifying children with acuity problems. One popular measure used in many school screening programs is the Snellen Test. You probably have seen the Snellen Wall Chart, which has lines of letters of decreasing size that children are asked to identify. You should know that although it serves a useful function in identifying some children with certain visual problems, the Snellen Chart has major flaws. First, it measures monocular acuity only. Second, it measures acuity only at the farthest range and not at the distance from which print is usually read. It provides no information pertaining to astigmatism, farsightedness, or aniseikonia, all of which may affect reading performance. If your school uses the Snellen Chart exclusively, you need to be more alert to the visual needs of your students, because your observation and analysis will be more effective than the chart in identifying visual problems. Other screening devices used in schools include:

Keystone Visual Survey Telebinocular Test
    Screens for myopia, hyperopia, color blindness, fusion, and depth perception.
Bausch and Lomb School Vision Tester
    Assesses binocular action of eyes, near point and far point vision, depth perception, color discrimination, and usable binocular vision.
Ortho–Rater Visual Survey
    Assesses visual acuity at far point and near point, depth perception, and binocular action.
Titmus Professional Vision Tester and Titmus Biopter
    Screens for nearsightedness, farsightedness, astigmatism, depth perception, color blindness, and binocular fusion.

Although these screening instruments are valuable, they do not replace ongoing observation by the teacher. This point is underscored by

Gillet and Temple (1986, 366) in their statement: "Teachers are sometimes the first line of defense against vision problems. They are usually in the best position to spot potential problems and refer children for appropriate screening because they, more than parents, observe children in close contact with reading and writing materials." If vision problems are detected, parents should be urged to take the child to an ophthalmologist (a medical doctor trained in diagnosing and treating diseases of the eye and performing surgery if necessary), or to an optometrist (a specialist in testing visual skills and prescribing corrective lenses or visual training).

Visual Discrimination.   Visual discrimination refers to the ability to recognize and identify differences and similarities among visual stimuli—letters, words, and phrases. Discrimination is predominantly a perceptual or mental act. It is a function more of the brain than of the eye. Visual discrimination is necessary to distinguish such forms as *b* and *d*, *p* and *q*, *bat* and *but*, or *call* and *cell*. Such distinctions are important in learning to read. Demands for visual discrimination differ, however, depending on the method of reading instruction. For example, if you use a linguistic, or spelling-pattern, approach, the demands for visual discrimination are extremely high. Consider the words *hat*, *bat*, *fat*, *rat*, *cat*, and *mat*, or the sentence, "The fat cat sat on the mat." The similar words require close attention and discrimination. On the other hand, if you use a sight word approach, the demands for visual discrimination may be quite low. The words to learn might be *boy*, *I*, *a*, *am*, *name*, *is*, *my*, *Mark*. These words might form the sentences, "My name is Mark; I am a boy." Since the words are dissimilar, discrimination confusion might rarely occur. Regardless of the program used, however, severe discrimination difficulties will probably eventually have a negative effect on reading performance.

There are a number of symptoms that will alert you to visual discrimination deficits in children. Some of the most prevalent are:

- Confusion of similar letters, e.g., *b* and *d*, *p* and *q*, *o* and *a*.
- Confusion of similar letter combinations, e.g., *br* and *dr*, *st* and *sk*, *br* and *tr*.
- Confusion of similar words, e.g., *them* and *then*, *if* and *of*, *horse* and *house*.

Visual Discrimination Training.   Many schools provide visual discrimination training for children in kindergarten and in first grade. Many of these programs use nonalphabetic forms (geometric shapes, environmental shapes) to train children in discrimination skills. Research does not support this practice. It seems that training in discriminating among nonprint forms results in a greater ability to perform the task, but does not transfer to discriminating among print-related forms such as letters, letter combinations, and words (Weaver 1980). A more appropriate strategy is to use letter and word forms in training for visual discrimination in reading.

There are also a variety of specialized visual-perceptual training programs available. Many parents and teachers turn to these programs out of frustration. The results have been unsatisfactory, leading the American Academy of Pediatrics, the American Academy of Ophthalmology and Otolaryngology, and the American Association of Ophthalmology to issue a joint statement stressing that visual training is ineffective in the treatment of learning disabilities (Dreby 1979).

If children in your classroom have visual discrimination problems, you may find a combination of the following strategies useful:

- Training in left to right directionality (d and b)
- Training in tracing words and letters
- Training in matching letters and words
- Adding a strong kinesthetic component to the reading program, such as writing, tracing, or using sandpaper letters and words
- Emphasizing meaning and using context to facilitate reading
- Teaching phonic analysis if auditory skills are strong
- Focusing on larger language units such as words and phrases, because more meaningful units are more easily processed
- Focusing on print immersion in whole language contexts (predictable print books, easy reading books, trade books)

Auditory Factors

A second factor that correlates with reading disabilities is hearing. Four subcategories of auditory functioning—acuity, discrimination, segmentation, and blending—are particularly important in reading performance. A discussion of each function and its effects on reading development follows.

Auditory Acuity.   Auditory acuity refers to the keenness or sharpness of one's hearing. Acuity is often measured with an audiometer. Audiometers measure two elements of sound: loudness, or intensity, and pitch, or frequency. Loudness is measured in decibels, and pitch is measured in cycles per second. Under normal conditions, the human ear can register frequencies between 20 and 20,000 cycles per second. The pitch of normal conversation usually ranges between 128 and 4000 cycles per second (frequency) and is about 60 decibels in loudness or volume (intensity).

Losses of hearing can affect loudness, pitch, or both. Losses in loudness affect one's ability to hear normal sounds. Normal classroom conversations, playground noises, and environmental sounds may not be perceived. Children with intensity losses may not be able to hear your voice if they are seated at the back of the classroom. If the losses are severe, you may need to stand directly in front of the children in order for them to hear you.

Loss in pitch has different results. Loss at the upper end of the pitch range results in difficulty hearing certain consonant sounds, including /t/, /l/, /s/, and their blends. These sounds are heard as muted, if at all. Loss at the lower end of the pitch range results in difficulty hearing certain consonant sounds, including /b/, /m/, /h/, /g/, and their blends. Vowel sounds are not heard clearly. Children with losses in auditory acuity have an extremely difficult time learning isolated phonics. A whole language approach is strongly recommended.

Your ongoing observation of children will help you identify students who may have hearing problems. Symptoms of hearing problems include the following:

- Not paying attention, particularly when oral directions are being given
- Speaking in a loud monotone
- Frequent rubbing of ears
- Frequent cupping of the hand behind the ear in order to hear
- Persistent requests to have oral directions or statements repeated
- Turning one ear in the direction of the speaker
- Complaining of aching, buzzing, or ringing in the ears
- Distorting facial expressions while listening
- Seeming restless when listening to speakers

If you note persistent symptoms of hearing loss, bring your observation to the attention of your school administrators and the children's parents. Parents should be encouraged to have their children checked by a hearing specialist.

Auditory Discrimination. Auditory discrimination refers to the ability to hear the similarities and differences between minimally contrasting sounds or words (e.g., /b/ and /d/, /k/ and /s/, not and nut, bat and bet). Auditory discrimination is particularly important in the learning of phonic analysis. Children with poor auditory discrimination skills often experience difficulty in learning phonics (Wilson 1981, Gillet and Temple 1986). Isolated phonic instruction is especially difficult for children who lack auditory discrimination skills. Consider the following example:

A child may not be able to hear the difference between the sounds /e/ (as in pen) and /i/ (as in pin). The child may experience less difficulty hearing the difference between the words pen and pin, and might have no difficulty at all understanding the differences between sentences containing these words, e.g., "My dress is ripped; I need a pin;" "I need to write a note; please give me a pen."

The more isolated the task the greater the demand for auditory discrimination.

Your observation of children's behaviors will allow you to identify children with auditory discrimination problems. Symptoms of auditory discrimination problems include the following:

- Confusion of minimally different words (*bet* and *bat*)
- Confusion on spelling tests (*pen* for *pin*, *them* for *then*, *drip* for *drop*)
- Confusion on phonic tasks that are orally presented (circles *rid* or *bed* when asked to circle *red*)

If you suspect a child has auditory discrimination problems, you might construct and administer an informal test. This is done by selecting minimally different words and asking children to say whether the words in the pairs are the same or different. In constructing your test, include words that differ at the beginning (*bat/rat*, *flap/strap*, *bay/day*), in the middle (*mat/met*, *flap/flip*, *map/mop*), and at the end (*mad/map*, *hope/home*, *ripe/ride*). Include words both with long and with short vowels. Choose some pairs that are the same to include among the pairs that are different. Some important tips follow for administering your test in a way that provides the most accurate results.

- The examiner should speak in approximately the same dialect as the child being tested.
- The child should know the concepts of "same" and "different." Include some practice items.
- If you present an identical pair, say both words with identical stress, volume, pitch, and tone.
- Face away from the child. The child could read your mouth formation to answer the questions.
- Ensure that the testing environment is free from distractions.

Some preconstructed auditory discrimination tests that are available include the Wepman Auditory Discrimination Test (1973) and the Goldman–Fristoe–Woodcock Test of Auditory Discrimination (1970).

Auditory Discrimination Training. Auditory discrimination does improve with training. As children progress through the first three years of school, they develop skills, primarily through exposure to phonic-oriented programs. Some suggestions for the development of auditory discrimination skills follow.

- Provide experience in rhyming. Say two words and have children tell you if they rhyme. Have children finish couplets with words that rhyme (e.g., The little frog *sat* on a ___).

- Recite pairs of words and have students say whether the words are the same or different, as in the auditory discrimination test.
- Show children two or three pictures. Say a word representing one picture, and have children identify the appropriate picture (e.g., picture of a pen, of a pan, and of a pin).

Again, remember to listen to children as they talk about their reading behavior. You can gain a great deal of information if you do. A personal experience will demonstrate the importance of listening.

CASE STUDY

Some time ago, I worked with a young boy who was at the end of first grade. After one year of school, he had a sight vocabulary of only eight words, an extremely poor self-concept, and almost nonexistent phonic skills. After listening to him attempt reading and informally testing his discrimination skills, I learned he was weak in auditory discrimination skills. I knew he had been in a strongly phonic-oriented program. In addition, he was in an ancillary program that stressed isolated phonic drill. I found that his visual skills were considerably stronger than his auditory skills. He was able to learn five words—*tiger*, *jungle*, *zoo*, *car*, *elephant*—quickly and accurately and to retain them over a one-hour period. I understood why he hadn't learned more than eight words in a year. The words he knew were his name, *the*, *a*, *and*, *will*, *call*, *she*, and *them*. Except for his name, these words were extremely low in meaning and difficult to learn. At the end of our meeting I asked him, "Why do you think you haven't learned to read?" He responded, "I keep on asking my teacher to write the words on the board so I can hear them, and she says you don't hear with your eyes."

The child was trying to tell the teacher that he couldn't hear the differences, but that if he could see the words, hearing would be easier. The teacher did not understand, however. Had the teacher observed and analyzed the child's skills and modified instruction to build on the child's strengths while working to remediate the weaknesses, the child's yearlong failure would have changed to success.

Auditory Segmentation and Blending. Auditory segmentation refers to the ability to segment speech into its individual parts (mat = /m/ + /a/ + /t/). Auditory blending refers to the ability to memorize the order of segmented sounds, blend the segments into a whole word, and retrieve the whole word from memory (/m/ + /a/ + /t/ = mat). The skills of segmentation and blending are essential to success in phonic-oriented programs. Lewkowicz (1980) examined several auditory abilities and found that auditory blending and oral segmentation were closely related to reading. She recommended that the relationship warranted the teaching of these skills in reading readiness programs.

Children who have difficulty segmenting auditorily have a hard time "sounding out" words in order to spell them. Their spelling is often random, showing little resemblance to the target word. Children who have difficulty blending sounds can produce individual sounds, but cannot hold the sounds in memory and blend them into a given word. If you observe these children when they read, you will notice that they may attempt to "sound out" or segment a word they do not know. They are often successful to this point, producing all the sounds correctly (e.g., *stand* = /st/, /a/, /nd/). You are sure the blended word will follow. Instead, however, they repeat the segments over and over and finally produce an incorrect word (e.g., /st/–/a/–/nd/, /st/–/a/–/nd/ = *step*). They seem unable to retrieve the appropriate word from memory.

Developing Segmentation and Blending Skills.   Auditory segmentation skills can be developed through ongoing practice. These skills are facilitated by what Elkonin (1973) terms "phonematic hearing." Phonematic hearing trains children to hear the separate sounds in words. Activities for developing the skill include games that segment words and require children to produce the whole word from the sounds (e.g., /c/ + /a/ + /t/ = child responds *cat*) and activities that help children segment complete words into individual sounds or syllables (e.g., *basket* = /bas/ + /ket/, *stop* = /st/ + /op/, *rat* = /r/ + /a/ + /t/).

Auditory blending may be developed by using the following procedures:

1. Provide two-syllable words and help children to blend the parts (e.g., /so/ + /fa/ = *sofa*, /clo/ + /ver/ = *clover*).
2. Provide one-syllable words separated into two parts, and have children blend the parts (e.g., /gla/ + /d/ = *glad*, /ha/ + /d/ = *had*, /pa/ + /t/ = *pat*).
3. Provide one-syllable words with the first sound separated from the remainder of the word (e.g., /h/ + /ad/ = *had*). Have the child blend the parts.
4. Provide one-syllable words, separate each sound, and have the child blend the parts (e.g., /h/ + /a/ + /d/ = *had*, /p/ + /a/ + /t/ = *pat*).
5. Move to words which contain four sounds (e.g., /stree/ + /ts/ = /str/ + /eets/ = /st/ + /r/ + /ee/ + /ts/ = *streets*).

Developing segmentation and blending skills is a process. Children in the primary grades may require short daily exposure to these skills for four to six months. Children lacking these skills who are expected to cope with phonic instruction should be trained in segmentation and blending skills. At the same time, emphasize meaningful whole word instruction. Alternative reading strategies should always accompany phonic remediation because of the length of time this form of remediation takes. Focusing on phonic remediation to the exclusion of other word recognition strategies (e.g., context, whole word, spelling patterns, language patterns) is not in children's best interests.

Language Factors

Children's oral language development has an effect on reading development. Reading is a language process, and while there are significant differences between the acquisition of oral language and the acquisition of reading, there are some striking similarities as well. Both oral language and reading are affected by syntax (grammar), semantics (meaning), and phonology (sound). The wealth of children's experiences adds significantly to the information and understanding they bring to the task of reading (Durr and Pikulski 1981, Devine 1986).

Many children with reading difficulties need more elaborate experiences with both oral and written language. Predictably, many disabled readers have difficulty with oral language. Research indicates that on intelligence tests children with reading disabilities have significantly more difficulty with the verbal subtests than with the performance subtests (Spache 1981, Moore and Wielan 1981). This is because verbal tests involve language operations while performance tests include nonverbal activities.

To appreciate the nature of language disorders, you need to have knowledge of normal linguistic development.

1. Language acquisition is an active process. From birth children are active processors of information. They are continually affected by and respond to their linguistic environment. Long before they speak in clear, adult-like speech, they understand that language is used for specific purposes such as communicating and meeting needs. They begin to build language through active involvement in the language experience.

2. Language is used for a variety of purposes. As children develop language, they use it to communicate with others, to satisfy their needs, to investigate unclear or unfamiliar concepts, and to please themselves and others. They learn to vary their vocabulary, tone, pitch, and volume according to their purposes.

3. Children pass through clearly identifiable language stages. They progress gradually through linguistic stages. Descriptions of the more well-defined stages follow:

- *The babbling stage* (birth to approximately one year). Babbling represents the first sounds made by the infant. During the first few months of life, the sounds produced by babbling are the same in all languages. By approximately three months of age, however, the child stops producing sounds that are not present in the linguistic environment, and continues practicing the sounds that are present (Norton 1980).

- *The holophrastic stage* (approximately one to two years). During this stage, children begin to use single words called holophrases to communicate the meaning of entire sentences. A child may say *wa-wa* to mean "I want some water" or *jacket* to mean "Please put on my jacket." Holophrastic speech allows children to begin using language for special and social reasons. During this time, children's naming vocabulary develops quickly.
- *The telegraphic stage* (approximately two to three years). During the telegraphic stage children develop syntax or grammar as they begin to use combinations of two or more words. Their language at this stage often sounds like the language adults use when they send a telegram—the function words are omitted. Children may use sentences like "All gone milk," "Mary dress," "No want night-night." As they mature linguistically, children start to develop telegraphic language into more complete sentence structure.

Table 2.1 shows the development of language through the more complex linguistic stages (Norton 1980).

4. Children learn the vocabulary and the conventions of language (Lund and Duchan 1988). They begin to realize that words carry meaning and that certain words fit into specific language slots and serve specific purposes. Children learn that words represent things (*table*), actions (*run*), descriptions (*big*), explanations (*slowly*), or connections (*and*). They also learn that certain language conventions must be observed during conversations. For example, specific words are used to open and close conversations; one takes turns in conversations and requests information in specific ways.

5. Children learn by being immersed in language. They are surrounded by language from birth. They hear language, see people responding to language, and hear the different tones of language expressing a variety of emotions. Through this immersion in language, children start to abstract certain consistencies and regularities (rules) and to gradually solve the problem of how to use and understand language.

By the time typical six-year-olds enter school, they are fairly proficient users and comprehenders of language. The 6,000 to 8,000 word forms they have mastered fit into one or more of the following vocabularies.

The *listening vocabulary* consists of words that children can understand when they hear them. They may not use the words, but they com-

TABLE 2.1   General Language Characteristics, 3 Months to 7 Years of Age

3 months	Child starts with all possible language sounds and gradually eliminates sounds not used in own linguistic environment.
1 year	Single words (e.g., *ma-ma*) used to express complex meanings.
1½ years	Two- or three-word phrases (*see baby*) used. Average vocabulary about 300 words.
2–3 years	Grammatical morphemes used (e.g., plural suffix *s*, auxiliary verb *is*, irregular past tense *went*). Simple and compound sentences, tense and numerical concepts develop (e.g., "many," "few," "whole lot"). Vocabulary of about 900 words.
3–4 years	Past tense appears. Children over-generalize the *-ed* and *-s* markers. Negative transformations appear. Exact numerical concepts develop (e.g., "three," "five"). Speech becomes more complex with more adjectives, adverbs, pronouns and prepositions. Vocabulary about 1500 words.
4–5 years	Language is more abstract. More basic language rules mastered. Children generally produce grammatically correct sentences. Vocabulary about 2500 words.
5–6 years	Complex sentences develop. Correct pronouns and verbs in the present tense are used. Average number of words per sentence is six to eight. Children understand approximately 6000 words.
6–7 years	Complex sentences are used. Adjectival clauses, conditional clauses beginning with *if* appear regularly. Language becomes more symbolic. Children understand concepts of time and seasons. Average sentence length is about seven and one-half words.

Source: D. Norton, *The Effective Teaching of Language Arts* (Merrill, 1980).

prehend them when the words are spoken by others. This vocabulary is usually the largest.

The *speaking vocabulary* consists of words children can recognize, understand, and produce orally. This vocabulary is constantly growing but is smaller than the listening vocabulary.

The *reading vocabulary* consists of words children can decode and comprehend. Most children entering first grade have at least a minimal reading vocabulary. Most recognize their names, signs for restaurants, names of cereals, and the like. Others recognize much more in print. This vocabulary is often small but becomes greatly expanded when reading instruction begins.

The *writing vocabulary* consists of words children can understand, produce orally, read, and spell. Because of the multiple demands of this vocabulary, it is usually the smallest.

Vocabulary development, particularly in the listening and speaking vocabularies, correlates with successful reading performance (Anderson and Freebody 1981). Limited listening and speaking vocabularies can seriously hamper reading development. Although most children enter school with appropriately developed linguistic abilities, many do not.

You should become aware of possible linguistic problems and understand their nature so that you can provide assistance. Children who are weak in their language development often demonstrate problems in two major areas: the development of receptive language skills and the development of productive language skills.

Underdeveloped Receptive Language Skills.   Receptive language refers to incoming language. Children who have underdeveloped receptive language skills do not appropriately comprehend oral, and often written, language. Difficulty in this area might be demonstrated in one or more of the following ways:

1. Children may not understand many commonly used words; they may have inadequate vocabulary development. They often have particular difficulty understanding abstract words. Many of these children have not been exposed to a sufficient variety of adult models of oral language. They may not have had adequate conversations. In the classroom, you will need to focus on direct instruction of vocabulary, discussion of concepts, exposure to a variety of words, and reading to children.

2. Children may not understand common sentence forms. Some children have difficulty processing even familiar sentences. This difficulty is magnified when you ask them to draw inferences from what they hear. Such chidren tend to perform poorly on reading comprehension or language comprehension tasks. In the classroom, discuss the material read and provide models for drawing inferences from language.

3. Children may have difficulty following directions. This may be due to their underdeveloped auditory skills or a failure to attend or to focus their attention. Since much school experience involves following directions, you must provide direct practice in the skill. Specific suggestions are offered in Chapter 12.

4. Children may have difficulty listening critically and making judgments. This may be the result of difficulty in appropriate listening, critical thinking, or both. Many children have not been exposed to purposeful listening in their home environments. Parents have not discussed issues with them. They have not questioned children at the levels that develop critical thought. In addition, many have not been listened to enough to develop good listening skills using adult models. Listening skills are vital to the development of appropriate comprehension. In your classroom, model good listening skills for children; read to them, discuss what was read, and use questions that develop critical thinking skills.

Underdeveloped Expressive Language Skills.   The term *expressive language* refers to the language produced by an individual. Children who have underdeveloped expressive language skills have difficulty communicating effectively with oral, and often written, language. Some of the more common concerns include the following:

1. Children may have difficulty formulating expressive sentences. Such children often speak in sentence fragments and use few words. They may seem hesitant to communicate orally or to participate in discussions. Some sociolinguists, such as Bernstein (1961), attempt to relate language production to social class variables. Bernstein identifies two basic categories of speakers: those using an "elaborated code" and those using a "restricted code." Elaborated-code users usually come from environments in which play, language activity, discussion, and verbal or social interaction are valued and encouraged. Problem solving and exploration of alternatives are also expected. Language becomes a tool for communicating, solving problems, analyzing, synthesizing, gaining information, and meeting needs. Speakers use complex language structures, varied vocabulary, and expressive language.

Restrictive-code speakers come from environments which discourage linguistic exploration and often have limited play space. Speakers use more controlling or disapproving language and emphasize single solutions rather than explorations of alternatives. Children in these environments rarely engage in expanded discussions with adults. They tend to prefer linguistically passive activities, such as watching television, instead of linguistically active experiences, such as reading and conversing with parents. Language in these environments includes simple sentences, a restricted range of grammatical forms, few subordinate clauses and abstract words, and a limited vocabulary.

Bernstein points out that the use of a restricted code does not mean linguistic deficiency or inability. It merely means that those children have a different language experience than elaborated-code speakers. They need an expanded language base. The importance of appropriate adult models for developing linguistic flexibility is stressed in the literature on reading and language instruction (Smith 1982, Speidel 1982). Vygotsky (1962, 1978) regards words as the tools of thought, and stresses the critical role of language in intellectual and conceptual growth. He emphasizes the importance of verbal interaction between children and adults in the development of advanced thinking. Instructional environments should therefore encourage discussion among children and teachers, and immersion in vocabulary development and use. In your classroom, model elaborated language, provide a variety of print, encourage memorization of familiar poems, rhymes, jingles, or riddles, and purposefully discuss events.

2. Children may have inadequate speaking vocabularies. Many children use a few words repeatedly and introduce few new words into their vocabularies. You should provide direct instruction, review, and practice in vocabulary. This should be your ongoing goal for all children.

3. Children may not practice appropriate language skills in school because they perceive school as a threatening environment. Feelings of rejection, hostility, and fear often cause children to withhold their language. You can help by creating an open and supportive classroom envi-

ronment. You can help children develop their productive language by providing opportunities for nonverbal activities (music, art, dance, play), for enhancement of self-concept and self-image, for acceptance of children's dialects, and for meaningful experiences with oral language and print. A detailed discussion of strategies for language development and remediation is presented in Chapter 12.

Neurological Factors

The possibility that children's learning problems might be related to neurological factors was first raised in the 1930s (Selzer 1933, Monroe and Backus 1937). One of the most useful discussions of neurological factors was provided by Strauss and Lehtinen in *Psychopathology and Education of the Brain-Injured Child* (1947). Strauss and Lehtinen discussed the relationship between brain dysfunction and learning disabilities, based on studies of children identified as mentally retarded or emotionally disturbed. Observation showed that the children behaved in many ways like a group of soldiers who had received brain injuries during World War II. The children and the soldiers both demonstrated attention fragmentation, perceptual problems, and hyperactivity. Strauss and Lehtinen hypothesized that the children had incurred damage to their central nervous systems, which caused their learning disabilities.

Since the 1930s many individuals in the fields of education, medicine, and psychology have discussed the relationship between learning disabilities and neurology (Rie and Rie 1980, Lerner 1981, Carpenter et al. 1984, Frith 1985, Patterson et al. 1985). To date, however, there is no general agreement on the exact nature of this relationship. One major reason for this ambivalence is the many diagnostic labels that lack explanatory power. For example, terms used interchangeably to describe children who have not learned in school include neurological deficit, brain damage, minimal brain dysfunction, learning disability, and psychological processing disorder. The labels might mean something to physicians or neurologists, but they have little practical, instructional, or remedial value for teachers. Bateman (1974) issues a strong statement against neurological labels, which she views as irrelevancies for educational practice and as excuses for poor teaching. She points out that the characteristics of such labels as "minimal brain dysfunction" can also be found in children labeled normal, gifted, emotionally disturbed, mentally retarded, and disadvantaged. She suggests replacing the term "learning disabled" with the term "teaching disabled." She advises teachers to remember that neurological labels reflect medical terminology. Teachers should focus on educationally relevant information affecting the children's learning.

Taylor, Harris, and Pearson make a related point (1988, 29) in the statement: "When all is said and done, once the labeling has occurred, you still have a student who cannot read. And your job as a teacher is to do as much as you possibly can to help."

One of the most widely used neurology-related terms for reading disabilities is dyslexia. Dyslexia has been defined as congenital word-blindness, primary reading disability, minimal cerebral dysfunction, and specific language disability. Little agreement exists as to the nature of dyslexia, its basic symptoms, or its treatment. The only agreement is that children categorized as dyslexic cannot read despite instruction and long-term remediation. In 1969, the Secretary of the Department of Health, Education, and Welfare appointed a committee (the National Advisory Committee on Dyslexia and Related Reading Disorders) to investigate and define the condition, and to make recommendations. The committee found it impossible to define dyslexia and concluded that the term served no useful purpose. The term nevertheless remains in the vocabulary of teachers, specialists, diagnosticians, parents, and medical personnel.

Teachers should refrain from using this term and other medically defined terms. Such terms may have medical value, but fail to give teachers any useful information. The causes, definitions, and treatments of all these "disorders" are confusing at best. As a teacher, you have little control over neurological disorders. What you do have control over is how you teach, what you teach, and how you modify your instruction according to the learning characteristics and needs of children.

No doubt many children have reading problems that seem to defy instruction and remediation. The answer does not lie in simply labeling children, but in modifying instruction based on the careful and professional analysis of their needs and learning characteristics.

CASE STUDY

Years ago, I worked with a second grade boy who had been classified as dyslexic. His reading skills were almost nonexistent. When I asked him what he thought his problem was, he responded, "I can't tell you. It's too weird." I promised I wouldn't laugh or think he was weird. He eventually confessed that when he read, the letters and words "jumped around on the page." Based on this information, I had him use a place marker. Using two shades of felt underliners I then blocked alternating words in different colors (e.g., *the* [blocked in blue], *man* [blocked in yellow], *ran* [blocked in blue], etc.). As print became more stabilized for him, I blocked phrases rather than words. As he learned to control print more effectively, I blocked whole sentences, then whole lines, and finally paragraphs. Within three months, the boy could control print and compensate for his "problem." His reading skills developed significantly. The following year, I retested him in order to place him in my reading clinic. His skills were so good that I could not justify including him in a remedial program.

Children's learning failure is a puzzle. Your job is to focus on a variety of strategies that may solve the puzzle—not simply to label the child.

INTELLECTUAL FACTORS

Discussions about the relationship between intelligence and reading can be most frustrating. Research into this relationship has yielded inconclusive results. One reason for the lack of clear results is that the relationship depends on the definition of reading used and on the test used to measure intelligence. If reading is defined as the decoding of combinations of letters into sounds, then the relationship between reading and intelligence is not very significant. Many individuals with significantly below average intelligence quotients have been successfully taught to read reasonably well. If reading is defined as interaction with print through critical, creative, and evaluative thinking, and application in a variety of contexts, however, then the relationship between reading and intelligence is more significant.

In general, research indicates that there is a positive relationship between intelligence test scores and reading ability. The scores from the verbal sections of these tests have a higher correlation with reading, particularly reading comprehension (between .60 and .85 levels of significance), than the scores from the performance sections (between .20 and .56) (Moore and Wielan 1981). Research also shows that although there is a relationship between intelligence and reading, intelligence tests are not predictive of success in reading (Kaufman 1979, Harris and Sipay 1980, Spache 1981, Brown 1982, Downing and Leong 1982). Most teachers can remember dealing with extremely intelligent children who were failing in reading.

The Nature of Intelligence

In our discussion of intelligence, it is necessary to describe its nature. One of the best-known names in the field of intelligence testing is David Wechsler, creator of the widely used Wechsler Intelligence Scale for Children. Wechsler (1974) defines intelligence as the overall capacity of individuals to understand and cope with the world. He emphasizes the fact that intelligence is not a narrow, single concept, but a global, multidimensional one. He further suggests that intelligence in its purest form cannot be measured accurately (1975). This view coincides with the point made by Green (1975, 90) as he states: "First of all, I.Q. is not a synonym for intelligence. The I.Q., intelligence quotient, simply represents a numerical score earned on a test. That test does not measure the broad range of experiences encompassed by all intellectual functions."

A controversial issue surrounding the concept of intelligence is whether intelligence is determined primarily by heredity or by environment. Some researchers suggest that intelligence predominantly results from environmental factors, including home experiences, exposure to social and learning experiences, the quality of health and nutrition, and exposure to a variety of vocabulary forms and problem-solving tasks. Research has shown that the I.Q. scores of children and adolescents can be raised if children are placed in enriching, positive environments stressing higher-level cognitive tasks (Herber et al. 1972, Feuerstein 1979). Other researchers suggest that intelligence is predominantly inherited and is therefore largely unresponsive to environmental manipulation (Jensen 1969, 1979). It seems clear that both heredity and environment affect intelligence. As teachers, you have no control over the genetic endowments of children. What you can control is your instruction and your expectations of children. By exposing children to a variety of experiences, both real and vicarious, and by directly attending to vocabulary development, concept development, and problem-solving tasks, you can affect children's ability to understand and cope with the world.

Measures Used to Assess Intelligence

There are a variety of intelligence tests, and children's I.Q. scores can vary significantly depending on the test taken. Some tests are group administered and require students to read test items and record their answers. Other tests are administered individually and require no reading ability whatsoever. Some tests require specially trained personnel to administer and score them, while others require no specialized training. Some tests measure receptive vocabulary, while others assess mathematical computation and other mental operations. Some tests assess a wide range of verbal tasks (specific factual information, vocabulary, common sense judgment, categorical thinking) and of nonverbal tasks (picture completion, sequential arrangements, whole-part analysis, short-term visual memory). A listing of the better-known and more widely used intelligence tests follows.

> *Cognitive Skills Assessment Battery*
> > (Psychological Corporation, 1981, 2nd edition)
> > Grades K–2
> > Individually administered: 15–20 minutes
> > Measures concepts required in the primary grades, e.g., parts
> > > of the body and story comprehension. Child answers orally.
> *California Short-Form Test of Mental Maturity*
> > (California Test Bureau, 1963)
> > Grades preschool through adult
> > Group administered: 40–50 minutes

Multiple choice items measuring concepts such as analogies and mathematical concepts. Has verbal and nonverbal sections.

Culture-Fair Intelligence Tests
   (Bobbs–Merrill, 1961)
   Ages 8 through adult
   Group administered: 25 minutes
   Nonverbal tests. Requires children to (a) complete pictorial series, (b) find pictures in a display that are different, (c) find missing parts, (d) state relationships between pictures.

Kuhlman–Anderson Intelligence Tests
   (Personnel Press, 1967)
   Ages 5 through 18
   Group administered: 45 minutes
   Consists of a multiple choice format that includes verbal and quantitative information.

Lorge–Thorndike Intelligence Tests
   (Houghton Mifflin, 1964)
   Ages 3 through 13
   Group administered: 1 hour
   Includes verbal and nonverbal tasks.

McCarthy Scales of Children's Abilities
   (The Psychological Corporation, 1972)
   Ages 2½ to 8½
   Individually administered: 45–60 minutes
   Created particularly for younger children.
   Assesses (1) verbal abilities, (2) perceptual performance, (3) quantitative abilities, (4) memory, (5) motor abilities, (6) cognitive abilities.

Peabody Picture Vocabulary Test—Revised
   (American Guidance Service, 1981)
   Ages 2½ to adult
   Individually administered: 10–30 minutes
   Consists of a series of pictures. Children indicate which picture represents a given word.

Otis–Lennon School Ability Test
   (Psychological Corporation, 1979)
   Grades 1 to 12
   Group administered: 45–80 minutes
   Multiple choice measures of verbal, figural, and numerical abilities

Slosson Intelligence Test
   (Slosson Education Publications, 1981)
   Ages infant through adult
   Individually administered: 20–40 minutes
   Primarily a test of vocabulary. Verbal and performance subtests. No reading required.

Stanford–Binet Intelligence Scale
   (Houghton Mifflin, 1973)
   Ages 2 years to adult
   Individually administered: 1 to 1½ hours
   Assesses vocabulary, maze tracing, obeying directions, observing differences between arrays.

Wechsler Intelligence Scales
   A. Wechsler Preschool and Primary Scale of Intelligence (Ages 4 to 6.6), 1967
   B. Wechsler Intelligence Scale for Children—Revised (Ages 6 to 16), 1974
   C. Wechsler Adult Intelligence Scale—Revised (Ages 15 to adult), 1981
   (Psychological Corporation)
   Individually administered: approximately 45 minutes.
   Each includes a verbal scale which assesses:
   1. Information (answering factual questions)
   2. Similarities (noting how things are similar)
   3. Arithmetic (solving timed questions)
   4. Vocabulary (defining words)
   5. Comprehension (discussing everyday issues and abstract concepts)
   6. Digit-Span (repeating digits, optional text)
   Each also includes a performance scale which assesses:
   1. Picture completion (finding missing parts)
   2. Block Design (duplicating designs)
   3. Picture Arrangement (sequencing pictures)
   4. Object Assembly (fitting puzzles together)
   5. Coding (matching and writing symbols with numbers)
   6. Mazes (following mazes, optional)

Woodcock–Johnson Psychoeducational Battery
   (Teaching Resources Corporation, 1977)
   Ages preschool to adult
   Individually administered: 1–2 hours
   Tests for picture vocabulary, spatial relations, memory for sentences, visual-auditory learning, blending, quantitative concepts, visual matching, antonyms and synonyms, analysis and synthesis, numbers reversed, concept formation, and analogies. Strongly language oriented.

A number of sources provide complete information about current, published tests. The sources describe and review tests. If your school uses particular instruments, you may wish to familiarize yourself with them before passing any judgments on children. Sources include:

Mental Measurement Yearbook (Oscar Buros, ed., 1978)
Tests in Print I (Buros, 1961)

Tests in Print II (Buros, 1974)
Reading Tests and Reviews (Buros, 1975)

Conclusions Regarding Intelligence Testing

Children's intelligence is a factor in their reading performance. Remember, however, that I.Q. test scores are not irrevocable measures of children's intelligence. In addition, I.Q. scores vary significantly depending on the I.Q. test used. If you are working with remedial readers, use an intelligence test that does not require reading ability, or else children will be unfairly penalized. The most accurate measure you can use with disabled readers is an individually administered I.Q. test that does not require reading and writing ability. Even so, however, you will not be measuring the "broad range of experience encompassed by all intellectual functions" (Green 1975).

Although intelligence affects reading potential, high intelligence does not ensure appropriate reading. Greenslade (1980) found that children must acquire specific concepts in order to read well. (1) They must be aware of the relationship between oral language and print. (2) They must understand that print is comprised of meaningful language units. (3) They must realize that reading is an interactive-thinking process that demands varied interpretations. Greenslade suggests that these concepts directly relate to the manner in which the teacher presents and teaches reading. When teachers do not help children to understand and develop these concepts and cognitive abilities, children invariably become "cognitively confused" about what reading really means.

As a teacher, you need to become aware of the instruments used to test the intelligence of your students. You also need to know the limitations of those tests. Your job is to analyze the children's strengths and weaknesses and to fit your instruction to their needs. This strategy results in children's growth. Labeling a child as "low I.Q." or basing your expectations for academic growth on such a label is a disservice to the child and to yourself as a teacher striving for competence and sensitivity.

ENVIRONMENTAL FACTORS

Children coming to school are affected by two dominant environments—the home and the school. Both environments affect children's learning, particularly learning to read. This section discusses the home environment. (See Figure 2.3.)

The role of parents in the development of children cannot be overestimated. The home climate parents provide for children either fosters and encourages learning or is not conducive to maximum learning.

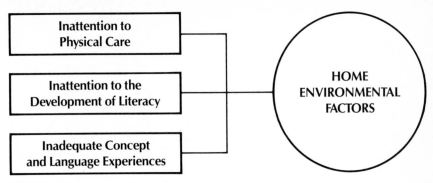

FIGURE 2.3   Home Environmental Factors Affecting Reading Failure

There are many factors in the home environment that may negatively affect reading development.

Inattention to Physical Care

One's general functioning is directly related to one's physical well-being. Many children are products of environments in which they are not cared for physically. Many have not had regular physical examinations (general, vision, hearing, etc.) that might detect and treat impairments or deficiencies. Some children are not required to get appropriate amounts of sleep or are not provided with sufficient nourishment. Many teachers cope daily with children who arrive at school tired, lethargic, and hungry. Since in most schools the reading period is in the morning, these children cannot accomplish the quality and quantity of work that is expected. Reading performance is directly affected. As a teacher you might wish to send a note to the parents of the children involved, telling them your observations (tiredness, hunger) and giving suggestions to solve the problems. Realistically, however, the children in the greatest need often live in environments that resist most teacher suggestions. In such cases, your ability to cause positive change is limited. Some teachers keep a supply of dried fruit, fresh fruit, or nuts for children. Food might be contributed by the PTA, by the school administration, by neighborhood businesses, or by government programs.

Inattention to the Development of Literacy

One of the most facilitating factors in the child's home environment is having parents who value literacy. Such parents continually help children to enjoy literature and to benefit from what it has to offer (Bettelheim and Zelan 1982). The parents read to and with children from books that entertain and fascinate them. Children react to print, discuss ideas from print with parents, and expect meaning, entertainment, information, and pleasure from print. They see the adults in their environment reading for these purposes as well (Dunn 1981, Heath 1983, Olson 1984, Wilson and Anderson 1985).

Children who grow up in an environment in which literacy is not valued are often at a disadvantage in school. This is particularly true if their teachers expect to immediately begin "drilling" reading instruction without attending to the development of this value. Valuing literacy is a prime prerequisite of fully developed reading. Unfortunately, many children from environments paying little or no attention to literacy often have teachers who also seem not to value literacy. The exposure of these children to print is therefore uninspiring, unattractive, and unfulfilling. It usually consists of drilling in isolated parts of reading which have no meaning.

Inadequate Concept and Language Experiences

A major factor in appropriate reading development, particularly in the development of comprehension, is the level of conceptual and linguistic stimulation that children experience. Children whose parents do not take opportunities to widen their language experiences (through such activities as reading to and with them, taking them on trips and discussing the events, listening and responding to them, and purposefully conversing with them) are often at a disadvantage in learning to read and in interacting with print. Similarly, home environments that fail to expose children to a variety of concepts (such as visits to and discussions about libraries, parks, zoos, shopping areas, transportation stations, and museums) often produce children who lack the basic information vital to the comprehension of much school-related print. For these children, understanding print is very difficult. Unless teachers provide a great deal of conceptual information prior to and during reading instruction, these children find reading comprehension to be nearly impossible. Conceptual development and text interaction strategies are discussed at length in Chapter 9.

Environmental factors are not necessarily related to socioeconomic class. A child from a low income family is not automatically deprived linguistically, experientially, or conceptually. Some extremely poor parents are very diligent about enriching their children's environment and use every opportunity to discuss, converse, and explain events. Similarly, children from affluent environments have not necessarily been exposed to enriched experiences, to quality time with others, or to conversation and nurturing. The positive or negative effects of an environment reflect parents' values and motivations more than their socioeconomic status.

There are several strategies teachers can use to work with the home environments of children. Teachers should provide parents with suggestions for helping them with academic tasks. Out of concern for their children, parents often use strategies that promote failure in reading. It is vital, then, that teachers share with parents ways that will help children. Other strategies for assisting parents are presented in Chapter 13.

EMOTIONAL FACTORS

Reading is an interactive process involving communication between a writer and a reader. As in all communication, emotional factors can inhibit performance (Figure 2.4) (Mathewson 1985). A major issue in the field of reading instruction is whether or not reading failure causes emotional disorders or emotional disorders cause reading failure. The issue is not a trite one because the position you take often affects your approach to remediation. If you believe that emotional problems cause reading failure, then the focus is on mitigating emotional trauma, establishing self-esteem, building confidence, and catering to children's interests. The emotional problem becomes the primary focus of remediation. The reading problem is addressed when the emotional climate improves. If, on the other hand, you believe reading failure causes emotional problems, you will focus on solving the reading problem as quickly as possible.

A middle position seems best. Undoubtedly, many children who have difficulty reading also have emotional problems. As teachers, you can probably recall many poor readers (or poor students in general) who displayed emotionally and behaviorally maladaptive actions. Spache (1981) estimates that three out of four disabled readers experience some degree of emotional problems. That children who fail in reading have these problems should not be surprising.

Most children who enter school expect to learn to do three things—to read, to write, to do math. In addition, they expect to accomplish these tasks quickly. Imagine the disappointment they feel when month after month they fail to read. Year after year they continue to fail. Imagine their embarrassment when they see their peers moving ahead, completing texts, and being recognized for their accomplishments in reading. No

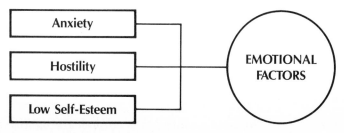

FIGURE 2.4   Emotional Factors Affecting Reading Failure

matter how kind teachers are or how hard teachers try to mask the failure, the children know they have failed; they feel like failures and the feeling hurts, as the following testimony shows.

> I recently tested a six-year-old girl who had just completed first grade and was being retained. She was extremely depressed as she spoke with me. It was sad to know that she was only six and had been in school for just one year. As she sat in my office, she said, "I am so dumb! All my friends can read, and I'll never read. School is so hard I wish I could drop out of school and become a garbage man."

Children who are failing in reading know it. Many teachers try to make performance levels less noticeable by giving reading groups motivating names. This is a good practice, but children know the composition of the group regardless of the name.

> This was made clear to me in a conversation I had with the son of a friend who was in the highest performing group in grade two. In our discussion he mentioned that he was in the highest reading group in his class.
> "What is the name of your reading group?" I asked.
> "The Raiders," he replied.
> "Did your teacher tell you that the Raiders was the highest reading group?"
> "No."
> "Well, how do you know that," I inquired.
> "Well," he said, "we have the hardest book, and we get the most work right. Anyway, I'm not sure that I'm in the highest group, but I know that all the smartest kids are in my group."

Children who are failing have similar insights. Some parents who know their children are failing pressure them, compare them with siblings or friends, or fail to understand the nature of their problems, adding to the stress these children face. The hurt these children feel is often expressed as anger, depression, withdrawal, anxiety, low self-esteem, aggression, or passive behavior. Many children who fail in reading do have a variety of emotional problems. Educators should focus on remediating children's reading problems in a way that builds their self-esteem, confidence, and enjoyment of learning. Three of the most important emotional problems affecting reading are discussed in this section.

Anxiety

An important requirement in learning to read is the ability to risk error and occasional failure. Risk-taking allows children to "solve" the problem of print by using their oral language knowledge to anticipate meaning and to correct themselves when this meaning does not occur. Anxiety results in fear of failure which destroys the willingness to take risks. This, in turn, undermines reading achievement. Anxiety can arise from a home environment that threatens children against failure in school, continually compares slow readers to high-achieving siblings or friends, punishes children for school failure, or pressures children unduly to excel. Anxiety can also arise from a school environment that punishes children for making errors, stresses accuracy at the expense of meaning, fails to compliment children for work well done, ridicules children for making mistakes, or persists in using strategies through which children cannot learn. Anxious children, therefore, approach reading sessions with fears of making mistakes, being yelled at, or failing (Gentile and McMillan 1987).

Hostility

Many children who read poorly develop an obvious hostility toward the task. They may seem relaxed and adjusted until the teacher announces the reading period, when their mood seems to shift to aggression and hostility. The hostility is often a mask for fear, embarrassment, or feelings of inadequacy.

CASE STUDY

I remember once working with a fourth grade boy who stomped into my office, obviously angry, sat down in a huff, and announced, "I hate reading and you aren't gonna make me do it!" I gave him a moment; then I asked, "Why do you hate it so much?" He replied gruffly, " 'Cause I can't do it—that's why." I understood exactly what he meant. I can remember telling my piano teacher, "I detest this piece," when what I was saying to myself was, "I can't play this piece." In a week or two (usually when my music teacher tired of hearing me massacre the selection), I moved on to another piece that I could play well and therefore liked. The fourth grade boy, on the other hand, never seemed to make any progress that was noticeable to him. For weeks—months—he was reminded of his failure. My strategy included the simplified rewriting of segments of *Return of the Jedi*, meaningful sight vocabulary, and exposure to the language experience approach. This is what it took to prove to him that he could learn to read and thus to reduce his hostility toward reading.

Hostility demands so much energy that children often have little energy left for productive effort. Hostility tends to be displayed more often in group situations to hide the embarrassment children feel when they fail or fear failing before their peers.

Low Self-Esteem

The relationship between self-concept and achievement has been discussed often in the literature (Eshel and Klein 1981, Eder 1983, Wigfield and Asher 1984). Young children associate school with the subjects of reading, writing, and math. Most expect to read in kindergarten or, certainly, in first grade. Many children who are unable to read and see their peers becoming good readers predictably question their self-worth and gradually lose self-esteem. Lack of self-esteem eventually leads to low motivation, insecurity, poor self-concept, and emotional imbalance (Quandt and Selznick 1984, Bristow 1985).

Self-esteem is enhanced when an individual sets and achieves goals or succeeds at valued tasks. You can heighten children's esteem by helping them to set realistic goals for learning to read and by using instructional strategies that will allow them to achieve those goals. When goals have been met, children should be recognized, praised, and encouraged. In addition, children should be exposed to material that motivates them. Poor readers often receive monotonous instruction from material with absolutely no interest for them. The "need" to read is therefore lacking. Lack of motivation and low self-esteem result in poor reading performance.

The importance of exposing disabled readers to meaningful material using familiar language and dealing with situations of interest to children cannot be over-emphasized. Such material not only motivates children to read but also allows them to use their own language abilities and knowledge in the decoding of print.

CASE STUDY

The importance of meaningful material was reinforced in my mind recently as I tested children for participation in reading clinics. I was interviewing a young girl who was at the end of her third year in school. She had been in a remedial reading program for three years. I began with my standard question, "Do you like to read?"

"I guess so," she replied, "but I hate to read in school."

"What makes you hate it?"

"I just hate those dumb stories. They're so stupid. They don't even make any sense. Why don't they use stories about real kids or people or neat stuff? They are so phoney!"

"What do you like to read?"

"Oh, I don't know. I guess I like *Curious George* or *Whistle for Willie* or *Clifford* and stuff. But my favorite is *Chicken Soup with Rice*. I know the whole book. Want to hear it?" At which point she recited Maurice Sendak's entire story. True, she might not have been able to "read" every word, but her strong motivation toward the language gave her incentive to read. Reflecting on the material she used in school, I could understand her resistance to reading.

While children should not be allowed to dictate their academic curriculum, they should have materials to which they can relate and which they can enjoy. This will result in the desire to read, which will affect progress in reading. When children succeed in learning, their self-esteem increases and their performance escalates.

EDUCATIONAL FACTORS

Reading failure often has its origins in inappropriate instructional strategies. Many children fail in reading because for extended periods of time they are exposed to teaching strategies from which they cannot learn and because instruction is not modified to meet their needs. Of all factors affecting reading performance, educational factors are most relevant to teachers because they are the only correlates of reading disability over which teachers have complete control. Educational variables are inherent in the ways in which teachers present reading to children. These ways reflect the instructional decisions teachers make about teaching children to read. Pay close attention to the six educational factors shown in Figure 2.5 and discussed below in order to recognize, avoid, or amend these behaviors in your instructional practices.

Beginning Reading Instruction before Children Are Ready

Before any content can be successfully taught, children must possess the underlying conceptual readiness that makes learning possible. Each skill, story, article, or passage demands a certain level of prior knowledge (Bransford 1985). This prior knowledge provides the concepts necessary for making incoming information meaningful and understandable. Before children learn the skill of syllabication, for example, they need to

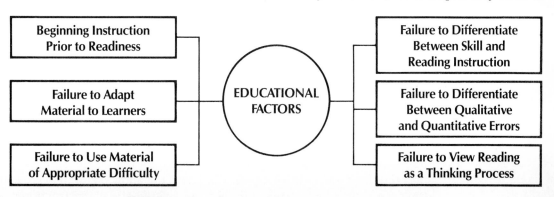

FIGURE 2.5   Educational Factors Affecting Reading Failure

hear and respond to the rhythm of oral language and to sense the natural sound segments in oral language (e.g., Ma/ry/had/a/li/ttle/lamb/li/ttle/ lamb/li/ttle/lamb). Before learning sequencing skills, they must first have such internalized concepts as "first," "next," "then," and "last." Similarly, before children read a story set on an Indian reservation, they must be familiar with concepts describing Indian life, values, beliefs, customs, and so on. Teachers who attempt to give instruction before ensuring conceptual readiness block children's learning. Extended exposure to instruction that ignores conceptual readiness will most likely result in reading failure. Before beginning instruction you should assess children's conceptual levels, analyze the conceptual demands of the task, and purposefully choose instructional strategies that will lessen the gap between what the children bring to the task and what the task demands of the children. This preparatory approach is called diagnostic instruction. A thorough discussion of conceptual readiness is presented in Chapter 9.

Failure to Adapt Existing Instructional or Remedial Programs to the Needs of Children

A fundamental premise of this text is that modification is imperative in reading instruction. Each instructional program is designed with a particular audience in mind. Each program has a specific set of prerequisites—skill requirements that are mandatory for expected progress in the program. Children will fail if they do not have the prerequisites and the instructional program is presented without modification. For example, a phonic-emphasis program demands strong auditory discrimination, segmentation, and blending skills. If some of the children you teach are weak in these skills, then your instruction should be modified to include sight vocabulary instruction and language immersion strategies. A variety of methods for teaching reading are available. Any one method will not be appropriate for all children. You should become familiar with the range of instructional methods in order to have teaching options to use for children with different learning characteristics. A variety of methods of reading instruction are presented in Chapter 7.

Failure to Use Material of an Appropriate Level of Difficulty

Children fail to make appropriate progress in reading when they use reading material that is inadequate for their performance level. Material that is too difficult frustrates children and leads to failure in reading. On the other hand, material that is too easy does not allow children to grow. Children should be instructed in material written at their instructional level. The material should not be simple enough to be read well independently, nor so difficult as to cause undue frustration. Prior to instruction children will not know all the words and ideas necessary for complete success. The teacher's instruction, however, will compensate for what the children do not know. It is careful instruction on the appropriate instructional level that makes reading a success.

Manning (1980) defines the instructional level as the level at which children continue to respond aggressively to print, using all learned phonic, semantic, and syntactic decoding strategies. They do this with the directed assistance of the teacher, and in spite of the fact that they occasionally meet with failure. The slight difficulty stretches children's performance daily and causes growth. Some teachers, in an effort to reduce children's frustration, use material so simple that it guarantees success. After one year, the children are successful, but their actual progress in reading is minimal. This also constitutes failure in reading. As you choose material for children, strive for the instructional level. Remember that teaching on the instructional level requires you to fill in the gaps in children's knowledge by using such strategies as vocabulary preinstruction, conceptual preparation, content preparation, and skill instruction.

Failure to Acknowledge the Difference between Skill Instruction and Reading Instruction

Skill instruction and reading instruction are not identical. While there is overlap, it is a mistake to assume that the teaching of isolated skills is the same as teaching "reading." Skill instruction, particularly for disabled readers, focuses on children's weaknesses—what they do not know. Reading instruction, on the other hand, focuses on children's strengths and on their knowledge of multiple clues in language. Skill instruction helps children to "learn" skills. Reading instruction helps children to "use" skills. There is no other reason for children to learn skills except to use them in actual reading. Programs that lock children in a spiraling pattern of skill instruction with little actual reading from connected print invariably force children struggling with skills into a pattern of failure. Teachers who day after day spend entire reading periods drilling children in isolated skills rather than exposing children daily to interesting print experiences contribute to reading failure. Remember that isolated skill instruction might not result in improved reading; but exposure to real reading almost always results in improved skill learning, as the following case shows.

CASE STUDY

As the director of the Reading Clinic at the University of Colorado at Colorado Springs, I had fifteen elementary age children who were involved in an eleven-week remedial program. The program consisted of one hour, forty-five minute weekly sessions during which children were exposed to the following instructional sequence:

1. vocabulary preinstruction (words and phrases)
2. concept preparation
3. content reading
4. oral and silent reading
5. relevant skill instruction
6. enrichment reading

The clinic is a one-on-one tutor-student program. In past years, by the fourth week children made significant progress. This term, however, there were two boys showing little or no progress. These two children were the clinic's most severe cases. I observed them closely and realized that though they would eventually "get" the skills, they would not transfer or apply that learning to actual reading. Immediately their program was changed. For the remaining seven weeks, they received two forms of instruction. First, they read for the entire session. Tutors recorded their errors on each page. Second, at the end of each page, tutors reviewed the errors with the children and taught or re-taught necessary skills. The children then reread the sentences they had read incorrectly. In this reading immersion no pre-determined skills or vocabulary were taught. The boys read the whole time. In post-testing at the end of the remaining seven weeks, the boys showed a minimum of six months growth for every assessed subtest on the Gates–McKillop Reading Test. They made admirable progress in fluency, word recognition, and comprehension. However, their greatest growth was on the phonic subtests. Because of their reading and immediate instruction on skills they had failed to use, their skill levels increased. Once instructed, they had to use the skills in actual reading. Reading results in better skill learning. Isolated skill instruction does not necessarily result in better reading.

Skill instruction is not synonymous with reading instruction. All skill instruction should include an application of skills in actual reading. Finally, although skill instruction is vital, daily exposure to real reading is imperative for appropriate growth in reading performance.

Failure to Differentiate between Qualitative and Quantitative Errors

One of the most unfortunate practices in reading instruction is habitually viewing all errors as negative. Errors are a source of information in all learning situations. Fear of making errors is detrimental to the learning process itself. Errors indicate both weaknesses and strengths. A child who sees the word *bench* and says *bent* certainly has made an error. That error tells us that the child does not know or does not apply the word *bench* as a sight word, nor the /*ch*/ as a sound combination; but it also tells us that the child does know the beginning consonant sound /*b*/, the vowel sound /*e*/, the sound /*n*/, and the phonemes /*ben*/. The child has a strong knowledge base on which to build remediation. It is important to remember that an error provides information about both strengths and weaknesses, which must be taken into account in planning remedial programs for children.

Many teachers often focus inappropriately on the number of errors rather than on the quality of errors. Knowing the number of errors tells us nothing of diagnostic or remedial value. Assume that two children have taken the same word recognition test and received identical scores of five out of ten correct. Assume that the words tested were *break, many, start, them, plate, wouldn't, between, rest, help,* and *fact.* The first child may have made the following errors: *beck* for *break, sat* for *start, pat* for *plate, ret* for *rest,* and *fat* for *fact.* The second child may have made the following errors: *man* for *many, breck* for *break, then* for *them, fast* for *fact,* and *pate* for *plate.* Although both children made the same quantity of errors, the quality of errors is significantly different. The two error types have different profiles and require different remediation strategies. Analysis shows that the first child knows beginning and ending single consonants, but does not know single vowels, vowel combinations, or consonant combinations. The second child knows initial single consonants, initial consonant combinations, and short vowel sounds, but needs practice with ending sounds, vowel combinations, and long vowels. Categorizing these children together on the basis of the number of their errors and providing both the same remediation would result in little growth and, ultimately, in failure.

Failure to View Reading as a Thinking Process

Instructional programs focusing on isolated skill drill and literal comprehension, providing little interactive instruction, inferential thinking, problem solving, and critical thinking experiences, do a great injustice to children. Reading is a thinking process demanding interaction and involvement. Reading depends on the child's ability to understand facts, draw inferences, think critically and creatively, evaluate clearly, and react personally to text. From the initial stages of reading instruction thinking skills should be the major thrust of teaching. The only reason for reading is understanding. Focusing on memorization of unimportant details and on isolated skill drill rather than on reading as a thinking process will result in failure.

SUMMARY   It is often impossible to trace reading failure to a single correlate. Reading is a complex process and many factors contribute to its success or failure. This chapter presented five major correlates of reading disability described in terms of factors related to failure in reading. The factors discussed were constitutional, intellectual, environmental, emotional, and educational. Knowing the correlates of reading failure allows teachers not only to better understand the origins of reading disability, but to modify instruction to meet the needs of children.

Although all factors are important to teachers, educational factors relate most directly to instruction. They are factors teachers can control.

R · E · F · E · R · E · N · C · E · S

Anderson, R. C., and P. Freebody. "Vocabulary Knowledge." In J. T. Guthrie, ed., *Comprehension and Teaching: Research Views.* Newark, DE: International Reading Association, 1981.

Bateman, B. D. "Educational implications of minimal brain dysfunction." *The Reading Teacher* 27 (April 1974): 662–668.

Bernstein, B. "Social Class and Linguistic Development: A Theory of Social Learning." In A. H. Halsey, J. Floud, and C. A. Anderson, eds. *Education, Economy and Society.* New York: Free Press, 1961.

Bettelheim, B., and Karen Zelan. *On Learning to Read.* New York: Vintage Books, 1982.

Bransford, J. D. "Schema Activation and Schema Acquisition: Comments on Richard C. Anderson's Remarks." In H. Singer and R. B. Ruddell, eds. *Theoretical Models and Processes of Reading,* 3rd ed. Newark, DE: International Reading Association, 1985.

Bristow, P. S. "Are poor readers passive readers? Some evidence, possible explanations, and potential solutions." *The Reading Teacher* 39 (1985): 318–325.

Brown, D. A. *Reading Diagnosis and Remediation.* Englewood Cliffs, NJ: Prentice–Hall, 1982.

Carpenter, P. A., M. A. Just, and J. L. McDonald. *Reading and Processing Differences Between Dyslexic and Normal College Students.* Technical Report. Pittsburgh, PA: Carnegie–Mellon University Department of Psychology, 1984.

Devine, T. G. *Teaching Reading Comprehension: From Theory to Practice.* Boston: Allyn and Bacon, 1986.

Downing, J., and Che Kan Leong. *Psychology of Reading.* New York: Macmillan, 1982.

Dreby, C. "Vision problems and reading disability: A dilemma for the reading specialist." *The Reading Teacher* 32 (April 1979): 787–795.

Dunn, N. E. "Children's achievement at school-entry age as a function of mothers' and fathers' teaching sets." *Elementary School Journal* 81 (1981): 244–253.

Durr, W. K., and J. J. Pikulski. *Reading Research and the Houghton Mifflin Program.* Boston: Houghton Mifflin, 1981.

Early, M. "Components of a Language Arts Program in the Primary Grades." In R. C. Aukerman, ed. *Some Persistent Questions on Beginning Reading.* Newark, DE: International Reading Association, 1972.

Eder, D. "Ability grouping of students and academic self-concepts: A case study." *Elementary School Journal* 84 (1983): 149–161.

Ekwall, E. T., and J. L. Shanker. *Diagnosis and Remediation of the Disabled Reader.* Boston: Allyn and Bacon, 1983.

Elkonin, D. "U.S.S.R." In John Downing, ed. *Comparative Reading: Cross National Studies of Behavior and Processes in Reading and Writing.* New York: Macmillan, 1973.

Eshel, Y., and Z. Klein. "Development of academic self-concept of lower-class and middle-class primary school children." *Journal of Educational Psychology* 73 (1981): 287–293.

Feuerstein, R. *Instrumental Enrichment.* Baltimore, MD: University Park Press, 1979.

Frith, U. "Beneath the Surface of Developmental Dyslexia: Are Comparisons Between Developmental and Acquired Disorders Meaningful?" In K. E. Patterson et al., eds. *Surface Dyslexia: Neuropsychological and Cognitive Studies of Phonological Reading.* Hillsdale, NJ: Erlbaum, 1985.

Gentile, L. M., and M. M. McMillan. *Stress and Reading Difficulties.* Newark, DE: International Reading Association, 1987.

Gillet, J. W., and C. Temple. *Understanding Reading Problems: Assessment and Instruction,* 2nd ed. Boston: Little, Brown, 1986.

Green, R. "Tips on educational testing: What teachers and parents should know." *Phi Delta Kappan* 57 (October 1975): 89–93.

Greenslade, B. "The basics in reading from the perspective of the learner." *The Reading Teacher* 34 (November 1980): 192–195.

Harris, A., and E. Sipay. *How to Increase Reading Ability,* 7th ed. New York: Longman, 1980.

Heath, S. B. *Ways with Words: Language, Life and Work in Communities and Classrooms.* New York: Cambridge University Press, 1983.

Herber, R. H., S. Barber, C. Hoffman, and C. Fallander. "Rehabilitation of Families at Risk for Mental Retardation." *Rehabilitation Research Training Center in Mental Retardation Progress Report.* Madison, WI: University of Wisconsin Press, 1972.

Jensen, A. "How much can we boost I.Q. and scholastic achievement?" *Harvard Educational Review* 39 (1969): 449–483.

_____. *Bias in Mental Testing.* New York: Macmillan, 1979.

Kaufman, A. S. *Intelligent Testing with the W.I.S.C.–R.* New York: Wiley Publishing Company, 1979.

Lerner, J. W. *Learning Disabilities: Theories, Diagnosis and Teaching Strategies*, 3rd ed. Boston: Houghton Mifflin, 1981.

Lewkowicz, N. K. "Phonemic awareness training: What to teach and how to teach it." *Journal of Educational Psychology* 72 (1980): 686–700.

Lund, N. J., and J. F. Duchan. *Assessing Children's Language in Naturalistic Contexts*, 2nd ed. Englewood Cliffs, NJ: Prentice–Hall, 1988.

Manning, J. C. *Reading: Learning and Instructional Processes*. Boulder, CO: Paladin, 1980.

Mathewson, G. C. "Toward a Comprehensive Model of Affect in the Reading Process." In H. Singer and R. B. Ruddell, eds. *Theoretical Models and Processes of Reading*. Newark, DE: International Reading Association, 1985.

Monroe, M., and B. Backus. *Remedial Reading: A Monograph in Character Education*. Boston: Houghton Mifflin, 1937.

Moore, D., and O. Wielan. "W.I.S.C.–R. scatter indices of children referred for reading diagnosis." *Journal of Learning Disabilities* 14 (1981): 511–514.

Norton, D. *The Effective Teaching of Language Arts*. Columbus, OH: Merrill, 1980.

Olson, D. R. "See! Jumping! Some Oral Language Antecedents of Literacy." In H. Goelman, A. Oberg, and F. Smith, eds. *Awakening to Literacy*. Exeter, N.H.: Heinemann, 1984.

Patterson, K. E., J. C. Marshall, and M. Coltheart, eds. *Surface Dyslexia: Neuropsychological and Cognitive Studies of Phonological Reading*. Hillside, N.J.: Erlbaum, 1985.

Quandt, I., and R. Selznick. *Self-Concept and Reading*. Newark, DE: International Reading Association, 1984.

Rie, H., and E. Rie, eds. *Handbook of Minimal Brain Dysfunction: A Critical View*. New York: John Wiley, 1980.

Selzer, C. A. *Lateral Dominance and Visual Fusion: Harvard Monographs in Education, No. 12*. Cambridge, MA: Harvard University, 1933.

Smith, F. "Demonstrations, engagements and sensitivity: A revised approach to language learning." *Language Arts* 58 (1981): 103–112.

Spache, G. *Diagnosing and Correcting Reading Disabilities*. Boston: Allyn and Bacon, 1981.

Speidel, G. E. "Responding to Language Differences." In *Oral Language in a Successful Reading Program for Hawaiian Children. Technical Report No. 105*. Kamehameha Early Education Program, 1982.

Strang, R. *Reading Diagnosis and Remediation*. Newark, DE: International Reading Association, 1968.

Strauss, A., and L. Lehtinen. *Psychopathology and Education of the Brain-Injured Child*. New York: Grune and Stratton, 1947.

Taylor, B., L. A. Harris, and P. D. Pearson. *Reading Difficulties: Instruction and Assessment*. New York: Random House, 1988.

Vygotsky, L. *Thought in Language*, Cambridge, MA: MIT Press, 1962.

_____. *Mind in Society*. Cambridge, MA: Harvard University Press, 1978.

Weaver, P. *Research Within Research: A Research-Guided Response to Concerns of Reading Educators*. Washington, D.C.: National Institute of Education, 1980.

Wechsler, D. *Manual: Wechsler Intelligence Scale for Children—Revised*. New York: Psychological Corporation, 1974.

_____. *The Measurement and Appraisal of Adult Intelligence*, 4th ed. Baltimore, MD: Williams and Wilkins, 1975.

Wigfield, A., and S. R. Asher. "Social and Motivational Influences on Reading." In P. D. Pearson, R. Barr, M. L. Kamil, and P. Mosenthal, eds. *Handbook of Reading Research*. New York: Longman, 1984.

Wilson, P. T., and R. C. Anderson. "Reading Comprehension and School Learning." In J. Osborn, P. T. Wilson, and R. C. Anderson, eds. *Reading Education: Foundations for a Literate America*. Lexington, MA: Lexington Books, 1985.

Wilson, R. *Diagnostic and Remedial Reading for Classroom and Clinic*. Columbus, OH: Charles E. Merrill, 1981.

Zintz, M. V., and Maggart, Z. R. *Corrective Reading*, 8th ed. Dubuque, IA: William C. Brown, 1986.

3 Formal Reading Diagnosis

FOCUS   1. How is formal reading diagnosis defined?
QUESTIONS   2. What part does formal diagnosis play in the total process of diagnosis?
3. What are the major strengths of formal diagnosis?
4. What are the major limitations of formal diagnosis?
5. What factors assist teachers in appropriately evaluating formal test results?
6. How can teachers use formal test results to plan appropriate instructional programs for children?

The terms "formal diagnosis" and "formal testing" have been used throughout the first two chapters. You might ask "What is formal diagnosis?" Formal diagnosis refers to the process of gaining information about the performance of learners through the use of commercially developed formal tests. Formal tests are of two basic types: norm-referenced tests and criterion-referenced tests.

NORM-REFERENCED TESTS

Norm-referenced tests are carefully constructed to assess learner performance on particular skills and competencies, and to provide a detailed comparative analysis of children's reading behavior. The tests are designed specifically to compare the scores of test takers to the scores of the sample of students used to "standardize" the test (Just and Carpenter 1987). The group of students used for standardization is referred to as the original norming sample. To determine the norms of a formal test, authors initially administer the test to a sample of children representing the total group to which the test should be given. For example, a test created for first through sixth grade students is first given to a cross-representation of first through sixth graders. More specifically, the average performance of second graders on the test is based on a sample of between 150 and 500 second graders, depending on the test. The average performance establishes second grade "norms." The performance of other second graders is then compared to the performance of the second graders in the original norming sample, leading to the use of the terms "on grade level," "above grade level," and "below grade level."

For norms to be valid, the number of children in the sample should be large enough to provide a fair average. The sample should also include representative numbers of boys and girls of different ethnic and socioeconomic backgrounds. Some authors administer tests separately to several groups of children (inner-city, gifted, rural, high socioeconomic status, low socioeconomic status, etc.) and produce individual sets of norms for different populations of children.

In summary, norm-referenced tests are initially administered to large numbers of children to establish norms. The norms represent the average performance of pre-selected groups of children. The performance of those subsequently taking the test is then compared to the norms.

Reporting Results

The results of norm-referenced tests are generally reported in one or more of the following formats (Plas 1985):

1. *Raw Scores.* Raw scores indicate the total number of correct items on each section (subtest) of a test. The scores show only the number correct and not the specific items answered correctly. Because of this, raw scores by themselves provide little useful information. For example, a child getting six out of ten correct on a consonant blend subtest would have a raw score of six. Referring to the raw score, you would not know which blends the child knew. You would need to refer to the actual test to identify the specific items. Because raw scores have so little meaning, they are usually converted to one of the other types of scores described in this section.

2. *Grade Equivalent Scores.* Grade scores are probably the most popular reporting formats. Raw scores are usually converted to grade-level scores. A raw score of fifteen, for example, might indicate a grade score of three and one half. This grade score is often interpreted incorrectly to suggest that the child should be reading at a third grade, fifth month level. Actually, the score means that the child answered as many items correctly as the average third graders in the fifth month of school who were in the original norming population. Norming procedures generally require testing of children at the start or end of the school year and not every month. Month values are statistically interpolated.

Grade equivalent scores require careful interpretation. In 1981 the International Reading Association passed a resolution urging teachers and diagnosticians to refrain from using grade equivalent scores to report students' performance. The resolution also suggested that publishers eliminate grade scores from tests. The reasons were that grade scores do not indicate at what level the child is actually reading or at what level the child should be reading. In addition, they do not assess appropriate progress or identify strengths or weaknesses. A grade score represents the level at which the child's reading broke down; it indicates a frustration level for the child.

3. *Percentiles.* Percentiles indicate the position of the individual's score in relation to the distribution of scores in the original norming

TABLE 3.1   Summary of Reporting Formats

Scores	Derivation	Advantages	Disadvantages
• Raw Scores	Actual number of items correct.	Easy scoring. Can be converted to other types of scores.	Do not identify specific correct and incorrect items.
• Grade Equivalent Scores	Comparison with scores received by norm group.	Can reflect students performance in comparison to a wider, more generalized group.	Do not assess progress. Do not identify strengths and weaknesses. May reflect frustration levels.
• Percentiles	Relative performance compared to norm group.	Reflect student's position compared to the wider norm group.	Do not identify actual performance profiles.
• Stanines	Distribution of possible scores divided into nine equal parts.	Identify student's position compared to the average of possible scores.	Provide no specific diagnostic and remedial information.

sample. Percentiles range from 1 to 99. A percentile score of 75 means that the child's performance was as good as or better than 75 percent of the norm group and poorer than 24 percent of the norm group. Percentile scores, then, show children's relative performance.

The distance between percentile points is not equal. Percentile scores therefore should not be averaged, added, or subtracted in order to describe reading growth. Be careful in reporting percentile scores to parents. Parents often interpret the score to mean the percentage of items correct rather than the relative position of the child's score.

4. *Stanines.* Stanines are somewhat similar to percentiles. The word stanine is an abbreviation for standard nine. Stanine scores have values ranging from 1 to 9, with 1 the lowest score and 9 the highest. In order to produce stanine scores, the distribution of possible scores is divided into nine equal parts. The mean score is 5. Most children's scores (54 percent) fall in stanines 4, 5, and 6; performance in these stanines is considered average. Fewer children's scores fall in stanines 1, 2, and 3 (23 percent) and stanines 7, 8, and 9 (23 percent). Stanines make raw scores more meaningful. For example, if a child's score falls in stanine 7, the child's performance is considered above average. This is more meaningful information than knowing that a child received a raw score of 73 or that the child's grade score is 4.5. Reporting formats are summarized in Table 3.1.

Types of Norm-Referenced Reading Tests

Standardized reading tests fall into three basic categories: survey tests, diagnostic tests, and literacy tests.

Survey Tests.   Survey tests are used to assess students' general reading level and to identify students with possible severe reading difficulties. Surveys indicate overall and general performance levels rather than specific skill strengths and needs (Gillet and Temple 1986). Survey tests usually consist of two to four subtests, such as reading vocabulary, comprehension, study skills, and reading rate. Most survey tests provide two similarly normed forms. One form is usually administered at the start of the school year or at the onset of intensive diagnosis. After the students have had instruction or remediation the second form is administered. The results of the forms are compared to assess growth.

Individually administered and group administered survey tests are available. Individually administered tests provide more information because teachers can directly observe the strategies readers use to answer the questions. Information such as response time, specific phonic analysis skills, speed, and confidence permit valuable insights into children's strengths and needs.

Survey tests are popular for their many advantages. They are comparatively easy to administer in both individual and group settings and have few directions demanding administration training or preparation. They can often be administered in one short sitting. They provide quick screening for large numbers of children, pinpointing students with reading difficulties in a short period of time.

Survey tests also have limitations. They are broad and general in content. Low scores on subtests therefore do not provide much information about specific skills children are missing (Taylor et al. 1988). Surveys tend to overestimate reading performance, particularly in group administered tests. Survey tests should therefore be supplemented by careful observation and performance monitoring, especially if scores are used for reading placement. Survey test results tend to give a more accurate estimate of average performance than of high or low performance. The abilities of very good readers are usually underestimated, while the scores of poor readers are often inflated.

In using survey tests with children, remember to analyze carefully the tasks children must perform. Since reading tasks vary greatly you should make sure the tasks reflect reading behavior as children practice it in your classroom. A listing of some of the better-known survey tests follows:

> *Comprehensive Test of Basic Skills: Reading*
>> (California Test Bureau/McGraw–Hill, 1970)
>> Group administered: 40 to 60 minutes
>> Grades 2.5 to 12
>> Tests reading, vocabulary, and comprehension.
>
> *Gates–MacGinitie Reading Tests*
>> (Teachers College Press, 1978)
>> Group administered: 40 to 60 minutes

Six levels, grades 1 through 9

Subtests in vocabulary, comprehension, accuracy and reading rate.

Peabody Individual Achievement Test (PIAT)

(American Guidance Service, 1981)

Individually administered: 30 to 40 minutes

One form, grades K through 12

Math, reading recognition, reading comprehension, spelling, and general information subtests.

Slosson Oral Reading Test

(Slosson Educational Publications, 1981)

Individually administered: 3 to 5 minutes

Grades 1 through 12

Students read aloud from 20 graded lists.

Wide Range Achievement Test (WRAT)

(McGraw–Hill, 1976)

Individually administered: 25 to 40 minutes

Two levels, 5 years through adult

Letter recognition, oral reading graded word lists.

Woodcock Reading Mastery Tests

(American Guidance Service, 1987)

Individual test: 30 to 40 minutes

Two forms, grades 1 through 9

Letter and word identification, word attack and word comprehension subtests.

A comprehensive listing and review of reading tests can be found in the *Ninth Mental Measurement Yearbook* (1985).

Diagnostic Tests.   Unlike survey tests, diagnostic tests are specifically constructed to provide a detailed analysis of readers' strengths and needs. They include a large number of subtests and a large number of items for each. Diagnostic tests generally fit into two categories: reading batteries and tests of specific reading skills.

Diagnostic reading batteries assess specific skills by means of specific subtests. Results are expected to yield a reading profile of the student. This profile identifies the student's strengths and weaknesses in specific skills. Reading batteries evaluate oral reading, silent reading, reading comprehension (literal, inferential, evaluative), vocabulary (sight and meaning), auditory discrimination, visual discrimination, a range of phonic analysis skills, and syllabication. Because of the many subtests in diagnostic batteries, they are often administered at more than one sitting. However, it is not sound diagnostic practice to give every subtest merely because it is provided. Teachers often begin with the major subtests of word recognition, comprehension, oral reading, and silent reading. The child's performance on these subtests might warrant further testing. The child's performance on each subtest should enable the teacher to ask and answer important diagnostic questions.

CLASSROOM APPLICATION

Subtest 1 – Word Recognition and Analysis

The child is asked to read a list of words. The teacher administers the test with the following questions in mind:

- What words are recognized immediately?
- What words are recognized after analysis or "sounding out?"
- What class of words is most easily or least easily recognized?
- What phonic strategies are used for analyzing unrecognized words?
- What parts of words are most or least successfully analyzed (beginning, middle, or end)?
- Which phonic skills are consistently misused or unused?

The child's performance might be assessed as follows:

Word Was	Child Said	Possible Problem
tree	tree	none
anything	thing	sight word any
she	see	sh
brown	bon	br
black	back	bl
from	from	none
would	____	sight word would
now	no	ow (or child read ow as in know)
like	lik	final e
hand	had	nd
said	said	none
home	hom	final e

Careful analysis of each item shows that this child demonstrates the following problems: basic sight words, consonant combinations in both beginning and ending positions, vowel combinations and the final e construction, and the ow digraph. The child also demonstrates clear strengths in short medial vowel sounds and initial single consonants. On the basis of the results of this subtest, the teacher should consider administering additional subtests on consonant clusters and on vowel combinations and forms.

In administering the second major subtest, oral reading, the teacher might ask the following questions:

- Are the error patterns detected in subtest one still evident in subtest two?

- Are some errors made in isolation (word recognition) that are not made in context (oral reading)?
- Does the child use context appropriately?
- Does the child use appropriate expression?
- Does the child observe punctuation appropriately?
- Does the child use non-word substitutions (e.g., *stet* for *street*) or contextually appropriate substitutions (e.g., *road* for *street*)?

The second subtest supports or does not support previously gained information, answers predetermined questions and raises new ones, and directs further testing. The results of the oral reading subtest might lead the teacher in a new direction.

CLASSROOM APPLICATION

Subtest 2 – Oral Reading

The child is asked to read a series of passages orally. Passage C reads:

> Peter got a bright new bike for his birthday.
> The bike was blue with red lines on it.
> Peter loved the bike. He wanted to ride it
> right away, but it was too dark after his
> party. He had to wait until the next day.

Comprehension check:

1. What did Peter get for his birthday?
2. What color was his present?
3. How did Peter feel about his present?
4. Why couldn't he use his present right away?

Child reads:

> Peter got a *big* new *bick* for his birthday.
> The *bake* was *big* with red *lins* on it. Peter
> love s the *bake*. He want s to *rip* it
> . . . , but it was too *dack* after
> his *pat*. He had to *wet* . . . the . . . day.

This passage is clearly at the child's frustration level; it is written beyond the level at which the child can cope. However, the reading provides useful information for the diagnostician, as the following analysis shows:

Word Was	Child Said	Possible Problem
bright	*big*	*br*, *ight*, and confusion of long and short vowels
bike	*bick*	final e

Word Was	Child Said	Possible Problem
bike	*bake*	short *i*
blue	*big*	sight word, *bl* and *ue*
lines	*lin*	final *e* and word ending
loved	*loves*	word ending
wanted	*wants*	word ending
ride	*rip*	final *e* and /*d*/
right	____	sight word
away	____	sight word
dark	*dack*	*ar*
party	*pat*	*ar*
wait	*wet*	*ai*
until	____	sight word
next	____	sight word

Analysis of the child's performance supports some of the conclusions of the first subtest. Recurring problems include basic sight vocabulary, consonant combinations, vowel combinations, and the final *e* construction. Further testing for consonant combinations, vowel combinations and vowel forms would be strongly recommended. The oral reading subtest also provides some important additional information, including the weak use of context and the pattern of nonword substitution. The child made many errors both in isolation and in context, and ignored meaning while reading.

The effective use of diagnostic batteries depends on careful analysis of children's performance. Analysis guides the teacher in making decisions about administering additional subtests.

The following chart demonstrates how one can analyze students' performance on tests and use that information to make decisions related to further subtest administration.

Major Question: Into which categories do the child's errors fall?

A. Auditory Memory and Blending

Observation:	The child sounds out word parts correctly but blends them incorrectly.
Question:	Can the child hold auditory stimuli in memory and blend the stimuli appropriately?
Subtest Indicated:	Auditory blending

B. Consonant Confusion

Observation:	Child misses a number of consonant combinations.

Question:	Does the child know consonant combinations?
Subtest Indicated:	Consonant combinations
Question (if child fails):	Does the child know the single consonants?
Subtest Indicated:	Single consonant sounds
Question (if child fails):	Does the child hear the differences among the sounds represented by the letters?
Subtest Indicated:	Auditory discrimination
Question (if child does poorly):	Does the child recognize the names of the letters?
Subtest Indicated:	Letter name
Question (if child confuses letters):	Does the child generally confuse visual forms?
Subtest Indicated:	Visual discrimination

C. Vowel Confusion

Observation:	The child misses a number of vowel combinations.
Question:	Does the child generally understand vowel combinations and forms?
Subtest Indicated:	Vowel combinations and vowel forms
Question (if child fails):	Does the child know single vowel sounds?
Subtest Indicated:	Single vowels
Question (if child fails):	Does the child *hear* the differences among the vowel sounds?
Subtest Indicated:	Auditory discrimination
Question (if child fails):	Does the child recognize the forms and names?
Subtest Indicated:	Letter name
Question (if child fails):	Does the child generally confuse visual forms?
Subtest Indicated:	Visual discrimination

Test administration involves much more than merely administering subtests. It requires close observation, analysis, and evaluation. The results of formal testing provide you with information about the strengths and needs of children. The results therefore have direct implication for instruction and remediation.

Diagnostic reading batteries provide broad, superficial coverage of a range of skills. Tests of specific reading skills, on the other hand, provide more extensive coverage, such as oral reading, phonic analysis, and word recognition. These tests give more comprehensive information about individual reading subskills. Specific tests are often administered as the result of specific weaknesses in children's performance, and give more extensive information than do particular subtests in a diagnostic battery.

Diagnostic tests have several strengths. They provide information on the strengths and weaknesses of children, including profiles of skill strengths and weaknesses. They provide teachers with initial directions for skill instruction and remediation. They also provide teachers the opportunity to observe closely children's reading performance and to perform a detailed analysis of individual skills.

Diagnostic tests have some serious limitations as well. They offer little assistance in remediation unless teachers analyze the actual responses of children and identify specific strengths and needs. Although many skills are tested in reading batteries, subtests assess only a sample of skills. Of approximately thirty consonant combinations, for example, a subtest might include ten or fifteen. The result, then, would indicate a child's knowledge of the selected consonant combinations and not others. The same is true of all skill areas, including sight vocabulary, meaning vocabulary, phonic skills, study skills, and comprehension. Diagnostic tests provide only a starting point for instruction and remediation. Because tests include only a sample of reading skills, ongoing informal diagnosis should always follow formal diagnosis.

Formal tests often predispose teachers to focus on children's weaknesses. The tests lure many teachers into accepting the medical model of diagnosis, which involves locating the illness (skill deficit) and concentrating directly on eradicating the problem, often without due attention to the rest of the "whole." Test results are too often used to identify specific skill deficiencies and to build total remedial programs around those deficiencies. This approach not only ignores children's strengths but dissects reading into isolated skill learning, which provides too little exposure to real reading. Because formal diagnostic tests are administered in a "one shot" fashion—usually at the beginning and end of a school year or of a long-term instructional period, there is often no systematic follow-up analysis. As a result many teachers tend to view diagnosis as a one-time procedure and fail to internalize its ongoing nature.

Most formal diagnostic tests are very limited in their assessment of comprehension skills. In general, the questions used to assess comprehension require only literal comprehension. Questions are seldom well written, often not text dependent, and require too few responses to provide valid conclusions. A listing of some of the better known and more widely used diagnostic tests follows.

Examples of Diagnostic Tests

Durrell Analysis of Reading Difficulty
(The Psychological Corporation, 1980)
Grades 1 through 6

Measures oral reading, silent reading, comprehension, listening comprehension, instant word recognition and word analysis, listening vocabulary, visual memory for words, identifying sounds in words and in isolation, phonic spelling of words, individual phonic tests (consonants, vowels, combinations), and spelling.

Individual test, one form: 30 to 90 minutes.

Gates–McKillop–Horowitz Reading Diagnostic Tests

(Teachers College Press, 1981)

Grades 1 through 6

Contains graded paragraphs for oral reading, instant vowel recognition and delayed word analysis, word attack (using nonsense words) syllabication, blending word parts, letter sounds and names, auditory blending and discrimination, and spelling.

Individual test, one form: 30 to 90 minutes.

Nelson Reading Skills Test

(Riverside Publishing Co., 1977)

Grades 3 through 9

Subtests include word meaning, reading comprehension, symbol/sound knowledge, identifying root words, reading rate, and syllabication.

Group test, two forms: 45 to 90 minutes.

Reading Diagnosis

(Jamestown Press, 1981)

Grades 1 through 6

Subtests include oral and silent reading, sight word recognition, listening vocabulary, letter and number recognition, handwriting, spelling and auditory and visual abilities.

Also includes an interest inventory and a parent interview form.

Individual or group, one form: approximately 30 to 90 minutes.

Stanford Diagnostic Reading Tests

(The Psychological Corporation, 1984)

Grades 1 through 12

Subtests include auditory discrimination, vocabulary, phonic analysis, word recognition, and reading comprehension.

Group test, two forms: approximately 60 to 120 minutes.

Woodcock–Johnson Psychoeducational Battery

(Teaching Resources Corporation, 1977)

Grades preschool to adult

Evaluates cognitive ability in 12 subtests: picture vocabulary, spatial relations, sentence memory, visual-auditory learning, blending, number concepts, visual matching, antonyms and synonyms, synthesis and analysis, numbers reversed, concept formation, and analogies. Four subtests directly relate to reading. These are letter-word identification, word attack, passage comprehension, and reading interest.

Individual test: approximately 120 minutes for the entire battery; approximately 30 to 45 minutes for reading related subtests.

Diagnostic Tests of Specific Skills

Doren Diagnostic Reading Test of Word Recognition Skills
   (American Guidance Service, 1973)
   Grades 1 through 3
   Subtests include letter recognition, beginning and ending sounds, whole word recognition, recognizing words within words, blending, rhyming, vowels, and spelling.
   Group test, one form: approximately 1 to 2 hours.

Gilmore Oral Reading Test
   (Psychological Corporation, 1968)
   Grades 1 through 8
   Assesses oral reading through the use of ten graded paragraphs. Each is followed by five comprehension questions.
   Individual test, four forms: approximately 15 to 20 minutes.

Gray Oral Reading Tests
   (Psychological Corporation, 1976)
   Grades 1 through 12
   Uses thirteen timed, graded reading passages, each followed by four questions assessing oral reading. Errors only in word recognition are used for grade placement.
   Individual test, four forms: approximately 15 to 20 minutes.

McCullough Word Analysis Test
   (Personnel Press, 1963)
   Grades 4 through 6
   Contains seven subtests, each using thirty items.
   Subtests include initial consonant blends and digraphs, vowel discrimination, matching letters to vowel sounds, sounding whole words, interpreting phonic symbols, dividing words into syllables, and root words.
   Individual or group test, one form: approximately 45 to 75 minutes.

Silent Reading Diagnostic Tests
   (Rand McNally, 1970)
   Grades 2 through 6
   Contains subtests such as words in isolation (select a word that describes a picture), words in context (select a word that completes a sentence), visual structural analysis (divide words with affixes), syllabication (given six rules, divide words into syllables), word synthesis (blend words hyphenated at the end of a line), beginning sounds (select sounds

similar to a stimulus word), ending sounds (select letters that represent stimulus words).

Group test, one form: approximately 60 to 90 minutes.

Literacy Tests.   Literacy tests assess an individual's ability to read functional material common in everyday contexts. These tests are often used with older remedial readers or to assess minimal competencies for high school graduation. The focus is on an individual's ability to function in society with the normal print in the environment—traffic signs, recipes, menus, bills, applications, and the like.

Teachers of intermediate grade remedial students need to know the content of literacy tests. Regardless of reading abilities, certain functional levels of reading should be achieved. Teachers should begin in the intermediate grades to ensure that children can cope in society. This thrust should parallel developmental or remedial programs. Some examples of literacy tests follow.

Examples of Literacy Tests

Adult Basic Learning Examination
　　(The Psychological Corporation, 1974)
　　Remedial through adult
　　Measures oral vocabulary, basic reading comprehension, problem solving, spelling, and math computation.
　　Individual test, two forms: approximately 40 to 60 minutes.
Adult Basic Reading Inventory
　　(Scholastic Testing Services, 1966)
　　Grades 6 through 12
　　Subtests include vocabulary (match pictures to words), beginning sounds (match beginning sounds to printed words), word matching (match words to synonyms), listening vocabulary, and contextual material (short passages).
　　Group tests, one form: approximately 45 to 60 minutes.

CRITERION-REFERENCED TESTS

Whereas norm-referenced tests compare the performance of one student or a group of students to norms established by a preselected group of students, criterion-referenced tests determine to what extent students have mastered specifically identified competencies. Norm-referenced tests compare student performance while criterion-referenced tests assess student mastery of specific skills (Sax 1980, Richek et al. 1983, McCormick 1987). The intent of criterion-referenced testing is to identify specific skills that have or have not been mastered (Rude and Oehlkers 1984).

Criterion-referenced testing was used as early as the 1960s. The basic concept has been embodied in a variety of terms, including domain-referenced testing, objective-referenced testing, content-referenced testing, maximum performance testing, and mastery testing. However, all criterion-referenced measures have the following characteristics.

1. Identification of essential skills. Criterion-referenced tests identify the skills essential for performance in a given domain. In reading, for example, identified skills might include word recognition, word analysis, phonic analysis, syllabication, vocabulary, and comprehension.

2. Translation of essential skills into clearly stated tasks. The term "criterion" refers to specific tasks to be mastered. A criterion-referenced test must therefore include items relating to a clearly defined set of tasks. Such tasks provide clear evidence of specific behaviors.

3. Precision in skill statements and clear evidence of whether or not students have met the criterion. Criterion-referenced tests require precise objectives (e.g., "Given a one second exposure per word, the child can correctly read with 90 percent accuracy a set of 15 words written at the first grade level"). Precisely stated objectives fulfill three mandatory requirements: defining the task to be accomplished, the conditions under which the learner will perform the task, and the exact level of performance required for mastery of the task.

After a criterion-referenced test is administered, emphasis is placed on directly teaching those skills that have not been mastered. This is not the same as the much criticized practice of "teaching to the test." Remember that the purpose of a criterion-referenced test is to evaluate student performance according to specific standards and to instruct children in the skills they are missing. Criterion-referenced tests, then, relate directly to instruction and remediation.

In criterion-referenced tests items are arranged in a sequence or skill hierarchy. The sequence is divided into grade levels, establishing specific criteria for each grade level. Many schools use criterion-referenced tests designed to accompany their basal reading series. Other schools use independently published tests. In any case, the sequence of skills presented in the tests must match the sequence in which skills are instructed to students.

Strengths and Limitations of Criterion-Referenced Tests

Criterion-referenced tests have some definite advantages. Their most significant strength is the fact that they can directly pinpoint the skills students can and cannot perform. This ability to diagnose exact skill deficits is useful in evaluating the success of remedial or instructional programs for teaching specific skills. Growth in specific skills can be measured easily through pre- and post-test measures. Criterion-referenced tests directly relate instruction to assessment, and provide a fair assessment of skills. In addition, they focus on individual rather than comparative skill development, and provide more comprehensive coverage of individual skills than do norm-referenced tests. Criterion-referenced subtests are usually longer, covering more items within each area.

Criterion-referenced tests also have limitations. Because the more literal and factual skills are more easily measured, these tests tend to emphasize basic skills over real higher-level reading skills, such as inferential thinking, prediction, critical thinking, problem solving, and creative thinking.

The segmentation of reading into numerous individual skills might give teachers the impression that reading is the sum of many splintered parts rather than a holistic process. Many teachers use the criterion-referenced skill sequence to define the parameters of their reading programs. As a result, they view reading as a series of skills, and emphasize children's mastery of individual skills rather than the reading process, which involves a range of higher-level thinking skills.

Some criterion-referenced tests include subtests dealing extensively with skills that have dubious value in actual reading (e.g., stress marks, dividing words into syllables, etc.). If these subtests are used to define program emphasis, children who most need exposure to real reading might be locked into hours of drill in skills that do not further their reading performance.

Finally, criterion-referenced test items have a hierarchical arrangement based on the assumption that there are a specific number of skills used in reading and that these skills are acquired in a specific order. Research does not support this assumption. Programs built around criterion-referenced tests often result in rigid and inflexible skill instruction. A listing of some of the better known criterion-referenced tests follows.

Examples of Criterion-Referenced Tests

Brigance Diagnostic Inventory of Basic Skills
> (Curriculum Associates, 1977)
> Diagnostic battery
> Grades 1 through 6
> Contains 141 criterion-referenced subtests for readiness, reading, reference skills, math, handwriting, spelling, and grammar.
> Reading subtests include word recognition, word analysis, oral reading, reading rate, and comprehension.
> Individual test, one form: approximately 90 minutes.

Comprehensive Test of Basic Skills: Reading, Expanded Edition
> (California Test Bureau, McGraw-Hill, 1976)
> Grades kindergarten through 12

Contains a wide range of reading and study skills subtests. Reading subtests include reading comprehension, word recognition, and word analysis.

Individual test, one form: approximately 30 to 60 minutes.

Cooper–McGuire Diagnostic Word Analysis Test

(Croft Educational Service, 1972)

Grades 1 through 5

Subtests include readiness for word analysis, phonic analysis, and structural analysis skills.

Group test, one form: 20 to 45 minutes.

Corrective Reading System

(Psychotechnic, 1976)

Assesses performance on a variety of subtests, including sight vocabulary, phonic analysis, structural analysis, upper- and lower-case letter recognition, vowels and vowel combinations, and consonants and consonant combinations.

Individual test, one form: approximately 30 to 90 minutes.

Doren Diagnostic Reading Test of Word Recognition Skills

(American Guidance Service, 1973)

Grades 1 through 3

Diagnostic test with subtests including letter recognition, beginning sounds, word recognition, blending, rhyming, and vowel sounds.

Group test, one form: approximately 45 minutes to 2 hours.

Group Phonic Analysis

(Dreier Educational Systems, 1971)

Grades 1 through 3

Diagnostic test assessing basic phonic skills such as long and short vowels, consonant sounds, vowel rules, and alphabetizing.

Group test, one form: approximately 20 to 30 minutes.

Oral Reading Criterion Test

(Dreier Educational Systems, 1971)

Grades 1 through 7

Consists of a number of graded oral reading passages.

Individual test: approximately 15 to 25 minutes.

Prescriptive Reading Inventory

(California Test Bureau, McGraw-Hill, 1977)

Grades 1 through 6

Subtests include symbol-sound knowledge, phonic analysis, structural analysis, and comprehension.

Group test: approximately 20 to 30 minutes.

Wisconsin Design for Reading Skill Development

(Multi-Learning Systems, 1972)

Grades kindergarten through 6

Diagnostic test including subskills in word recognition, word attack, study skills, comprehension, interpretive and creative reading.

Individual or group test: approximately 30 to 60 minutes.

Performance Assessment in Reading

(California Test Bureau, 1978)

Grades 7 through 9

Literacy test assessing minimal competency in reading.

Seventy-two items focusing on survival reading, including warning signs, card catalogues, telephone directories, bus schedules, and encyclopedia entries.

Group test, one form: approximately 30 to 60 minutes.

Reading/Everyday Activities in Life (REAL)

(Westwood Press, 1978)

Grades 4 through adult

Assesses functional reading.

Individual or group test, one form: approximately 45 to 90 minutes.

CAUTIONS REGARDING FORMAL TESTS

Educators continually use formal test results to make important decisions about individual children and groups of children. These decisions include grouping children for instruction, placing children in special programs, and retaining children in programs or grade levels. Results of these formal instruments are weighted so heavily that often one percentage, percentile, or raw score point determines the decisions. It is therefore imperative that you understand the fundamental concepts underlying test construction and the factors that should lend caution to your judgment of children based on test results (Mitchell 1985). The factors of which you should be aware are:

1. Date of publication
2. Norming population
3. Reliability
4. Validity
5. Standard error of measurement
6. Standardization procedures

Date of Publication

Tests are usually revised every five to eight years. Often, however, test editions continue to be used even after ten, fifteen, or twenty years. Since groups of children change significantly over time, however, it is unwise to use the norms developed for one group of children to judge other groups ten or fifteen years later. Although the content of some subtests might not alter significantly over time (e.g., phonic subtests), other subtests might be greatly affected. For example, words change in familiarity over time. Such words as *video* and *computer* are commonplace today, but would have been unknown to the children of a few years ago. Similarly, such words as *parasol* and *divan* were far more familiar years ago than they are today. Teachers should analyze word recognition subtests on older tests to assess the general familiarity of the words.

Comprehension tests might be "dated" because comprehension depends to a large degree on prior knowledge. Passage content generally familiar to children facilitates comprehension. Unfamiliar content blocks comprehension. Reading passages designed for comprehension assessment tend to reflect the issues prevalent in society, in which case children using older tests might be unfairly penalized for lacking information that is outside their realm of experience. You should assess the general familiarity of the content of reading passages in tests. Publication dates should be considered before you completely accept test results.

Norming Population

The concept of norming was explained earlier in this chapter. You should have information about the norming population of tests. The children to whom the test is administered should have the same basic characteristics as the norming population. When this is not the case, instruments tend to "test high" or to "test low." In addition, the norm group should be large enough to provide a representative sample of children's performance.

Reliability

Reliability refers to the consistency or stability of test results. It refers to the test results and not to the test itself. Reliability is a basic requirement of formal tests. Test results are reliable if they remain basically the same after repeated testing, assuming that no further instruction in test content was provided. Kavale (1979) identified the most critical factors affecting the reliability of a test.

1. The length of the test: longer tests tend to be more reliable than shorter ones.
2. The homogeneity of the items: tests with similar types of items are more reliable than those with dissimilar items.
3. The difficulty of the items: tests with large numbers of easy or

difficult items are less reliable than those with items of moderate difficulty.

4. The homogeneity of the norming sample: tests based on a norming population with a wide range of ability levels are more reliable than those based on more homogeneous populations.

The three important forms of reliability are stability, equivalence, and internal consistency. Stability refers to the consistency of results in one group of students from one administration of the test to another. If one group of students repeatedly took the same test, each person's score would be slightly different at each sitting. However, the general rank of each student should remain the same. The student who received the highest score in the first sitting should have the highest or near highest score in the second or third sitting. Similarly, the student receiving the lowest score should rank in the lowest range in subsequent retesting. Test results could not to be trusted if they were completely unpredictable sitting after sitting.

Stability is built into tests in two main ways. The first way relates to test length. The longer the test, the more reliable the results (Sax 1980). A test with forty items is usually more reliable than one with six items. However, a test with 300 items might be unreliable because of the fatigue factor introduced by the length. Test constructors try out different numbers of items to find an appropriate length. The second way stability is built into tests is through the standardization procedures. The test directions specify the time of year, time of day, and general administration conditions under which the test should be given. Tests given in the same conditions tend to provide more stability among results. Stability of test results is assessed through the test-retest method. The same test is administered twice to the same group of students after a short time lapse. The results are analyzed to ensure similar ranking of scores (Arter and Jenkins 1979).

Equivalence refers to the consistency of results among different forms of the same test. Many companies provide more than one form of a test for pre- and post-testing purposes. Results gained from all forms should be the same.

The equivalent-form method is used to assess equivalence. The various forms of a test are administered within a short period of time, and the results are compared to establish equivalence. Forms of similar length and content give the best results.

Internal consistency refers to the consistency among items on the test. It allows you to judge whether students perform as well on one portion of a test as they do on another. Internal consistency is assessed by comparing results on half of the test items with the results on the other half. You might think this would be an unfair practice, since the second half of tests is usually more difficult than the first half. Test constructors avoid this problem by using the split-half or odd-even procedure, which compares odd-numbered to even-numbered items. Therefore, comparative difficulty does not interfere with determining internal consistency.

Formal tests should have a reliability coefficient (or rating) of at least 0.80 for individual tests and 0.70 for group administered tests. If results are less reliable, the tests should not be used. Tests are rarely 100 percent reliable (1.00). Unfortunately, there is always some error.

Validity

Validity refers to a test's success in measuring what it states it measures (Rupley and Blair 1983, Farr and Carey 1986). Reliability measures answer the question, "How consistent are the results?" Validity measures answer the question, "Does the test accurately assess the behavior it claims to assess?" While reliability can be objectively or quantitatively measured, validity requires a degree of subjective decision making.

The most important types of validity are content validity, construct validity, concurrent validity, and predictive validity. A discussion of each type follows.

Content validity refers to the test's success in measuring an appropriate sample of the content it purports to measure. For example, a test that claimed to measure comprehension but included only literal comprehension questions would not have high content validity because it did not assess all the different levels of comprehension. Similarly, a test that purported to assess word recognition but tested phonic analysis and not contextual use or structural analysis would have questionable content validity. Tests measuring a broader sample of skills have more appropriate content validity.

Many human characteristics that people attempt to measure are hypothetical constructs—ideas that we use to explain human behavior. Characteristics such as intelligence, sensitivity, creativity, and comprehension fall into this category. Construct validity refers to the success of a test in measuring the "construct" it says it is measuring. In a test with good construct validity, the discrete skills measured are consistent with the skills that experts in a field identify as comprising a given construct. In reading, for example, a reading test that contained subtests on vocabulary, phonic analysis, structural analysis, comprehension, and the like would have higher construct validity than one containing subtests on math computation, fine and gross motor movement, and dexterity. Construct validity relates to theoretical beliefs about the reading process— the "construct" of reading.

Concurrent validity refers to the degree to which one test is related to another test or group of tests. The concept assumes the existence of established, respected instruments that are valid measures of a given construct. Results of newly constructed tests are correlated with results of established tests. The findings are expressed as correlation coefficients ranging from + 1.0 (a perfect positive correlation in which both tests measure identical abilities) to – 1.0 (a perfect negative correlation in which the tests measure totally different abilities). Tests usually range from + .20 to + .90. Correlations of + .80 and above are acceptable. It is generally required that tests achieve a minimum level of + .80 on all validity measures.

Predictive validity refers to the ability of test scores to predict performance at a later point in time. For example, do scores on a reading survey test given at the start of the school year predict reading performance at the end of the year? Do the results of a reading readiness test administered at the start of first grade predict scores on a reading survey test administered at the end of first grade?

Standard Error of Measurement

The scores children receive on tests are rarely a reflection of their true scores. So many variables affect test scores that any given score is only an approximation of the true score. Variables range from the degree of error within the test to the natural variations in the behavior of individuals. The true score might be higher or lower than the achieved score. An estimate of the difference between true and achieved scores is termed the standard error of measurement. If a student achieves a raw score of 50 on a reading comprehension test with a standard error of measurement of 5.0, then the true score of that child would be between 45 and 55. A low standard error of measurement indicates that there is a smaller range in which a true score may be found, and therefore less difference between true and achieved scores. More reliable tests tend to have lower standard errors of measurement.

Standardization Procedures

Standardization refers to the directions given in the test ensuring that the conditions of administration match as closely as possible the conditions in the initial norming of the test. These conditions include the month of year in which testing occurred, the time of month (beginning, middle, end), the time of day, and the exact verbal directions given to the children. Standardization procedures must be followed exactly to ensure valid results.

You might correctly conclude that it is impossible to gain completely accurate results through the use of formal tests. There are many opportunities for error within any instrument—for example, a lack of reliability, a lack of validity, or the improbability of finding a true score. There are also opportunities for error within any individual—for example, guessing, lack of motivation, lack of prior knowledge, or anxiety.

Formal test results are therefore never truly accurate measures of performance. Although formal measures have specific strengths, they should be used cautiously (Farr and Carey 1986). Results of formal tests should never be the only (or even the most important) factors in making decisions about children. Formal testing should always be accompanied by ongoing teacher observation and informal diagnosis.

SUMMARY   Formal diagnosis is the process of gaining information about the performance of learners through the use of formally developed and constructed tests. Two major categories of formal tests are norm-referenced tests, which compare children's performance to the performance of students used in the original norming population, and criterion-referenced tests, which determine whether or not students have mastered specific competencies. Both types of test have strengths and limitations. They can provide teachers with helpful profiles of student strengths and needs, but also contain many opportunities for error. Test results, then, should always be viewed flexibly and be followed by ongoing informal assessment.

R · E · F · E · R · E · N · C · E · S

Arter, J. A., and J. R. Jenkins. "Differential diagnosis—Prescriptive teaching: A critical appraisal." *Review of Educational Research* 49 (1979): 517–555.

Buros, O. K. "Reading Tests and Reviews." In O. K. Buros, ed. *Eighth Mental Measurement Yearbook*. Highland Park, NJ: Gryphon Press, 1978.

Farr, R., and R. F. Carey. *Reading: What Can Be Measured?* 2nd ed. Newark, DE: International Reading Association, 1986.

Gillet, J. W., and C. Temple. *Understanding Reading Problems: Assessment and Instruction*. Boston, MA: Little, Brown, 1986.

Just, M. A., and P. A. Carpenter. *The Psychology of Reading and Language Comprehension*. Newton, MA: Allyn and Bacon, 1987.

Kavale, K. "Selecting and Evaluating Reading Tests." In Robert Shreiner, *Reading Tests and Teachers: A Practical Guide*. Newark, DE: International Reading Association, 1979.

McCormick, S. *Remedial and Clinical Reading Instruction*. Columbus, OH: Merrill, 1987.

Mitchell, J. V. Jr., ed. *The Ninth Mental Measurements Yearbook*. Lincoln, NE: The Buros Institute of Mental Measurements, 1985.

Plas, J. M. "If Not Grade Equivalent Scores–Then What?" In A. J. Harris and E. R. Sipay, eds. *Readings on Reading Instruction*. New York: Longman, 1985.

Richek, M. A., L. K. List, and J. W. Lerner. *Reading Problems: Diagnosis and Remediation*. Englewood Cliffs, NJ: Prentice–Hall, 1983.

Rude, R., and W. J. Oehlkers. *Helping Students with Reading Problems*. Englewood Cliffs, NJ: Prentice–Hall, 1984.

Rupley, W. H., and T. R. Blair. *Reading Diagnosis and Direct Instruction: A Guide for the Classroom*. Boston: Houghton Mifflin, 1983.

Sax, G. *Principles of Educational and Psychological Measurement and Evaluation*, 2nd ed. Belmont, CA: Wadsworth, 1980.

Taylor, B., L. A. Harris, and P. D. Pearson. *Reading Difficulties: Instruction and Assessment*. New York: Random House, 1988.

4 Informal Reading Diagnosis

FOCUS   1. How is informal reading diagnosis defined?
QUESTIONS   2. What part does informal diagnosis play in the total process of diagnosis?
          3. What are the major formats of informal measurement?
          4. How can formal and informal diagnosis be combined in meeting
              children's needs?
          5. What forms of teacher-constructed tests can be used to assess children's
              reading needs?

In its most basic form, informal diagnosis involves the continual analysis of reading behavior in order to identify children's strengths, weaknesses, and specific skill needs, and to develop remediation activities. Whereas formal diagnosis relies on sporadic, intermittent assessment, informal diagnosis relies on ongoing observations of pupils. Observation is a skill that should become a natural and regular part of instruction. Any effort to remediate deficient reading skills certainly depends on a well-developed ability to use informal diagnostic techniques.

The general definition of diagnosis offered in Chapter 1 refers more accurately to informal diagnosis than to formal diagnosis. It is an ongoing procedure that involves continual analysis of students' behavior, measurement of samples of their behavior, careful evaluation of the measurement results, and changes in instructional strategies resulting in improvements in students' behavior. By the end of this chapter, you will see how formal and informal diagnosis work in concert to provide a complete diagnostic profile of each child. The forms of informal diagnosis include teacher observation, oral reading used for diagnostic purposes, the cloze procedure, teacher-made tests, informal reading inventories, and reading miscue inventories.

ONGOING TEACHER OBSERVATION

At the core of all diagnosis, and particularly informal diagnosis, is the concept of observation. While testing instruments are valuable in providing important information about children, no test can replace or equal your eyes, ears, and sensitivity to children. McCormick underscores the importance of teacher observation in the following statements:

> One of the most powerful forms of informal assessment is daily observation, which provides teachers with a chance to diagnose what students can and cannot do in real reading. Most teachers make

judgments about the ability of students to handle material in daily work and note areas where more instruction should occur, but many feel hesitant to assume that this is a legitimate form of assessment (1987, 119–120).

Observation supplies much information about children that cannot be pinpointed by tests, as the following case studies show.

CASE STUDY A: Jerry A.

Jerry A. is an eight-year-old boy in mid-second grade. He is reading on the mid-first grade level. Jerry repeated first grade. The primary cause of his retention was his inadequate reading performance. Jerry has received extensive testing. Most of the results were not remarkable. His visual and auditory skills tested appropriately. He had no clear learning disability, and therefore did not qualify for any of the ancillary educational services provided by his school. His second grade teacher, Ms. Ray, felt frustrated because of Jerry's lack of progress in reading. She could find no reason in his test results for this persistent lack of growth. Ms. Ray began an intensive and purposeful observation of Jerry's behavior during reading class and reading-related tasks. She recorded these observations in a notebook:

1. Jerry confused several sounds, but his confusion followed a pattern. He confused similar sounds, such as /p/ for /d/, /t/ for /v/, and /b/ for /d/. This led Ms. Ray to question his auditory discrimination skills.
2. Jerry was consistently unable to put sounds together into appropriate whole words. For example, given the word *stop*, Jerry would sound out /st/−/o/−/p/, but then he would say *step*. This led Ms. Ray to question his auditory blending skills.
3. Jerry would confuse similar words in spelling. For example, he often spelled *bad* as *bed*, *fed* as *fod*, or *do* as *to*. This led Miss Ray to question his auditory segmentation and discrimination skills.

Considering these observations, Ms. Ray assessed her reading program. She found that it was strong in phonics, the very skills Jerry lacked. She decided to make some specific modifications for Jerry.

1. She de-emphasized phonic instruction for Jerry, viewing phonics as readiness rather than as instruction.
2. She paired Jerry with a high-performing partner to do phonic worksheets or workbook pages that demanded the skills he lacked. She did this to minimize Jerry's frustration. Practicing with a child who could perform the tasks exposed Jerry to the skills and heightened his level of readiness for learning them.
3. She emphasized meaningful whole-word instruction.

4. She trained a mother helper to provide Jerry with 20 minutes of auditory training per week.
5. She asked the fifth grade teacher to send a fifth grader to work with Jerry ten minutes a day on sight words.

Although Jerry had been extensively tested, his major problems were detected not by the tests but by the teacher's careful observation. Because of the teacher's modifications, Jerry began to show clear progress in reading.

CASE STUDY B: Mara H.

Mara H. is a ten-year-old girl in mid-fourth grade. Records show that in her first three years of school Mara performed consistently in the top third of her class. She was an outgoing, friendly child with clear leadership potential. In third grade, however, Mara's grades began to drop, particularly in reading. By the last third of third grade, Mara's teacher was quite concerned. Mara was making what seemed like careless errors and her reading comprehension was clearly declining. At the same time, Mara's general behavior was not markedly different, and she certainly was not becoming less adept at processing orally presented information.

By mid-fourth grade, Mara's performance had significantly declined. Her comprehension was weak and her word recognition poor and erratic. Ms. Graef, her fourth grade teacher, requested testing. The results showed poor performance but no clues to help pinpoint the specific causes of Mara's weak reading skills. Ms. Graef decided to observe Mara's reading behavior more closely.

1. It was true that Mara's whole passage comprehension was weak. However, her comprehension of the first part of a selection was very good. Her comprehension became poorer as the selection continued, particularly if she was reading silently. This led Ms. Graef to ask two questions: Does something negative happen to Mara *visually* as selections wear on? Does something negative happen to Mara *motivationally* as selections wear on? Further observations answered these questions.
2. It was true that Mara's word recognition was weak. However, her word recognition started out well, but became less accurate and more erratic as the selection continued. This observation led Ms. Graef to ask the same two questions as she had in the first observation: Visual problems? Motivational problem?
3. Mara began reading selections with a normal posture and with her book held in a natural manner. As sessions wore on, however, Mara became more inattentive. She squirmed in her seat, turned her book to different angles, and frequently

moved the book closer or farther away as she read. This observation led Miss Graef to question Mara's visual skills.

The first thing Ms. Graef did was to ask Mara if she could see the page clearly when she read.

"Sometimes," Mara answered.

"When?"

"When I start to read. Then later it seems like the words are kind of blurry and sometimes they look like they are moving."

"Why didn't you tell me before?"

Oh, I don't know. I guess I didn't remember," replied Mara.

Although Mara had been formally tested, the nature of her problem was detected by her teacher's keen use of eyes, ears, and sensitivities. Miss Graef made the following changes based on her careful observation.

1. She recommended that Mara's parents take her to a vision specialist who would provide an accurate account of Mara's actual visual behavior during reading.
2. She encouraged Mara to use a marker. This seemed to help stabilize the print.
3. During the reading period, Miss Graef asked Mara to read and respond at the start of the reading selection.
4. On long independent reading assignments, Miss Graef helped Mara to divide the selections into three or four segments and to take a break after each segment.
5. Ms. Graef encouraged Mara to monitor her own comprehension by stopping to allow her eyes to refocus or by rereading a section if she did not understand what she read.

As the year wore on, with the glasses the vision specialist prescribed for Mara and with Ms. Graef's adjustments, Mara's reading performance showed quick and steady growth. Her confidence and self-esteem improved as well.

As you can see, observation is central to successful informal diagnosis. Clues to children's reading behavior can be found in the learning environment if you observe the whole child within that environment and analyze what you find. The factors on which you can focus your attention are summarized in Figure 4.1.

Observation of Emotional and Motivational Factors

The analysis of these factors involves answering three main questions:

1. How does the child approach the reading task? Feelings of anxiety, fear, hostility, disappointment, depression, rigidity and apathy show

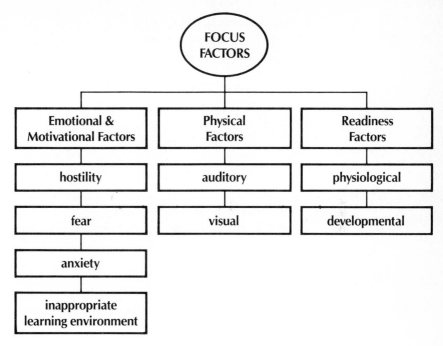

FIGURE 4.1   Focus Factors for Informal Diagnosis

up in the child's body posture, body movements, facial expression, and verbal behavior. Emotional factors contributing to reading failure are discussed in Chapter 2. You should become aware of these feelings in children and encourage physical and emotional readiness prior to instruction. Much academic information is not even processed because of counter-productive emotional sets.

2. What motivates the child to read? Children's performance often accelerates under specific motivating conditions, such as success, a structured environment, specific content of reading material, or self-competition. Careful observation will assist you in assessing these various patterns.

3. What distracts the child from reading? Many children's academic problems are related to simple, avoidable distracters. A child with visual or auditory acuity problems should be seated in the front row. Children with behavioral problems should not be seated next to each other. Children should be separated who either like each other so much that they want to "visit" throughout the session or who can't stand each other and continuously annoy each other. Class troublemakers should not be seated in the middle of the classroom but as near as possible to the teacher. Many academic problems would be mitigated if children's seating arrangements were changed.

The question of distracters also involves observing the children who do not do well in competition with other children. Competition against other students (e.g., Who can read the most words in one minute? Who can read the most books in one month?) makes some children become frustrated, doubt their own abilities, fear failure, or simply give up.

Observation of Physical Factors

This level of observation involves analysis of the visual, auditory, and readiness factors within the child. These factors, discussed in part in Chapter 2, include answering the following questions:

How Does the Child Behave in the Auditory Domain?

- Can the child discriminate among similar sounds and words?
- Does the child confuse similar words?
- Can the child hear the discrete sounds in words?
- Can the child blend segmented sounds into an appropriate whole word?
- Does the child lean forward or lean the head to one side when listening?
- Does the child often ask that oral directions be repeated?
- Does the child misunderstand oral directions?

Answers to these and other questions will provide information about children's auditory skills and about their receptiveness to phonic instruction as a primary mode of reading instruction.

How Does the Child Behave Visually?

- Does the child strain forward to see the chalkboard or the book?
- Does the child hold the book too far away or too close to the eyes?
- Does the child confuse visually similar words?
- Does the child frequently lose his or her place during reading?
- Does reading accuracy and speed improve with the use of a marker?
- Does the child frequently miscall words with no visual similarity to the correct word (e.g., *through* for *house*); can miscalled words be found above or below the word in question?
- Does accuracy of word recognition deteriorate with more bizarre errors as the child progresses through a selection?

These and other signals should alert you to possible problems in visual acuity, visual discrimination, or to other visual problems, such as fading or moving print.

Observation of Readiness Factors

One of the reading teacher's most important skills, particularly with children who have previously failed at reading, is the ability to assess the type of reading for which each child or group of children is ready. Some children are ready for intense phonic instruction after failing the first time because they were not ready or because phonics was presented in an isolated way. Such children may display some or all of the following characteristics:

- They seem "suddenly ready for phonics."
- They have good auditory discrimination, segmentation, memory, and blending skills.
- They make rapid real progress with phonic instruction.
- They learn and retain phonic information at an appropriate pace.

Other children might be ready for a strong visual approach to reading, yet show no readiness for phonic instruction. Such children may display some or all of the following characteristics:

- They have weak or nonexistent auditory discrimination, segmentation, memory, and blending skills.
- They have a slow learning rate and low retention for phonic information.
- They easily learn meaningful or emotionally important vocabulary (e.g., personal names, such words as *elephant*, *monster*, *school*, and *house*.)
- They generally perform better on visual than on auditory tasks.

You should remain open to observing the ways in which children most easily learn to read and should support them in their needs.

Another important form of readiness is developmental readiness. Attention to developmental readiness is particularly critical if you are teaching young children in kindergarten through beginning second grade. Developmental readiness refers to children's physical, emotional, and social growth. Children develop at different rates. Some children entering first grade at chronological age six might be developmentally more like children age seven or eight. Others might be more like children of four or five years of age. Developmentally young children might not be ready for a formal first grade classroom, much less formal reading instruction. Although chronologically and intellectually ready to learn, they might not be developmentally ready to function in a structured first grade classroom. Being pushed into a somewhat rigid school environment causes frustration and failure for some children (Ilg et al. 1978, Ames and Chase 1981). Developmentally young children benefit by waiting an extra year to start kindergarten, repeating kindergarten, or repeating the first grade. In this way they would have what specialists at the Gesell Institute of Child Development call "the gift of time." Such children might display some or all of the following characteristics:

- They seem overly anxious about being right.
- They become easily frustrated by difficult tasks.
- They cry easily.
- They have noticeably short attention spans.
- They have difficulty getting their work done.
- They perform far below the expected or predicted levels.
- They express feelings of inadequacy.
- They seem able to perform "if they would only try."

These children might require a less structured method of reading presentation, such as language experience, language immersion, or environmental reading (see Chapter 7). Each time you observe student behavior, analyze the behavior, evaluate the behavior's meaning, and change instruction to meet student needs, you are practicing the essence of informal diagnosis.

USING ORAL READING DIAGNOSTICALLY

Children who have difficulty in reading are often given a great amount of practice in oral reading. Most of their actual reading is oral reading, which provides important and useful information. Teachers often ignore or underutilize this valuable information because they fail to analyze and evaluate oral reading appropriately. The diagnostic use of oral reading begins with a set of realistic expectations of performance. First, oral reading is rarely flawless. Like speech, it is plagued with stops and starts, errors, miscalled words, hesitations, repetitions, and corrections. This is true of most oral reading, including that of skilled readers. Second, comprehension is understandably less efficient while reading orally than while listening or reading silently. Oral reading stresses calling words correctly and "sounding" accurately. Inefficiency in comprehension becomes more pronounced as textual material increases in difficulty. Third, the errors in oral reading fall into two broad categories: those based on the reader's expectation of meaning, and those based on the reader's insensitivity to meaning. These two sources of error are different and need to be treated in different ways. Realistic expectations of oral reading should include the following assumptions:

- It will contain errors.
- Errors either take into account or ignore meaning.
- Comprehension decreases, especially of more difficult material.

Oral reading is a valuable diagnostic tool. If you listen carefully and analyze children's oral reading, you will develop a clear picture of their word recognition and phonic analysis needs. You will also acquire firsthand information about their use of higher-level skills, such as the use of context, self-monitoring, self-correction, and the willingness to take risks.

The best way to acquire this information is to monitor carefully children's oral reading behavior over time. Keep a written account of each child's oral reading errors and analyze that information about twice a week. You might keep a small note pad (for example, a stenographer's pad) for each small group of children. Divide each page into two columns, "Word Was" and "Child Said." As each child reads, record error(s) and the corresponding correct word(s) in the appropriate columns. It is not necessary or practical to record every error. Your goal should be to record between eight and ten errors per session for each child. Avoid recording errors in people or place names or in unfamiliar words rarely seen in print. Errors in such words are common and tend to "throw" children, fooling them into anticipating, and thus making, errors. This is true even of comparatively good readers. By the end of a session, your record might resemble the example in Table 4.1. Show each child the "Word Was" column at the end of a session, and ask the child to read each word. This allows you to distinguish words that were accidentally or carelessly misread from those that the child genuinely cannot decode because of underdeveloped or unlearned skills. At the end of each week, analyze the errors of each child and attempt to determine a pattern. Patterns of error greatly assist you in planning children's reading programs.

Table 4.2 presents an error analysis sheet for a one-week period for the student, John H. If you analyzed single errors, you would become frustrated because the errors appear random. However, if you look at the overall picture you will see strengths in initial consonants and in ending

TABLE 4.1   Error Analysis Sheet

	Date	Word Was	Child Said
	4/14/84		
	John H.	*beach*	*bench*
		owned	*oned*
		mouth	*moth*
		playing	*paying*
		angry	——
		strange	*stand*
		watched	*what*
		dangled	*daled*
		threw	*though*
	Julie S.	*hotel*	*house*
		owned	*had*
		almost	*most*
		beach ball	*big ball*
		threw	*throw*
		watched	*waited*
		dim	*dark*

TABLE 4.2   Error Pattern Analysis

Date	Word Was	Child Said
John H.		
4/14	beach	bench
	owned	oned
	mouth	moth
	playing	paying
	angry	——
	strange	stand
	watched	what
	dangled	daled
	threw	though
4/15	stopped	stepped
	wooden	wood
	color	clear
	fir	for
	rolled	ralled
	special	——
	match	met
	weak	walk
4/16	towel	——
	stuffing	stuff
	clean	can
	cloth	clothes
	sore	so
	felt	fell
	cast	case
	brushing	brush
4/17	sometimes	something
	longer	long
	shape	sap
	scary	sorry
	hugged	had
	spin	spill
	pack	pake
	chill	call
	summer	same
4/18	slight	——
	place	plack
	cases	casses
	tea	to
	thank	talk
	problem	——
	broken	broke
	front	font

sounds. On the other hand, the one overriding weakness is complete disregard for meaning. Notice how the errors destroy meaning. Most even fail to maintain the same grammatical class (e.g., *watched* for *what*, *strange* for *stand*, *tea* for *to*). Notice also the number of uncorrected nonword substitutions, such as *casses*, *pake*, and *oned*. In almost every case, the child's word could not fit the given language context without completely destroying meaning. Secondary weaknesses include some consonant blends, vowel combinations, and the final *e* construction. Focusing immediately on the secondary problems might not significantly change the primary weakness. However, focusing immediately on the primary problem in conjunction with giving practice in the specific skills would greatly help John H. to improve his overall reading performance.

Table 4.3 presents the case of Julie S. Analysis of Julie S.'s errors shows that she attends to the meaning of the passage as she reads. Notice that the majority of her errors make some sense and at least fit the same class as the correct words. She uses context to help her when her comprehension fails and to correct herself appropriately. Her secondary strength is initial consonants. Weaknesses include reading through to the ends of words and confusing some vowel combinations. In this case, the child understands that the purpose of reading is to gain meaning. She needs instructional support in the use of specific skills and focusing on those individual skills would be appropriate. Notice how an overall profile reveals an error pattern which guides you to an appropriate skill remediation focus.

TABLE 4.3   Error Pattern Analysis

Date	Word Was	Child Said
Julie S.		
4/14	hotel	house
	owned	had
	almost	most
	beach ball	big ball
	threw	throw
	watched	waited
	dim	dark
4/15	switch	stick
	dangled	dropped
	beyond	behind
	rose up	rang up
	entry	enter
	famous	funny
	strips	stripes
4/16	seven	seen
	recently	rekent*
	throat	thumb

(continues)

TABLE 4.3 Continued

Date	Word Was	Child Said
	scaly	scary
	shape	shade
	chilled	cold
	repeat	reply
	several	seven
4/17	older	old
	patch	place
	frayed	____
	especially	special
	growling	going
	likely	like
	sewn	sewed
	usually	usual
4/18	result	____
	sign	sig*
	beach	bech*
	sponge	(finished line then said *sponge*)
	patch	piece
	string dangled	string danced
	famous	funny
	declared	decided

*Self-corrected.

Informal Reading Inventory

One of the most valuable and most frequently used informal diagnostic tools is the informal reading inventory (I.R.I.) (McKenna 1983, Dechant 1981). Informal inventories are used primarily to determine children's initial placement in graded reading or content area series. They also provide information about children's general reading strategies (McCracken 1984, Harris and Lalik 1987).

Informal inventories consist of reading passages of between 50 and 300 words taken from graded series. Sets of six to ten comprehension questions follow each passage. The questions generally address details, main ideas, inferences, evaluation, cause and effect, and vocabulary. Inventories include word lists of ten to twenty words accompanying each graded passage. Children read the vocabulary items, then the passage, and then answer the assigned questions. Teachers keep a record of children's errors, analyze those errors, and determine the appropriate placement of children in the series.

Many basal series provide an I.R.I. for placing children at appropriate levels. Many published informal reading inventories are available for ascertaining children's general reading levels and for deciding initial

group placement. Use the informal inventory provided with a basal series to place children in that series. Use commercially available inventories only for generic skills and general placement. A listing of some of the
best known informal inventories follows:

    Analytical Reading Inventory
        (Charles Merrill, 1981)
        Grades 1 through 9
        Approximately 30 minutes
        Contains word recognition lists and oral reading passages for
           each grade level.
        Six to eight questions follow each passage. Questions tap vo-
           cabulary, details, cause and effect, inference, and main idea.
        Identifies independent, instructional, listening, and frustra-
           tion levels.
    Basic Reading Inventory
        (Kendall Hunt, 1978)
        Grades preprimer through 8
        Three forms: approximately 30 minutes
        Contains word recognition lists and reading passages for each
           grade. Five to eight comprehension questions follow pas-
           sages. Identifies independent, instructional, and frustration
           levels.
    Classroom Reading Inventory
        (William C. Brown, 1979)
        Grades 1 through 8
        Three forms: approximately 20 minutes
        Contains word lists and oral reading passages for each grade
           level. Includes a spelling inventory. Identifies independent
           instructional and frustration levels.
    Contemporary Classroom Inventory
        (Gorsuch, Scanisbrick, 1980)
        Grades 2 through 9
        Three forms with literature, social studies, and science con-
           tent: approximately 30 minutes
        Five to eight questions follow each passage.
        Questions tap main idea, inference, vocabulary, and details.
           Identifies independent, instructional and frustration levels.
    Ekwall Reading Inventory
        (Allyn and Bacon, 1979)
        Grades 1 through 9
        Four forms: approximately 30 minutes
        Contains word recognition lists and oral and silent reading
           passages for each grade level. Five to eight questions follow
           each passage. Questions focus on literal recall, inferences,
           and vocabulary. Also includes a phonic survey. Yields inde-
           pendent, instructional, and frustration levels.

Informal Reading Assessment Tests
    (Houghton Mifflin, 1980)
    Grades 1 through 12
    Four forms: approximately 30 minutes
    Contains word recognition lists and reading passages for each
       grade. Eight to ten questions follow each passage. Questions
       focus on main idea, details, cause and effect, vocabulary, se-
       quence, and inference.
    Identifies independent, instructional, and frustration levels.
Sucher–Allred Reading Placement Inventory
    (Economy, 1973)
    Grades 1 through 9
    Two forms: approximately 30 minutes
    Contains word recognition and reading passages for all levels.
       Five questions on vocabulary inferences, factual data, and
       main idea follow each passage.
    Identifies independent, instructional, and frustrational levels.

Although published inventories are available, many teachers prefer to prepare their own tests for use with their basal or content-area series. Teacher-made inventories can be valuable in assessing children's general reading strategies. Informal reading inventories are simple though time consuming to construct. Their advantages far outweigh the time spent in their construction.

Preparing an Informal Reading Inventory

To prepare an I.R.I. you need a series of graded texts. These might be reading, social studies, or science texts, or any series in which you place students for instruction. Obtain texts two grade levels above and two below your current grade assignment. This will allow you to accommodate the wide range of reading abilities in your students.

Step 1. Choose two reading selections of 50 (for grade one) to 300 (grade 6 and above) words from the middle of each text. Use one passage for oral reading and the other for silent reading evaluation. (Some teachers choose passages from the beginning, the middle, and the end of their texts. This allows them to more specifically determine appropriate placement in each text.) Each passage should make sense in isolation. You will need one copy of each selection for yourself and as many other copies as there are students, so you can record individual children's reading errors.

Step 2. Count and record the number of words in each sample.

Step 3. Create a short and simple introduction to each passage. This introduction sets the stage for reading and provides a conceptual context for students.

Step 4. Prepare six to ten comprehension questions for each selection. Include a variety of questions to assess different levels of comprehension. For example, construct questions that require factual recall, inferential thinking, vocabulary, cause and effect reasoning, evaluating, predicting, sequencing, and characterization.

The following is an example of a teacher-made I.R.I. passage constructed from a reading selection.

CLASSROOM APPLICATION: Level 3.2

Second half of third grade; 201 words, 17 sentences.

Introduction: Peek was a little field mouse. He was on his own for the first time in his life. He was by a river bank. There, some children were floating toy boats down the river. Peek jumped into one of the boats. As the story begins, he is in the middle of the river. Read this passage and find out about Peek's adventure.

Passage: The little mouse was only two weeks old. He knew nothing about life. He didn't know how to search for food, hide from his enemies, or find shelter from wind and water. He didn't even know that he had enemies. But worst of all, he was unaware of the unseen dangers that were all around him.

One of these dangers was circling above him right now. A white gull had spied him. Soon Peek heard a whole flight of gulls screaming. They settled down on the water and paddled up alongside the little boat. Peek was in trouble! What he didn't know was that a fish had seen the gulls and had come to the surface. The fish was waiting for the gulls to tip the boat over, so that he could snap up the mouse in his sharp jaws. As the gulls came toward him, Peek closed his eyes.

Just then a fish hawk appeared overhead. Seeing the boat, the mouse, the gulls, and the waiting fish, the hawk swooped down. With the tip of his wing, he brushed the boat, turning it over. When the hawk flew off, he had the fish, and Peek was in the water.*

Comprehension Questions:

1. How old was Peek when this story took place? (Literal detail)
2. What did the flight of gulls do in the story? (Literal detail)
3. How did Peek's boat happen to turn over? (Literal detail)
4. What might be a good title for this story? (Main idea)
5. What happened after the fish hawk appeared above Peek's boat? (Sequence)
6. Why did Peek close his eyes as the gulls came toward him? (Inference)
7. What does the word "spied" used in the story mean? (Vocabulary)

*From "Two Weeks Old and On His Own," in *Peek the Piper*, by Vitali Bianki, © 1964, George Braziller Publishers. Used with permission.

8. How do you think Peek felt when the hawk flew off with the fish? (Evaluation)
9. Why didn't Peek know about the dangers around him? (Inference)
10. Why had the fish come to the surface of the water? (Literal detail)

Administering the Informal Reading Inventory

An informal reading inventory is administered to each child individually. Start the child reading orally a passage approximately one year below her or his estimated reading level. This procedure avoids immediate frustration over passage difficulty. The following steps may be taken.

Step 1. Briefly provide a context for the selection. If an introductory statement is not provided, then create one for the child. For example, you might say, "The passage you are going to read is about a young mouse who is out on his own. Read the passage and find out about some of his adventures."

Step 2. Have the child read the selection orally.

Step 3. As the child reads, record the errors on your copy. If the child encounters an unknown word, encourage sounding out. Wait a few seconds and then provide the word. Have a clear and consistent marking system to record oral reading errors, like the marking system presented in Table 4.4. Mispronunciations of names of people and places, brief hesitations, pronunciations reflecting the child's dialect, and self-corrections are not counted as errors.

Step 4. After the child has read the passage and you have recorded the errors, ask the comprehension questions and record responses. If the child correctly answered 60 percent or more of the comprehension questions, proceed to the next level. If the child's comprehension falls below 60 percent, stop the oral reading.

Step 5. Begin the silent reading passages, starting at the difficulty level at which you begin the oral reading passages.

Step 6. At the end of the reading of the first passage, ask the child the comprehension questions. Again, if the child receives a score of 60 percent or higher, proceed to the next level. When comprehension falls below 60 percent, stop the silent reading.

Step 7. When the child has reached the frustration point in the test (comprehension below 60 percent), you might use the I.R.I. to estimate the child's listening comprehension. Listening comprehension refers to the highest level of written material a reader can comprehend when the material is read to the reader. Many teachers use listening comprehension to get a general idea of children's potential for reading improvement. Continue reading aloud the silent reading selections and asking the comprehension questions until the child's score falls below 60 percent. At that time, stop the test.

TABLE 4.4   Oral Reading Marking System

Error	Marking	Example
Substitutions (a real word used in place of the key word):	Underline the key word and write in substituted word above	The little mouse *is* <u>was</u> only two weeks old.
Omission (a word or words omitted from the text):	Circle omitted word.	A ⟨white⟩ gull had spied him.
Addition (inserted word or words not in the text):	Write in added word.	He didn't even know that he *his* had　　 enemies.
Mispronunciation (a word or words pronounced incorrectly resulting in a nonword substitution):	Underline word and write in the mispronunciation.	Just then a fish *hawg* <u>hawk</u> appeared overhead.
Hesitation (an unduly long pause before a word or set of words):	Place a slash mark (/) before the word or words.	Soon Peek heard a whole /flight of gulls / screaming.
Unknown word (words pronounced for the child):	Place a "P" above the word.	P Peek was in trouble.
Repetition (part of a word, a whole word, or several words are repeated):	Underline repeated word(s) and write "R" to indicate.	R Peek <u>was in</u> the water.
Reversals (the correct word order is reversed):	Use the reversal symbol (‿⌢) to show errors in word order.	He ⟨didn't / even⟩ know he had enemies.
Self-corrections (child corrects error without assistance):	Write "C" beside the record of error.	speed Ⓒ A white gull had spied him.

Scoring the Informal Reading Inventory

In scoring the I.R.I., you need to analyze both oral reading accuracy and comprehension. In scoring oral reading, not every departure from the text is counted as an error, as previously explained. Mispronunications due to the student's dialect, disregard of punctuation, one-word repetitions of correct words, and self corrections are usually not counted as errors. They are, however, noted by the teacher and analyzed for diagnostic information. In addition, if the same error is made repeatedly, it should be counted only once.

In order to find the student's oral reading score, compute the percentage of words in the passage read correctly. The following formula makes it easy to find this percentage.

$$\frac{\text{Number of words correct}}{\text{Total words in passage}} \times 100 = \text{percentage correct}$$

For example,

$$\frac{183 \text{ (words correct)}}{201 \text{ (total words in passage)}} = .9104 \times 100 = 91.04 = 91\%$$

The oral reading score for this student would be 91 percent. This score represents the level of accuracy with which the student read the passage.

In scoring comprehension keep a record of students' incorrect responses. This allows you to analyze the errors and to identify patterns of errors. For example, you might note that the child has difficulty drawing conclusions or making inferences or predictions.

Strange (1980) proposes a useful scheme for categorizing and understanding children's comprehension errors. It includes the following explanations for miscomprehension.

- No existing schemata. Children lack the appropriate schemata—concepts—for understanding the content.
- Naive schemata. Children have underdeveloped or insufficient concepts for understanding. Their comprehension is superficial.
- No new information. The text provided no new information. Consequently the child was bored and inattentive.
- Poor story or passage. The passage was poorly written and thus failed to activate children's existing knowledge.
- Many schemata appropriate. The material was ambiguous or open to several interpretations.
- Schemata intrusion. Children's existing knowledge blocked comprehension, resulting in responses that have little or no relation to the text.
- Textual intrusion. Children focused on irrelevant, incidental, or unimportant segments of the text and failed to attend to critical elements.

When you have identified the general patterns of miscomprehension, you can help students acquire the concepts necessary for understanding. The comprehension segment of the I.R.I. is scored by assessing the percentage of questions answered correctly. The chart presented in Figure 4.2 will assist you in quickly determining the percentage of correct answers.

Results of the I.R.I. can be used to place children at one of three reading levels:

1. Independent. (The child scores 95 percent or above on word recognition and 90 percent or above on comprehension.)
2. Instructional. (The child scores 90 to 94 percent on word recognition and 70 to 89 percent on comprehension.)
3. Frustration. (The child scores 89 percent or below on word recognition and 69 percent or below on comprehension.)

Assessing Listening Comprehension

Another important use of the I.R.I. is estimating children's listening comprehension. Listening comprehension refers to the highest level or greatest difficulty of text that a listener can comprehend when someone reads the passage aloud. Many teachers use the listening comprehension level as a general estimate of student potential for comprehension devel-

Number of Correct Responses

		1	2	3	4	5	6	7	8	9	10	11	12
	1	100											
	2	50	100										
	3	53	67	100									
	4	25	50	75	100								
Number of Items	5	20	40	60	80	100							
	6	17	33	50	67	83	100						
	7	14	26	43	57	71	86	100					
	8	12	25	38	50	62	75	88	100				
	9	11	22	33	44	56	67	78	89	100			
	10	10	20	30	40	50	60	70	80	90	100		
	11	9	18	27	36	45	55	64	73	82	91	100	
	12	8	17	25	33	42	50	58	67	75	83	92	100

FIGURE 4.2   Easy-to-Find Percentages

opment. Remember, however, that no test can accurately assess a human being's potential.

In order to identify the listening comprehension level, begin one level below the level at which the child failed to comprehend passages. Read a passage aloud to the student and ask the comprehension questions. Continue reading passages and asking the questions until the child's comprehension falls below 60 percent. The listening comprehension level is the highest level at which the child gains a score of 60 percent or above.

As you can see, the informal reading inventory is a valuable tool for placing children in reading or content area materials. In addition, it is useful in assessing strengths and weaknesses in oral reading, silent reading, and comprehension, and in estimating listening comprehension. However, informal reading inventories also present some problems of which you should be aware. A listing of some of these problems follows.

- Passages chosen from books might not accurately represent the difficulty of the book. Students might score on the instructional level on one passage, yet experience difficulty with the book as a whole (McKenna 1983).
- Questions asked can affect students' scores. Peterson et al. (1978) have shown that different sets of questions constructed for the same passage produced different results. Depending on which set was used, 37 out of 57 students were placed on two different instructional levels.
- Students' performance is influenced by interest in the content.
- The scoring criteria for word recognition and comprehension passages are still being debated.
- Word lists for indicating starting points for oral and silent reading should be used with caution. Reading listed words is different from reading them in context (Jongsma and Jongsma 1981, McKenna 1983). Word lists are more appropriate at the lower grade levels than at the upper grade levels (Froese 1971). You should be aware of these limitations as you use informal reading inventories.

The Reading Miscue Inventory

The Reading Miscue Inventory shares some features of the informal reading inventory, but utilizes passages of greater length. Each passage is a self-contained selection or story. The basic purpose of the Reading Miscue Inventory is to assess students' strategies of interaction with the text and to assess their levels of comprehension based on oral reading (Goodman and Burke 1972).

Administration of the Reading Miscue Inventory requires students to read a passage at the instructional level. The selection must be written at this level because the child's reading must generate a number of miscues or errors (approximately 25). Material should not be written at the frustration level, which might cause the child to make errors that are not true indicators of reading strategies. As the student reads the passage, the teacher records all the miscues using a marking system similar to that of the I.R.I. After reading the passage, the student is asked to retell the story. The teacher scores responses for accuracy and completeness of retelling.

One widely used commercially constructed instrument is the Reading Miscue Inventory (Goodman and Burke 1972, McCormick 1987). The student orally reads a four to eight page passage written at the instructional level. The reading is taped, and the miscues are analyzed according to the following factors:

1. Dialect. (Does the miscue represent the child's natural dialect?)
2. Intonation. (Does the miscue involve an inappropriate shift in intonation?)
3. Graphic Similarity. (Are the miscue and the correct word visually similar?)
4. Sound Similarity. (Are the miscue and the correct word similar in sound?)
5. Grammatical or Syntactic Function. (Do the miscue and the correct word share the same grammatical class?)
6. Correction. (Does the child spontaneously self-correct the miscue?)
7. Grammatical or Syntactic Acceptability. (Is the miscue grammatically acceptable?)
8. Semantic Acceptability. (Does the miscue result in a semantically acceptable sentence?)
9. Meaning Change. (Does the miscue result in a change of initial meaning?)

These questions help you assess the student's strategies for decoding print. For example, if the child's uncorrected miscue was similar to the text in graphic configuration and in sound, and did affect meaning ("the *bid* boy" for "the *bad* boy"), the child might need instruction in context use and in phonic analysis, particularly in short vowel sounds. If children's miscues are self-corrected, this means they are monitoring their comprehension and taking steps to correct miscomprehension. They view reading as a meaning-gaining process. Miscues resulting in meaning change, showing that the student is not monitoring comprehension and meaning, are considered serious errors. Miscues maintaining meaning are not considered serious errors. In miscue analysis, the teacher concentrates on the child's interaction with print and strategies for gaining meaning from print.

You can use the nine analysis questions of the Reading Miscue Inventory with informal reading inventories or with oral reading analysis to gain further insights into children's reading strategies.

The Cloze Procedure

The cloze procedure is a method of assessing a reader's passage comprehension by omitting words (for example, every fifth word or every seventh word) and having readers fill in the blanks with the deleted word or with a semantically acceptable one (Taylor 1953, Warwick 1978, McCormick 1987). This procedure identifies the accuracy with which students can supply deleted words by depending on context clues. It allows you to assess students' ability to interact with print in a meaningful way, to monitor their comprehension, and to supply words creating "closure" in the passage (Jongsma and Jongsma 1980). The cloze procedure is generally used for three major purposes:

1. For placement (to determine the level at which children should be placed for instructional purposes).
2. For diagnosis (to diagnose the extent of a student's ability to use context).
3. For remediation (to provide practice in comprehension and word recognition skills).

The Cloze Procedure Used for Placement Purposes.   The three generally accepted levels of reading include the independent, instructional, and frustration levels. The independent level is the level at which an individual can read without assistance and with high levels of word recognition and comprehension. Readers at this level find the material easy to read. The instructional level is the level at which readers succeed if direct instruction is provided. At first the reader does not know all the words and concepts required for comprehension. Direct instruction of vocabulary and concepts closes the gap between what the reader knows and what the reader needs to know in order to succeed. The frustration level is the level at which the reader cannot succeed because the material is too difficult. The reader knows so few words and concepts that even excellent instruction cannot close the gap. The cloze procedure is often used to identify material written on the instructional level. Many teachers use the procedure to place children appropriately in reading series or content area texts (Anderson and Coates 1984, Gillet and Temple 1986).

Suggestions for constructing cloze passages for placement purposes follow.

1. Select a passage 50 (second grade) to 300 (sixth grade) words long. The passage should be new to children.
2. Leave one or two opening sentences intact so that readers get the initial context.
3. Count words, replacing every fifth word with a blank. If the fifth word is a proper noun, replace the next word instead. It is often recommended that every tenth word be deleted from material intended for use in grade three and below.
4. Continue until you have fifty blanks. This suggestion should begin approximately at the fourth grade level because of the length of the paragraph needed to get fifty blanks.

The following is an example of a cloze passage.

CLASSROOM APPLICATION

The little mouse was only two weeks old. He knew nothing about life. He didn't know how __(1)__ search for food, hide __(2)__ his enemies, or find __(3)__ from wind and water. __(4)__ didn't even know that __(5)__ had enemies. But worst __(6)__ all, he was unaware __(7)__ the unseen dangers that __(8)__ all around him.

One __(9)__ those dangers was circling __(10)__ him right now. A __(11)__ gull had spied him. __(12)__ Peek heard a whole __(13)__ of gulls screaming. They __(14)__ down on the water __(15)__ paddled up alongside of the __(16)__ boat.

Peek was in __(17)__. What he didn't know, __(18)__ that a fish had __(19)__ the gulls and had __(20)__ up to the surface. __(21)__ fish was waiting for __(22)__ gulls to tip the __(23)__ over, so that he __(24)__ snap up the mouse __(25)__ his sharp jaws. As __(26)__ gulls came toward him, __(27)__ closed his eyes.

Just __(28)__, a fish hawk appeared __(29)__. Seeing the boat, the __(30)__, the gulls and the __(31)__ fish, the hawk swooped __(32)__. With the tip of __(33)__ wing, he brushed the __(34)__, turning it over. When __(35)__ hawk flew off, he __(36)__ the fish, and Peek __(37)__ in the water.

Peek __(38)__ down. Then he came __(39)__. And somewhere in between __(40)__ had learned to swim. Paddling __(41)__ with all four feet, __(42)__ swam to the wooden __(43)__ and clung to it __(44)__ his teeth. A little __(45)__, the boat crashed into __(46)__ rocks and was flung __(47)__ a sandy shore. Peek __(48)__ for the bushes. He __(49)__ soaked. Also, he was __(50)__ hungry. To find food, Peek had to leave his hiding place beneath the bush.*

(278 words)

---

*From "Two Weeks Old and On His Own," in *Peek the Piper*, by Vitali Bianki, © 1964, George Braziller Publishers. Used with permission.

Words Deleted

1. to	18. was	35. the
2. from	19. seen	36. had
3. shelter	20. come	37. was
4. He	21. The	38. went
5. he	22. the	39. up
6. of	23. boat	40. he
7. of	24. could	41. furiously
8. were	25. in	42. he
9. of	26. the	43. boat
10. above	27. Peek	44. with
11. white	28. then	45. later
12. Soon	29. overheard	46. some
13. flight	30. mouse	47. upon
14. settled	31. waiting	48. leaped
15. and	32. down	49. was
16. little	33. his	50. very
17. trouble	34. boat	

Administering the cloze procedure is easy. Begin by providing students with practice in using context to fill in blanks. You might do a number of practice sentences at the chalkboard. When you are sure students understand the task, give the following directions: (1) use only one word in each blank; (2) you might want to read the passage through first, then go back and fill in the blanks. Provide enough time for the students to complete the task without rushing.

Scoring the Cloze Procedure. In scoring cloze passages, only exact matches are accepted. This might seem to be a severe requirement. However, the cloze is being used for placement in this case and not for diagnosis. Demanding the exact match provides the most valid results for placement purposes (Gillet and Temple 1986). Count the number of exact matches and calculate the percentage of correct responses. If you have exactly fifty deletions, simply calculate two percent for each correct response. Use the following chart to evaluate the scores.

60% to 100%	Independent Level
40% to 59%	Instructional Level
39% and lower	Frustration Level

Some authors suggest that 40% is an appropriate minimum for the instructional level in the early intermediate grades. However, higher percentages (50% to 59%) should be required for students at higher reading levels (Duffelmeyer 1983).

The cloze procedure is an informative tool for quickly placing children in textual material. Like any placement instrument, it should be used in conjunction with teacher observation and evaluation of student performance in order to ensure appropriate placement.

The Cloze Procedure Used for Diagnostic Purposes. The cloze procedure also helps in diagnosing students' overall passage comprehension and use of context in text comprehension. The construction of passages for diagnosis is similar to the construction of passages for placement. However, the length of the passage is variable (between 50 and 400 words), as well as the interval between deletions. Students may complete the passage by reading the passage and independently writing in the missing words, or by reading the passage aloud and having the teacher write in their responses. The oral reading approach allows the teacher to assess word recognition strategies, as well as context use and general comprehension.

When used diagnostically, the cloze procedure can be manipulated to diagnose specific skills. For example, if you have a question about children's ability to use pronouns, delete all the pronouns from a passage. Similarly, if you wish to diagnose children's use of signal words (e.g., *since, because, but, although*), delete the signal words from a passage. It is often easier to construct cloze passages for the diagnosis of specific skills than it is to find appropriate prewritten exercises.

The cloze procedure can be adapted to assess students' knowledge of the vocabulary and concepts in a reading selection. To do this, delete the main vocabulary items or key concepts from the cloze passage. Used prior to reading, such passages give you a good idea of students' vocabulary and concept levels in relation to the demands of the selection. You can then modify your prevocabulary and conceptual development instruction to meet the children's needs. Used after reading, the cloze passage can provide a good assessment of comprehension—the kind and amount of understanding the children have gained from reading the selection.

When the cloze procedure is used diagnostically, scoring is not restricted to exact matches. Words are accepted as correct if they make sense grammatically and semantically (in meaning).

The Cloze Procedure Used for Remediation and Practice. The cloze procedure is also used for remediating or practicing missing, unused, or confused skills. In this context cloze passages are manipulated to focus on the specific skills that require attention (Gunn and Elkins 1984). Use the procedure to reinforce such skills as comprehension, decoding, sight vocabulary, and meaning vocabulary. The following example shows how a passage is manipulated in different ways to reinforce each of these skills.

CLASSROOM APPLICATION

Original Passage

John was drawing a picture of a dragon one night before bed. His eyes began to droop, so he shut the drapes and went to sleep.

John began to dream. In his dreams, he saw the dragon in his picture come to life! The dragon played on John's drum and woke up his family. Then the noisy dragon went to the kitchen for a drink and dripped water all over the floor.

Just then, John woke up. He looked around his room, but there was no dragon. "What a crazy dream," thought John. "I won't draw dragon pictures before bed again."*

Passage Modified for General Comprehension Development

John was drawing a _____ of a dragon one night before bed. His eyes began to droop, so he _____ the drapes and went to sleep.

John began to dream. In his _____ he saw the dragon in his picture come to life! The dragon _____ on John's drum and woke up his _____. Then the noisy dragon went to the kitchen for a drink and dripped _____ all over the floor.

Just then, John woke up. He looked around his _____, but there was no dragon. "What a _____ dream," thought John. "I won't _____ dragon pictures before _____ again."

As with all cloze passages used for remediation or practice, you may use the exercise in two ways. First, you may allow the child to fill in the blanks with any word that makes sense in the slot. Second, you may supply a scrambled list of the missing words and have the child select from the list the appropriate word for each slot.

Deleted Words

bed	picture
crazy	dream
water	family
played	room
shut	draw

Choosing from a list is a slightly more difficult task. With either strategy you should work with the children to do the task so you can directly observe the strategies they use to arrive at the answers.

Passage Modified for Decoding

John was _____ a picture of a dragon one night before bed. His eyes began to droop, so he shut the _____ and went to sleep.

John began to dream. In his _____, he saw the _____ in his picture come to life! The _____ played on John's _____ and woke up his family. Then the noisy dragon went to the kitchen for a _____ and dripped water all over the floor.

*Franka Hopwood, graduate student, University of Colorado, Colorado Springs, 1983.

Just then, John woke up. He looked around his room, but there was no ____. "What a crazy ____," thought John. "I won't ____ dragon pictures before bed again."

Deleted Words

drawing	*dream*
drapes	*dragon*
dragon	*drum*
drink	*dragon*
dream	*draw*

This modification reinforces the /dr/ consonant combination. You would direct the child to fill in the blanks with words that begin with /dr/.

The cloze procedure can be modified for vocabulary development and practice as well. Simply delete previously taught vocabulary items from the passage and direct children to fill in the blanks. As you can see, you may construct passages focusing on any skill, including short and long vowel sounds, consonant and vowel combinations, contractions, signal words, word endings, meaning vocabulary, sight vocabulary, and compound words.

A variation of the cloze procedure is the maze format (Guthrie et al. 1974). The maze format provides students with three choices for each deleted word. The three choices include the correct word, an incorrect word of the same grammatical class as the correct word (e.g., both verbs), and an incorrect word of a different grammatical class (e.g., one noun, one verb). The child chooses the correct word from the multiple choice display. This format allows you to observe the child's general comprehension, ability to use context, types of error, and error patterns.

The maze format is easier than the typical cloze format because it limits choices and allows the child to focus on a few words. The maze format is a good choice for children who have difficulty using context. Figure 4.3 presents an example of the maze format.

Notice how you can construct the choices to analyze different skills. For example, the words in block B are all forms of the verb *to sleep*, but the choice children make will tell you how they use syntax. The choices in blocks E and F, on the other hand, will tell you how well children read through initial consonant combinations and decode the middles and ends of words. Word choices also provide information about children's use of context.

You can make any cloze task easier for children by including one or more of the following aids:

- the first letter(s) of the word (e.g., John was drawing a p____ of a dragon.)
- the first and last letters of the word (e.g., He shut the drapes and went to sl____p.)

- one short dash for each letter in the missing word (e.g., He saw the dragon in his picture come to ————!)
- combinations of the above (e.g., The dragon played on John's drum and woke up his f——————.)
- one short dash for each letter in the word and the first and last letters in the word (e.g., The dragon dripped water all over the fl——r.)

The cloze procedure and its variations give you many options for assessing children's performance on a number of levels in both comprehension and word analysis.

John was drawing a

A
1. picture
2. flower
3. paint

of a dragon one night before bed. His

eyes began to droop, so he shut the drapes and went to

B
1. slept.
2. asleep.
3. sleep.

John

began to dream. In his dream he saw the dragon in his picture come to

C
1. drawing!
2. life!
3. grow!

The dragon played on John's drum and woke up his whole

D
1. family.
2. brother.
3. coming.

Then the noisy dragon went to the kitchen for a drink and

dripped water all over the

E
1. fly.
2. floor.
3. flying.

Just then, John woke up. He looked

around his room, but there was no dragon. "What a crazy

F
1. dreams,"
2. dreaming,"
3. dream,"

thought John. "I won't draw dragons before

G
1. night
2. bed
3. sleeps

again."

FIGURE 4.3 Maze Format

Teacher-Made Tests

Tests constructed by teachers are among the most valuable forms of measurement. Teachers construct tests to answer questions about students' performance. For example, if a student's oral reading indicated a problem recognizing consonant combinations, the teacher might make a list of all the consonant combinations and ask the child to respond. The teacher could then provide instruction and practice in the combinations the child did not know. Similarly, observing that the student had difficulty using context, the teacher could construct and administer cloze exercises in order to pinpoint the kind of context practice needed. Teacher-made tests may be uncomplicated or detailed in construction. They may be used year after year or only once or twice to provide quick measurement of students' behavior. There are four basic questions you need to answer as you construct a test:

1. For whom is the test intended? You should identify the specific group of children for whom you are writing the test. This will guide your decisions about the length of the test, its complexity, and its content in relation to what you have taught.

2. What is the purpose of the test? Tests are basically diagnostic or comparative in purpose. If the test is meant to be diagnostic, it should focus on identifying students' strengths and weaknesses. If it is meant to be comparative, it should focus on comparing students' performance. Most teacher-made tests can serve either purpose, depending on how the results are used.

3. What specific skills are to be measured? Each test typically focuses on one skill. This allows teachers to directly observe children's performance on individual skills. When observing and measuring a variety of skills, as in oral reading tests, teachers should identify categories of skills, such as phonic analysis, structural analysis, word recognition, and comprehension.

4. What form of response will be required? There are several response formats for assessing performance. These include true-false, multiple choice, matching, fill in the blanks, short answer, oral responses, and written essays. Teachers should analyze the task to choose the most appropriate response format.

If a test has written directions that children must read independently, take care to write clear directions using appropriate vocabulary. Unclear or overly difficult directions invalidate the test results, which fail to reflect children's true performance.

Chapters 3 and 4 have explored both formal and informal methods of assessing children's reading behavior. Assessment methods can be conceptualized as a continuum ranging from formal, infrequently ad-

ASSESSMENT METHODS

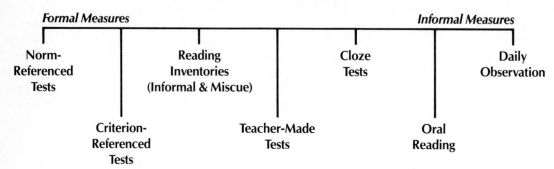

FIGURE 4.4   Assessment Methods

ministered measurements to informal, routinely administered measurements. Figure 4.4 presents a model of this continuum.

Diagnosis occurs throughout the range of assessment. Formal measures provide you with general patterns of information that help you to determine the starting points of instruction and remediation. As instruction progresses, informal methods give you specific information about the appropriateness and effectiveness of instruction, and also give you ongoing data for use in further diagnosis and remediation. Both forms of assessment work together to give you a complete picture of each child and the information you need for making sound instructional decisions.

SUMMARY   Informal reading diagnosis begins with the keen and continual observation of children and the factors that affect their performance. Oral reading testing is a valuable diagnostic technique. Specific methods include informal reading inventories, reading miscue inventories, the cloze procedure and its variations, and teacher-made tests. Teachers need to understand and appreciate the advantages and limitations of each diagnostic instrument in order to choose the best format for any given learning situation.

R · E · F · E · R · E · N · C · E · S

Ames, L. B., and J. A. Chase. *Don't Push Your Preschooler.* New York: Harper and Row, 1981.

Anderson, J., and A. Coates. "The Teacher's Dilemma: How to Gauge the Suitability of Reading Material. In A. J. Harris and E. R. Sipay, eds. *Readings on Reading Instruction.* New York; Longman, 1984.

Dechant, E. *Diagnosis and Remediation of Reading Difficulties.* Englewood Cliffs, NJ: Prentice–Hall, 1981.

Duffelmeyer, F. A. "The effect of grade level on cloze test scores." *Journal of Reading* 26 (February 1983): 436–441.

Froese, V. "Word recognition tests: Are they useful beyond grade 3?" *Reading Teacher* 24 (February 1971): 432–438.

Gillet, J. W., and C. Temple. *Understanding Reading Problems: Assessment and Instruction*, 2nd ed. Boston: Little, Brown, 1986.

Goodman, Y. M., and C. L. Burke. *Reading Miscue Inventory Manual: Procedures for Diagnosis and Evaluation*. New York: Macmillan, 1972.

Gunn, V. P., and J. Elkins. "Clozing the Reading Gap." In A. J. Harris and E. R. Sipay, eds. *Readings on Reading Instruction*. New York: Longman, 1984.

Guthrie, J., M. Seifert, N. A. Burnham, and R. Caplan. "The maze technique to assess and monitor reading comprehension." *The Reading Teacher* 28 (November 1974): 161–168.

Harris, L. A., and R. M. Lalik. "Teachers' use of informal reading inventories: An example of school constraints." *The Reading Teacher* 40 (March 1987): 624–630.

Ilg, F., L. B. Ames, A. B. Haines, and C. Gillespie. *School Readiness*. New York: Harper and Row, 1978.

Jongsma, E. A. *Cloze Instruction Research: A Second Look*. Newark, DE: International Reading Association, 1980.

Jongsma, K. D., and E. A. Jongsma. "Test review: Commercial informal reading inventories." *The Reading Teacher* 34 (1981): 697–705.

McCormick, S. *Remedial and Clinical Reading Instruction*. Columbus, OH: Merrill, 1987.

McCracken, R. A. "Using an Informal Reading Inventory to Affect Instruction." In A. J. Harris and E. R. Sipay, eds. *Reading on Reading Instruction*. New York: Longman, 1984.

McKenna, M. C. "Informal reading inventories: A review of the issues." *Reading Teacher* 36 (March 1983): 670–679.

Peterson, J. M., J. Greenlaw, and R. Tierney. "Assessing instructional placement with an I.R.I.: The effectiveness of comprehension questions." *Journal of Educational Research* 71 (May/June 1978): 247–250.

Sax, G. *Principles of Educational and Psychological Measurement and Evaluation*, 2nd ed. Belmont, CA; Wadsworth Publishing, 1980.

Strange, M. "Instructional implications of a conceptual theory of reading comprehension." *Reading Teacher* 33 (January 1980): 391–397.

Taylor, W. "Cloze procedure: A new tool for measuring readability." *Journalism Quarterly* 30 (Fall 1953): 415–433.

Warwick, B. E. "Cloze Procedures as Applied to Reading." In O. R. Buros, ed. *Eighth Mental Measurements Yearbook, Vol. 11*. Highland Park, NJ: Gryphon Press, 1978.

5 The Poor Reader: Child of Concern

FOCUS   1. How do underachievers and children with specific reading deficiencies
QUESTIONS   differ?
          2. What are the characteristics of children with limited reading ability?
          3. What is the concept of slow learning rate, and how does this concept
             affect instruction in reading?
          4. What is priming and why is it necessary for appropriate learning?
          5. How are poor readers handicapped in the way they decode words?
          6. How are poor readers handicapped in the way they comprehend
             connected text?

If you have taught reading for any length of time, you know that no one
definition or description fits all poor readers. Children with reading difficulties display a wide variety of often baffling characteristics. They are
also given a wide variety of labels. Depending on which text you read,
you may encounter such labels as reading impaired, slow reader, dyslexic, reading handicapped, retarded reader, and reading delayed. In this
text, children with reading difficulties are placed in four broad and basic
categories: underachiever in reader, reading disabled, specific reading
deficiency, and limited reading ability.

UNDERACHIEVERS

Underachievers in reading include children who read adequately for
their age and grade placement, but perform below their reading potential
or capacity (Ekwall and Shanker 1983, Zintz and Haggart 1986). Reading
potential or reading capacity refers to the reading performance you can
expect given the child's chronological age, mental age, and intellectual
development. Several expectancy formulas exist for calculating potential
or capacity. One of the best known is the Harris formula (Harris and Sipay 1985):

$$\text{Reading expectancy} = \frac{2\ (\text{mental age})\ +\ \text{chronological age}}{3}$$

$$\text{Mental age} = \frac{\text{I.Q.} \times \text{chronological age}}{100}$$

Based on these formulas, a ten-year-old child (beginning fifth grade) with
an I.Q. of 120 would have a mental age of:

$$\frac{120 \times 10}{100} = \frac{1200}{100} = 12.0 \text{ years}$$

That child's reading expectancy would be:

$$\frac{2(12) + 10}{3} = \frac{24 + 10}{3} = \frac{34}{3} = 11.3 \text{ years}$$

Some educators subtract 5.2 years to transform the reading expectancy to a grade level, because children begin kindergarten at an average age of five years and two months (Stauffer et al. 1978). The reading expectancy age of 11.3 would therefore yield a grade level of 11.3 − 5.2 = 6.1. The fifth grade child in question would be expected to be reading at the beginning sixth grade level. Although reading well at the fifth grade level, based on the expectancy, the child could be considered an underachiever in reading.

A child with a chronological age of 10 years and an I.Q. of 95, on the other hand, would have a mental age of:

$$\frac{\text{I.Q.} \times \text{chronological age}}{100} = \frac{95 \times 100}{100} = 9.5 \text{ years}$$

The child's reading expectancy would be:

$$\frac{2 \text{ (mental age)} + \text{chronological age}}{3} = \frac{2(9.5) + 10}{3} = \frac{29}{3} = 9.6 \text{ years}$$

The grade level expectancy would be 9.6 years − 5.2 = 4.4. If this child was in fifth grade and was reading on the low fourth grade level, she or he would be performing appropriately based on reading expectancy.

The results of expectancy formulas vary considerably. You should realize that reading capacity is merely a score derived from a formula, which should not be used to place a ceiling on children's abilities. You should treat the concept of reading expectancy flexibly, since no formula can accurately indicate the true potential of a human mind. In addition, remember that calculations of mental age depend on I.Q. scores. The measurement of I.Q., however, is often inaccurate and dependent on the test used.

READING DISABLED

Many children who perform poorly in reading have average or above-average intelligence and perform adequately in other school subjects. Despite efforts to give appropriate instruction and long-term remediation in reading, these children fail to make expected progress and continue to perform one or more years below their grade placement. These children are often labeled reading disabled. Reading disabled children tend to have a weak profile of reading skills and inadequate subskills, such as sight vocabulary, phonic analysis, structural analysis, and comprehension. The entire complex of reading is incomplete and underdeveloped. For the most part, these children seem to miss the entire point of reading. Reading disabled children have long-standing reading difficulties often lasting for several years (Swaby 1984). Reading disabled children generally perform below their reading expectancy, or potential.

SPECIFIC READING DEFICIENCIES

Children with specific reading deficiencies have fairly well-developed overall reading skills, but experience marked difficulty in one or more specific skills. For example, some children might have good comprehension skills but inadequate phonic analysis skills. They can somehow understand most of what they read but have severe difficulties sounding out words, retaining phonic rules, and reading orally. Children with excellent phonic skills and a strong ability to decode almost any word they encounter may nevertheless have little or no comprehension of what they read. The reading problems of these children are more specific and more clearly identified than those of the reading disabled. Children with specific reading deficiencies require less extensive intervention programs than disabled readers.

LIMITED READING ABILITY

Some children demonstrate poor reading skills because they have limited intellectual capacity. They have below average intelligence, which results in significantly slower rates of learning. These readers are often referred to as "slow learners" (Ekwall and Shanker 1983). They often require considerably more practice and reteaching than other children of the same chronological age and grade placement. Slow learners usually experience moderate to severe difficulty in other school subjects as well. Their academic problems seem more generalized than those of children with other kinds of reading problems. They also read very near to their potential level. Table 5.1 summarizes the categories and characteristics of poor readers.

Teachers are often confused about the differences between children with "reading disabilities" and those with "learning disabilities." This confusion is justified. There is considerable confusion in the litera-

TABLE 5.1   Characteristics of Poor Readers

Reading Disabled	Underachiever in Reading	Specific Reading Deficiencies	Limited Reading Ability
• average and above intelligence	• read adequately for age and grade placement	• well-developed general skills	• limited intellectual capacity
• perform adequately in other subjects	• read below potential	• marked difficulty in one or more specific skills	• below average intelligence
• often have received long-term remediation			• very slow learning rates in reading
• weak general profile of skills			• moderate to severe difficulty in other school subjects
• perform one or more years below grade placement			• read close to potential
• read below potential			

ture about the definition and treatment of these disabilities. In general, learning disabled children are identified as having central nervous system dysfunctions. These dysfunctions are viewed as the cause of their reading or learning difficulties. Reading disabled children do not have known central nervous system dysfunctions, although their performance and skill deficits resemble those of learning disabled children. Despite similar performance profiles, these children might be treated differently by a learning disabilities specialist than by a reading disabilities specialist. Weaver and Shonkoff (1978, 112–113) elaborate on these differences in the following statement:

> Traditionally, classroom teachers enlist the help of reading specialists for students who are behind in reading. . . . Remediation focuses on skills that are found to be deficient, not on what might have caused the deficiencies. Although the pace of the lessons might be different, the methods and materials used by the remedial teacher are, for the most part, quite similar to those used by the teacher in the classroom.
>
> The field of learning disabilities was developed more recently than that of remedial reading. It evolved from the notion that a few of the children with reading problems (about 2%) have difficulty because of central nervous system dysfunction. Generally, learning disabilities specialists believe that this group should be isolated and treated differently from the larger group whose reading difficulties

are not neurophysiologically based. . . . Reading specialists emphasize reading skills. Skill deficits are identified and remediated using methods and materials similar to those used in classroom instruction. In contrast, the learning disabilities specialist emphasizes the perceptual, cognitive, and linguistic processes assumed to underlie reading skills. Deficits in these processes are identified; the instruction is designed to remediate the deficits.

Clear differences between learning disabled and reading disabled children might not exist in reality. Many reading disabled children are identified as learning disabled because programs designed for learning disabled children do exist.

All children with reading problems of any kind require careful ongoing diagnosis, and skillful, effective remediation. They can all show progress in reading. This does not mean they can all be taught to read on grade level. It is unrealistic to expect individuals with vastly different abilities and skills to perform at the same level in any content area. With appropriate intervention, however, all children can improve their reading skills. Helping all children to improve is the teacher's primary responsibility. Improvement should be appropriately relative to the starting point of each child.

The single most important characteristic of an effective reading program is its ability to promote progress in children without causing harmful side effects. Whatever their starting points, day by day and session by session children will become slightly more proficient at learning to read. As a result children will learn the process of reading to the best of their abilities.

CHARACTERISTICS OF POOR READERS

Regardless of the category in which we place them, children who have difficulty learning to read tend to share the following characteristics:

- Slow learning rate
- Nonautomatic priming abilities
- Single clue usage in decoding words
- Difficulty in applying skills
- Difficulty in abstracting
- Attention deficits
- Maladaptive behavior

You should recognize these characteristics in children and their implications for your instructional strategies.

Slow Learning Rate

Many poor readers have slow learning rates in reading. It takes them longer to learn written content. In one hour they might thoroughly learn only half of the content taught during that hour. At the end of a year, test scores predictably show that they have not achieved a year's growth. At the end of the elementary grades, many have learned five or fewer years of material in reading.

A slow learning rate has important instructional implications. Because they learn slowly and cannot realistically be expected to assimilate the entire curriculum in any given year, you should limit instructional content to the most important and necessary skills. For example, if the reading scope and sequence includes such skills as recognizing and marking stress, using context in decoding, dividing words into syllables, and prediction and drawing inferences, you should prioritize these skills and emphasize those with the greatest potential for enhancing long-term learning. Predicting, using context, and inferring are more critical to reading than marking stress and syllabication. Given limited time and children with limited learning rates, you must decide the priority of content. It makes sense to focus on the most usable and vital information.

Lack of Priming Abilities

Priming refers to cognitive preparation for incoming information (Swaby 1984). Masses of information are available to the mind at any given time. This information comes from both external and internal sources. For example, external information in a typical classroom includes the variety of personalities, clothing colors and styles, gestures, voices, bulletin boards, posters, and the like. Internal information comes from the thoughts, ideas, memories, wishes, and interests of the individual. Because of external and internal stimuli, the mind must be directed to appropriate content in order to process that content. Directing the mind to content activates prior knowledge. The activation of prior knowledge permits more efficient comprehension (Langer and Nicolich 1981, Shantz 1981, Johnson 1982, Devine 1986). If children do not direct their minds to specific content, they become distracted by irrelevancies and ignore appropriate incoming information. The result is failure to learn.

Children who are primed for content have an alert posture. They tend to sit straight and orient themselves toward the teacher. They ask questions and make comments relevant to incoming content. Children who are not primed for content tend not to display alert postures. They seem inattentive and mentally uninvolved in the sharing of information. Teachers often feel compelled to direct them to "sit up" or "sit straight." Unprimed children also make comments and ask questions that have nothing to do with the content, as the following case study shows.

CASE STUDY

Recently, I was observing a social studies lesson in a fifth grade classroom. The teacher called the session to order and instructed the children to take out their texts. She announced the heading and title of the day's lesson, "Endangered Species: The Great Slaughter of the Roo." On the page were pictures of a bald eagle, a wallaby, a kangaroo, and a crane. As the teacher spoke, I could see and hear the "self-primed" children. They were alert and attentive. They sat straight. They were making comments and asking questions (Is this like the story of the bald eagle here in the U.S.? Is the roo a kangaroo? Is this about Australia? Did you know that people eat kangaroo meat and use it for pet food too? I really think hunting is awful). The primed children had obviously identified the content and had activated their prior knowledge relevant to the incoming information. The result was mental priming and readiness for learning.

I could also see and hear the nonprimed children. They were nearly lying on their desks and were obviously distracted. Their comments and questions (Do you know what? Next Thursday my mom is going to take me to buy new tennis shoes. Are we going to read the whole thing? My paper didn't get put up on the board this morning) showed that these children had not identified the incoming content and had not activated their prior knowledge. As a result, they were not primed, not ready for learning.

The most important instructional implication of the lack of priming abilities is that the teacher must help these children to prime themselves for learning. The teacher must show them how to focus their attention on relevant information, how to use the incoming information to activate their relevant prior knowledge, and how to use that knowledge to prime themselves for learning. Smith (1982) suggests using prediction as a natural strategy for priming students' cognitive systems. Prediction sets up expectations and taps prior knowledge in anticipating outcomes. If you help children use prediction in reading, you will be helping them to develop their priming abilities. The following questions and comments might help.

- Look at the heading of the selection. What do you think the selection will be about?
- Look at the title. What do you think the article will be about?
- Look at the illustrations, pictures, charts and graphs. What do you expect to find in the story?
- Notice the captions, boldface type, italics, etc. What do you think the selection will be about?
- Based on the heading, title, illustrations, etc., what are some words you expect to find in the selection?
- Based on the heading, title, and illustrations, what do you think is the setting of the story?

- Do you think the selection is fictional or factual? How do you know?

Single Clue Usage in Decoding Words

Many poor readers use single clues in the decoding of words. However, many strategies or clues exist for decoding unknown words in print. A listing of some of the most important and useful clues follows.

- Spell the word, allowing readers to look at the word and to isolate its parts.
- Use context to predict the appropriate word.
- Skip the word, read to the end of the sentence, return to the word and predict meaning from context.
- Block the known part of a word and analyze the remaining part.
- Sound out the word.
- Ask someone.

Many of the weakest readers, however, systematically use one strategy to decode unknown words. They usually sound out the word or skip the word without returning for self-correction. Students with auditory blending deficits and slow learning rates for phonic information find single strategies unsuccessful in decoding. In addition, many words cannot be decoded by sounding out (i.e., *island*, *are*, and *eight*). They tend not to use a variety of strategies in decoding. The following case study illustrates the problems of decoding with single clues.

CASE STUDY

Recently I was involved in the informal testing of a fourth grade boy. He was a very weak reader, not only because he lacked many basic decoding skills, but also because he had missed the entire point of reading—gaining meaning. I asked the child to read a number of sentences to get a basic idea of how he went about the task of reading. One of the sentences in question read, "The man cut the grass with the lawn mower." The boy began reading. When he got to the words *lawn mower*, it was obvious that he did not know them as sight words. Had he been aware of context he would have realized that by far the most common thing used to cut grass is a lawn mower. The *l* and *m* at the beginning of the words would have confirmed his prediction. Instead, he reverted to the only strategy he knew and used. He sounded out /l/, /aw/, /n/, but ended with the word *lag*. He then began sounding out *mower*. He said /m/, /o/, /w/, /er/, and blended it as *mugger*. Quite in awe, I asked him to reread the sentence. He read, "The man cut the grass with the lag mugger," and he didn't look the least bit uneasy. Notice that in spite of the many clues available, he used a single clue that was unproductive for him.

Teachers must continually teach children to use a variety of strategies and must reinforce these strategies during all reading experiences (McClelland and Rumelhart 1985, Just and Carpenter 1987).

Difficulty in Applying Skills

Many poor readers find it difficult to apply isolated skills to real reading situations. They can often learn or memorize individual skills, perform well on worksheets, and respond appropriately to skill lessons. However, when they are placed in real reading contexts with connected narrative, they fail to apply these skills (Weaver 1980, 1988). The children often have difficulty generalizing information. They learn in specific contexts and do not generalize to others. In addition, they do not read enough on their own to strengthen their whole reading skills—the reading of connected content that makes sense in the whole. In whole reading, children learn to use the entire context of language to solve the problem of print. In isolated reading, children read sentences contrived for the purposes of specific skill development.

The major instructional implication is that teachers must provide daily experiences with whole reading (Weaver and Shonkoff 1980). The specific skills taught must be practiced in whole language so that children have opportunities to apply the skills in real reading contexts. All skills are means to one end, which is whole reading.

Difficulty in Abstracting

Poor readers often have difficulty grasping abstract concepts. Reading and reading instruction are filled with abstractions. Think of the terms "long o," "short a," "silent e," "hard g," "soft g," and "main idea." Many children have great difficulty grasping such abstract ideas, as the following case illustrates.

CASE STUDY

Years ago, I observed a teacher teaching a skill lesson to a slow reading group. The lesson was on vowel digraphs such as oa and ea. The teacher used a skill chart and then switched to a workbook page. Students listened attentively and seemed to understand the content. The teacher used the well-known rhyme, "When two vowels go walking, the first one does the talking," to help children internalize the rule. At the end of the session, she asked if everyone understood and everyone said "Yes." They returned to their desks to complete the workbook assignment. Soon, I saw a hand up. As the teacher was occupied, I walked over to the child and asked if I could help.

"I don't understand this page," he said.

"Well," I said, "It really is exactly like the material you just did in your reading group."

"It is?"

"Yes."

"Well," he said thoughtfully, "I understand that."

"Explain it to me."

"I understand that when two vowels go walking the first one does the talking."

I felt hopeful. "Great," I said. "What don't you understand?"

"I don't understand where they are going."

He had memorized the rule but he had not understood the abstract concept.

To help children grasp abstractions, teachers should as much as possible provide actual experience with the application of skills. The more children experience reading, the more they learn to apply reading concepts and to focus on using their skills. Application helps them to better understand the concepts, and tells you whether children are using skills or are merely repeating skill information.

Attention Deficits

Poor readers often fail to direct their attention and concentrate on relevant information (Ekwall and Shanker 1983). They seem unable to focus on the most useful and productive clues to meaning. For example, they tend to miss relevant material in a reading selection, such as the title, the heading, the illustrations, the charts or graphs, the italicized words, and the like. As they read, they tend to be attracted to trivia. In some children, attention deficits result from confusion about the process of reading. They don't know where to look to receive maximum information. In other children the problem might be related to stress, anxiety or other emotional states. Sometimes they are so involved in reacting to stress that they have little energy left for attending appropriately to the text (Stauffer et al. 1978).

Teachers can assist these children by teaching them that the specific material provides them with maximum information. You should model for students the process of reading, the use of clues in print, the focus on important information, and the practice of self-monitoring in order to check comprehension.

Maladaptive Behavior

Some children with reading difficulties demonstrate maladaptive behavior. They lack basic self-discipline and often disrupt the class (Ekwall and

Shanker 1983). Because of their erratic behavior, their academic performance is also erratic. When they behave well and listen to directions, they learn content and perform well. When they behave badly and ignore directions and content, they perform poorly. The maladaptive behavior of children is sometimes the cause of their poor performance in academic areas. However, maladaptive behavior is sometimes a result of children's feelings of inadequacy in school. They use disruptive behavior as a distraction from their feelings.

Regardless of the reasons for children's behavior, the teacher should ⸻ the classroom environment to ensure that the structure ⸻nt of the classroom are not contributing to disruption. ⸻ggestions offer ideas for creating and maintaining de- ⸻avior.

⸻xpectations for student behavior from the first day of ⸻r expectations with children and post important ⸻ne teachers accept inappropriate behavior at the ⸻e they feel children need time to "fit in" or "adjust" ⸻ed to conform to expectations. During this time, ⸻most disruptive ones—are setting the tone of the ⸻uation becomes intolerable and the teacher de- ⸻me to restore order, it may be too late. The con- ⸻respecting rules after they have been routinely ⸻trategy is to set the expectations immediately. ⸻ed in establishing criteria for appropriate be- ⸻rate that they can follow the rules, they may

⸻fective consequences for the breaking of ⸻consequences as the repeated writing of ⸻entire group for the infractions of one ⸻out, and cruel humiliation. More effec- ⸻privileges, removal from the classroom ⸻ification, parent-teacher-student-prin-

⸻r. Motivate positive behavior with re- ⸻recognition in school newsletters, ⸻rds, and special privileges or certif-

p⸻ ⸻a behavior on one occasion and

no⸻ ⸻sure that disruptive children are rate⸻ ⸻k of the room. Keep them sepa- ⸻within your sight.

them⸻ ⸻to reason with students who are angry. Allow ⸻wn. Do not argue with children.

7. Be sure that students, parents, and the principal receive a writ-

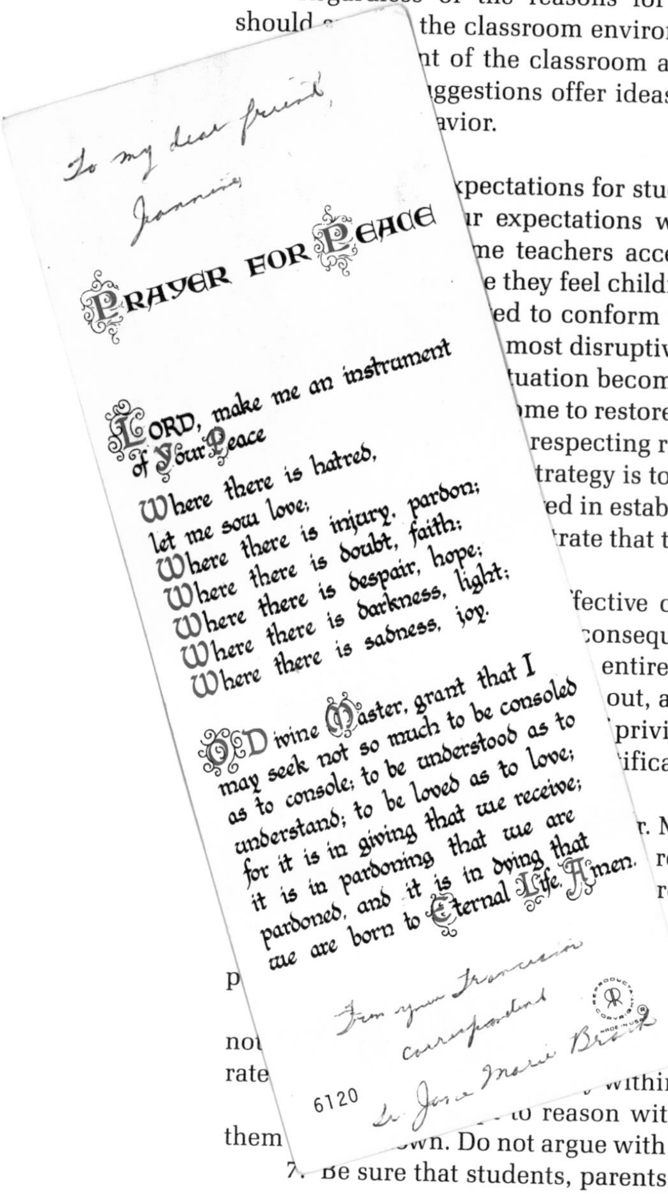

(Handwritten prayer card overlaying the page text:)

To my dear friend, Jeannine,

PRAYER FOR PEACE

LORD, make me an instrument of Your Peace

Where there is hatred, let me sow love; Where there is injury, pardon; Where there is doubt, faith; Where there is despair, hope; Where there is darkness, light; Where there is sadness, joy.

O Divine Master, grant that I may seek not so much to be consoled as to console; to be understood as to understand; to be loved as to love; for it is in giving that we receive; it is in pardoning that we are pardoned, and it is in dying that we are born to Eternal Life. Amen.

From your Jeannine, correspondent

Sr. Jose Marie Br⸻

6120

ten copy of classroom rules along with the consequences for breaking the rules.

8. Provide children with meaningful work that they can accomplish.

SUMMARY   Poor readers include the reading disabled, underachievers, students with specific reading deficiencies, and children with limited reading abilities. Regardless of the category into which they are placed, children who are poor readers share some common characteristics. These characteristics include a slow learning rate, a lack of self-priming abilities, a reliance on single clues for decoding words, difficulty in applying skills, attention deficits, and maladaptive behavior. Each problem has specific instructional implications. Awareness of the characteristics of poor readers allows you to monitor student behavior and performance and to modify your instruction in order to better meet students' needs.

R·E·F·E·R·E·N·C·E·S

Devine, T. G. *Teaching Reading Comprehension: From Theory to Practice.* Newton, MA: Allyn and Bacon, 1986.

Ekwall, E. E., and J. L. Shanker. *Diagnosis and Remediation of the Disabled Reader,* 2nd ed. Boston: Allyn and Bacon, 1983.

————. *Teaching Reading in the Elementary School.* Columbus, OH: Merrill, 1985.

Harris, A., and E. Sipay. *How to Increase Reading Ability,* 7th ed. New York: Longman, 1985.

Johnson, B. "Helping children construct meaning: Comprehension strategies that work." *Reading Horizons* 22 (Summer 1982): 268–274.

Just, M. A., and P. A. Carpenter. *The Psychology of Reading and Language Comprehension.* Newton, MA: Allyn and Bacon, 1987.

Langer, J. A., and M. Nicolich. "Prior knowledge and its relationship to comprehension." *Journal of Reading Behavior* 13 (Winter 1981): 373–379.

McClelland, J. L., and D. E. Rumelhart. "An interactive activation model of context effects in letter perception: Part I. An account of basic findings." In H. Singer and R. B. Ruddell. *Theoretical Models and Processes of Reading.* Newark, DE: International Reading Association, 1985.

Shantz, M. "Briefs: Readability." *Language Arts* 58 (November/December 1981): 943–944.

Smith, F. *Understanding Reading*, 3rd ed. New York: Holt, Rinehart & Winston, 1982.

Stauffer, R. G., J. C. Abrams, and J. J. Pikulski. *Diagnosis, Correction, and Prevention of Reading Disabilities*. New York: Harper and Row, 1978.

Swaby, B. E. R. *Teaching and Learning Reading: A Pragmatic Approach*. Boston: Little, Brown, 1984.

Weaver, C. *Psycholinguistics and Reading: From Process to Practice*. Cambridge, MA: Winthrop, 1980.

———. *Reading Process and Practice: From Socio-Psycholinguistics to Whole Language*. Portsmouth, NH: Heinemann, 1988.

Weaver, P., and F. Shonkoff. *Research Within Reach: A Research-Guided Response to Concerns of Reading Educators*. Washington, D.C.: National Institute of Education, 1978.

Zintz, M. V., and Z. R. Haggart. *Corrective Reading*. Dubuque IA: William C. Brown, 1986.

PART TWO

CORRECTION

6 Effective Instruction and Remediation

FOCUS 1. What are the primary characteristics of effective instruction?
QUESTIONS 2. According to Brophy's research, what are the most important characteristics of effective teachers?
3. How are reading diagnosis and remediation principles interdependent?
4. What are the basic prerequisites of effective remediation?
5. What is the difference between individualizing instruction and individualizing children?
6. What are the characteristics of direct instruction identified by Rosenshine?
7. How can teachers apply the principles of effective remediation in actual classroom instruction?

FUNDAMENTALS OF EFFECTIVE INSTRUCTION

The issue of teacher effectiveness has received significant attention during the past decade (Rupley 1975; Medley 1977; Rosenshine 1979; Edmonds 1982, 1979; Brophy 1982, 1983; Allington 1984; Rosenshine and Stevens 1984). Researchers have attempted to identify the specific instructional characteristics related to academic achievement. Interest in teacher effectiveness is not a recent development. As early as the 1930s Gates and Bond (1936) attempted to assess the relationship between mental age and reading success. In the 1930s there was significant support for the view that a mental age of 6.5 was a prerequisite for success in beginning reading. It was recommended that children receive no formal reading instruction until they had achieved the appropriate mental age. Gates and Bond disagreed with this entrenched view. They believed that certain characteristics of teachers and instruction affected reading readiness and performance. To test their hypothesis, they identified the ten lowest-achieving students in four first grade classes and assigned them to tutors. Within three months all ten children were successful in reading. The study demonstrated that readiness for reading could be developed, and also sparked interest in teacher effectiveness and ineffectiveness and in the impact of teacher characteristics on student performance.

Research on teacher effectiveness began in the 1960s. In one of the earliest studies, Wade (1960) designed an instrument for identifying and measuring teacher strategies in reading instruction in grades two through five. The strategies included:

- Placement of students in homogeneous groups
- Use of readability levels in the choice of material
- Assessment of growth after instruction

- Diagnosis of reading difficulties
- Categorization of word recognition errors
- Knowledge of the goals of workbook assignments

Wade administered the instrument to inservice teachers, prospective teachers with sixteen weeks of training in reading, and undergraduates with no instruction in the teaching of reading. He found that inservice teachers outperformed prospective teachers, and prospective teachers outperformed undergraduates. Wade also found that students whose teachers scored in the top quartile outperformed students whose teachers scored in the bottom quartile. This finding suggested that teachers using the strategies enhanced student performance.

The 1970s saw a significant increase in teacher effectiveness studies. In an extensive review of the literature, Medley (1977) reported five teacher characteristics that consistently contributed to improved pupil performance. These included:

- Devoting more class time to academic activities
- Involving students in structured learning experiences
- Running more orderly classrooms
- Providing more direct instruction to students in small groups
- Encouraging positive self-concepts and higher achievement in students

Brophy (1979) drew similar conclusions in his review of the literature, and made the following generalizations.

1. Teachers do make a difference. Some teachers promote student learning better than others because of their instructional behavior.
2. Teachers who define their primary role as providing instruction and who expect students to learn are more successful.
3. Effective teachers know how to organize and maintain classroom environments that maximize the time spent on academic activities.
4. Effective teachers practice direct instruction.
5. Effective teachers monitor learning to ensure overlearning before undertaking a new objective.

Brophy (1979, 34) summarized effective instruction in the following way:

The instruction that seems most efficient involves the teacher working with the whole class (or with small groups in the early grades), presenting information in lectures/demonstrations and then following up with recitations or practice exercises in which the students get opportunities to make responses and get corrective feedback. The teacher maintains an academic focus, keeping the students involved in a lesson or engaged in seatwork, monitoring their performance, and providing individualized feedback. The pace is rapid in the sense that the class moves efficiently through the curriculum as a whole (and through the successive objectives of any given lesson) but progress from one objective to the next involves very small, easy steps. Success rates in answering teacher questions during lessons are high (about 75%) and success rates on assignments designed to be done independently are very high (approaching 100%).

McDonald (1976) reported the results of the six-year Beginning Teacher Evaluation Study, which led him to the following conclusions.

1. The more time teachers spend in direct instruction, the more children learn.
2. Time-on-task (the time students successfully spend on academic tasks) relates positively to student learning.
3. The more time teachers devote to teaching reading, the more children learn.
4. Teachers with an academic focus and high expectations for student learning stimulate higher student performance.
5. Classroom environments that foster cooperative learning and mutual respect stimulate higher student achievement.

The term "direct instruction" appears throughout the literature on teacher effectiveness. Rosenshine (1979) identified seven basic components of direct instruction. These components include:

- An academic focus
- Teacher-directed instruction with extensive content coverage and high levels of student involvement
- Clear goals that students understand
- Sufficient time for teaching
- Monitoring of student performance through the use of direct questions
- Little time for students' choice of activities
- Large-group rather than small-group instruction
- Immediate, academically oriented feedback
- An orderly, task-oriented, relaxed environment

The Association for Supervision and Curriculum Development (1981) identified the following characteristics of effective teachers:

- Well organized, avoiding problems that arise from confusion
- Give students more time for academic tasks, spending less time on classroom routines

- Teach the class as a whole or in large groups, relying less on independent seat work
- Emphasize academic achievement, expecting that students will achieve
- Select and direct classroom activities
- Ensure that students master a unit before beginning the next one
- Involve students in learning activities whenever possible
- Assign tasks in which students can succeed
- Know subject matter
- Use excellent presentation skills, explaining, demonstrating, and leading discussion
- Monitor student progress, asking questions and moving around the room
- Give adequate feedback so that students know what they learned and what remains to be learned
- Find ways to get students to cooperate with one another and to take responsibility for their work
- Direct questions more to specific students than to volunteers
- Use guides and probing questions when students do not know the answers
- Encourage positive behavior and control negative behavior
- Do not grade papers during class
- Do not socialize or allow students to socialize in class
- Do not permit interruptions of class activities

The 1970s also produced several studies investigating the characteristics of effective reading instruction. Harris (1979) made the following conclusions about effective reading instruction.

1. In terms of student performance, teacher-directed reading programs are superior to student-centered programs in which students choose activities.
2. The amount of time devoted to reading instruction relates positively to achievement, particularly at the lower grade levels.
3. The amount of time-on-task relates positively to student achievement.
4. Effective reading teachers use more praise and verbal reinforcement than less effective teachers.
5. An orderly, well-disciplined environment relates positively to student achievement.
6. Effective reading teachers monitor students' behavior and resolve potential problems before serious difficulties arise.

The research on effective teaching therefore concurs on the importance of teachers in students' learning. However, the academic growth of students is not solely the responsibility of the teacher. There are several other factors that contribute to effective schools, including the following ones:

- Principal's instructional leadership (Edmonds 1979, Goodlad 1979, Wynne 1981, Stallings 1981)
- General school climate (Edmonds 1982, Goodlad 1984, Wynne 1981)
- Parent and community involvement (Henderson 1981, Stallings 1981, Thomas 1981)
- Accountability and long-range planning (DePew and Hennes 1982, Thomas 1981)
- Quality of staff development experiences available to teachers (Pinero 1982, Cawelti 1980)

The fact remains, however, that the behavior and instructional practices of teachers profoundly affect student academic performance. Guthrie, Martuza, and Seifert (1979, 177) stated, "We are compelled to draw the conclusion that what children learn about reading in one year is determined primarily by the quality of instruction they receive." According to Brophy (1979, 33), "Teachers make a difference. Certain teachers elicit much more student learning than others, and their success is tied to consistent differences in teaching behavior."

The research findings on teacher effectiveness provide valuable information about classroom organization and instruction. The identified characteristics are behaviors that any individual can learn, practice, and refine. The research findings give guidance in the development of effective patterns of organization and delivery. The findings therefore have major implications for preinstructional and instructional teaching.

Implications for the Preinstructional Phase

Many teacher behaviors relating positively to student achievement occur before actual content instruction begins. A listing of some of the most important preinstructional behaviors follows.

1. Expect children to learn, and control contingencies toward that end (Brookover 1979, Edmonds 1981, Association for Supervision and Curriculum Development 1981). Children are learners. Although they learn at different rates and at different levels, they can make progress in school. Your expectations of learners are important to their learning and academic growth. If you see children as learners, you will seek ways of helping them achieve rather than accept their failures as a reflection of their inadequacies.

2. Make your expectations clear to children. Tell them exactly what you want them to do, and make sure they understand your expectations

(Emmer 1980, Edmonds 1981). Provide them with clear, specific directions for the completion of work, and check their understanding of your directions. Such preparation will help eliminate unwanted interruptions during instruction and will allow students to complete their work more successfully.

3. Organize the instructional environment effectively (Brophy 1979, Association for Supervision and Curriculum Development 1981, Gage 1978). For example, make classroom rules clear. Review rules often, and have consistent consequences for infractions. Set up a system that allows children to attend to their personal and procedural needs without teacher attention. For example, provide a couple of times per day when children may perform their personal chores. This time might precede assigned seat work. Show children where supplies are kept, so they can help themselves without your attention. Establish that only one or two students may be out of their seats at any given time. Have restroom passes (one for girls, one for boys) allowing children to go to the restroom without your permission.

4. Arrange the learning environment to minimize interruptions during small group instruction (Association for Supervision and Curriculum Development 1981, Stallings 1981, Brophy 1982, Fisher et al. 1979). It is important that you have a period of uninterrupted teaching time during small group (e.g., reading group) instruction. Children typically interrupt small group instruction to ask permission to go to the restroom, to report on other children, to ask for clarification of seat work directions, or to check answers. Suggestions of direct strategies for reducing interruptions follow.

- Assign practice-oriented seat work. Use material children know, and need only to practice to achieve automaticity, or overlearning. You should expect high levels of success (approximately 95%) on children's practice work (Brophy, 1982; Fisher et al. 1979).
- Move around the room to monitor children's work and answer questions. Let children know you will be doing this so they can save questions until an appropriate time.
- Assign daily student helpers, preferably one from each reading group, to assist other children while you are providing small group instruction.
- Assign students to partners. Stronger students can help partners who encounter greater difficulty.

Implications for the Instructional Phase

Many behaviors characteristic of effective teachers are performed during actual instruction of content. A listing of some of the most important instructional behaviors follows.

1. Provide sufficient time for reading instruction (Good 1979, Harris 1979). Allocate enough time for teaching reading. If you are frequently unable to complete reading sessions, consider extending instructional time. Manning (1980) suggests that instructional time should be directly related to group need. The greater the need, the longer the time needed for instruction.

2. Provide direct instruction (Medley 1977, Brophy 1979, Harris 1979, Association for Supervision and Curriculum Development 1981, Brophy and Good 1986). Direct instruction includes the following key behaviors (Rosenshine 1979).

- Making lesson goals clear to students
- Allowing enough time for teaching
- Maintaining an academic focus
- Directing instruction rather than having children work independently at their own pace
- Using frequent questions to check students' understanding or need for specific assistance

3. Provide for maximum time-on-task (Rosenshine 1979, Harris 1979, Association for Supervision and Curriculum Development 1981). Time-on-task is the time during which students successfully work on academic tasks.

4. Monitor students' progress and provide direct and appropriate feedback (Harris 1979, Edmonds 1979, Stallings 1981). During instruction, observe students' responses to check their understanding of content and to provide clarification. This is best done through interactive instruction in which teachers elicit students' responses and clarify content to help students integrate the content with their prior knowledge. The correction of seat work or workbook material is best done in the presence of children, which allows you to give immediate feedback about their performance and to discuss, clarify, and correct errors. Table 6.1 summarizes the preinstructional and instructional implications for the teaching of reading based on the teacher effectiveness research.

The concept of student success in learning underlies the effective teaching research. Success reduces failure-related stress, which can cause further failure. Researchers have shown a direct relationship between stress and reading failure. Clay (1972) suggested that many poor readers have negative emotional reactions arising from the knowledge of reading failure. Failure-related reactions might start as early as six months after instruction begins. Sherman (1968) noted that everyone is socialized to expect reading to occur. Children sense this expectation even before they come to school. Failing to learn to read in school makes them frustrated and anxious because they are constantly reminded of their failure.

TABLE 6.1 Implications of Effective Teaching Research for Reading Instruction

Preinstruction	Instruction	Post-Instruction
• Expect children to learn • Make expectations clear to children • Organize the instructional environment • Prepare students for instruction	• Provide sufficient time for teaching • Tolerate no interruptions during small group instruction • Provide direct instruction • Provide for maximum time-on-task • Monitor students and provide feedback	• Provide adequate guided practice • Practice should ensure 95 percent success rate • Monitor practice and provide feedback • Ensure adequate time-on-task • Maintain whole print focus

Downing and Leong (1982, 242) identified a "failure-threat-anxiety syndrome" in many failed readers. Children are trapped in a "vicious cycle of failure—anxiety—more failure." Children suffering this syndrome show one or a combination of the following behaviors.

- Overt fear reactions demonstrated by fear of making mistakes, of reading poorly, and of failing in front of their peers
- Non-specific emotional behavior, including being shy and withdrawn, evading reading tasks, lacking concentration, and being inattentive and distractable
- Escape behavior, including withdrawal, daydreaming, psychosomatic disorders, rigidity, and other avoidance strategies
- Attack behavior, including resentment, hostility, and antisocial behavior

Downing and Leong noted the positive effects of improved self-concept and reading success in reducing stress and anxiety and in improving performance and attitudes toward reading. Effective teaching behaviors therefore benefit children in terms of emotional development as well as academic performance.

FUNDAMENTALS OF EFFECTIVE REMEDIATION

Recall that this text defines diagnosis as an ongoing procedure involving continuous analysis of students' behavior, measurement of samples of their behavior, careful evaluation of the measurement results, and changes in instructional strategies leading to positive changes in students' behavior. Changes in instructional strategies relate directly to remediation. Remediation is intervention through the application of teaching strategies designed to give learners the skills, competencies, or behaviors they need to improve their performance in a given area. These strategies are chosen on the basis of careful analysis of needs. The goal of remediation, then, is to create positive change in learner performance. For this change to occur, the delivery and the focus of instruction must change. You might present material in a different way or with a different slant, orientation, focus, intensity, or frequency.

The characteristics of effective instruction have direct implications for remediation as well as for instruction. General elements of effective instruction and remediation include positive expectations, appropriate organization, time for teaching, direct instruction, time-on-task, continual monitoring, and academically oriented feedback. In addition, however, there are specific prerequisites for effective remediation.

1. Remediation must be specific to the individual and to the context.
2. Remediation must be accompanied by a change in instruction.
3. Remediation must be related to the classroom curriculum.
4. Remediation must address both the strengths and the weaknesses of children.
5. Remediation must focus on whole print.
6. Remediation must focus on individualizing instruction rather than on individualizing children.
7. Remediation must focus on the most critical content.

A discussion of these prerequisites follows.

Remediation Must Be Specific

The concept of remediation assumes that the expected pattern of growth in reading has not been achieved. Each reader, however, has a different reading profile with different strengths and needs. A child might desperately need help in decoding vowels, or in developing an appropriate sight vocabulary, or in learning to use context in reading. Although children have common needs, they might also have specific needs requiring direct attention. Children's reading problems are specific to print. Since they make errors within connected discourse, remediation should begin with an analysis of children's specific errors during actual reading and with a focus on the building of skills in real reading contexts. Remediation, then, should be specific to individual needs and to the actual reading of print.

Remediation Must Be Accompanied by Change in Instruction

Children with reading problems are often placed in ancillary programs for remediation. These programs generally provide more individualized instruction tailored to children's needs. Ancillary teachers might complain, "The child is doing really well in my room, but when he returns to the classroom, he fails continually." Although this complaint might point to the use of inappropriate material in the ancillary room, it often reflects a lack of instructional modifications in the classroom. Children with reading difficulties need instruction that addresses their learning characteristics. Instruction needs to include such strategies as priming for learning, preinstruction of vocabulary, modeling of the comprehension process, application of skills, and conceptual preparation. Successful remediation requires a modification of daily classroom instruction to meet the special learning needs of children.

Remediation Must Be Related to the Classroom Curriculum

Children who are removed from the classroom for special remedial assistance should receive instruction that relates to the classroom curriculum. Remediation should not duplicate classroom materials and strategies, but should relate to children's needs in the classroom, and should assist them in achieving more appropriate performance in that environment. Ideally, classroom and special teachers cooperatively plan and implement productive experiences for children. When teachers share expectations, remediation can focus on using a variety of materials and strategies to meet those expectations. Remedial programs that are independent of and unrelated to classroom realities are not in the best interests of children.

Remediation Must Utilize Both Strengths and Weaknesses of Children

Remediation should focus on both the strengths and the weaknesses of children. As they are being remediated in missing skills, children should be allowed to extend their reading through their areas of strength. For example, a child who fails in learning phonics but succeeds in learning meaningful sight vocabulary should certainly be remediated in phonics. At the same time, however, the child should have the opportunities for extending meaningful sight vocabulary. Remediation utilizes both strengths and weaknesses.

Remediation Must Focus on Print

A critical prerequisite of remediation is a whole print focus. Many children with reading difficulties cannot apply isolated skill knowledge to whole reading contexts. It is important, then, to follow skill instruction with immediate whole print experience. The most vital component of any reading program is exposure to and immersion in whole reading. Children must be shown how the skills they learn are used in print. The goal of all reading instruction and remediation is reading with comprehension. Reading, therefore, must form the core of all such experiences.

Remediation Must Focus on Individualizing Instruction Rather Than on Individualizing Children

Direct instruction is an important aspect of appropriate teaching. Children with reading problems depend on the teacher's awareness of their needs and the teacher's willingness to modify instruction. In many remedial programs children are placed in individualized, programmed skill materials, and progress through these materials at their own rates. Such programs often center on isolated skills and rarely help children transfer their skill learning to the actual reading of print. As a result children do improve in skills, but not necessarily in reading. Teachers might view these programs as effective because children improve in isolated skills and because the programs seem to involve positive individualized instruction. However, such programs can be more accurately described as ones that individualize children. Children are placed on individual paths, but no real instruction is provided.

Individualized instruction operates within an instructional framework. Children are instructed by a knowledgeable teacher who observes their needs and modifies instruction to meet those needs. Children are placed in individual programs or skill strands only after receiving instruction matched to their individual needs. The following example illustrates the concept of individualizing instruction.

CLASSROOM APPLICATION

Ms. Hunt is working with a small reading group of five children. She begins the session with a quick review of the previous day's skills. She then starts the preinstruction of vocabulary and thoroughly teaches six new words. As she asks for responses, she notices that four children are reasonably sure of the words. The fifth child, however, is inaccurate with the words. At this point, Ms. Hunt usually flashes the words quickly to each child, and each is asked to respond. Realizing that the fifth child is in the greatest need of help, Ms. Hunt decides instead to individualize her instruction. First, she asks child number five to read the words and provides assistance as needed. Next, she asks children number one and number five to read the words. In this way, the target child is receiving additional practice. Next children number two and number five read the words. Again, the fifth child receives more practice. In this way, Ms. Hunt has made her instruction more appropriate to the individual.

Effective remediation relies on the effective individualization of instruction. The independent placement of children in separate material relating to their skill needs does not ensure appropriate learning. Individualization should be more related to the monitoring of individuals than to the delivery of instruction individually.

Remediation Must Focus on the Most Important Content

Remedial programs should focus on content that is most critical to reading performance. Teachers need to analyze the content of their programs to ensure that the information children are taught represents the skills, competencies, and experiences essential to reading. Time spent on such skills as marking stressed syllables cannot be justified when students do not know how to draw appropriate inferences. Since many poor readers learn slowly and are limited in the amount of information they can learn in a given instructional period, teachers must take care to ensure that the information taught is the most essential to reading growth.

SUMMARY　During the past decade, many researchers have given attention to the factors characterizing both effective instruction and effective reading instruction. Several studies identify the instructional factors that make a difference in student performance. Factors leading to improved student performance include time-on-task, direct instruction, monitoring of student performance, and academically oriented feedback. Teachers need to assess carefully their instructional environments and to thoughtfully apply effective teaching strategies. In addition, there are basic prerequisites for effective remedial programs. Essential ingredients of effective remediation include such factors as maintaining a print focus, modifying instruction, and addressing both the strengths and the weaknesses of children. Instructional behaviors that positively affect student performance can be learned, practiced, and refined. Knowledge of these behaviors helps teachers to analyze classroom situations and to create necessary changes.

R • E • F • E • R • E • N • C • E • S

Allington, R. "Content coverage and contextual reading in reading groups." *Journal of Reading Behavior* 16 (1984): 85–96.

Anderson, L. M., C. M. Evertson, and J. E. Brophy. "An experimental study of effective teaching in first-grade reading groups." *Elementary School Journal* 79 (March 1979): 193–223.

Association for Supervision and Curriculum Development. "Teacher and school effectiveness." *Leaders Guide* (1981): 5.

Brookover, W. *School Social Systems and Student Achievement: Schools Can Make A Difference*. New York: Bergin Publishers, 1979.

Brophy, J. "Teacher behavior and student learning." *Educational Leadership* 37 (October 1979): 33–38.

———. "Successful teaching strategies for the inner-city child." *Phi Delta Kappan* 63 (April 1982): 527–530.

———. "Classroom organization and management." *Elementary School Journal* 83 (1983): 265–285.

Brophy, J., and T. Good. "Teacher Behavior and Student Achievement." In M. Wittrock, ed. *Third Handbook of Research on Teaching*. New York: Macmillan, 1986.

Cawelti, G. "Effective instructional leadership produces greater learning." *Thrust for Educational Leadership* 9 (January 1980): 8–10.

Clay, M. M. *Reading: The Patterning of Complex Behavior*. Auckland, New Zealand: Heinemann, 1972.

DePew, K., and J. Hennes. *1980–81 Annual Report: Overview of Educational Accountability and Accreditation in Colorado*. Denver, CO: Colorado Department of Education, 1982.

Downing, J., and C. K. Leong. *Psychology of Reading*. New York: Macmillan, 1982.

Edmonds, R. "Some schools work and more can." *Social Policy* 9 (1979): 28–32.

———. "Programs of school improvement: An overview." *Educational Leadership* 30 (December 1982): 4–12.

Emmer, E. T. "Effective classroom management at the beginning of the school year." *Elementary School Journal* 80 (May 1980): 219–231.

Fisher, C., R. Marliave, and N. Filby. "Improving teaching by increasing academic learning time." *Educational Leadership* 37 (October 1979): 52–54.

Gage, N. L. "The yield of research on teaching." *Phi Delta Kappan* 60 (November 1978): 229–235.

Gates, A. I., and G. L. Bond. "Reading readiness: A study of factors determining success and failure in beginning reading." *Teachers College Record* 37 (May 1936): 679–685.

Good, T. L. "Teacher effectiveness in the elementary school." *Journal of Teacher Education* 30 (1979): 52–64.

Goodlad, J. I. "Can our schools get better?" *Phi Delta Kappan* 60 (January 1979): 342–347.

————. *A Place Called School: Prospects for the Future.* New York: McGraw–Hill, 1984.

Guthrie, J. T., V. Martuza, and M. Seifert. "Impacts of Instructional Time in Reading." In L. B. Resnick and P. A. Weaver, eds. *Theory and Practice of Early Reading*, Vol. 3. Hillsdale, NJ: Lawrence Erlbaum, 1979.

Harris, A. J. "The effective teacher of reading revisited." *The Reading Teacher* 33 (November 1979): 135–140.

Henderson, A. *Parent Participation—Student Achievement: The Evidence Grows.* Columbia, MD: National Committee for Citizens in Education, 1981.

McDonald, F. J. *Teachers Do Make A Difference.* Princeton, NJ: Educational Testing Service, 1976.

Manning, J. C. *Reading: Learning and Instructional Processes.* Geneva, IL: Paladin House, 1980.

Medley, D. *Teacher Competence and Teacher Effectiveness: A Review of Process—Product Research.* Washington, D.C.: American Association of Colleges of Teacher Education, 1977.

Pinero, U. C. "Wanted: Strong instructional leaders." *Principal* 61 (March 1982): 16–19.

Rosenshine, B. V. "Content Time and Direct Instruction." In P. L. Peterson and H. J. Walburg, eds. *Research on Teaching: Concepts, Findings and Implications.* Berkeley, CA: McCutchan, 1979.

Rosenshine, B. V. and R. Stevens. "Classroom Instruction in Reading." In P. D. Pearson, ed. *Handbook of Reading Research.* New York: Longman, 1984.

Rupley, W. H. "Relationship between Selected Areas of Teacher Emphasis and Students' Achievement in Reading." Ph.D. dissertation, University of Illinois, 1975.

Sherman, M. "Psychiatric Insights into Reading Problems." In D. G. Schubert and T. L. Torgerson, eds. *Readings in Reading: Practice, Theory, Research.* New York: Crowell, 1968.

Stallings, J. "What Research Has to Say to Administrators of Secondary Schools About Effective Teaching and Staff Development." Paper prepared for the conference, Creating Conditions for Effective Teaching, University of Oregon College of Education, July 1981.

Thomas, M. D. "Variables of educational excellence." *The Clearing House* 54 (February 1981): 251–253.

Wade, E. W. "The Construction and Validation of a Test of Ten Teacher Skills Used in Reading Instruction, Grades 2–5." Ph.D. dissertation, Indiana University, 1960.

Wynne, E. A. "Looking at good schools." *Phi Delta Kappan* 62 (January 1981): 377–381.

7 Utilizing Methods of Reading Instruction

FOCUS
QUESTIONS

1. Why should teachers become familiar with a variety of reading methods?
2. How is the language experience method used in reading remediation?
3. How can the linguistic method be integrated into remedial programs?
4. How can the phonic and sight word methods be combined in teaching reading?
5. How can combinations of methods aid in reading remediation?

One of the advantages in teaching reading is the existence of a variety of methodologies for helping individuals learn to read. Each methodology approaches reading differently, uses different instructional strategies, demands from learners a different set of competencies, and focuses initially on different aspects of the reading process. These differences affect the teaching of reading and the remediation of reading problems. For every child who needs help, you have several possible instructional options to take. You are not tied to one method or to any set of strategies that proves ineffective with a given student. You may use a variety or a combination of methods or strategies to assist children. Knowing the options is the first step.

The five methods of teaching discussed in this chapter include the phonic method, the linguistic method, the language immersion method, the sight word method, and the developmental basal methodology. Each method is evaluated in terms of the following concerns.

1. *Definition of reading and consequent teaching.* Every methodology rests on a stated or implied definition of reading. The definition determines the instructional strategies endorsed by each method.

2. *Content.* The content of each methodology suggests both a scope (the individual skills to be taught) and a sequence (the sequence in which those skills should be taught) of reading instruction.

3. *Prerequisites for the child and the teacher.* All methodologies are successful with some children, and all will fail with others. Success or failure depends in part on the extent to which the teacher and the children possess the skills prerequisite for success in the methodology. Knowledge of the prerequisites helps you to modify instruction, ensuring the success of children who lack the prerequisite skills.

4. *Cautions.* All methodologies have certain weaknesses. Their effectiveness rests on the teacher's ability to identify the weaknesses and to compensate for them in instruction.

5. *Strengths.* All methodologies have certain strengths. Effective teachers identify strengths and build on them.

THE PHONIC METHODOLOGY

The phonic methodology places heavy initial emphasis on symbol-sound or letter-sound relationships. It emphasizes the rules that are necessary to help children make the transition from letters to sound.

Philosophy of the Phonic Method

Phonic methodology implicitly defines reading as the decoding of graphemes—letters—into phonemes—sounds, and the understanding of the rules governing decoding. The underlying philosophy is that reading is a code system, an oral language coded by letters. The key to reading is learning how to break the code hidden in the combination of letters. Once the code is broken, meaning is released. Because reading is defined as decoding, instruction initially concentrates on teaching children to break the code as quickly as possible. Instruction thus focuses on teaching the forms and names of letters, the association of the letters with the sounds they represent, the blending of individual letter pairs and of strings of letters into words, and the rules of pronunciation and syllabication. In initial instruction, learning sight vocabulary and processing literal information get secondary attention. Because the philosophy is committed to code breaking, initial instruction in nonliteral comprehension is not a priority. Once children have adequately learned to break the code, they can use their comprehension abilities to consider the actual content of reading material.

Content of the Phonic Method

The content of the phonic method consists of instruction in letters, sounds, blending, and the rules explaining how graphemes represent phonemes. This content is communicated to children through two basic strategies: the inductive, or analytic, strategy and the deductive, or synthetic, strategy (Smith and Johnson 1980, May 1986).

The inductive strategy involves reasoning from particular experiences with words to the rules or conclusions about the words. For example, children might be presented with whole language experiences involving the words *boy*, *book*, *bird*, and *ball*. They then would be presented with the same words as sight words, and would be encouraged to generalize. They would see that (1) the words begin with the same sound; (2) the words begin with the same letter; (3) the letter is *b* and the sound is /b/; and (4) words that begin with the letter *b* begin with the sound /b/. Children would then practice responding appropriately to the letter *b* and to the sound it represents. Phonic rules progress from the whole language experience to the verbalization and practice of specific rules.

The deductive strategy, on the other hand, involves reasoning from a specific rule to the applications of the rule. For example, in the same lesson, children would be presented with the letter *b* and with the rule that the letter *b* represents the sound /b/. Examples of words that demonstrate this rule would be presented. Children would also be asked to generate appropriate words, which would be written on the chalkboard. Children would do a worksheet designed to practice the skill. The sheet would include pictures of items that begin with different letters and children would be asked to identify those beginning with the letter *b* and the sound it represents. They would also receive drill, practice, and reinforcement in the skill. Other letters would be presented in the same way. Finally, children would be taught to blend sounds to make words.

Phonic Method Prerequisites

To successfully learn phonics, children should have good auditory skills, including auditory discrimination, blending, segmentation, and memory (Swaby 1984). Because the phonic method emphasizes the sound system of written language, learners must be able to differentiate easily among sounds. This is no simple task since many sounds are closely related, e.g., /b/ and /p/, short /i/ and short /e/. Many words in isolation are also similar, e.g., *pen* and *pin*, *big* and *beg*, *bat* and *bet*. Auditory discrimination is particularly important if phonics is presented through deductive strategies. Most children come to school with appropriate discrimination abilities (Harris and Smith 1986). Some do not, however, and for them phonic learning is often laborious and slow.

Auditory segmentation and blending are also important. Auditory blending allows children to blend isolated sounds into whole words (e.g., /b/ + /a/ + /t/ = *bat*). Auditory memory affects blending. Memory allows children to remember individual sounds in the appropriate order long enough to blend them. Segmentation refers to the skill of hearing the isolated sounds in whole words. Many programs use phonics to develop spelling skills by having children listen to words and identify the individual sounds they hear (e.g., *bat* = /b/ + /a/ + /t/).

In addition to auditory skills, children need fast learning rates and good memories. They must be able to quickly learn and remember many specific bits of information. This is necessary because phonics consists of isolated sounds that often hold little meaning for children.

The teacher of phonics must possess certain characteristics as well, including the following:

1. Ability to know which children lack the necessary prerequisites and to provide immediately other word recognition strategies for them. Phonics is presented as readiness experiences while more effective strategies are used for instruction.

2. Knowledge of the comparative usefulness of phonic rules. Phonic rules are not all equally useful in reading (May and Eliot 1978, Moskowitz 1973, Vaughn–Cook 1977, Bailey 1967, Clymer 1963). The teacher must know when it is necessary to teach a rule and when it is not (see Chapter 10).

3. Commitment to providing children with many experiences in realistic, meaningful, and motivating language and commitment to developing high level comprehension skills through reading and listening. Because phonic material rigidly controls vocabulary, initial reading content is often dull and irrelevant to children's experiences or language.

Phonic Method Cautions and Strengths

The phonic methodology has pitfalls. As a teacher of reading you should be aware of these pitfalls in order to modify instruction as necessary. A discussion of cautionary concerns follows.

1. Phonics should not be taught as if letters and sounds have a one-to-one correspondence. There are twenty-six letters and approximately forty-four sounds in the English language. Phonics can certainly be used to eliminate several alternatives in reading and to provide close approximations of appropriate pronunciation. However, phonics should not be thought of or taught as the only strategy or even the major strategy of word recognition (Smith 1979, 1982, Larrick 1987). It should be presented in conjunction with other word recognition strategies, especially the use of context.

2. Phonics content includes information not essential to the process or the act of reading. For example, children are taught to mark accented syllables and to divide words into syllables. If children can read a word, they have successfully syllabicated and accented it, and if they can't, phonic strategies do not necessarily help. Emphasize skills that make a direct, positive difference in reading.

3. Realize that teaching phonics and teaching reading are not the same. Phonics is essentially a word analysis strategy. Reading involves connected discourse and interaction between the writer and the reader (*Becoming a Nation of Readers*, 1985). Children achieve mastery in phonics mainly through paper and pencil tasks, such as workbooks, tests, skill pages, and activity pages. Transfer to real reading situations is often neglected. In many remedial reading situations, teachers provide phonic skill instruction and assume that reading instruction is taking place. However, phonics (a strategy of word analysis) is not the same experience as reading (interaction with print). Phonics is one way of helping children read better—a means to an end.

4. Because of the heavy emphasis on decoding, many children internalize a definition of reading as sounding out words rather than as

seeking meaning. The restricted language of phonic programs makes it difficult to focus on meaning acquisition and higher level comprehension skills. It is important, therefore, to expose children to other print more relevant to their interests and experiences, and to use that print to develop critical thinking.

Phonic-oriented programs unquestionably provide children with a strategy for systematic word analysis (Beck 1981, Shimron and Navon 1981). A considerable body of research supports systematic phonic instruction (Beck 1981, Calfee and Pointkowski 1981, Johnson and Baumann 1984). Children with the prerequisites quickly develop independent reading abilities. They acquire a strong background in letter-sound knowledge that gives them orderly and productive strategies for decoding words. Remember, however that many children lack the auditory skills to learn phonics (Carbo 1987). A listing of some better-known phonics materials follows.

Phonic Materials
Keys to Reading Series (Economy Company)
Merrill Phonics Skill Texts (Merrill)
Phonics Is Fun Series (Modern Curriculum Press)
Phonics Plus (Prentice–Hall)
Phonics We Use Series (Rand McNally)
Breaking the Code (Open Court)
Speech to Print Phonics (Harcourt Brace Jovanovich)

THE LINGUISTIC METHODOLOGY

The linguistic methodology capitalizes on the regularity of English spelling. It emphasizes existing patterns in the alphabetic spelling system and uses those patterns to teach children the relationships among combinations of letters and sounds.

Philosophy of the Linguistic Method

The linguistic methodology defines reading as a decoding activity in which readers use the patterns in the spelling system to derive sounds from letter combinations. The key to learning to read is breaking the code of writing implicit in the spelling patterns of written language.

Since reading is basically decoding spelling patterns, instruction concentrates on teaching children to recognize the spelling patterns of printed language. Instruction begins with groups of words that conform to specific spelling patterns (e.g., *an, man, fan, pan*), and focuses on combinations of letters and sounds. Children are encouraged to discover for themselves the relationships between individual letters and their sounds. One spelling pattern is presented first. Once that pattern has been learned, another is introduced and contrasted against the first pattern, as in the following example.

Pattern 1	Pattern 2
an	in
pan	pin
man	min
tan	tin
fan	fin

Notice that nonsense syllables (e.g., *min*) are used. These are permissible because the major emphasis is on decoding, not on meaning. Nonsense words contribute to the eventual decoding of larger words, such as "*minister*" and "*minstrel*."

The linguistic method presents regular spelling patterns first (e.g., *man*, *rod*, *mug*), and then less regular patterns (e.g., *fine*, *week*, *lead*). Words with irregular spelling (e.g., *the*, *enough*, *said*, *through*) are taught as sight words. These are presented infrequently during initial instruction so as not to disturb pattern learning. Because breaking the code is the primary objective of reading instruction, low priority is given to initial development of comprehension skills beyond the literal level.

Content of the Linguistic Method

Programs using the linguistic method contain regularly spelled patterns (*man*, *pat*), irregularly spelled patterns (*mine*, *beat*), and sight vocabulary (*the*, *enough*). Because attention is drawn to whole patterns, individual letters are not sounded out, and phonic rules are not verbalized. Children are expected to discover these relationships through inductive reasoning on the basis of their experiences with print. Nonsense syllables may be used because patterns and not meaning are initially important. The child concentrates on the contrasting patterns of words.

Linguistic Method Prerequisites

To succeed in linguistic programs, children must automatically recognize letter names and sounds. Isolated practice in these skills is not provided once actual reading instruction begins. Visual discrimination is another important prerequisite. Children must discriminate among visually similar words, such as *pat* and *bat*, *lat* and *tat*, and *pat*, *pit*, and *pet*. Auditory discrimination is necessary because children must learn the letter names and the individual sounds letters represent.

Because letter-sound relationships and phonic generalizations are usually not taught directly, children must also be able to infer or abstract phonic information, which requires an inductive learning style.

Teachers need a clear understanding of inductive instruction and the ability to modify such instruction for children who do not learn inductively. Teachers must also familiarize children with a variety of meaningful literature, because the linguistic method uses material containing improbable and unfamiliar language (e.g., "Nan can fan Dan. Fan Dan, Nan. Dan can fan Nan. Fan Nan, Dan"). Teachers must have the ability to develop children's higher-level comprehension skills. The language and the content of these programs rarely stimulate questions requiring high-level thinking. Teachers should use meaningful graphic material with meaningful language to extend children's thinking abilities.

Linguistic Method Cautions and Strengths

Teachers using linguistic materials must consider the drawbacks. The unrealistic content of the material often leaves children with the idea that reading is decoding rather than meaningful interaction with print. This can be avoided by extending children's exposure to meaningful literature and to a rich variety of vocabulary. Teachers must use more realistic material to develop appropriate high-level thinking skills in children. Linguistic readers, particularly at the early levels, are inadequate for the development of nonliteral comprehension. Finally, teachers must be aware of children who are not making appropriate progress, and must use alternative instructional strategies that work better for those children.

Programs based on linguistic methodology structure experience through a specific decoding strategy, which is a strength. The spelling pattern focus might facilitate decoding because of the contrasting pattern instruction (Ekwall and Shanker 1985). The focus on spelling patterns in reading makes children aware of those patterns, which might improve spelling performance. In addition, because decoding focuses on words conforming to patterns rather than on isolated letters and sounds, children are almost immediately confronted with connected print. The following list names some of the more widely used materials based on the linguistic method.

Linguistic Materials
   Merrill Linguistic Reading Program (Merrill)
   Miami Linguistic Readers (Heath)
   Programmed Reading (McGraw–Hill)
   The Basic Reading Series (Science Research Associates)
   Sullivan Reading Program (McGraw–Hill)
   The Palo Alto Reading Program (Harcourt Brace Jovanovich)

THE WHOLE WORD METHODOLOGY

The whole word, or sight word, method uses complete words as the basic elements of initial instruction. Children learn and practice specific words that are presented as discrete visual units.

Philosophy of the Whole Word Method

Whole word methodology views reading as a meaning-seeking activity. To find meaning, however, children must have at their disposal a number of words they can recognize in print. These words are taught as sight words. Words are reinforced through practice and drill. An effort is made to have children locate, identify, and use the words in actual reading contexts.

Content of the Whole Word Method

Instruction based on this philosophy teaches words to children by sight. The words include (1) high-frequency words chosen from high-frequency word counts, and (2) meaningful words chosen by the teacher, by text authors or by children themselves. One sight word method is the key vocabulary, or key word, method (Veatch et al. 1979). This method has its origins in the work of Sylvia Ashton–Warner (1963). Ashton–Warner developed the "first word" or "organic word" concept, which recommended that children be allowed to choose the first words they learn to read in school. She endorsed student choice of words because student-chosen words:

- Have immediate and intense meaning.
- Function actively and positively in the child's life.
- Carry with them the emotional ties that facilitate easy learning and retention.

The content of a sight word approach, then, includes the following components.

1. Chosen or assigned sight words
2. Working with the word (printing, tracing, copying, or illustrating the word)
3. Print transfer (circling the word on a page of print, writing a short story or paragraph using the word, finding the word in an article, or identifying the word in a graphic display)
4. Daily review
5. Reinforcement (categorizing words; making picture dictionaries

of words; illustrating words; and writing or dictating sentences, paragraphs, or stories about words)

Whole Word Method Prerequisites

For success in the whole word methodology, children need good visual memory abilities to retain the visual images of the words. They also need good memory abilities to retain and retrieve the words.

Teachers need the ability to help children derive phonic information from the words they learn. For example, after teaching the words *boy*, *baseball*, and *bus*, the teacher might teach children the rule *b* = /*b*/. Teachers must also be skilled in presenting whole language to children. This enables children to begin learning unchosen words that are essential to reading print (e.g., *the*, *was*, *enough*, *them*).

Whole Word Method Cautions and Strengths

All reading materials include a sight word component. Many teachers view this component as an alternative to phonic instruction. They believe that children having difficulty with phonics will build a meaningful reading vocabulary through the sight component. However, particularly in the initial stages of reading, the words selected for sight presentation hold little meaning for children, and tax their memory abilities much the same as isolated phonics. For example, in one reading program, the eighteen sight words chosen for presentation to kindergartners and first graders included *will*, *is*, *said*, *a*, and *in*. Sight words should carry strong meaning and emotional impact (e.g., *school*, *dog*, *toy*, and *jump*, particularly in initial reading instruction. After children learn meaningful sight vocabulary, add less meaningful words to form phrases or sentences. For example, after children have learned *ship*, present the phrase *the ship*. Children are more likely to learn the word *the* in connection with a meaningful word than as an isolated word. Finally, whole word methods provide little context in the practice and reinforcement component. Children need extensive language exposure to help them transfer word learning to actual reading.

On the other hand, the whole word approach provides children with an alternative strategy for word recognition. In choosing words, children form emotional attachments to the words that help in recall. In addition, children unable to learn phonics can learn whole words and possibly infer phonic information from them.

Materials for applying this methodology are usually taken from children's language. As a result, formal published programs do not exist. A short list of programs using whole word instruction follows.

Whole Word Materials
    Instructional Aid Kits: For Sight Words (Barnell Loft)
    Dolch Word Cards (Dolch)

THE LANGUAGE IMMERSION METHODOLOGY

Language immersion methods capitalize on the common language patterns and vocabulary of children, which are used as the graphic material for initially teaching children to read. This methodology emphasizes the strong relationships between oral and written language and between the processes of understanding speech and of understanding print.

Philosophy of the Language Immersion Method

The language immersion approach defines reading as a process in which readers use all possible language cues to derive meaning from print. Learning to read involves viewing written language as spoken language. Readers apply skills of interpreting speech to the process of interpreting print. The goal of reading is to extract meaning. The primary objective in instruction, therefore, is to teach children to anticipate and expect meaning from print. Programs achieve this objective by presenting children with interesting, meaningful, familiar, and predictable print. Children are immersed in this print through listening activities. As children listen to the words, they follow the print. As they begin to memorize the print, they predict meaning. The first step in reading, then, is recognizing that print is meaningful. Sight words are subsequently isolated, taught, and practiced. Finally, children learn phonic information extracted from known sight words.

Content of the Language Immersion Method

Language immersion programs include a strand offering varied, familiar literature used for listening. Programs also provide predictable, simplified literature for initial reading instruction, and a strong, meaningful sight vocabulary. Phonic instruction is based on the sight vocabulary. Oral discussion is emphasized and a strong literal and inferential comprehension strand is incorporated from the beginning of instruction.

Consider the following example of language immersion content from a beginning grade one selection.

A girl got on the bus
Then the bus went fast.

A boy got on the bus
Then the bus went fast.
A fox got on the bus
Then the bus went fast.
A hippopotamus got on the bus
Then the bus went fast.
A goat got on the bus
Then the bus went fast. . . .*

Large, brightly colored illustrations accompany the story. First, the story is read to children, who discuss content and ask many literal and inferential questions. Next, the children "read along" by following the printed version of the story. Memorization comes easily because of the predictability of the language and the clarity of the illustrations. When children understand the story well enough to recite it fluently, they learn *boy*, and *bus*, and other words as isolated sight words. Children practice words extensively. They are encouraged to find the words in the story and in other printed material. Finally, letters and sounds are isolated from the words and presented, e.g., *b* in *boy* and *bus* = the sound /*b*/. All phonics instruction is done after the children have learned sight words and the teacher has demonstrated phonic skills, using meaningful material. Both inferential comprehension and meaningful sight vocabulary have primary importance.

The most extreme form of language immersion is the language experience approach developed by the Allens in the late 1950s. They created this approach in reaction to the existing phonic-oriented methods, which they felt favored word-by-word reading over comprehension. The language experience method begins with children dictating sentences or stories, which teachers write down for them. Teachers guide the children to read and illustrate their own stories. Vocabulary items are isolated and taught from this material, and then phonic relationships are taught. Emphasis is placed on helping children realize that many of the clues they use in oral language also operate in graphic language, and that they should actively anticipate meaning from print (Stauffer 1980, Allen and Laminack 1982, Mallon and Berglund 1984, Vacca et al. 1987).

Language Immersion Prerequisites

The language immersion methodology has few prerequisites for children. They must be able to use oral language and to process language through auditory skills. They should have some interest in literature, some motivation toward reading, and good memory. Prerequisites for teachers are more significant. Language immersion programs are nondi-

*"The Bus Ride," *Reading Unlimited*, Scott, Foresman (1976), 1–10.

rective and expect high levels of knowledge and flexibility from teachers. Teachers need skill in asking questions that develop broad levels of comprehension, since this is the major purpose of reading instruction. They must help children use all language cues in order to unlock print. Teachers must also be able to present phonic information in a variety of ways to a variety of children, provide consistent oral language reinforcement for children with slow or ineffective language development, and identify and instruct children who need a more systematic presentation of phonic skills.

Language Immersion Method Cautions and Strengths

Language immersion programs tend to be teacher dependent and nondirective. The skill strand is less extensive and sequential than skill strands in other approaches. Immersion programs often lack the internal structure of other methods.

Strengths of the language immersion programs include their emphasis on language, comprehension, and meaningful discourse from the beginning stages of reading. Multiple clues are used in teaching reading (e.g., sight, phonics, meaning, language, patterns). This method promotes interest in and motivation toward reading (Smith 1986, Larrick 1987).

Language Immersion Materials
   Instant Readers (Martin and Brogan; Holt, Rinehart & Winston)
   Language Experience Activities (Allen and Allen; Houghton Mifflin)
   Sounds of Language Series (Martin and Brogan; Holt, Rinehart & Winston)

THE DEVELOPMENTAL BASAL METHODOLOGY

The developmental basal reader, often referred to simply as "the basal," is a package of reading materials including readers, workbooks, teachers' manuals, and assessment instruments. The package is organized around a developmental approach to the teaching of reading. The developmental approach identifies important reading skills and arranges them in logical sequences for specific grade levels. Vocabulary counts are used to select appropriate vocabulary for each grade level. Appropriate literature is chosen and assigned to each grade level. An appropriate instructional design is created and the material is organized around this design. The developmental basal is the most widely used method for teaching reading in the United States today.

Philosophy of the Developmental Basal Method

This method views print as a language code. Reading is breaking the code to gain meaning from print. Breaking the code leads to early independence in reading, and gaining meaning leads to interest in and enjoyment of print. Since both code breaking and meaning in reading are valued, the developmental basal begins with a strong emphasis on phonic instruction. Children are expected to master word analysis early. In keeping with the emphasis on meaning, skills are taught in the context of sentences rather than in complete isolation. In addition, children learn a strong sight vocabulary, which is then used in reading material employing natural language. Since comprehension is important, teachers are directed to ask questions at the beginning of and throughout instruction.

Content of the Developmental Basal Method

The developmental basal reader consists of a skill strand and a literature strand. The skill strand provides a system in which skills are introduced by the teacher, practiced in a workbook, and reinforced periodically throughout the text and workbooks. Each skill is tested, and if children have not mastered a particular skill, it is retaught and retested. The literature strand consists of literature created or selected for specific grade levels. Each selection introduces new vocabulary and content, and assigns questions to answer during and after reading.

Developmental Basal Method Prerequisites

To succeed in a developmental basal framework, children must be able to learn a wide variety of skills and content in a comparatively short time. Skill demands are quite high. Children also need good memories because of the heavy emphasis on decoding. They must remember phonic information until they are exposed to meaningful print.

The developmental basal is very structured. Material is introduced, presented, taught, and reinforced in the same way throughout each text. Skills that are not learned are often retaught the same way they were taught initially. Children must be able to tolerate the usual routine of instruction and to learn the material in the way it is presented. Because of the strong phonic element, auditory discrimination is also important.

Developmental basals are created for widespread adoption; therefore, they are written with the average child in mind. Teachers must be able to modify the basal to meet the needs of both slow and gifted readers. For children who fail to learn in a developmental basal format, success depends on the teacher's knowledge of different ways to teach skills and content. Teachers must be able to teach reading, not merely a series. Teachers should be willing and able to vary the structure to overcome the pervasive sameness of basal programs and to keep children interested and involved.

The developmental basal has a complex, well-defined structure. Teachers easily overdepend on the manual, doing exactly as the manual dictates, and fall into a professional rut in which little growth, innovation, or life occurs. Teachers using developmental basals must be committed to flexibility and professional growth.

Cautions and Strengths of the Developmental Basal Method

The formats of basals are often so structured that little room is left for teachers' creativity and innovation. Skills are taught and retaught using one strategy, offering no alternative strategy for children who cannot learn from the basal structure. Basals do not adequately provide for children on either side of the norm—gifted or learning disabled.

Although major efforts have been made during the past decade to include literature representative of the broad racial, ethnic, environmental, and social differences in society, much more attention to these areas is needed. In addition, basal series are written around a developmental theme, and, particularly at the initial stages, literature is written using a controlled vocabulary. This often results in very contrived beginning reading material. The basic format of the developmental basal is often the same throughout the grades, making a series seem monotonous.

Strengths of developmental basal series include their systematic presentation of phonic skills and a variety of literary genres. Emphasis is on the development of comprehension skills from the initial stages of reading, and a range of supportive material is available for practice and enrichment. Basal series provide a complete structure for teaching reading, which might be helpful to beginning teachers. The assessment strand provides teachers with a way of keeping abreast of children's strengths and deficits. Vocabulary and skills are introduced at a well-defined pace, and a series maintains a continuity of skill development. A listing of some widely used basal programs follows.

Developmental Basal Materials
Addison–Wesley Reading Program (Addison–Wesley)
American Readers (Heath)
Ginn Reading Series (Ginn)
HBJ Bookmark Reading Program (Harcourt Brace Jovanovich)
Headway Program (Open Court)
Holt Basic Reading (Holt, Rinehart & Winston)
Houghton Mifflin Reading Program (Houghton Mifflin)
Lippincott Basic Reading (Harper & Row)
Macmillan Reading: Series R (Macmillan)
Scott, Foresman Reading Program (Scott, Foresman)

INTEGRATING THE METHODOLOGIES IN REMEDIATION

Whatever material you use to teach children, for remediation you may integrate strategies from a variety of methodologies. One strategy from one set of materials is rarely effective in the remediation of children with reading difficulties (see Chapter 5). It is necessary to use several approaches to help them internalize what reading is and how it works. But how does a teacher merge multiple strategies in a remedial session? Consider the following example.

CASE STUDY

Ms. Williams is a Chapter I reading teacher in an elementary school. She works with small groups and individual children. Today, she is working with Abby, an eight-year-old beginning third grader, who has serious auditory perception problems and has not responded well to instruction in her basal reader. Abby is reading on approximately the beginning second grade level. She has had significant difficulty learning the phonic elements of reading. This is not surprising considering her auditory deficits. Abby is learning to sound out words but many of her attempts are unsuccessful. She makes several oral reading errors that destroy meaning, but rarely self-corrects. She seldom regards punctuation, and her comprehension is poor. Ms. Williams views Abby's major problems as not attending to meaning, missing the point of reading, and lacking interaction with print. Her secondary problems are inappropriate phonic and word recognition skills. Ms. Williams has identified the following goals for working with Abby during the first quarter of school.

1. Teach Abby that reading should make sense.
2. Teach Abby to self-monitor and self-correct.
3. Improve Abby's performance in short and long vowels and in consonant combinations.
4. Increase Abby's sight vocabulary.
5. Focus on comprehension, particularly literal comprehension, prediction, and inferential thinking.

Because the main focus for Abby is on meaningful reading, Ms. Williams teaches a language experience lesson one day each week. Today is such a day. Abby has been excited for the past week about a visit from her grandmother. After a long discussion about the topic again this morning, Abby decides to write a story about her grandmother. Ms. Williams writes the words as Abby dictates them. Here is Abby's unaltered story.

My Grandmother

My grandmother is coming for a visit on Saturday. She is going to bring me a Cabbage Patch doll. She is bringing my little brother one too. My grandmother calls me "Bright Eyes." She says my eyes light up. She is coming on the plane. My granddaddy is not coming. He's staying at home. I call my grandmother "Nana." I love her.

Once the story has been transcribed, Ms. Williams discusses it with Abby and reads it aloud for her. As she reads, she runs her fingers under the words and has Abby look at the print. She then has Abby read the story with her.

Next comes skill instruction. Ms. Williams chooses five words to teach Abby as sight words. The words are _bring_, _bringing_, _bright_, _brother_, and _plane_. The words were chosen because of Abby's needs in the area of consonant blends. Ms. Williams writes each of the words on a note card, and teaches the words. As she does, she calls Abby's attention to the letters in the word ("Let's spell the word together"), the meaning of the word ("Can you remember how you used this word in your story?"), the phonic elements in the word ("Look at the way this word begins. Listen to the sounds at the beginning. Can you think of another word that begins this way?"), and the patterns in the word ("What is this word, Abby? Good, it is _bright_. Now Abby, what would happen if I took the _br_ off and wrote _fight_? Good. What would _right_ say? How about _light_? Good. Now back to _bright_? Good job").

At the end of the session, Abby was asked to reread her story. She was also allowed to take it home, read it for her parents, and draw a picture illustrating it. On the following day, Ms. Williams reviewed the sight words and gave Abby two skill related worksheets. One required Abby to identify words beginning with the blend _br_. The sheet came from a skill workbook. The other sheet was made by Ms. Williams. It listed the five words that were taught on the previous day, and required Abby to write each word and to draw a picture representing each word. Abby then added the five words to her sight word ring.

Notice that in the sessions Ms. Williams integrated all the methodologies. She used language immersion, sight word, phonic, and linguistic strategies.

Integration of methodologies is also effective in group settings in traditional classroom contexts. Consider this example.

CASE STUDY

Ms. Bailey is a first grade teacher. Her class is in the second quarter of the school year. Her school has adopted the Macmillan Reading Program as the basal reading series. The basal attempts to use eclectic methodologies to meet the needs of a variety of children. Ms. Bailey is concerned about her lowest reading group, which consists of seven children. She realizes that she must make instructional modifications in order to meet the needs of these children. The group is reading at the pre-primer level in the series. Today they will begin to read the story, "I Can," in the book, *Who Can?* The story reads:

> I can jump.
> Can you jump too?
> I can ride.
> Can you ride too?
> I can run.
> Can you run too?
> I can read.
> Can you read too?*

First, Ms. Bailey reviewed the sight words identified by the series and taught during the previous week. The words were *can*, *you*, *I*, and *too*. She then taught three personally selected words, *jump*, *run*, and *ride*. As she taught the words, she had a blank sheet of paper and a pencil beside her. She went over each word in the following way. First she told the children the word, pronouncing and spelling the word ("This word is *run*. *R, u, n, run*").

Second, she gave meaning to the word ("How many of you like to run? Where should you run? Where should you not run?"). Third, she emphasized the phonic elements of the word ("Listen to the sounds in this word—/r/, /u/, /n/. Listen to how the word begins—/r/. Who can give me another word that begins like *run*?"). She wrote the words that children volunteered on the chalkboard so that they could see.

Fourth, she extended the word through patterns. (She wrote the word *run* on a piece of paper. "What is this word?" Children replied "run." "Now, if *r, u, n* is *run*, what is this word?" She wrote *fun* under the word *run*. Children responded "fun." She did the same with the words *bun*, *sun*, and *gun*.) She then had children read each word as she pointed to it.

Fifth, she had children visualize the word and react kinesthetically to the word. ("Look at this word. Look at the letters in the word. Now I am going to remove the word. Look up and see the word again in your mind. Let's spell the word. Let's trace the word with our fingers. Good. *R, u, n*. Good job. Look at the word again. Now make a picture of yourself running in your favorite place. Look at your picture. Now see the word *run* again. *R, u, n, run*.")

Sixth, she provided two skill practices for the words.

1. She gave each child a sheet of paper with the three words in addition to those previously taught. The sheet looked like this:

*Reprinted with permission of Macmillan Publishing Company from *Who Can?* (Pre-Primer I, Macmillan Reading Series r—Carl B. Smith & Ronald Wardhaugh, Senior Authors). Copyright © 1980 Macmillan Publishing Company.

I   *can*
you   *jump*
too   *run*
ride

She gave each child a pencil and then did a quick recognition exercise. She said, "Circle the word *you*," or "Put a number 1 before the word *ride*," or "Circle the word that begins like *bus*," or "Put a number 3 before the word that means something that you can do with a skipping rope."

2. Each child received another piece of paper. On it was one of the words taught and the pattern extension of that word. For example:

run

fun

bun

gun

sun

Children were asked to "Circle the word that is something you can eat," or "Circle the word that means something that is in the sky." Each word was included. Finally, when all the words were taught, she did a quick flash review of all the words.

The children were then introduced to the new story and assisted in reading the story. As they read, Ms. Bailey discussed the story with them and asked a number of interactive questions. At the end of the reading, the children were allowed to choose their favorite word from the story and to dictate a sentence or a short paragraph using their word. Their sentences or paragraphs were written for them on a sentence strip. They then copied their words at the bottom of a sheet of paper and illustrated the material during independent seat work time. The lesson lasted two instructional periods.

Notice, again, the integration of language immersion, sight word, phonic, and linguistic strategies into the traditional basal reader approach.

SUMMARY   Children who are experiencing difficulty in reading often need multiple strategies for coping with print. All the methodologies offer strategies that can be helpful in remediation. Knowledge of the methods and the strategies each has to offer provides the teacher with the instructional variety essential to meeting children's needs. One of the hallmarks of a good remediation program is the way it integrates strategies and formulates a varied and effective instructional plan.

R·E·F·E·R·E·N·C·E·S

Allen, E., and L. Laminack. "Language experience reading—It's natural." *Reading Teacher* 35 (March 1982): 708–714.

Allen, R. V. "How a Language Experience Program Works." In E. C. Vilscek, ed. *A Decade of Innovations: Approaches to Beginning Reading.* Newark, DE: International Reading Association, 1968.

Ashton–Warner, S. *Teacher.* New York: Simon and Schuster, 1963.

Bailey, M. H. "The utility of phonic generalizations in grades one through six." *Reading Teacher* 20 (February 1967): 413–418.

Beck, I. L. "Reading Problems and Instructional Practice." In G. L. Mackinnon and T. G. Waller, eds. *Reading Research: Advances in Theory and Practice*, Vol. 2. New York: Academic Press, 1981.

Becoming a Nation of Readers: The Report of the Commission on Reading. Washington, D.C.: National Institute of Education, 1985.

Calfee, R. C., and D. C. Pointkowski. "The reading diary: Acquisition of decoding." *Reading Research Quarterly* 16 (1981): 346–373.

Carbo, M. "Deprogramming reading failure: Give unequal learners an equal chance." *Phi Delta Kappan* 69 (November 1987): 197–202.

Clymer, T. "The utility of phonics generalizations in the primary grades." *The Reading Teacher* 16 (1963): 252–258.

Ekwall, E. E., and J. L. Shanker. *Teaching Reading in the Elementary School.* Columbus, OH: Merrill, 1985.

Harris, A. J., and C. B. Smith. *Reading Instruction: Diagnostic Teaching in the Classroom*, 4th ed. New York: Macmillan, 1986.

Johnson, D. D., and J. F. Baumann. "Word Identification." In P. D. Pearson, R. Barr, M. Kamil, and P. Mosenthal, eds. *Handbook of Reading Research.* New York: Longman, 1984.

Larrick, N. "Illiteracy starts too soon." *Phi Delta Kappan* 69 (November 1987): 184–189.

Mallon, B., and R. Berglund. "The language experience approach to reading: Recurring questions and their answers." *The Reading Teacher* 39 (1984): 867–871.

May, F. B. *Reading As Communication: An Interactive Approach*, 2nd ed. Columbus, OH: Merrill, 1986.

May, F. B., and S. B. Eliot. *To Help Children Read: Mastery Performance Modules for Teachers in Training*, Columbus, OH: Merrill, 1978.

Moskowitz, A. "On the Status of Vowel Shift in English." In T. E. Moore, ed. *Cognitive Development and the Acquisition of Language.* New York: Academic Press, 1973.

Shimron, J., and D. Navon. *The Dependence on Graphemes and on Their Translation to Phonemes in Reading: A Developmental Perspective.* Technical Report 208. Urbana, IL: Center for the Study of Reading, University of Illinois, 1981.

Smith, F. *Reading without Nonsense.* New York: Teachers College Press, 1979.

————. *Understanding Reading: A Psycholinguistic Analyses of Reading and Learning to Read.* New York: Holt, Rinehart, & Winston, 1982.

————. *Insult to Intelligence: The Bureaucratic Invasion of Our Classrooms.* New York: Arbor House, 1986.

Smith, R. J., and D. D. Johnson. *Teaching Children to Read*, 2nd ed. Reading, MA: Addison–Wesley, 1980.

Stauffer, R. G. *The Language Experience Approach to the Teaching of Reading*, 2nd ed. New York: Harper & Row, 1980.

Swaby, B. *Teaching and Learning Reading: A Pragmatic Approach.* Boston: Little, Brown, 1984.

Vacca, J. A., R. T. Vacca, and M. K. Gove. *Reading and Learning to Read.* Boston: Little, Brown, 1987.

Vaughn–Cook, A. F. "Phonological rules and reading." In R. Shuy, ed. *Linguistic Theory: What Can It Say About Reading?* Newark, DE: International Reading Association, 1977.

Veatch, J., F. Sawicki, G. Elliott, E. Flake, and J. Blakey. *Key Words to Reading: The Language Experience Approach Begins.* Columbus, OH: Merrill, 1979.

8 Neurolinguistic Applications for Teaching Reading

1. What implications does neurolinguistic programming have for the remediation of literal comprehension skills?
2. How do eye movements play a role in the assessment of reading difficulties?
3. How can neurolinguistic strategies be used to remediate skills in spelling?
4. What is the role of positive anchoring and reinforcement in neurolinguistics?
5. How can visualization strategies be used to remediate word recognition and comprehension skills.

Neurolinguistic programming (N.L.P.) is a recently introduced concept in the field of education. The techniques involved, however, have been implemented in communication and counseling for many years. Neurolinguistic programming describes an effort to match language with thinking processes. Specifically, N.L.P. stresses making educational inferences on the basis of individuals' behavioral responses (Arnold and Swaby 1984). Neurolinguistics should not be confused with psycholinguistics, which focuses on "the psychological processes by which language is learned, and on a detailed study of exactly what is learned when one learns language" (Gillet and Temple 1986, 20). The psycholinguistic view of reading instruction is discussed at length in Chapter 9.

Neurolinguistic programming can be viewed as an observational science. The basic techniques derive from the systematic observation and analysis practiced by individual therapists highly respected in their field. Certain therapists, including Milton Erickson, Virginia Satir, and Fritz Perls, were able to help clients change their unwanted behaviors quickly and maintain the changes over extended periods of time (Perls 1973; Satir 1972; Erikson 1980, 1982, 1984). Leaders in the field discovered that these master therapists succeeded because they performed specific, observable, and identifiable procedures. Once the successful procedures were identified, other individuals could learn them and achieve similar positive results. Intensive observation of the master therapists and their techniques formed the basis of neurolinguistic programming.

It is important to understand the observational basis of neurolinguistics. The underlying assumption is this: To achieve success in a given skill, carefully observe the performance of a master of that skill, identify as accurately as possible the many discrete details of a master performance, and then attempt to replicate those details of successful performance. The intensive observation and imitation of successful behaviors is a fundamental principle of neurolinguistic programming. Neurolinguists are less concerned with the history—etiology—of success or failure. They focus on the following issues: (1) What is the unwanted behavior? (2) What processing patterns are observed as the unwanted behavior is performed? (3) What processing patterns are observed as the desired, successful behaviors are performed? (4) How can unsuccessful individuals be taught the successful patterns? The assumption is that the behavior patterns used by unsuccessful individuals do not work, and therefore need to change.

One of the patterns of performance observed in the successful therapists was their ability to establish a strong rapport, or synchrony, with their clients. Careful analysis of this pattern revealed the following details of performance.

MATCHING

Therapists initially imitated clients' body posture, eye movements, hand gestures, speech rate, and representational language. This imitation of behavior is called matching. Matching seemed to facilitate feelings of empathy and rapport.

1. *Body posture.* Neurologists believe that individuals' inner emotional states are clearly reflected in the body's outer appearance. When the inner self is open and positive to learning, the individual has a "straight body line." The body is straight and alert. When the inner self is closed or depressed, or negative to learning, the body bends or slumps. If a client sat in a slumped position, the therapist tried to express empathy for the client by matching the posture.

2. *Eye movements.* Neurolinguists strongly support current eye-movement theory. Eye-movement theory holds that eye movements reflect cognitive and linguistic processing. Theorists analyze cognitive phenomena, such as perceptual span, fixations, duration of fixations, spacing of eye movements during reading, and fixation distance (Shebilske 1975, Young 1976). Other theorists analyze linguistic variables, such as eye-voice span—the distance eye focus precedes the voice during oral reading (Wanat 1971, 1976; Rayner 1977).

Using these studies as a foundation, neurolinguists make a connection between observable eye movements and the storage and retrieval of categories of information (DeMille 1973, Bandler and Grinder 1979, Dilts et al. 1979, Harth 1983). They believe that certain categories of information are stored in specific parts of the brain, and that observation of individuals' eye movements provides clues to the area of the brain where specific information is stored. Neurolinguists have observed and defined a strategy of using eye movements to pinpoint different modes of thinking. Eye movements directed upward or straight ahead indicate the retrieval of visual images. Those directed from side to side (in line with the ears) indicate the retrieval of auditory stimuli. Eye movements directed downward indicate the retrieval of emotional or kinesthetic thought. Therapists observed that emotionally depressed clients displayed predominantly downward eye movements. The therapists would match these movements.

3. *Hand gestures.* It was noted that in individuals with an open, positive learning mode, hand gestures tended to move upward. In individuals with negative, depressed feelings, gestures tended to move downward. Notice your hand gestures when you are excited or positive. For example, when you say "Boy, was I excited," or "I am so happy about this," your hands naturally point upward. On the other hand, notice your gestures when you make comments like "I am so depressed," or "This makes me so unhappy." Your hands automatically point downward. Therapists matched the client's hand gestures in order to establish rapport.

4. *Speech rate.* Positive, open emotional sets usually produce faster, higher-toned speech. Less positive, emotionally laden sets produce slower, lower-toned speech. If clients spoke in low, depressed tones, the therapist matched the tone to show empathy and acceptance.

5. *Representational language.* Neurolinguists believe that the language one uses, particularly the predicates, provides valuable information about thought processes and the way experience is represented. Individuals tend to code most of their experiences either visually, kinesthetically, or auditorily. The language you use to represent thought provides information about the way you coded experiences. For example, an individual who codes in predominantly visual terms repeatedly uses certain predicates: It *looks* good; I *see* your point; I can't *see* it that way; It seems *vague* to me; It is not *clear*; It seems *hazy*; I *see* it from your perspective; I get a *picture* of it. Individuals who code predominantly auditorily use other predicates: This *sounds* good; It *rings* a bell; I *hear* you; Let me tell you how that *sounds*; I hear the *tone* of that. Those who code in primarily kinesthetic modes use the following language: I get a *grasp* on that; This *feels* good; I am *backed* against the wall; I have a *handle* on this; *Back* me up here; I am in *touch* with this. With clients using mainly visual predicates (I can't see what I should do; I wish I could see this more clearly) rather than responding in auditory language (I hear you; That sounds like you are unhappy) or in kinesthetic language (I'm in touch with your feelings; I know it doesn't feel good to you), the therapist would match their language (I see what you mean; That sheds some light on your decision).

In matching clients in representational language, the therapist created rapport, which formed the basis of effective communication. Matching, then, became a key behavioral pattern in neurolinguistic programming.

LEADING

After empathy and rapport were established, the therapists gradually changed their gestures and language to lead clients into more positive mind sets. The assumption is that an individual must be in a positive physiological state in order for positive learning or change to occur. The physiological changes of the therapist bring slow but noticeable changes in the client. Attempting to create positive change when posture, eye movements, speech rate, tone, gestures, and language are negative is a waste of time. Leading was identified as another major neurolinguistic behavior pattern.

ANCHORING

Anchoring refers to the recalling of a strong, positive, and successful past experience in order to recreate the "success physiology" and "expectation of success." This positive state sets the stage for positive learning in the present. For example, people often associate a special song or place with the experience of being in love. Years later, hearing the song or visiting the place causes them to re-experience the physical feelings of being in love. The song or place recalls them to a past time and recreates in them the old feelings. The same phenomenon holds for negative experiences. Auto accident victims might re-experience their fear every time they pass the intersection where the accident occurred. These are examples of emotions that have been associated with or "anchored to" given experiences. Individuals who have experienced what they view as failure associate failure with the physical environment or with related experiences, which tend to anchor the negative. For example, for many children, the word "reading," the reading table, or the reading book recall feelings of failure, the humiliating comments of peers or teachers, and the frustration and embarrassment of not being able to perform. Negative anchoring predisposes them to further failure. Notice the negative cycle: past failure — expectation of probable present failure — present failure. The cycle is not only validated but accepted as a rule for future experiences.

To circumvent this negative loop, the therapists led clients to recall positive, successful past experiences. They fully discussed all aspects of the experience, including visual details (How did you look? What did others look like?), auditory details (How did you sound? What were others saying?), and kinesthetic details (How did you feel? How did others feel?). As individuals fully recalled positive experiences, their physiological bearing changed for the better. Clients were encouraged to believe that the success would be repeated. Recalling the visual, auditory, and kinesthetic positives, clients achieved a physical and mental state allowing them to successfully receive and process information they had previously interpreted as threatening. Anchoring became a major behavior pattern in neurolinguistic programming. The three patterns— matching, leading, and anchoring—underlie the basic strategies in neurolinguistic programming.

EYE MOVEMENTS AND LEARNING

Eye-movement theory underlies neurolinguistic applications to the instruction of children. Neurolinguists have observed and identified eye movements that pinpoint storage and retrieval strategies. Their observations are presented in Figure 8.1.

When asked to construct or create a visual image (imagining a large pink elephant with green spots), most individuals automatically look up and to the right. When asked to recall an exact picture (the pattern on the living room sofa), most individuals look up and to the left. In the auditory domain, questions requiring the recall of previously heard sounds or words (the sound of a close friend's voice) elicit automatic lateral eye movements to the left. Questions relating to constructed sounds (listen to rain falling on a metal surface) elicit automatic lateral eye movements to the right. Eye movements directed down and to the left usually indicate internal dialogue (talking to yourself), while those directed down and to the right indicate that you are experiencing emotions or physical sensations.

RIGHT	LEFT
Visual Constructed Images	Visual Remembered Images
Auditory Constructed Sounds or Words	Auditory Remembered Sounds or Words
Kinesthetic Feelings	Internal Dialogue

FIGURE 8.1   Eye Movements

These observations are true for most people, but not all. Neurolinguists ask questions relevant to each category (visual construct, visual remembered, auditory construct, auditory remembered, kinesthetic, and internal dialogue). For example, in order to observe where visual remembered information is accessed, questions ask for the recall of exact visual images.

- What is the color of your front door?
- How many windows are in your bedroom?
- Describe the house in which you grew up?
- What was your best friend wearing the last time you saw her or him?

Questions or tasks revealing the retrieval of visual construct information might include the following:

- How would you look if you weighed 300 pounds?
- How would your livingroom look if you rearranged the furniture?
- See yourself dressed in a suit of pure gold.
- How would you look if you were ten feet tall?
- See an ice cream cone with scoops of orange, chocolate, and cherry sherbet.

Questions or tasks revealing retrieved auditory remembered information might include:

- How does a barking German Shepherd sound?
- Remember the sound of thunder.
- Remember the sound of your favorite friend saying your name.
- Remember the sound of the telephone ringing.

Tasks revealing auditory construct retrieval:

- Imagine how you would sound if you talked like Donald Duck.
- Imagine how you would sound if you had a very deep voice.
- Imagine how it would sound if you dropped a tray full of dishes into a swimming pool.

Internal dialogue:

- Tell yourself that you are performing well.
- Ask yourself why you did the last dumb thing you did.
- Convince yourself that you should save more money.
- Tell yourself how good you look.

Kinesthetic information:

- Think about how it feels when a cat licks you with its rough tongue.
- Think about how it feels when you bite into a fresh lemon.
- How does your favorite perfume smell?
- Think about how it would feel if a spider crawled on your leg.

Unexpected eye movements can usually be explained by asking for clarification. For example, a child asked to retrieve kinesthetic information (How does it feel when a cat licks you?) might first respond by constructing a visual image of a cat licking.

The categories of retrieved stimuli are used in instruction. For example, teaching a word involves the visual aspects of the word (individual letters, letter forms, word configuration), which students hold in the visual remembered field. Auditory aspects of the word (sounds of letter combinations, phonic elements) are held in the auditory remembered field during instruction. The word would be finger traced, written, or drawn in the kinesthetic field.

On the basis of the observation of eye movements, neurolinguists have noted that many children with histories of learning failure display a sequence of reactions identified as a "negative learning loop" (Jackson and Brownell 1985). The loop involves the following steps:

1. Seeing pictures and hearing sounds of failure (eye movements in visual and auditory remembered)
2. Talking to oneself and hearing negative dialogue relating to failure (eye movements in internal dialogue)
3. Feeling badly about failure (eye movements in kinesthetics)
4. Talking to oneself about feeling badly (eye movements in internal dialogue)
5. Feeling worse (eye movements in kinesthetics)

The negative loop blocks effective learning. The pattern is often accompanied by physiological states portraying inadequate learning, which contributes to learning failure. Anchoring is used to combat the negative loop.

Although neurological aspects of reading failure have long been discussed in the literature (Money 1962; Myklebust 1968, 1971, 1975, 1978; Mattis 1978), Neurolinguistic programming is distinctly different from earlier views. Earlier views focused on specific reading disabilities such as dyslexia. Studies identified syndromes, including language disorders (e.g., anomia—a disorder in comprehension, imitative speech, and speech sound discrimination), articulatory and graphomotor dyscoordination, visual-constructional difficulties, and maturational lag. Children with severe reading problems were evaluated to identify those who could be classified as neurologically impaired. Intensive step by step language and reading programs were then recommended. Neurolinguistics takes a less clinical or medical approach, and is not concerned with labeling children. The behavioral patterns children actually use during reading are closely observed, and unproductive patterns are changed to more successful ones.

IMPLICATIONS FOR REMEDIATION

Neurolinguistic programming provides the teacher of language arts a variety of strategies for use in remediation. Strategies may be implemented in three stages of instruction—preparation, delivery, and maintenance and reinforcement.

Preparation for Instruction

Neurolinguistics emphasizes the importance of an appropriate physiological state for effective learning. Many poor readers begin a reading session in an inefficient posture. They tend to slump, bow their heads forward, speak slowly and low, and show inattention. At the beginning of instruction, make sure students have appropriate posture reflecting alertness and readiness to learn.

Teachers must create a climate in which students recall previous successes and anticipate success in their current learning context. Many poor readers have long-standing experiences with reading failure that prime them for continued failure. They see themselves failing, hear themselves failing, see and hear others responding to their failure, and feel badly about failing. To break the negative loop, positive anchoring is essential. Remind students of successful experiences, discuss these experiences with them, and tell them they can anticipate success again. Ask children questions in order to identify their successful or positive experiences.

- What do you do best when you are at home?
- What is the thing that you like to do the best?
- Of all the things you know how to do, which one do you do best?
- If you could choose anything to do, what would that be?
- Of all the things you can do, what makes you the most proud?

Observe children during the school day to identify areas of strength, and use that information to anchor children positively.

Many poor readers become so defeated and negative about reading that they are unable to think of any positive outcomes. Because of this, it is vital that teachers isolate, discuss, and reinforce success experiences with students, and use these experiences for future positive anchoring. An example of positive anchoring of a group follows. The context is a group of third grade low readers at the start of a reading lesson.

> Boys and girls, I was so pleased with several things that happened during reading yesterday. Bob, see yourself yesterday when I complimented you on your posture. Good posture helped you to be very successful during the lesson. How were you sitting? Good, let us all sit in that way again. Mary, yesterday you did a beautiful job of paying attention. Your eyes were on me or on your books all session. Let me see all eyes on me right now. Good job. Yesterday, you all did so well making clear pictures as you read. Remember how well you understood what you read? Today as we read, you will make those same, clear pictures, and your comprehension will be just as good and maybe even better. Now, let's get into our straight reading positions, get ready to make clear pictures, and have a successful lesson.

At times, teachers work with individual children who have severe emotional blocks against reading. More intensive anchoring techniques may be required. The procedure follows:

- Have the child tell you about one thing that she or he does extremely well. ("Tell me about something you do really well, or like to do a lot.")
- Have the child discuss fully the visual, auditory, and kinesthetic aspects of the experience. ("How do you look when you . . . ? How do the people around you look when you . . . ? What do you sound like when you . . . ? What do the people around you say when you . . . ? How does it feel when you . . . ? How do you think the people around you feel?")

  As the child fully recalls the positive experience, you will notice a difference in the physiology. The body becomes straighter, the voice rises, speech is faster, and the eye movements are more in the visual modes.
- Tell the child that the positive experiences will be recreated in reading as the task gets easier and easier, more and more fun, and they feel better and better about it.

Neurolinguists suggest that children with a history of reading failure are unable to discriminate between appropriate and inappropriate behavior. For example, surrounded by other poor readers, they do not distinguish good reading from poor reading, good posture from poor posture, good responses from poor responses, good strategies from poor strategies. In time, children lose their sense of appropriate expectations in a learning context.

"Separating the states" is a strategy for teaching appropriateness as preparation for instruction. Children are asked to perform opposing behaviorally exaggerated tasks. For example, ask children to "sit slow," then "sit smart"; to "look dumb," then "look smart"; to "read poorly," then "read smartly." You may further exaggerate the differences by asking children to "Do it worse than that." Do this only in a humorous, light-hearted way. The result is that children learn the differences between appropriate and inappropriate behavior. Children asked at a later time to "Sit smart, please" have a clear picture of what to do.

Neurolinguistics holds that all learning progresses from the known to the unknown. All incoming information, then, is linked to previously learned information. Preinstruction should build a foundation for learning by using known concepts to introduce new content. New information should be associated with students' repertoires of knowledge.

Delivery of Instruction

An application of neurolinguistics to instruction is the teacher's use of gestures, facial expressions, tone, and pace to lead students into positive learning modes. Teachers of slow readers often tend to speak slowly, softly, and in low tones. They also tend to use low gestures and to take a long time in delivering short lessons. Neurolinguists believe that these behaviors cause students to sink deeper into the negative learning loop (Bandler and Grinder 1979, Arnold and Swaby 1984, Jackson and Brownell 1985). Instead, teachers should speak in higher, faster-paced tones, and use gestures that guide students into the visual-auditory fields. The lessons should be quickly paced. Present information in different ways several times during the lesson instead of covering the material once, slowly, by only one method. Model a high level of enthusiasm for and interaction with material. This gives students an opportunity to become motivated toward content.

Among the most important instructional applications from the field of neurolinguistics is the concept of visualization. It is believed that many reading disabled students are blocked in their learning by over-reliance on their auditory skills. This auditory block can be seen clearly in children who spell poorly and fail to comprehend content. Good spellers have a consistent strategy of looking up into the visual remembered field to spell the word and making a quick kinesthetic check. They avoid the auditory field unless the word cannot be located in the visual field. Poor spellers use a different strategy involving internal dialogue ("I know I can't spell this word") and auditory constructs (sounding it out). Unfortunately, many of these children have auditory deficits which distort sounds. As a result, the word *when* might become *win*, *stop* might become *sop* or *step*, and *for* might become *fir*.

Neurolinguists have created a spelling strategy based on good spellers' spelling practices. The strategy maximizes the visual field and avoids the auditory except in the case of spelling a word for which no visual form is established. The strategy includes the following steps (Jackson and Brownell 1985):

1. Write the word on a note card.
2. Ask visual remembered questions to determine the student's organizational pattern. If in doubt, assume that the student is normal in organization.
3. Anchor a positive experience.
4. Hold the card in the visual remembered field. Have the student visually trace each letter. Discuss the shape of the word, the letters above and below the line, and the beginning and ending of the word.
5. Remove the card. Guide the student back to the visual remembered field to "see" the word again and spell it. Check the student's internalized picture of the word. Questions you might ask include Does the child see the word more clearly with eyes closed or open? How much of the word is remembered? Are there any trouble spots? If the child is having trouble "seeing" the word, use the expressions "Remember," "Just notice," "Imagine how it looks," or "Pretend your eye is a TV screen and bring the word into view."
6. Show the card again in the visual remembered field. Have the child look at the word until the eyes become tired.
7. Remove the card and have the child spell the word.
8. Show the card again. Have the child pretend that the eyes are a camera. Focus the word clearly and take a picture of it.
9. Remove the word. Have the child spell the word forward and then backward as proof that the child sees the word as a picture.
10. Have the child look at the word, write the word on a piece of paper (kinesthetic), and check the word against the picture. If the word is written incorrectly, you will see a physical response. The child's brow will wrinkle or the hand will pull back. Bring the response to the child's attention. A kinesthetic response alerts the student to check the picture.
11. If a particular part of a word is causing difficulty (e.g., *broccoli* misspelled as *brocoli*), use exaggeration to draw attention to the correct letter combinations. Say to the student, for example, "Place a huge red circle around the two *c*'s; "see the word in black letters and place the two *c*'s in red letters; place the two *c*'s in a green box."

The strategy will take less time as it is practiced. Children can be taught to install words into visual memory by themselves. The strategy can also be modified for whole groups, using the same steps. Encourage students to use the visual field for spelling. If children ask for the spelling of a word, first encourage them to see the word. If it is not correct, write the word for them to help them install the word visually. This strategy works for the installation of any visual stimulus, including math facts, rules, formulae, and the like.

Neurolinguists also use intensive visualization to help children with serious deficits in literal comprehension. The auditory block discussed earlier applies in this case as well. When asked to tell what they have read, many of these children resort to starting the retelling at the end of the passage or trying to relate the exact content verbatim. This tendency demonstrates their reliance on what they hear. Again, the strategy is inefficient. A more effective learning aid is getting students to visualize by building pictures of the information they read. The neurolinguistic literal comprehension strategy contains the following steps:

1. Have the child read a sentence or a short paragraph.
2. Stop the reading and have the child look up into the visual field and "build a picture" of what was read.
3. Discuss the picture. Analyze the "wholeness" of the picture and identify omitted parts.
4. Help the child build a more complete picture by asking questions that guide the child in elaborating on the visual, auditory, kinesthetic, and sequential aspects of the picture. Use the following questions to help the child elaborate:

Visual Detail

- Color (What colors . . . ?)
- Size (How big is . . . ? How small is . . . ? What size is . . . ?)
- Season (What season of year is it? How do you know?)
- Time of Day (How can you tell the time of day?)
- Light (How bright is it?)
- Shape (Describe the shape of . . . ?)
- Appearance (How does . . . look?)

Auditory Detail

- Sounds (What kind of sounds do you hear?)
- Volume (How loud is . . . ?)
- Sequence (What do you hear first? Next?)
- Location (Where does the sound come from?)

Kinesthetic Detail

- Movement (What movement do you observe?)
- Smell (What odors or fragrances can you identify?)

- Emotions (How does . . . feel?)
- Texture (How does . . . feel?)
- Temperature (What is the temperature . . . ?)

5. Have the child go back to the beginning, look at all the pictures, and then retell sequentially. The following case study demonstrates the effectiveness of this strategy.

CASE STUDY

I recently worked with a nine-year-old third grade student, Michael, who was having severe reading difficulties. He was reading laboriously on a mid-second grade level. Michael was in the Special Education program primarily because he could not comprehend even the most simple material he read. He seemed to make a sincere effort but could not construct meaning from either oral or silent reading. His decoding skills were relatively good. He also could understand material written on his grade level when the material was read to him. Michael was reading a story, "The Bluebird's New Adventure," which begins:

(Page 1)   Baby bluebird popped his tiny feathered head out of his nest and looked out at the world about him.

"Go," said mother bluebird gently. "Fly around and take a look at your world."

(Page 2)   "I'm too scared to fly," said baby bluebird quietly, trying hard not to show quite how much his tiny body was trembling.

"Too scared to fly!" said mother bluebird somewhat surprised. "But you are a bird, and birds fly."

(Page 3)   "Well . . . I'm too small to fly," said baby bluebird, pulling his tiny, shaking body deeper into his nest.

"Too small to fly!" said his mother, somewhat amazed. "You are big enough. You'll see. You are a bird, and birds fly."

(Page 4)   "But I'll be all alone," said baby bluebird sadly. "I'll be all alone and I'll be lonely."

"Come, come," said his mother gently. "You'll not really be alone. You'll make new friends in your new world. I promise you will. You are a bird, and birds fly."

(Page 5)   "But what will I do if I come home and you are not here?" Baby bluebird was really upset now, and big tears welled up in his tiny bluebird eyes.

"My, my," said mother bluebird calmly. "I am your mother. I'll be around when you return. You'll see. Remember, you are a bird, and birds fly."

After giving a brief introduction, I began by asking Michael to read the first two pages orally. He did so very slowly but accurately. I then asked him to tell me what he had read. He responded, "There was a bird that wanted to fly." I asked him if he could remember anything more. He replied, "No." At this point, I chose not to prod with specific questions, because I wanted to see how much he could pull from his memory without assistance. Notice that several elements are missing:

- sequence
- accuracy of factual recall
- elaboration of facts
- wholeness of recall

I then began the neurolinguistic comprehension strategy. I asked Michael to reread the passage, stopping at the end of each sentence to look up in his visual field, see the picture, and discuss it. For example:

(Page 1) **Text**	Baby bluebird popped his tiny feathered head out of his nest, and looked out at the world about him.
Teacher	Stop. Look up, and build a picture of what you read. Tell me about your picture.
Michael	Well, there is this little bird who is blue, and he is in his nest. I think it is in a tree, and the bird is looking all around.
Teacher	How does the little bird look?
Michael	Well, he is blue, and he has feathers on his head.

Notice the completeness of recall. Because he had visualized so well, I extended the print to two sentences.

Text	"Go," said mother bluebird gently. "Fly around and take a look at your world."
Teacher	Stop and build your picture, then tell me about it.
Michael	Well, his mother told him to go and fly around and look around at the world.

Again, notice the wholeness of recall. Michael was ready to read a bit more.

Text	"I'm too scared to fly," said baby bluebird quietly, trying hard not to show quite how much his tiny body was trembling. "Too scared to fly!" said mother bluebird somewhat surprised. "But you are a bird, and birds fly."
Teacher	Stop. Check your pictures.
Michael	Well, the little bluebird was scared, and he was trembling. He said that he was too afraid

to fly, but his mom said that he was a bird, and birds are supposed to fly.

We continued to the end of the story. Then I asked Michael to check all his pictures from the beginning of the story to the end and to tell me the whole story. Michael looked up in his visual field and began.

Michael Once there was a little bird. It was a bluebird. He was in his nest with his mother. One day, he popped his little head outside the nest and he looked around. But he got scared because it was so big. His Mom told him that he should go and fly around and see the world, but he began to make up all these excuses like he was too scared, or too small, or too lonely to fly. His mother kept on telling him that he was a bird and that's what birds did.

Notice the completeness with which Michael recalled the material. The detail, the sequence, the accuracy, and the elaboration are all significantly improved. Michael continued training in the visualization strategy until he was able to perform the task more automatically. His comprehension steadily improved.

Visualization strategies should be applied to expository material as well. Children often need more assistance in comprehending content material than in understanding stories. Visualization strategies are valuable tools for children and should be applied to all material (Clemes and Bean 1981, DeMille 1973, Bry 1978, Harth 1983).

Visualization should not be limited to reading and spelling instruction. It should also be emphasized during "read aloud" sessions with children. As you read aloud, encourage children to create images based on the content of the passage. Encourage students to share and elaborate on their "pictures." Students' images are often sparse, recalling few helpful details. Reread the passage to the children and have them revisualize the content. Again, elaborate on the visual, auditory, and kinesthetic details.

Visualization also helps children use clear pictures to assist them in drawing inferences. If they "see" accurate pictures, they can draw inferences more easily. Consider the following passage. As you read the selection, concentrate on building clear pictures; then answer the question at the end.

Susan walked on. Decaying plants and dried twigs cracked under her feet. She could smell the damp, heavy air. Small creatures scurried through the undergrowth. She felt uneasy. She had to bend lower and lower in order to clear the dense overhanging growth. As she went farther, it got darker and darker, and she had to use both her hands to make a path large enough to squeeze through. Susan looked up, but only thin streaks of sunlight were visible. She got more and more afraid. It seemed that she was lost for good. Then, just ahead she saw a ray of light. She walked toward the light. As she got closer, she realized that there was a clearing up ahead. It began to get lighter and lighter. Susan knew that she had made her way out. She sighed with relief.

Question: Where is Susan?

Notice how visualizing the passage assisted your inference regarding a forest. Read similar passages to children. After each sentence, guide children to visualize and discuss their pictures in terms of accuracy and prediction (e.g., What picture do you see? Where do you predict Susan is? What clues are you using to make your prediction?). As they proceed through the selection, children use additional information to revise their predictions. As they gain confidence in drawing inferences from visualized material presented orally, they can read similar passages by themselves and perform the same visual and inferential tasks.

Maintaining and Reinforcing Information

Neurolinguists use a strategy called "future pace" to help children "see themselves" being resourceful with their new strategies in future work experiences. Children are asked to visualize themselves using new successful strategies in new work. Ask them to step into their picture, look out with their eyes, and notice what they see around them (Jackson and Brownell 1985). Children discuss these pictures and elaborate on them. They share and analyze their behavior, posture, learning patterns and strategies, and the responses of others to their performance. Lead children through the strategies they just learned and practiced successfully. Future pacing uses statements like the following to help students anticipate future success and enjoy greater self-esteem.

- Notice how your work is getting easier and easier.
- Notice that learning is getting faster and faster.
- You are becoming much more accurate.
- You are acting smarter and smarter.
- You are seeing your spelling words easier and easier.
- You are building clearer and better pictures of what you read.

Future pace experiences are also useful in anchoring. Positive feelings and expectations can serve as content for anchoring.

When students are reviewing material or preparing for tests, guide them to recall the pictures of the concepts they previously created. The pictures help them recall content more easily. The importance of using visual images productively cannot be over-emphasized. Spelling, reading comprehension, content retention, and self-esteem can be improved by training children to use their visual abilities (Harth 1983, and Lankton 1980).

SUMMARY   Educators have only recently recognized the powerful effects of neurolinguistic programming on learning. The effect is an intensified effort to apply and evaluate educational applications in classroom and clinical settings. Analysis of currently available data shows that the strategies derived from neurolinguistic programming are highly effective with a wide range of children and content. The strategies are particularly effective with children for whom learning is difficult.

R·E·F·E·R·E·N·C·E·S

Arnold, D., and B. Swaby. "Neurolinguistic applications for the remediation of reading problems." *The Reading Teacher* 37 (1984): 831–834.

Bandler, R., and J. Grinder. *Frogs into Princes.* Moab, UT: Real People Press, 1979.

Bry, A. *Visualizations.* New York: Harper & Row, 1978.

Clemes, H., and R. Bean. *Self-Esteem.* New York: Putnam, 1981.

DeMille, R. *Put Your Mother on the Ceiling.* New York: Viking Press, 1973.

Dilts, R. B., J. Grinder, R. Bandler, J. DeLozier, and L. Cameron–Bandler. *Neuro-Linguistic Programming I.* Cupertino, CA: Meta Publications, 1979.

Erickson, M. H. *Innovative Hypnotherapy.* Edited by E. L. Rossi. New York: Irvington, 1980.

———. *The Essential Erickson: Selected Papers on Hypnosis, Psychotherapy.* Edited by E. L. Rossi. New York: Irvington, 1984.

———. *The Nature of Hypnosis and Suggestion.* Edited by E. L. Rossi. New York: Irvington, 1982.

Gillet, J. W., and C. Temple. *Understanding Reading Problems: Assessment and Instruction,* 2nd ed. Boston: Little, Brown, 1986.

Harth, E. *Windows on the Mind.* New York: Quill Publishing, 1983.

Jackson, J., and M. J. Brownell. *Excellence in Teaching Handbook.* Denver, CO: New Learning Pathways, 1985.

Lankton, S. *Practical Magic.* Cupertino, CA: Meta Publications, 1980.

Mattis, S. "Dyslexia Syndromes: A Working Hypothesis that Works." In

A. L. Benton, and Pearl, D. eds. *Dyslexia: An Appraisal of Current Knowledge.* New York: Oxford University Press, 1978.

Money, J. "Dyslexia: A Post Conference Review." In J. Money, ed. *Reading Disability: Progress and Research Needs in Dyslexia.* Baltimore, MD: Johns Hopkins Press, 1962.

Myklebust, H. R., ed. *Progress in Learning Disabilities,* Vol. 1 (1968), Vol. 2 (1971), Vol. 3 (1975), Vol. 4 (1978). New York: Grune and Stratton.

Perls, F. *The Gestalt Approach and Eyewitness to Therapy.* Lomond, CA: Science and Behavior Books, 1973.

Rayner, K. "Visual attention in reading: Eye movements reflect cognitive processes." *Memory and Cognition* 4 (1977): 443–448.

Satir, V. *Peoplemaking.* Palo Alto, CA: Science and Behavior Books, 1972.

Shebilske, W. "Reading Eye Movements from an Information-Processing Point of View." In D. W. Massaro, ed. *Understanding Language.* New York: Academic Press, 1975.

Wanat, S. F. "Linguistic Structure in Reading: Models from the Research of Project Literacy." In F. B. Davis, ed. *The Literature of Research in Reading with Emphasis on Models.* New Brunswick, NJ: Rutgers University Press, 1971.

———. "Relations between Language and Visual Processing." In H. Singer, and R. B. Ruddell, eds. *Theoretical Models and Processes of Reading.* Newark, DE: International Reading Association, 1976.

Young, L. R. "Physical Characteristics of the Eye Used in Eye-Movement Measurement." In R. A. Monty, and J. W. Senders, eds. *Eye Movements and Psychological Processes.* Hillsdale, NJ: Erlbaum, 1976.

9 Remediating Skills in Comprehension

FOCUS
QUESTIONS

1. How do traditional and psycholinguistic approaches to comprehension differ?
2. What skills are involved in metacognition and how can they be developed?
3. What are some strategies for developing children's inferential comprehension skills?
4. How are questions used in comprehension development?
5. How does visualization develop literal comprehension skills?
6. How does conceptual preparation function in comprehension-centered instruction?
7. Why must learners and teachers share responsibility for comprehension?

Comprehension is one of the most complex internal processes in human learning. While conclusions about it must be speculative, the product of comprehension is easy to observe. Teachers observe it daily when asking children questions or giving them tasks to perform. Theorists use the products of comprehension to hypothesize about the processes individuals use to make sense of experience.

Two major views of comprehension dominate the field of reading instruction. These are the traditional and the psycholinguistic views. This chapter presents both positions, discusses the instructional implications of each view, and presents several strategies for improving the product of comprehension. A basic sensitivity to the ways children comprehend is central to all instruction.

THE TRADITIONAL VIEW OF COMPREHENSION

In the traditional view comprehension is a major skill comprised of a number of individual subskills. Theorists have attempted to delineate the subskills on the premise that instruction in those subskills results in comprehension. The four main types of comprehension subskills are literal comprehension, inferential comprehension, evaluative comprehension, and critical comprehension skills.

Literal comprehension refers to the accessing of information explicitly stated in oral or written communication. Skills include recalling facts, details, and sequence, and knowing word meanings.

Inferential comprehension refers to the combined use of literal information and prior knowledge to make inferences extending beyond the explicitly stated information. Skills include inferring central ideas, comparing and contrasting, identifying causes and effects, explaining, and making predictions.

Evaluative comprehension is the forming of personal opinions based on communicated information. Skills include judging worth, making and justifying choices, taking stands on issues, and defending or rejecting actions.

Critical comprehension is the ability to analyze material in terms of style, content, and form. Skills include distinguishing fact from opinion; recognizing logic or consistency of thought; distinguishing among literary forms; and recognizing mood, intention, or point of view.

The traditional view of comprehension argues that children should be taught the identified comprehension skills, which will result in their understanding of material. Most reading texts adopt this position. Comprehension skills are identified, allocated to specific grade levels, and taught directly and individually. Skills are often presented in isolated skill sessions and practiced and reinforced in workbooks. Throughout the grades, questions following reading selections monitor skill development.

The traditional approach assumes that once children learn the comprehension skills, they automatically transfer them to actual reading situations. Children with inadequate reading comprehension are often referred to remedial reading programs that follow the traditional model of comprehension. Such children are given a diagnostic test to identify their specific comprehension skill deficits. Children are then usually placed in a skill program consisting of graded books that deal specifically with individual skills (e.g., drawing conclusions, understanding the main idea, understanding sequence, recalling details). After a few weeks of successfully working through the appropriate books, children are assumed to have gained competence in the given skills and to have remediated their previous comprehension skill problems.

Many children acquire appropriate comprehension skills through this traditional approach. Many can transfer the learned, isolated skills to the reading of textual material. Many can understand skill lessons, practice the skills in workbooks, and apply them in the reading of connected discourse. Some children, however, cannot. Some can comprehend only certain textual material or subjects. Some can comprehend one teacher's instruction and not another's. One reason is that some children cannot transfer their knowledge of isolated skills to actual reading tasks. Another reason is that comprehension skills do not necessarily result in comprehension. Comprehension is much larger than the sum of its parts, which states the fundamental position of the psycholinguistic school of thought.

THE PSYCHOLINGUISTIC VIEW OF COMPREHENSION

Theorists of the psycholinguistic view regard comprehension as a bridge between the known and the unknown (Smith 1982, Goodman 1976, Pearson and Spiro 1981). Figure 9.1 offers a representation of this relationship. Comprehension is something that humans do from birth. While the quality of comprehension might be limited by low native intelligence, by narrow experiences, or by restricted interests, you can successfully learn to comprehend information.

According to the psycholinguistic view, you comprehend incoming information by relating it to information already stored in your "knowledge bank." To comprehend incoming information, you must have in your cognitive structure pre-established concepts about the incoming information. In other words, you must already know something—some conceptual knowledge—that you can relate to new information before you can comprehend it.

Consider the fact that a lawyer might comprehend extremely complicated legal briefs, while a doctor might read them with only minimal comprehension. Similarly, the doctor reads and comprehends medical reports that an equally intelligent teacher might minimally understand. In the psycholinguistic view of comprehension, the more you know about a subject, the more you can know about it. Comprehension depends largely on prior knowledge.

The psycholinguistic approach delineates two major functions of comprehension—forming concepts and interrelating concepts.

The Formation of Concepts

The first task of comprehension is the formation of concepts. To comprehend you must already have a concept of incoming information. If you

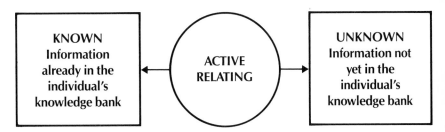

FIGURE 9.1   Comprehension as a Bridge between the Known and the Unknown

are learning about an island, you must already have some concept of island such as land, water, land surrounded by water. Without a concept of
"islandness," you cannot appropriately comprehend island. Similarly,
children must have concepts of the rhythm of verbal language before they
can learn syllabication.

The comprehension system abstracts concepts from meaningful
experiences, real or vicarious. Once you have the concepts, you develop,
expand, and enrich them through speech, print, and added experiences.
Smith (1982) suggests that, lacking concepts for incoming information,
you have three options. First, you might investigate the issue, consulting
other people, the media, or books to find out about the "unknown." You
are more likely to take this option if you are highly motivated, or if you
must learn information for a test or for your job. As you learn, you continually relate incoming information to previously understood and stored
information. Few elementary students take this option because they have
limited conceptual repertoires and sometimes lack the motivation to investigate unfamiliar school material.

A second option is to simply discard the information. If you cannot
connect the information to what you already know, you might reject the
new information as essentially irrelevant. It simply does not compute.
As a third alternative you might misfile or miscategorize the information
because it is unfamiliar or too difficult for you to comprehend. Unsuccessfully conceptualized information is often stored in inappropriate
categories. The misfiled material is extremely difficult to retrieve. Children often take this option. Conceptually unprepared for incoming information, they place fragments of the information in available related
categories. They then are unable to retrieve the information if and when
they need it.

In the psycholinguistic view, then, comprehension is seen as a conceptual filing system. Each concept has a file, and you add to that file by
relating additional information to it. The creation and expansion of this
conceptual filing system establishes the basis of comprehension.

Interrelations among Concepts

The second major function of the comprehension system is to interrelate
the concepts. It is not enough to have individual concepts. You need to
know how the concepts relate to one another. In processing incoming
information, you need to know how that information relates to concepts
pre-established in your cognitive framework.

The cognitive structure is a network of rich connections where
nothing of meaningful and lasting value remains an isolated entity.
These connections help you to categorize and use past experiences to
understand present experiences and to accurately predict the future. The
ability to interrelate concepts permits the use of existing information to

develop, elaborate, enrich, expand, and complement new information, leading to greater comprehension.

The psycholinguistic view of comprehension, diagrammed in Figure 9.2, suggests some reasons children might not comprehend print. Aside from a lack of comprehension skills, the problem might stem from inexperience with the concepts in the material, from an inability to categorize the information appropriately, or from difficulty in connecting new material to relevant, meaningful, and familiar information.

Schema Theory

The psycholinguistic view of comprehension is supported by a conceptually parallel theory, schema theory (Rumelhart 1976, Adams 1979, Adams and Collins 1979, Stefferson et al. 1979). Schema theory explains how information is stored in memory, retrieved from memory, and used in comprehension. Schema theory rests on the assumption that everything a person learns is organized and stored hierarchically. Information "files" are open to constant growth and modification as a person learns through new experiences (Rumelhart 1976). A schema consists of existing information relevant to a given concept. A schema (plural "schemata") is more than a concept, in that a concept involves the fundamental or distinctive features of information, but a schema involves those con-

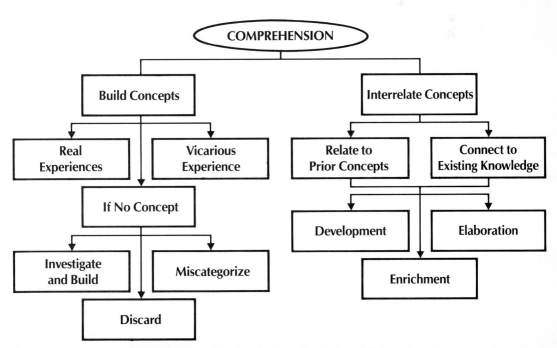

FIGURE 9.2 The Psycholinguistic View of Comprehension

cepts in addition to associations, experiences, and whole meaningful relationships connected to concepts. For example, a concept of "chair" might include distinctive features, such as "seat," "legs," "back support," "hard," and "elevated from the floor." A schema for chair, on the other hand, also includes associations, such as "my favorite overstuffed chair," "being rocked to sleep in my grandmother's old rocking chair," or "relaxing and reading a wonderful book in my favorite arm chair." A schema, then, includes a set of associations and experiences that is evoked when you see or hear a word, phrase, sentence, picture, story, or event.

Because information files are constantly open to change, schemata are incomplete. Conceptual files and schemata become more complete as you hear, read, see, or experience, adding relevant and meaningful information. Comprehension results when incoming information interacts with existing schemata, resulting in understanding and in the schemata's expansion.

Schema theory therefore acknowledges a symbiotic relationship between the reader and the print. The reader brings to the print the appropriate concepts and schemata. The print supplies the reader with opportunities for expanding and refining the existing schemata. Reading and comprehension occur when the reader and the print interact. This model of reading has been called an "interactive model" (Rumelhart 1976). This model contrasts with the "top-down" or concept-driven view, which gives supremacy to the reader's prior knowledge and sees the print as secondary (Smith 1982, Goodman 1976, Weaver 1980). The interactive model also contrasts with the "bottom-up" or text-driven view, which gives supremacy to print, and sees the reader's knowledge as important but secondary (Gough 1972, LaBerge and Samuels 1974).

The implications of schema theory include the importance of building conceptual readiness for new information, alerting children to their existing relevant schemata prior to instruction, and encouraging mental interaction with print through discussion and questioning.

The Memory Process

The process of comprehension and the process of memory are directly related. Psychologists describe a four-part memory process that includes the attention stimulus, the sensory system, short-term memory, and long-term memory.

Attention.   Samuels (1976) states that attention is a primary requisite for any learning and is partially a selective process. Inundated with stimuli in any given environment, you attend to only the more important or more blatant stimuli. In addition, attention is "all or nothing"; you can attend to only one element at a time. Seeming to attend to more than one thing at a time is actually an effect of rapidly switching attention among stimuli or of performing subskills automatically or unconsciously.

Attention switching has been called "the cocktail party phenomenon." You arrive at a party and begin to converse with another guest, when you hear someone across the room mention your name. You stare intently at your conversation partner, but switch your attention quickly back and forth to the conversation across the room. Attention switching succeeds only if you know enough about both conversations. If you do not know enough about one to fill in when you are at the other, you miss the trend of that conversation.

Many children try to use attention switching in class. They fail because they do not know enough about the newly taught information to fill in when they daydream or fail to attend. These children miss important instruction.

Everyone has experienced doing two things at the same time: talking on the phone while fixing a meal, driving a car while reading directions, reading notes on a page while playing an instrument. According to Samuels, you can divide your attention if you have learned to perform certain subskills or behaviors automatically. As you listen and talk on the phone automatically, you can attend to preparing a meal. If you read music automatically, you can turn your attention to playing with expression. Samuels suggests that readers need to decode print automatically so that their attention is free for comprehending. Comprehension diminishes if decoding is not automatic.

Sensory System.   Information from the environment is transmitted to the cognitive system through the physical senses. Printed information enters the cognitive system through the senses of sight, hearing, or touch. When the senses are functioning normally, information is transmitted to memory. Recall the problems arising from impaired or underdeveloped sight and hearing (see Chapter 2). Underfunctioning sensory systems cause distortions in the memory system.

Short-Term Memory.   Short-term memory retains meaningful information and discards the rest. Two characteristics of short-term memory—its brevity and its limited capacity—significantly affect comprehension. Short-term memory is the place in the cognitive system where you temporarily store a telephone number you have just looked up in the directory. You usually look up the number, repeat it, close the directory, and repeat the number until you dial it. Barring distractions, you can dial the number successfully. If someone calls your name or starts a conversation, you usually must consult the directory again.

Information in short-term memory decays rapidly—within approximately fifteen seconds—unless you continuously rehearse it or encode it into long-term memory. Meaningful information relating to existing concepts is passed on and otherwise abandoned—forgotten.

Short-term memory also has limited capacity—between five and nine chunks or units of information at a time (Lindsay and Norman 1977). When capacity is reached, information must be transmitted to long-term memory or discarded. Meaningful units of information associ-

MEMORY

ATTENTION STIMULUS Attention must be demanded; is a selective process.	SENSORY SYSTEM Information is processed through the senses.	SHORT-TERM MEMORY Characterized by brevity and limited capacity.	LONG-TERM MEMORY Consists of concepts, schemata, and interrelations.

FIGURE 9.3   Elements of the Memory Process

ated with prior knowledge are retained in long-term memory. The amount of information in a unit is more important than the number of units. Consider the following sentences: "The man ran to the door and opened it quickly. He hoped that the package he was waiting for had arrived." A child with no fluency in reading might decode, "Th . . . e . . . m . . . a . . . n . . . r." The child processed six units but the units consist of six meaningless sounds—/th/e/m/a/n/r/, which will be rejected and discarded because the child lacks conceptual files making the information meaningful. It would not be surprising if the child remembered little of the passage. In more fluent reading ("The man . . . ran . . . to the door . . . and opened . . . it quickly. He hoped . . ."), the child would again process six units, but the larger units would contain more meaningful information. This information would more likely be encoded into long-term memory, which would aid comprehension. The brevity and limited capacity of short-term memory indicate a need for fluency in decoding and word recognition to aid comprehension.

Long-Term Memory.   Long-term memory stores prior knowledge —concept files and schemata. Long-term memory is the natural link between memory and comprehension. Comprehension depends on relating incoming information to information stored in long-term memory. The more information you have stored, the more you can extend, expand, interrelate, complement, and comprehend incoming information. Figure 9.3 summarizes the memory process. Comprehension and memory, then, are both crucial in information processing. Teaching in ways that facilitate memory assists comprehension, and comprehension-centered instruction facilitates memory.

MERGING THE TRADITIONAL AND PSYCHOLINGUISTIC VIEWS

The traditional view of comprehension emphasizes the importance of learning individual comprehension skills. The psycholinguistic view emphasizes the importance of conceptual and prior knowledge. Skills and conceptual readiness are both certainly essential to comprehension. Conceptual readiness must be attained prior to reading. When necessary concepts are activated before reading, the reader can apply the individual skills to the task of comprehension. The role of the teacher, then, is to instruct children in comprehension skills and to ensure that children have the conceptual knowledge to apply those skills successfully.

REMEDIATING SKILLS IN COMPREHENSION

Before attempting to remediate comprehension deficits, you must identify the specific reasons for inadequate comprehension. Six causes of inadequate comprehension are listed below.

- Inadequate conceptual background
- Unawareness of print structure
- Underdeveloped interactive and critical thinking skills
- Underdeveloped metacognitive skills
- Lack of fluency
- Failure to visualize

1. *Inadequate conceptual background.* Many comprehension deficits have their roots in inadeqeuate conceptual background (including vocabulary). Research supports the existence of a strong relationship between prior conceptual knowledge and comprehension (Langer and Nicolich 1981, Stevens 1982, Adams and Bruce 1980, Shantz 1981, Hayes and Tierney 1982). Strange (1980) suggested that children comprehend poorly when they lack appropriate or sufficient concepts for understanding content. Without needed background, children comprehend less.

2. *Unawareness of print structure.* Research suggests that readers process print successfully when they know the textual structure or format for specific genre (expository narrative, poetry, drama, etc.). These formats help readers to understand, store, and retrieve the information in selections. Students who do not know the inherent structures of different types of material are often at a disadvantage in comprehending (Bruce 1978, Guthrie 1979, Nezworski et al. 1982, Stein and Glenn 1979).

3. *Underdeveloped interactive and critical thinking skills.* Some children cannot comprehend material because they do not interact mentally with print. They do not apply to print a variety of appropriate thinking strategies, which would allow them to process the information critically (Cassidy 1981, Swaby 1984). These children view reading as a passive activity, something to be "got through."

4. *Underdeveloped metacognitive skills.* The importance of metacognitive development is well documented (Kavale and Schreiner 1979, Brown 1980, Adams 1980, Collins et al. 1980). Metacognition refers to the

ability of individuals to monitor their learning and to select and apply those strategies that result in appropriate comprehension. There are two main metacognitive skills: learners' knowledge (about their learning processes, their limitations as learners, and the complexities and demands of the learning task); and learners' self-regulating strategies. Strategies include consciously relating incoming information to prior knowledge, monitoring the learning process, testing and evaluating the learning outcomes, and taking corrective action when comprehension fails. Poor readers are less likely to practice these skills (Weber 1970, Clay 1973, Isakson and Miller 1976, Kavale and Schreiner 1979). Research suggests that poor readers are also less likely to receive direct instruction and practice in metacognitive skills in school (Au 1980).

   5. *Lack of fluency.* Fluency affects short- and long-term memory, as has been noted. Nonfluency prevents appropriate coding of information. Research into the area of linguistic phrasing ("chunking") suggests that poor readers do not phrase appropriately. When phrasing is taught, readers achieve more appropriate comprehension (Stevens 1981, Brozo et al. 1983).

   6. *Failure to visualize.* Visual imagery affects comprehension (Anderson and Kulhavy 1972, Lesgold et al. 1975, Pressley 1976). Some poor readers fail to visualize as they read. They make no effort to remember what is "said" as they read, which decreases their comprehension.

STRATEGIES FOR REMEDIATING INADEQUATE COMPREHENSION

Teachers can play a central, active role in helping children develop more appropriate comprehension skills. Remediation of comprehension skills, however, is a long-term commitment. It is not accomplished by single or short-term interventions. The teacher must continually help children learn, internalize, and practice new strategies.

   The following list identifies six general strategies for remediating inadequate comprehension.

- Activate children's prior knowledge
- Assist children in abstracting print structure
- Develop critical thinking through appropriate questioning
- Train metacognitive skills
- Train fluency
- Encourage visualization

Activate Children's Prior Knowledge

Without conceptual activation, children learn and retain little information. Teachers must ensure that children have the needed concepts in their cognitive frameworks and activate them for use. Children some-times have the concepts, but do not realize the necessity or desirability of using them in their reading. Teachers need to help children actively use prior knowledge to comprehend material. The following strategies are useful in activating prior knowledge.

Vocabulary Preinstruction.   Prior knowledge can be activated by preinstructing and discussing important vocabulary items and making predictions about relationships between the words and text content. As Pearson (1985, 729) states, "Reader's knowledge about topic, particularly key vocabulary, is a better predictor of comprehension of text than any measure of reading ability or achievement." Prior to instruction, teachers should select vocabulary items central to appropriate comprehension of the reading selection. Preinstruct these items. Discuss the words with the children in an effort to relate the new words to children's prior knowl-edge. Ask, "What do the children already know in connection with this new word; how can I use their knowledge to help them comprehend this new word?" Teachers often introduce new vocabulary by having children look up words in the dictionary, write definitions, and use words in com-plete sentences. There is increasing evidence that this approach to vo-cabulary instruction is less effective than a more experience-oriented, concept development approach (Beck et al. 1982, Johnson 1983, Johnson and Pearson 1984). Pearson (1985) suggests that vocabulary instruction should focus on semantic elaboration rather than on definition and us-age. The following suggestions might serve as guidelines for vocabulary preinstruction:

- Encourage students to search their memories for experiences with the word. (Have you ever heard this word used before? In what context have you heard the word? What do you think it might mean?)
- Provide an experience-oriented context rather than a simple defi-nition of the word. (The word is *enraged*. Provide an experience such as: "Last month I sent a very expensive suit to the laundry. It came back with a huge scorch mark on the sleeve. I was enraged." Experience can also be provided through illustrations, pictures, or models.)
- Discuss the meanings. Involve students' actual experiences as much as possible. ("What might *enraged* mean? What are the clues? Have you ever felt enraged? What might make you en-raged?")
- Show children where the word fits in relation to words or con-cepts they already have. ("How is the word *enraged* like the word *angry*? How is it unlike the word *angry*? The word *enraged* is like the word *mad*, except that . . .")
- Provide the definition of the word. Often, teachers move too quickly from the initial presentation of the word to its definition. The intermediate steps of semantic elaboration and interaction

are ignored. The result is inappropriate vocabulary learning and failure to interact with the words.

When the vocabulary pertaining to a selection has been taught, have students make predictions about the content, using the words and elements such as selection title, pictures, illustrations, and headings. Chapter 11 provides more information on vocabulary development.

Structural Prediction.   Prediction is a major skill in reading. Prediction not only enhances interaction with print; it focuses relevant prior knowledge on incoming content. Structural prediction is using the structural elements in print (heading, title, pictures or illustrations, sections in boldface or in italics) to make appropriate predictions about incoming content. These predictions prime prior knowledge, heightening comprehension. Consider a selection entitled "Endangered Species: The Great Slaughter of the Roo," with pictures of a bald eagle, a wallaby, and a kangaroo. Children with good predictive skills and with appropriate prior knowledge might anticipate the following:

- The selection is about animals in danger of extinction. This would eliminate animals such as dogs, cats, and cattle.
- Someone or something is killing the animals in question (clue: *slaughter*).
- "Roo" might mean a kangaroo. The pictures support this prediction.
- If the passage is about kangaroo, the setting is probably a country like Australia rather than the United States (clue: prior knowledge).
- People might kill kangaroo for their skin or meat, for sport, or for some other reason (prior knowledge).
- The article probably opposes killing kangaroo since many people want to protect endangered species.

Imagine the high level of interaction predictive readers have with print before they actually read. This interaction is vital to comprehension (Eeds 1981, Burmeister 1983). Teachers can help children develop this skill by directly instructing them in structural prediction. Before children read selections, direct them to:

- Look at the title and predict selection content.
- Look at the pictures, illustrations, charts, graphs, captions, etc., and refine previous predictions.
- Look at the section headings, words or phrases in heavy type, etc., and continue predictions.
- Use the information to predict whether the content is factual or fictional.

Tell children the reasons for structural prediction. Teachers should let children know that attention to structural elements will help them to activate prior knowledge, which, in turn, helps them to better understand and remember content. Discuss children's predictions. Encourage them to justify their predictions. Write predictions on the chalkboard, and check them for accuracy as children read the selection. This also provides a purpose for reading. Involving readers in the learning process allows them to see the reasons for instruction and aids comprehension.

As children gain confidence and success in making predictions, help them to use the strategy independently. Ask, "What are you going to look for before you begin reading? What questions are you going to ask yourself based on the title, pictures, etc.?"

Advance Organizers.   A useful strategy for activating and engaging prior knowledge is the advance organizer. An advance organizer organizes students' thinking so that they know what information they already have will help them in comprehending new information. This conceptual organization takes place before reading.

The idea of an advance organizer is not new. It was discussed and researched by Ausubel in 1960. The concept of an advance organizer remains popular, although the terms used for it today are schema preparation, or conceptual preparation (Weaver 1980, Pearson and Spiro 1981, Smith 1982).

The concept of advance organizers is compatible with the psycholinguistic view of comprehension. Organizers alert learners to the prerequisite concepts needed for comprehension, and guide learners to the appropriate conceptual files so that understanding can occur. An advance organizer is any effort on the part of a teacher to prepare students for reading by linking new concepts with students' existing concepts. Constructing advance organizers involves three steps.

- Identify the main ideas or concepts of the selection to be read.
- Establish parallels between the concepts and the children's prior experiences.
- Tell children how their prior experience directly relates to the selection they are going to read.

The following example shows how to prepare an advance organizer.

CLASSROOM APPLICATION: THE SELECTION

President Lincoln's Reconstruction Plans

Early in 1865, President Lincoln announced his reconstruction plans. The President decided that the division between the North and the South should end and that the country should be reunited once more. In his Second Inaugural Address, President Lincoln had promised the American people to "bind up the nation's wounds," and that was what he was determined to do.

First, Lincoln offered full pardon to all Southerners who would take an oath of allegiance to the Union, and who would promise to uphold the antislavery laws. Second, he announced that each state could make new laws, elect new officials, and eventually return without penalty as equal members of the Union.

Although President Lincoln believed firmly in his reconstruction, or rebuilding, plan, some Northerners were opposed to his ideas. Several congressmen, for example, wanted Southerners to be punished. They believed that former Confederates should not be pardoned, and should not be allowed to hold public office or to vote. In addition, the congressmen did not trust the former Confederates to treat black Americans fairly, in spite of the antislavery laws.

Despite this opposition, President Lincoln held his position that the South should be rebuilt and reunited with the rest of the country. He believed in civil and political equality between black and white Americans, and he believed in the principle of amnesty.

Unfortunately, President Lincoln died before he could convince critics to accept his reconstruction plan. He was assassinated while watching a play at the Ford's Theater by an actor named John Wilkes Booth. Some witnesses thought that as Booth fled, he shouted, "Thus be it ever to tyrants." On that evening April 14, 1865, the American nation lost a great leader.

Advance Organizer

Step 1. Identify major concepts: Reconstruction after a disagreement might be difficult to achieve.

Step 2. Find parallels between the selections and children's experiences: Have you ever been in a situation in which two of your close friends have had a huge quarrel? Think back to that situation. Do you remember how angry they were at each other and how it seemed as if they might never forgive, trust, or like each other again? You have at least two options at such a time. First, you might take sides, saying one person is right and the other wrong. You might even wish to see the "wrong" party punished. Second, you might realize that there are two sides to every argument. You might try to bring the two people together again. Reunion is a name for bringing people together again. Reconstruction is a name for building a relationship again. Countries or groups at war are like individuals in an argument. After war, people and their leaders might take sides or might try to reunite and reconstruct.

Step 3. Make a bridging statement: The selection you are about to read is about President Lincoln's efforts to reunite the North and the South after the American Civil War.

Discuss advance organizers with children so they can verbalize the links necessary for comprehension. Discussion gives teachers an opportunity to observe the effectiveness of the parallels.

Advance organizers are not time-consuming additions to teaching loads. They are simple to construct and require only that teachers read selections beforehand to extract the key concepts. The strategy helps children create and activate concepts. This benefits children who lack the necessary experiences or the organizational skills for comprehending content.

Overviews.   Overviews are used to give children an advance synopsis of the content to be learned. Unlike advance organizers, which are concept-bound (tied to children's prior concepts and experiences), overviews are content-bound (related to the facts or content to be presented). An overview tells readers what they will read and acts as a comprehension check after reading. Comprehension after reading should minimally include the facts in the overview.

An overview of the selection in the foregoing application might include the following information:

> The selection you are about to read describes President Lincoln's plan to reunite the country after the Civil War. As you would expect, the people of the North and the South had hostile feelings toward one another. This made the job of reuniting the country very difficult. Unfortunately, President Lincoln died before the problems could be resolved.

Overviews are appropriate when children already have the necessary concepts and experiences to deal with the material. They are also appropriate for presenting the people and places named in the selection.

Combination Advance Organizer and Overview.   A combination of strategies can be very effective. This technique prepares children conceptually and gives them an overview of the selection as well. Combine strategies by adding an overview to step 3 of the procedure for constructing an advance organizer.

CLASSROOM APPLICATION

1. Identify major concepts. Reconstruction after a disagreement might be difficult to achieve.

2. Establish necessary parallels between the major concepts and children's experiences. Have you ever been in a situation in which two of your close friends have had a huge quarrel? Think back to the situation. Do you remember how angry they were at each other, and how it seemed as if they might never forgive, trust, or like each other again? You have at least two options at the time. First, you might take sides. Second, you might realize that there are two sides to each argument. You might try to bring the two people together again. Reunion is a

name for bringing people together again. Reconstruction is a name for building a relationship again. Countries or groups at war are like individuals in an argument. After a war, people and their leaders might continue to take sides or might try to reunite and reconstruct.

3. Make a bridging statement and give an overview. The selection you are about to read is about President Lincoln's attempt to reunite the country after the Civil War. Because of the war, the people of the North and the South had hostile feelings toward one another. The job of reconstruction was therefore very difficult. Let us read and find out how President Lincoln attempted to achieve this goal.

Combined strategies provide both conceptual and factual information. Some might regard this as "spoon feeding" children. However, instructional reading is the teacher's primary responsibility. The teacher should be teaching the children how to read more effectively. The less prior knowledge children bring to print, or the less able they are to organize their prior knowledge for comprehension, the more they need this kind of instruction.

Listing.   Advance organizers and overviews are more effective with narrative or story-form factual material. Listing is a more useful strategy for preparing children to read expository, non-fiction selections, particularly in science or social studies. Unlike advance organizers, which prepare children conceptually, listing alerts children to facts they know, or provides them with facts pertaining to the content. Listing thus gives them useful information before reading that serves as a basis for comprehension.

Listing consists of eight steps. These steps are applied to the following selection.

CLASSROOM APPLICATION

The Great Barrier Reef

Out in the Pacific Ocean, waves curl and break, crash and foam in a long line. The waves are striking a reef lying near the surface of the water. It is the Great Barrier Reef. It is the longest coral reef in the world. If it were placed beside the United States, it would stretch from Philadelphia to Miami.

What is truly wonderful about a coral reef is the way it is made. The building begins with tiny animals called polyps. Polyps look like brightly colored flowers growing in an ocean garden. But they are a very simple form of animal life. Each little animal makes a coral cup around itself. The coral is hard, like stone. The animal unfolds from the cup to feed. It folds into the cup for safety. When the animal dies, the hard cup remains. New polyps build their cups on top of the remaining cups. As more and more cups are added, the coral takes different shapes. In time, masses of coral form a reef.

The reef is not safe from danger. Waves crash and beat at its edges. With each sweep of waves, bits of coral are carried away. Some kinds of fish feed on live polyps. When live polyps are killed, the reef breaks down. People also cause damage. They pollute the waters. They even tear off pieces of beautiful coral.

It has taken millions of years to build the Great Barrier Reef. Day by day parts of it are destroyed. Day by day the building goes on.*

Listing

Step 1. Write the title on the chalkboard.

Step 2. Read the title to the children. Ask if anyone has heard the phrase "coral reef" before. Ask children to tell you anything they know about coral reefs.

Step 3. If there is no response, give a clue, such as, "It has to do with something in the ocean." (If students cannot provide information about the content, this means they are not ready to read and comprehend the selection. They must be provided with "prior knowledge" through pictures, illustrations, vicarious or real experiences, or discussion.)

Step 4. List all responses on the board. Delay discussion until many responses are listed. Responses for "coral reef" might include the following:

hard
different colors and shapes
sharp
easily broken
found in the ocean
people collect pieces of them

Step 5. Stop when you feel you have enough responses.

Step 6. Reread the list and ask for clarification or discussion as necessary.

Step 7. Have children identify general categories, such as size, uses, location, color, shapes.

Step 8. Leave the information in sight to give children a purpose for reading and a check on information as they read.

Listing helps children establish content, enabling them to read better and to augment existing knowledge.

---

*From "Great Barrier Reef," by Brenda Hamilton, in Pleasant T. Rowland, ed. *Abracadatlas,* © 1982 Addison–Wesley.

Assist Children in Abstracting Print Structure

Textual material, whether narrative or expository, has internal structure. This internal structure contains predictable components. For example, stories (narratives) typically include such elements as setting, characters, problem, and problem resolution. Similarly, expected components of articles (expository) include descriptions, facts, comparisons or contrasts, or issues and their arguments. Children's expectation, understanding, and use of internal structures allow them to better process, understand, and recall the content (Bruce 1978, Stein and Glenn 1979). Many children are unaware of these structures. Thus, they have diminished understanding and memory of what they read (Taylor and Beach 1984). Descriptions follow of strategies for helping children learn print structure.

Story Form.   A useful strategy for helping children internalize narrative print structure is the story form, created by Enfield and Greene (1987). They pointed out that stories contain the following elements:

- characters
- setting
- main idea or point
- sequence representing the points of rising action
- climax
- sequence representing the points of falling action

These elements are arranged in a graphic representation called a story form. The graphic representation is first discussed with children. They are encouraged to identify each segment of a given story. The segments are filled out on the story form. The teacher assists children in filling out the story form for several stories. When children understand the idea of the narrative structure, they can complete the form independently after reading selections. The strategy reinforces comprehension skills of identifying sequence, climax, main idea, characterization, setting, and the appreciation of plot.

Story Grammar.   The importance of children's ability to internalize the structure of a story cannot be overestimated. During the past decade, psychologists have investigated the processing of whole language units such as stories, and have found that stories have identifiable, internal structures consisting of syntactic or structural elements (setting, plot, episodes), and semantic elements (time frame, location, specific events). Semantic elements vary from story to story, but syntactic elements remain comparatively stable. Internal syntactic structures are called story grammars (Whaley 1981, Sadow 1982). Research suggests that many children are successful in processing narrative material because they have abstracted the concept or schema for story structure. This helps them to understand, store, and retrieve information in a story (Bruce 1978, Nezworski et al. 1979, Stein and Glenn 1979).

Stein and Glenn (1979) proposed that a simple story usually contains two main components—setting and episode. The setting includes the following elements:

- place
- character
- general background information

The episode includes the following elements:

- an initiating event that sets the stage for a problem
- a response that sets up a goal
- an attempt to accomplish the goal
- a consequence indicating the result of the attempt
- a reaction indicating the concluding response to the situation

In the following example story grammar is applied to a simple story, "The Clever Chipmunks."

CLASSROOM APPLICATION: "The Clever Chipmunks"

Setting

Once upon a time there was a family of chipmunks who lived *in a great and green forest.* The chipmunks were the smallest of the forest animals, for all around them lived tigers, wolves, foxes, bears and most feared of all, the lion, king of the beasts.

Initiating Event

One day, the chipmunk family went hunting for food. They came to a huge oak tree which bore the largest, most succulent nuts in the forest. One nut could feed almost the entire chipmunk family for a meal. The nuts were so large, however, that try as they might, *the chipmunks could not get the shells open* to enjoy the delicious nuts inside. On this day, lion lay under the huge tree, taking a rest from the blazing noon sun.

Response

Now, though the chipmunks were small, they were very clever. They thought of *a way to trick the powerful lion into helping them.* They knew that the lion was extremely strong and was the most feared beast in the forest. They also knew that he had one great flaw: lion was terribly vain.

Attempt

The chipmunk family gathered into a huge pile the largest nuts that were lying on the ground. They then ran around the pile, making just enough noise for lion to open one sleepy eye. At that, the first chip-munk said in a loud clear voice, "These nuts are so huge and so hard that there is *no animal in the whole forest—except fearless wolf, of course—who could crack this whole pile before nightfall.*" The vain lion sat up quickly and roared, "Wolf, eh? I am king of the beasts. Wolf is no match for me. I can crack all those nuts before the tigers go down to the river for their after-lunch drink. That is way before nightfall." And so saying, the lion took each nut in his huge jaws, and in no time, he had cracked every one.

Consequence

The clever chipmunks praised the lion's power and strength. They cheered loudly as he strutted proudly off, muttering to himself about how much stronger he was than poor, feeble wolf. *On the ground lay the large pile of succulent, cracked, ready-to-eat nuts.*

Reaction

The chipmunks were proud of their clever trick. They began gathering the cracked nuts and carrying them to their home, where the nuts were stored. The chipmunks were thrilled that the entire family would have plenty of food all winter long.

A story grammar not only explains a story, but also serves as a tool for analyzing the story. Introduce the story grammar after children have internalized the story structure and can do the story form (elements of sequence, problems and their resolution, characters, and setting). Once children conceptually understand the structure of a story, they can master the more complex elements of events, responses, attempts, consequences, and reactions.

Report Form.   In the primary grades children have comparatively little exposure to expository material. In the secondary grades expository material abounds. Many children with reading problems find the transition difficult because the strategies for reading narrative and expository materials differ considerably. In narrative text the "whole" is supreme—plot, characterization, main idea. In expository text, discrete units are important. Each sentence might state an essential fact.

Enfield and Greene (1987) devised a visual representation of expository writing, called a report form. They based the report form on the observation that each paragraph in expository selections often contains a key fact and supporting details.

The report form helps children abstract key facts and relevant details from expository material. The internal structure also helps children in reading texts. The report form aids analysis of structure, of major facts, and of supporting details. It also provides a foundation for outlining and a good structure for test review. Teach children the technique before expecting them to do it on their own.

Expository Text Structure.   Research supports the fact that teaching expository paragraph structure results in greater recall and comprehension of textual material (McGee 1982, Taylor and Samuels 1983, Meyer and Freedle 1984, Taylor and Beach 1984). McGee and Richgels (1985) developed an effective method of teaching expository paragraph structure to elementary school students. They identified five common expository text structures: description, collection, causation, problems and solutions, and comparison. Description and collection are common in elementary content, while the other three structures appear less frequently. Nevertheless, students benefit from learning all five of the structures (Meyer and Freedle 1984). McGee and Richgels provided descriptions and examples of each structure, presented in Table 9.1.

TABLE 9.1   Expository Text Structures

Structure and Definition	Sample Passage	Clue Words
Description: Specifies something about a topic; presents attributes or setting of a topic.	The Summer Olympic Games are the biggest entertainment spectacles of modern times. Every four years they offer two weeks of non-stop pageantry and competition.	
Collection: A number of descriptions (specifics, attributes, settings) presented together.	The Summer Olympics have so many different things to offer. First, there are many kinds of events, big shows like the opening and closing ceremonies, pure competitions like the races and games, and events that are partly artistic and partly competitive like the subjectively scored diving and gymnastics contests.	*first, second, third, next, finally*
Causation: Elements grouped in time sequence (before and after); causative relationship specified.	There are several reasons why so many people attend the Olympic Games or watch them on television. The first Olympics were held in Greece over 2,000 years ago. As a result of hearing the name "Olympics," seeing the torch and flame, and being reminded in other ways of the ancient games, people feel that they are escaping the ordinariness of daily life.	*so, that, thus, because of, as a result of, since, and so, in order to*

(Table 9.1 continues)

TABLE 9.1   (Continued)

Structure and Definition	Sample Passage	Clue Words
Problem and Solutions: Includes relationship between a problem and its causes, and a set of solutions, one of which breaks the link between the problem and its cause.	One problem with the modern Olympics is that they have gotten so big and so expensive to operate. A city or country often loses a lot of money by staging the games. A stadium, pools, and playing fields are built for the many events and housing is built for the athletes, but it is all used for only two weeks. In 1984, Los Angeles solved these problems by charging companies for permission to be official sponsors and by using many buildings that were already there.	*a problem is,* *a solution is,* *have solved this problem by*
Comparison: Contains no element of time sequence or causality; organizes elements in terms of their similarities and differences.	The modern Summer Olympics are really very unlike the ancient Olympic Games. Individual events are different. For example, there were no swimming races in the ancient Games, but there were chariot races. There were no women contestants and everyone competed in the nude. Of course, the ancient and modern Olympics are also alike in many ways. Some events are the same, like the javelin and discus throws.	*different from,* *same as,* *alike,* *similar to,* *resemble*

Source: Adapted from B. J. Meyer and R. O. Freedle, "Effects of Discourse Type on Recall," *American Educational Research Journal* 21 (Spring 1984), 121–124.

McGee and Richgels (1986) devised a five-step approach to teaching students to identify and understand print structure.

Step 1: Selecting Passages. First, teachers search content material for paragraphs using the five expository structures (description, collection, causation, problem and solutions, and comparisons). Collection and description are more common in expository passages written for young children than causation, problem/solution, and comparison. Teachers should rewrite, revise, or compose paragraphs to demonstrate the less common structures. It is important to find (or construct) passages that use the appropriate clue words. Clue words such as those presented in Table 9.1 help students to identify structures.

Step 2: Preparing Graphic Organizers. After selecting a passage, prepare a graphic organizer. The graphic organizer shows the key ideas, which are arranged in a "map" revealing the specific organization of ideas in the passage. Figure 9.4 shows a graphic organizer for a causation paragraph structure.

Step 3: Introducing the Graphic Organizer. The teacher next introduces the graphic organizer to the children, and discusses the main ideas. The relationships among the ideas are given particular attention. The actual passage is not shown at this point.

Step 4: Composing a Passage. Children then compose passages based on the information in the graphic organizer. The teacher helps them use the organizer to guide their composition and draws their attention to the structure and to the relationships among the ideas. Students revise their passage by rearranging sentences, combining sentences, refining word choices, adding appropriate topic sentences, or adding appropriate concluding sentences. Figure 9.5 presents a paragraph created by a group of fifth grade students based on the graphic organizer for "Camels in the Desert."

Camels in the Desert

Camels are still ridden by the people of the desert today. They are well suited for carrying people and heavy burdens for long distances in hot, dry places because they can go for a long time without water. As a result of their thick hooves, camels can easily walk on the hot sand. Finally, camels can live off the desert because they are able to find even the smallest plant to eat hidden in the desert soil.

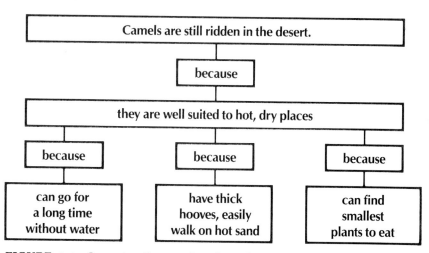

FIGURE 9.4   Causation Paragraph and Graphic Organizer

Source: L. M. McGee and D. J. Richgels, "Teaching Expository Text Structure to Elementary Students," *The Reading Teacher* 38 (April 1985), 743. Reprinted with permission of Lea M. McGee and the International Reading Association.

Camels in the Desert

Camels have been used in the desert for many years. They are still ridden in the desert today. Camels are excellent desert animals. They are well suited to hot, dry places. You can tell that because they can go for a long time without water. A desert animal would have to be able to do this. They also have thick hooves, therefore they can easily walk on hot sand. Finally, they are suited to the desert because they can find the smallest plant to eat. You can see that camels make great desert animals.

FIGURE 9.5 Understanding Print Structure: Step 4: Fifth-Graders Use a Graphic Organizer to Compose a Passage
Source: Adapted from L. M. McGee and D. J. Richgels, "Teaching Expository Text Structure to Elementary Students," *The Reading Teacher* 38 (April 1985), 743. Reprinted with permission of Lea M. McGee and the International Reading Association.

Step 5: Comparing the Student-Composed and the Original Passages. In this final step, students see the original passage for the first time. The teacher helps the students compare and contrast their passage with the original. Students also locate additional paragraphs in content area material that illustrate the print structure.

This strategy comprehensively presents the complex concept of print structure to children in an understandable and effective way.

Develop Critical Thinking through Appropriate Questioning

Questioning students about what they have read is a standard strategy in both developmental and remedial reading instruction. Questions serve two purposes. First, they determine whether or not comprehension has taken place. Second, they positively affect students' processing of and response to material read. Research shows that the questions teachers ask affect students' abilities to respond critically to print (Hansen and Pearson 1983, Gordon and Pearson 1983, Hansen and Hubbard 1984). Teachers' questions affect children's abilities to think about print on a variety of levels from simple, factual to complex, inferential levels. Perhaps the best-known attempt to describe these levels of thought is Bloom's taxonomy of educational objectives (Bloom et al. 1956). The taxonomy grew from an effort to standardize examination questions for evaluating comprehension. Bloom and other educators tried to identify various levels of thinking. The resulting taxonomy has since become a landmark in the field of education. While the taxonomy identifies different cognitive functions and categorizes certain patterns of thought, it does not imply that levels of thought are mutually exclusive. The taxonomy identifies six levels of thought: knowledge, comprehension, application, analysis, synthesis, and evaluation. A discussion of each level follows.

Level 1: Knowledge. Knowledge refers to the recall of facts and details and does not necessarily include comprehension. At this cognitive level individuals can state facts, recall events, list specific details, and name items or conventions. The individual might make the statement, "I know and can state what I know."

Level 2: Comprehension. Comprehension refers to the ability to understand information. At this level, individuals process information and translate it into their own words. They can explain information and compare and contrast elements of content. Because comprehension involves relating new information to prior knowledge, individuals can also predict events. A person at this level might state, "I can understand and explain."

Level 3: Application. Application refers to the ability to apply information to real or hypothetical situations by manipulating elements to the abstract and apply rules. Individuals can use application abilities to solve problems. A person at this level might state, "I can use information; therefore I can solve problems by manipulating and applying elements or ideas."

Level 4: Analysis. At the level of analysis individuals can discover elements, principles, and relationships by pulling apart a whole in order to better understand its parts. People can analyze reactions, characters, patterns, settings, motives, and vocabulary use. Because it involves the critical investigation of information, analysis is the beginning of critical thinking. A person at this level might state, "I can pull selections apart and analyze the parts in order to better understand the whole."

Level 5: Synthesis. Synthesis refers to the ability to reintegrate parts into a new whole. In the process, individuals add personal meaning and creative perspective to the whole. Synthesis is therefore the beginning of creative thinking. A person at this level might state, "I can put the parts back together and add my own creative perspective to the whole."

Level 6: Evaluation. Evaluation is the ability to place value on an idea and to judge it in terms of inherent logic or external principles. An individual at this level might say, "I can state and support my opinions and can share my values with others."

At each cognitive level individuals engage in specific thinking behaviors, listed in Table 9.2.

One of the goals of education is to help children operate effectively at all levels of thought. This goal should apply to all children in the development and teaching of comprehension skills. Teachers can help children in this endeavor by exposing them to questions that activate and stimulate each cognitive level. Questions stimulate children's thinking, increase their interaction with content, and enrich and extend comprehension.

TABLE 9.2 Possible Operations at Each Level of Bloom's Taxonomy

Cognitive Level	Behaviors
1. Knowledge	tell, cite, show, list, locate, state, recite, repeat
2. Comprehension	describe, explain, review, translate, paraphrase, predict, summarize, discuss
3. Application	use, model, try, operate, manipulate, diagram, apply, demonstrate, utilize
4. Analysis	organize, categorize, analyze, scrutinize, dissect, take apart, break down, prove, inspect
5. Synthesis	create, imagine, suppose, compose, hypothesize, improve, reorder, originate, formulate, elaborate, design
6. Evaluation	justify, appraise, recommend, criticize, support, reject, judge, award, censure

Source: From *Taxonomy of Educational Objectives: The Classification of Educational Goals: Handbook I: Cognitive Domain*, by Benjamin S. Bloom et al. Copyright © 1956 by Longman Inc. Reprinted by permission of Longman Inc., New York.

Developmental and remedial reading materials always include a variety of questions. Research shows, however, that these questions tend to tap low-level, literal thinking (Beck 1984, Durkin 1979, 1981). Such questions restrict performance to the first two cognitive levels, knowledge and comprehension. Many children with reading problems in the area of comprehension have difficulty applying higher level thinking to print. This is often because they have received little practice. Teachers should continually provide opportunities for children to answer a full range of questions. In addition, the development of thinking skills through the use of questions should not be limited to the reading program. Teachers should ask appropriate questions in all content areas.

Gallagher (1965) offered a useful questioning scheme including narrow and broad questions. Narrow questions are text-bound; the answers are stated directly in the text. They have one right answer, and require little or no mental interaction. Answers depend heavily on memory. Broad questions are reader-bound; the answers begin in the text but end in the mind of the reader. These questions elicit varying responses and demand a high level of mental interaction.

Gallagher identified two types of narrow questions: cognitive-memory and convergent. Cognitive-memory questions require students to recall information, identify facts, answer yes or no, give definitions from the text, and name information. These questions tap only the first cognitive level, knowledge. Cognitive-memory questions begin with the words *who*, *what*, *when*, and *where*—by far the most often asked questions in school. Convergent questions are also text-bound, but their answers require students to locate and use information from different parts of the text. Students use the information to explain content, state explicit relationships, and compare and contrast. Convergent questions tap the second cognitive level, comprehension. They often begin with the words *why, how, explain, compare,* and *contrast.* The great mass of questions asked of children during any school day are narrow questions of the cognitive-memory and convergent types. It is little wonder, then, that studies such as the National Assessment of Educational Progress (1981) show that children nationwide perform well on factual comprehension tasks but poorly on tasks requiring critical thinking, creative thinking, and problem solving abilities.

Gallagher also identified two types of broad questions: divergent and evaluative. Divergent questions require students to predict, hypothesize, infer, reconstruct, solve problems, and trace alternatives. Divergent questions tap the cognitive levels of application, analysis, and synthesis. They often begin with the following phrases and words: What if . . . ? Suppose . . . ? How do you know that . . . ? What might happen next? What leads you to believe that? How many ways can you think of to . . . ? How might the outcome have been different if . . . ? Predict. . . . Such questions utilize many levels of thinking, which is important to the development and extension of comprehension.

Evaluative questions require students to state and support an opinion, justify a choice, defend a position, place a value, and make a choice. These questions tap the sixth cognitive level, evaluation. They begin: What do you think about . . . ? Do you agree? Why or why not? Can you support . . . ? How do you feel about . . . ? Would you . . . ? and Would you suggest . . . ? Gallagher's scheme is represented in Table 9.3.

Teachers should read textual material prior to instruction and then construct questions to stimulate children's thinking on all levels of thought. The question types are equally useful, but none should be overused or underused. Questioning strategies apply to all grade levels and content. Teachers should strive to extend thinking skills in children of all ages and in all areas of the curriculum.

Recent research points to the value of constructing a "line of questions" for narrative material (Singer and Donlan 1982; Beck, Omanson, and McKeown 1982; Gordon and Pearson 1983; Beck 1984). Beck, McKeown, McCaslin, and Burkes (1979) analyzed the questions contained in basal manuals. They found that most questions were low-level and nonchallenging. They also found that the questions represented a random selection with no clear purpose or pattern. This second finding clearly relates to other research indicating that randomly constructed questions are inferior to question patterns that focus students' attention on "salient story elements." Patterned questions promote more appropriate comprehension and retention.

Beck (1984) interpreted "story elements" as a "story map" including (1) main character(s), (2) main character's problem in the story, (3) attempts to solve the problem, (4) actual solution and resolution, and (5) lessons about life. Beck suggested that teachers first read the story, de-

TABLE 9.3   Questioning Scheme

Question Type	Level of Thinking	Purpose	First Words
Narrow			
Cognitive-memory	Knowledge	Recall Identify Observe Answer yes/no Define Name	Who What When Where
Convergent	Comprehension	Explain State relationships Compare Contrast	How Why Explain Compare Contrast
Broad			

Divergent	Application
	Analysis
	Synthesis
		Predict
		Hypothesize
		Infer
		Reconstruct
		Trace
		  alternatives
		Guess
			What if
			Suppose
			How do you
			  know
			How many ways
			Predict

Evaluative	Evaluation	Judge
		Give an
		  opinion
		Justify
		Choose
		Support
		Value
			What do you
			  think
			Do you agree
			Can you
			  support
			How do you
			  feel about

Source: Adapted from J. J. Gallagher, *Productive Thinking with Gifted Children, Cooperative Research Project No. 965,* Urbana, IL: Cooperative Research on Exceptional Children, University of Illinois (1965): 24–27.

velop a story map (important information in the story), and then create questions that focus children's attention on the content of the story map. During guided reading periods (instructional or remedial) ask questions that relate to the story map to help children identify what is important. Construct questions that not only stimulate and enrich comprehension, but also highlight essential story elements. Research also supports the use of questions in the pre-reading phase (Hansen 1981, Hansen and Pearson 1983). Questions asking students to predict story content and to relate predictions to their own experiences facilitate comprehension and recall.

Some researchers recommend alternatives to questioning for extending comprehension. Herber (1978), for example, uses statements rather than questions because he feels that questions give the impression of having one exact answer. This expectation greatly limits students' critical and creative thought. In Herber's method students are asked to accept or reject declarative statements according to textual information. All supportable responses are viewed as correct.

Herber views comprehension as a three-level process. Level 1 is the literal level, in which readers determine what the writer says. Level 2 is the interpretive level, in which readers use prior knowledge and literal information to infer what the author means. Level 3 is the applied level, in which readers search for broad principles or generalizations relating content and previously acquired concepts. The three levels of comprehension are used in the form of a three-level guide, which is a discussion tool for developing and extending comprehension. An example of Herber's method, based on "Binding the Wounds," follows. Children would be guided to find information in the text to support or dispute each statement.

CLASSROOM APPLICATION: THE HERBER GUIDE

Literal Level: What did the author say?

_____ There was a division between the North and the South.
_____ Reconstruction means rebuilding.
_____ Congressmen from the North disagreed with President Lincoln's plan for reconstruction.

Interpretive Level: What did the author mean?

_____ President Lincoln was not afraid to go against public opinion.
_____ The issue of slavery complicated Lincoln's reconstruction plans.
_____ President Lincoln's political views contributed to his death.

Applied Level: Do you agree based on the story and on what you know about life?

_____ True freedom is often difficult to achieve.
_____ Taking a stand for what you believe in can be extremely dangerous.
_____ In the midst of hope there is often despair.
_____ Being a leader can be very challenging.

The Herber guide can be used as a discussion aid until children become familiar with the process and adept at the critical reading skills required. The method can then be modified. For example, assign independent reading material and direct children to respond to the literal statements before coming to the reading group. Then discuss the interpretive and applied statements during the group reading period. Children might read a selection in the group, discuss some of the statements, and then respond to other statements in writing.

During the past five years, researchers have conducted studies to determine whether children can be trained to answer inferential questions appropriately (Hansen 1981, Gordon and Pearson 1983, Hansen and Pearson 1983, Holmes 1983, Hansen and Hubbard 1984). The research consistently shows that poor readers can be taught to draw inferences from print.

Gordon and Pearson (1983) created an inference training strategy that proved effective in significantly improving the inferential thinking abilities of poor readers. The strategy is based on four subskills of inference tasks:

- Asking the inferential question
- Answering the inferential question
- Finding the clues in the text that support the inference
- Telling how to get from the clues to the answer

The following example applies the subskills to a line of text reading, "Outside, the kites flew high in the sky."

- "What was the weather outside like?" (Ask the question.)
- "Windy." (Answer the question.)
- "The text said that the kites were flying high in the sky." (Provide textual support.)
- "I know that when kites are flying in the sky, the only thing that keeps them in the air is the wind. If the kites are flying high then, I know that there is a lot of wind outside. It is, therefore, windy." (Provide a line of reasoning.)

Gordon and Pearson designed an eight-week training strategy providing instruction in inferential thinking skills. The training was conducted in four stages.

In Stage One, the teacher assumed the responsibility of asking the questions, answering the questions, finding the clues, and identifying the lines of reasoning. This stage, then, was a modeling stage in which the teacher showed students how inferences are drawn. Example:

Teacher	What kind of weather is there outside? (Question)
Teacher	It is windy. (Answer)
Teacher	The text says "Outside the kites flew high in the sky." (Clues)
Teacher	I know that if kites are flying high, then the wind is holding them in the air; therefore, I know that it is windy. (Reasoning)

In Stage Two, the teacher asked and answered the question and students found the clues and provided the line of reasoning:

Teacher   What kind of weather is there outside? (Question)
Teacher   It is windy. Jane, read the clue that lets you know that it is windy. (Answer)
Student   Outside the kites flew high in the sky. (Clues)
Teacher   How does the clue lead you to the answer?
Student   Because I know that if the kites are flying high in the sky, then the wind is keeping them up. (Reasoning)

In Stage Three, the teacher asked the question, the students answered the question, the teacher found the clue and the students identified the line of reasoning:

Teacher   What kind of weather is there outside? (Question)
Student   It is windy. (Answer)
Teacher   Good. I see the clue on the page. The sentence says "Outside the kites flew high in the sky." Jane, how does this clue lead you to the answer? (Clue)
Student   Because I know that when kites are flying high, it is windy outside. (Reasoning)

In Stage Four, the teacher asked the question and the students did the rest:

Teacher   What kind of weather is there outside? (Question)
Student   It is windy. (Answer)
Student   Outside the kites flew high in the sky. (Clue)
Student   I know that when kites are high in the air, there is a lot of wind outside. (Reasoning)

Table 9.4 outlines the entire procedure. Notice that the teacher initially assumes the responsibility of modeling. Students are led to greater independence during each successive stage. The process of thinking must be modeled for children who have problems with inferential comprehension. Often, they simply do not know how to come up with the answer. Typically, these children continually hear the product of others' thought, but do not know the process leading to the product. Consider the following example.

Teacher   John, what kind of weather was it outside?
John   I don't know.
Teacher   Mary, do you know? (The teacher proceeds to a student who is sure to know the answer.)

TABLE 9.4   **Stages of Inference Training**

Stages	Ask Question	Answer Question	Add Clue	Provide Reasoning
1. Modeling	Teacher	Teacher	Teacher	Teacher
2. Guided Practice	Teacher	Teacher	Student	Student
3. Guided Practice	Teacher	Student	Teacher	Student
4. Independent Study	Teacher	Student	Student	Student

Source: Adapted from P. D. Pearson, "Changing the Face of Reading Comprehension Instruction," *The Reading Teacher* 38 (April 1985), 731. Used with permission of P. David Pearson and the International Reading Association.

Mary   It is windy outside
Teacher   Good job, Mary. It is windy outside. Now let's keep on reading.

While John has received the product of Mary's thinking, he does not know the process Mary used to come up with the correct answer. He now knows two things for sure. He failed again, and Mary was right again. The next time that John is asked an inferential question, the product of Mary's thought ("It is windy") will be useless to him, because the question will pertain to different content. John needs to know how to produce the appropriate product. He needs not only to be shown the process, but to be provided with multiple opportunities for practicing his newly acquired skill.

Another training strategy comes from Raphael (1984), who conducted a study on training children to locate information and find answers in text. Three response situations were taught:

1. Both the question and the answer came from the same sentence in the text.
2. The question and the answer came from different parts of the text.
3. The question came from the text, but the answer came from readers based on their experiences.

Raphael trained children to label the first situation, "right there," the second, "think and search," and the third, "on my own." Consider the following example.

Text   Carol was so excited. She lay in bed, eyes open, mind racing, unable to sleep. She just knew that she would be

awake all night long. Tomorrow was Christmas day, her
favorite day of the year.

Question Who was excited?
Location of information: Right there (Carol was so excited.)

Question Why was Carol excited?
Location of information: Think and search (Carol was
so excited. . . . Tomorrow was Christmas Day.)

Question Why was Carol excited about Christmas Day?
Location of information: On My Own (Tomorrow was
Christmas Day. On Christmas I get lots of presents and
that's exciting. I bet Carol was excited because she was
going to get lots of presents too.)

Children learned to identify questions as right there, think and
search, or on my own questions. When children classified the question-
answer relationship, they were asked to justify their choice. The four sub-
tasks included ask the question, answer the question, classify the
question-answer relationship, and justify the classification. Children
were first told that the answer to a question can be found in one of three
places: (1) in one word or phrase in the text, (2) in more than one place in
the text, or (3) in their own minds. Then the labels (right there, think and
search, on my own) were taught using many examples. Children received
intensive training in the classification. The teacher first modeled the sub-
tasks. For example:

Teacher Who was excited? (Question)
Teacher Carol was excited. (Answer)
Teacher This fits in the "Right There" category. (Classification)
Teacher I know it fits in this category because the answer is right
there in the sentence, "Carol was so excited." (Justifica-
tion)

The teacher then provided guided and independent practice as in the
Gordon and Pearson inference training strategy. Finally, the students
were encouraged to construct and answer their own questions. Table 9.5
outlines the entire procedure.

Raphael found that students of all ability and grade levels who
learned this strategy better understood new textual material. The importance of training remedial readers in inferential thinking strategies cannot be overemphasized. Recent research shows that teachers tend to treat
higher and lower reading groups differently (McDermott 1978, Au 1980).
Teachers ask children in higher reading groups higher-level questions
and require more indepth discussion. Teachers of children in low reading groups, on the other hand, seldom ask them to read, frequently drill
them in decoding and pronunciation, and ask them primarily low-level

TABLE 9.5 Stages of Question-Answer Relationship Training

Stages	Ask Question	Answer Question	Question-Answer Relationship Classification	Justification
1. Modeling	Teacher	Teacher	Teacher	Teacher
2. Guided Practice	Teacher	Teacher	Teacher	Student
3. Guided Practice	Teacher	Teacher	Student	Student
4. Independent Practice	Teacher	Student	Student	Student
5. True Independence	Student	Student	Student	Student

Source: Adapted from P. D. Pearson, "Changing the Face of Reading Comprehension Instruction," *The Reading Teacher* 38 (April 1985), 731. Used with permission of P. David Pearson and the International Reading Association.

questions. The children least likely to have opportunities to develop higher-level comprehension skills are those who most desperately need those skills. Because of this, teachers of poor readers must give priority to the instruction of comprehension and higher-level thinking skills.

Develop Children's Metacognitive Skills

Metacognition refers to individuals' knowledge of and control over their thinking and learning. Metacognition involves not only a tacit knowing, but the ability of individuals to discuss their knowing process (Kavale and Schreiner 1979; Brown 1980, 1982; Bransford et al. 1980; Brown et al. 1981; McGee 1982; Ehrlich and Rayner 1983; Baker and Brown 1984; Meyer 1984).

Two forms of metacognition have particular bearing on remediation in comprehension. These are the awareness learners have of their behavior during reading, and the strategies learners use to regulate and monitor their reading. Both forms are crucial for learning from print. Research demonstrates that poor readers use metacognitive skills less often than good readers. Poor readers seldom monitor their reading activities (Adams 1980). They make more meaning-distorting errors and fewer spontaneous corrections of their errors (Kavale and Schreiner 1979, Clay 1973), infrequently question themselves about content (Andre and Anderson 1979, Collins et al. 1980), and have difficulty reading for different purposes (Forrest and Waller 1979). The research suggests that teachers should directly instruct children in metacognitive skills, especially less efficient readers.

Teachers can use several strategies to develop children's metacognitive skills. Discussion and application of three main strategies follow.

Teach Children to Read for Different Purposes.   Skimming, scanning, and close reading are three different monitoring strategies. Skimming refers to the ability to go through a selection quickly to determine general information such as the overall content and general point of view. In skimming a selection, readers read the title, major headings, the first and last sentences in each paragraph, italicized or boldtype words, illustrations and captions. They also look at the pictures, charts, or graphs.

Skimming helps readers to gain general information. In teaching the skill, teachers might ask questions like the following.

- Is the selection you are going to read fiction (true) or nonfiction (made up)? How do you know?
- Will the selection you are going to read help in writing a report on . . . ? How do you know?

Scanning refers to the ability to locate specific information very quickly. In helping readers develop systematic scanning strategies, ask the following questions.

- Look at the index of a book. In what chapter would you find . . . ? How did you find out?
- Look at a page of print. What is the name of the person you will be reading about? How did you find out?
- What town is the setting? What did you do to find out?
- In what year was the story set? What clues did you use?

Notice that asking "How do you know?" allows children to verbalize helpful clues. Children who do not know the strategies can hear the process used to find the answer.

Thomas and Robinson (1982) identify three levels of scanning:

Level 1: Scanning for information that stands out readily (dates, names, numbers, etc.) to answer questions such as "In what year did the war begin?"

Level 2: Scanning for an answer that contains the same words as the question, such as "Does the tribe depend on fishing or hunting for its survival?"

Level 3: Scanning for an answer that requires different words from the question, such as "Can you find any support for the idea that the people were angry?"

Teachers can develop children's scanning abilities by asking them to find specific facts in a limited time. Many expository selections are appropriate for practicing this strategy. At the start of training, use the first level of scanning, and introduce the other levels as children gain confidence and success. If students cannot perform the strategies, the teacher should model the process.

Close reading refers to the process of reading connected discourse for understanding and discussion. Use the following strategies.

- Prereading techniques: scanning, using structural prediction, formulating predictions and questions, and reading to check predictions and answer questions.
- Reading techniques: continuous interaction, self-monitoring, self-questioning, and self-correcting.
- Postreading techniques: reflecting on content, clarifying questions by rereading and discussion.

Children need to be taught to perform these tasks and to know the purposes for which each task is appropriate.

Teach Children Self-Monitoring and Self-Correction Skills.   If you have worked with remedial readers, you know they tend to ignore errors that completely destroy the flow of meaning. They seem unable to monitor their comprehension, to recognize when meaning is absent, or to take corrective action to restore comprehension. This behavior reflects a lack of interaction with print and with content, which might partly be the result of a child's history of failure.

Teachers must teach children to monitor their comprehension and to correct themselves when errors distort meaning. When children make such errors, allow them to finish the sentence. If they do not correct themselves, stop them and ask, "Did that make sense?" If the child does not know, repeat exactly what the child read. "Listen to what you read. . . . Did that make sense?" Provide and explain miscalled words that are not in the child's listening vocabulary. This "forced" monitoring for meaning is necessary and should be provided consistently. When the child identifies a sense-making word, help the child use sense (context) in conjunction with word attack strategies to confirm the prediction. Teachers might remind children of strategies to use when they come to a word they do not know. These strategies include spelling the word; using context; skipping the word, finishing the sentence, and then returning to the unknown word; blocking the parts that are known; and sounding out the word. Consider the following example. The selection might read:

> The day was very hot.
> Susan was happy that
> she was going swimming
> in the lake with her
> friend Mary.

The child read:

> The day was very hot.
> Susan was happy that
> she was going swimming
> in the *lak* with her
> friend Mary.

Teacher Did that make sense?
Child   Yes.
Teacher Listen to what you read. "Susan was happy that she was going swimming in the *lak* with her friend Mary." Did that make sense?
Child   No.
Teacher What word did not make sense?
Child   *Lak.*
Teacher What might make sense there?
Child   *Lake.*
Teacher Look at that word. Could that word be *lake*?
Child   Yes.
Teacher Good job. Notice the *e* at the end of the word. It makes the *a* have a long sound. *L, a, k, e* is *lake*. Let's read the sentence again.

As the child gains practice in self-correction, the number of clues can be reduced. "Did that make sense?" might be all that is required. As you train children in self-correction, watch for spontaneous self-corrections to encourage and praise. Before children read silently, review the strategies so children can transfer them to independent reading.

Teach Children to Verbalize Their Strategies.   As children become independent in their use of appropriate strategies, help them to verbalize the processes. For example, ask questions like the following.

- What are you going to do before you start reading a selection? (structural prediction)
- What are you going to do when you are reading and you find a word you do not know? (spell, block, etc.)
- What are you going to do when you read something that doesn't make sense? (Go back and make it make sense.)
- What should you do if you are reading silently and you don't understand what you are reading? (Stop, go back, and reread.)

Train Children in Fluency

Fluency is important in reading comprehension, as previously explained. Fluency is not speed, but reading in the phrasing and pace of natural speech. Reading in natural linguistic units, such as meaningful phrase units, is termed "chunking." Consider the following example of a selection in its original and "chunked" forms.

Original Form

Once upon a time there was an old man who lived in a little house at the edge of a forest. He lived with his wife Sarah and his faithful dog Pedro. They were very poor but very happy.

Chunked Form

Once upon a time / there was / an old man / who lived / in a little house / at the edge / of a forest. / He lived / with his wife Sarah / and his / faithful dog Pedro. / They were / very poor / but very happy.

Listening to poor readers read orally, you can easily hear their inappropriate chunking. They tend to read word by word. Research shows that when passages are divided into meaningful chunks, if children have practice in reading pre-chunked passages, then children comprehend better and chunk material more appropriately on their own (Brozo et al. 1983). Stevens (1981) suggested that teachers read chunked material with children, discuss the segments, and then help children to chunk new material. A discussion of five main strategies for improving phrasing and fluency follows.

Provide Systematic Phrase Instruction.   One reason children read word by word is that they receive much of their instruction in that way. Teachers teach isolated vocabulary items, ignoring larger, more meaningful units. Remedial readers benefit from phrase instruction. Manning (1980) recommends that teachers give systematic phrase instruction not only by preteaching target words but also the phrases that include the target words. Consider the following example.

CLASSROOM APPLICATION

Ribbit's mother laid her eggs among the soft slimy weeds of the bottom of a large fresh water lake. She laid more than 1,500 eggs at one time. The eggs were very close together. Being close together protected the tiny eggs. Inside one of those tiny eggs was Ribbit. Of course, he didn't look like he does now. He started out as a tiny speck of life inside a tiny shell.

Target Words for Preinstruction

laid
bottom
close
protected
speck

Phrases for Preinstruction

laid her eggs
at the *bottom*
very *close* together
protected the tiny eggs
speck of life

Children exposed to phrase instruction develop more appropriate eye spans and learn to expect phrases rather than isolated words. As they feed larger, more meaningful chunks into short-term memory, children better succeed in comprehension.

Encourage Children to Read Fluently and with Expression.   The key to developing fluency is letting children know what "good reading" sounds like and that you expect it of them. Remind children before oral reading that there are two kinds of reading: choppy, meaningless reading, and smooth, meaningful reading. Model both kinds, and tell children to try for smooth, meaningful reading during the session.

As children read, help them monitor their reading by such questions as Did that sound smooth to you? Did your reading make sense to you? Do you think you could read that again more smoothly? "Would (a character) have said that the way you did? Can you make it sound the way (a character) would have said it? Praise and encourage children when they do read fluently and when they realize they read poorly and correct themselves.

Use Echoic Reading.   Echoic reading is particularly helpful to nonfluent readers. In this activity the teacher reads a section of print and a child rereads the section attempting to match the teacher's accuracy, fluency, and expression. The rationale for this strategy is that poor readers seldom hear good models. They daily hear the poor oral reading of other children.

In reading a section, the teacher provides the appropriate word attack, fluency, and expression for students to imitate, or echo. Extended use of echoic reading helps poor readers to read more fluently with more appropriate expression (Manning 1980). Consider carefully the length of the passage. It should be long enough so that children cannot recall it from memory, but short enough for children to retain words and expressions and to use memory in decoding the text well. With some practice, teachers can determine the appropriate passage length for individual children. In using echoic reading, ensure that children look at the text as you read. Children will intuitively look up at you as you read, and unless they look at the print, they will lose the benefits of echoic reading. Use echoic reading during oral reading when children read non-fluently with poor expression, as in the following example.

Text   Camile opened the door and went outdoors. The air smelled fresh and clean.

Child	Camile / opened / the / door / and went / outside the / air / smelled / fresh / and / clean. /
Teacher	Did that sound smooth to you, Helen?
Child	No.
Teacher	You said most of the words really well, but your reading was slow and choppy. Follow along as I read it for you; then you can read it again.

Incorporate Repeated Reading into Your Instructional Program. Repeated reading refers to the strategy of practicing a selection until fluency is achieved. The procedure includes the following steps: Choose a short paragraph of 50 to 250 words depending on the grade level. Ensure that the passage is written at the children's instructional level, such as a passage children have already read for comprehension.

- Have the child read the passage. As the child reads, record the time taken to finish.
- Discuss any errors.
- Have the child practice reading the selection until completion time is reduced by at least one third, preferably by one half.

Children might record reading times to monitor their own progress. Repeated reading gives children the opportunity to practice a selection until they read fluently and expressively. Stress fluency rather than speed, and use this strategy for individual instruction.

Use Instructional Repeated Reading.   Instructional repeated reading is a modification of the repeated reading strategy. The modification addresses the needs of children who focus solely on print, disregard syntax and semantics, ignore context clues that make reading predictable, fail to self-correct, and read slowly in a detached and labored manner (Swaby 1982). The instructional repeated reading strategy includes the following steps:

- Choose a short passage written on the child's instructional level. Make copies of the passage for the child and for yourself. Choose material the child has already read for comprehension or ensure that the content is well within the child's conceptual abilities.
- Divide the passage into two to four paragraphs or segments. If the child previously read the material, review the major concepts. If the material is new, discuss the major concepts briefly.
- Have the child read the first segment aloud. On your copy, record each error and keep track of the time the child takes to finish. Be sure to note all miscues accurately.
- After the child finishes, reread the segment sentence by sentence exactly as the child read it. The child follows along and tries to discover and correct all the miscues.

- Help the child analyze each discovered error. Discuss the reasons for specific errors, and have the child contrast miscues with the correct word. Direct the child to use context clues. For example, the child might read, "John sat down on the *care* and pulled it up to the table." Point out the semantic clue "sat down," and ask the child to think of things to sit down on. Point out the *ch* combination as a phonetic clue to combine with semantic clues such as "pulled it up to the table." The child can discover how to avoid miscues by analyzing them in this way.
- After the miscues have been detected and analyzed, have the child reread the segment as fluently as possible. Aim for shorter reading time, fewer miscues, more frequent self-correction, and greater expression.

This strategy has proven effective in increasing fluency and the use of multiple clues in reading (Swaby 1982).

Encourage Visualization

Research solidly establishes the importance of visualization or mental imagery in reading comprehension. The ability to create visual images while reading and to describe images in detail enhances comprehension and involvement in print. Kulhavy and Swenson (1975) studied imagery in 119 fifth and sixth grade children. They read a twenty-paragraph text to the children and instructed half the group to draw detailed pictures of what they heard. Results showed that the children who were told to create images outperformed the others.

Pressley (1976) taught third graders to construct mental pictures from read sentences and paragraphs. Compared to a control group, children who were taught to visualize content consistently remembered more information. Mayer (1980) found that visualization helped secondary students not only to remember more technical content, but to better draw inferences.

Instruction and practice in visualization should be used in teaching remedial readers. In both oral and silent reading encourage children to build pictures as they read. Children with severe comprehension problems may need to stop at the end of each sentence to build and discuss pictures. As accuracy increases, increase the length of passages.

SUMMARY   Comprehension should be the major focus in reading instruction. The development of comprehension includes many factors. Teachers should prepare children by providing necessary concepts, eliciting previously acquired concepts, clarifying unfamiliar vocabulary, building motivation and interest, and stimulating prediction of content. Teachers should promote interaction with and comprehension of text by continuing prediction, having children retrieve facts, questioning children to develop their thinking and inferential comprehension skills, stressing fluency, and encouraging visualization. Finally, teachers should extend children's understanding and motivation by elaborating on the material they read and by helping them use information in a variety of situations.

Research in reading instruction indicates that educators need to review their instructional priorities. While the educational system admirably teaches decoding and literal recall of information, it falls short in the teaching of inferential thinking, a cornerstone of comprehension. Comprehension must be taught to children through modeling and training. Priorities in instruction must shift from having children merely regurgitate details to helping them develop, recognize, use, and extend their thinking abilities as they practice reading tasks. The strategies presented in this chapter are designed to help teachers build, enhance, and remediate children's comprehension skills during all phases of reading instruction.

R·E·F·E·R·E·N·C·E·S

Adams, M. J. "Models of word recognition." *Cognitive Psychology* 11 (1979): 133–176.
———. "Failures to Comprehend and Levels of Processing in Reading." In R. J. Spiro, B. C. Bruce, and W. F. Brewer, eds. *Theoretical Issues in Reading Comprehension.* Hillside, NJ: Erlbaum, 1980.
Adams, M., and B. Bruce. *Background Knowledge and Reading Comprehension, Reading Educational Report No. 13.* Urbana, IL: Center for Study of Reading, 1980.
Adams, M. J., and A. Collins. "A Schema–Theoretical View of Reading." In R. O. Freedle, ed. *New Directions in Discourse Processing,* Vol. 2. Norwood, NJ: Ablex, 1979.
Anderson, R. C., and R. W. Kulhavy. "Imagery and prose learning." *Journal of Educational Psychology* 63 (1972): 242–243.
Andre, M. D. A., and T. H. Anderson. "The development and evaluation of a self-questioning study technique." *Reading Research Quarterly* 14 (1979): 605–623.
Au, K. "A test of the social organizational hypothesis: Relationships between participation, structures and learning to read." Ph.D. dissertation, University of Illinois, 1980.
Ausubel, D. P. "The use of advance organizers in learning and retention of meaningful material." *Journal of Educational Psychology* 51 (1960): 267–272.

Baker, L., and A. L. Brown. "Metacognitive Skills and Reading." In P. D. Pearson, ed. *Handbook of Reading Research*. New York: Longman, 1984.

Beck, I. L. "Developing Comprehension: The Impact of the Directed Reading Lesson." In R. Anderson, J. Osborn and R. Tierney, eds. *Learning to Read in American Schools: Basal Readers and Content Texts*. Hillsdale, NJ: Erlbaum, 1984.

Beck, I. L., M. G. McKeown, E. S. McCaslin, and A. M. Burkes. *Instructional Dimensions That May Affect Reading Comprehension: Examples from Two Commercial Reading Programs*. Pittsburgh, PA: University of Pittsburgh Learning Research and Developmental Center, 1979.

Beck, I. L., R. C. Omanson, and M. G. McKeown. "An instructional redesign of reading lessons: Effects of comprehension." *Reading Research Quarterly* 17 (1982): 462–481.

Beck, I. L., C. A. Perfetti, and M. G. McKeown. "The effects of long-term vocabulary instruction on lexical access and reading comprehension." *Journal of Educational Psychology* 74 (1982): 506–521.

Bloom, B. S., M. D. Engelhart, E. J. Furst, W. H. Hill, and D. R. Krathwohl. *Taxonomy of Educational Objectives: Handbook I, Cognitive Domain*. New York: Longman, 1956.

Bransford, J. D., B. S. Stein, T. S. Shelton, and R. A. Owings. "Cognition and Adaptation: The Importance of Learning to Learn." In J. Harvey, ed. *Cognition, Social Behavior and the Environment*. Hillsdale, NJ: Erlbaum, 1980.

Brown, A. L. "Metacognitive Development and Reading." In R. J. Spiro, B. C. Bruce, and W. F. Brewer, eds. *Theoretical Issues in Reading Comprehension*. Hillsdale, NJ: Erlbaum, 1980.

———. "Learning How to Learn from Reading." In J. A. Langer and M. T. Smith–burke, eds. *Reader Meets Author: Bridging the Gap*. Newark, DE: International Reading Association, 1982.

Brown, A. L., J. C. Campione, and J. Day. "Learning to learn: On training students to learn from texts." *Educational Researcher* 10 (1981): 14–21.

Brozo, W. G., R. V. Schmelzer, and H. A. Spires. "The beneficial effect of chunking on good readers' comprehension of expository prose." *Journal of Reading* 26 (February 1983): 442–445.

Bruce, B. "What makes a good story?" *Language Arts* 55 (1978): 460–466.

Burmeister, L. *Foundations and Strategies for Teaching Children to Read*. Reading, MA: Addison–Wesley, 1983.

Cassidy, J. "Grey power in the reading program: A direction for the eighties." *The Reading Teacher* 35 (December 1981): 287–291.

Clay, M. *Reading: The Patterning of Complex Behavior*. Auckland, NZ: Heinemann, 1973.

Collins, A., J. S. Brown, and K. M. Larkin. "Inference in Text Understanding." In R. J. Spiro, B. C. Bruce, and W. F. Brewer, eds. *Theoretical Issues in Reading Comprehension*. Hillsdale, NJ: Erlbaum, 1980.

Durkin, D. "What classroom observations reveal about reading comprehension instruction." *Reading Research Quarterly* 14 (1979): 481–533.

———. "Reading comprehension instruction in five basal reading series." *Reading Research Quarterly* 16 (1981): 515–544.

Eeds, M. "What to do when they don't understand what they read: Research based strategies for teaching reading comprehension." *The Reading Teacher* 34 (February 1981): 565–571.

Ehrlich, K., and K. Rayner. "Pronoun assignment and semantic integration during reading: Eye movements and immediacy of processing." *Journal of Verbal Learning and Verbal Behavior* 22 (1983): 75–87.

Enfield, M. L., and V. Greene. *Project Read: Report Form and Story Form Reading Guide.* Bloomington, MN: Language Circle Enterprises, 1987.

Forrest, D. L., and T. G. Waller. "Cognitive and Metacognitive Aspects of Reading." Paper presented at the meeting of the Society for Research in Child Development, San Francisco, March, 1979.

Gallagher, J. *Productive Thinking with Gifted Children.* Cooperative Research Project No. 965. Urbana, IL: Cooperative Research on Exceptional Children, University of Illinois, 1965.

Goodman, K. "What We Know About Reading." In P. D. Allen and D. J. Watson, eds. *Findings of Research in Miscue Analysis: Classroom Applications.* Urbana, IL: National Council of Teachers of English, 1976.

Gordon, C., and P. D. Pearson. *Effects of Instruction in Metacomprehension and Inferences on Students' Comprehension Abilities, Technical Report No. 269.* Urbana, IL: University of Illinois, 1983.

Gough, P. G. "One Second of Reading." In J. F. Kavanagh and I. G. Mattingly, eds. *Language by Ear and by Eye.* Cambridge, MA: M.I.T. Press, 1972.

Guthrie, J. T. "How we understood the news." *Journal of Reading* 23 (1979): 162–164.

Hansen, J. "The effects of inference training and practice on young children's comprehension." *Reading Research Quarterly* 16 (1981): 391–417.

Hansen, J., and R. Hubbard. "Poor readers can draw inferences." *The Reading Teacher* 37 (March 1984): 586–589.

Hansen, J., and P. D. Pearson. "An instructional study: Improving the inferential comprehension of good and poor fourth-grade readers." *Journal of Educational Psychology* 75 (1983): 821–829.

Hayes, D. A., and R. J. Tierney. "Developing readers' knowledge through analogy." *Reading Research Quarterly* (1982): 256–280.

Herber, H. *Teaching Reading in the Content Areas.* Englewood Cliffs, NJ: Prentice–Hall, 1978.

Holmes, B. C. "A confirmation strategy for improving poor readers' ability to answer inferential questions." *The Reading Teacher* 37 (November 1983): 144–148.

Isakson, R. L., and J. W. Miller. "Sensitivity to syntactic and semantic cues in good and poor comprehenders." *Journal of Educational Psychology* 68 (1976): 787–792.

Johnson, D. D. *Three Sound Strategies for Vocabulary Development. Occasional Paper No. 3.* Lexington, MA: Ginn, 1983.

Johnson, D. D., and P. D. Pearson. *Teaching Reading Vocabulary*, 2nd ed. New York: Holt, Rinehart, & Winston, 1984.

Kavale, K., and R. Schreiner. "The reading process of above average and average readers. A comparison of the use of reasoning strategies in responding to standardized comprehension measures." *Reading Research Quarterly* 15 (1979): 102–128.

Kulhavy, R. W., and I. Swenson. "Imagery instructions and the comprehension of text." *British Journal of Educational Psychology* 45 (1975): 47–51.

LaBerge, D., and S. J. Samuels, "Toward a theory of automatic information processing in reading." *Cognitive Psychology* (1974): 293–323.

Langer, J. A., and M. Nicolich. "Prior knowledge and its relationship to comprehension." *Journal of Reading Behavior* 13 (Winter 1981): 373–379.

Lesgold, A. M., C. McCormick, and R. M. Golinkoff. "Imagery training and children's prose learning." *Journal of Educational Psychology* 67 (1975): 663–667.

Lindsay, P. H., and D. A. Norman. *Human Information Processing: An Introduction to Psychology*, 2nd ed. New York: Academic Press, 1977.

Manning, J. C. *Reading: Learning and Instructional Processes.* Geneva, IL: Paladin House, 1980.

Mayer, R. C. "Elaboration techniques that increase the meaningfulness of technical text. An experimental test of the learning strategy hypothesis." *Journal of Educational Psychology* 72 (1980): 770–784.

McDermott, R. D. "Some Reasons for Focusing on Classrooms in Reading Research." In P. D. Pearson and J. Hansen, eds. *Reading: Disciplined Inquiry in Process and Practice.* Clemson, SC: National Reading Conference, 1978.

McGee, L. M. "Awareness of text structure: Effects on children's recall of expository text." *Reading Research Quarterly* 17 (1982): 581–590.

———. "The Influence of Metacognitive Knowledge of Expository Text on Discourse Recall." In J. Niles and L. Harris, eds. *New Inquiries in Reading Research and Instruction.* Rochester, NY: National Reading Conference, 1982.

McGee, L. M., and D. J. Richgels. "Teaching expository text structure to elementary students." *The Reading Teacher* 38 (April 1985): 739–748.

———. "Attending to Text Structure: A Comprehension Strategy." In E. K. Dishner, T. W. Bean, and J. E. Readence, eds. *Reading in the Content Areas: Improving Classroom Instruction*, 2nd ed. Dubuque, IA: Kendall Hunt, 1986.

Meyer, B. J. F., "Organizational Aspects of Text: Effects on Reading Comprehension and Applications for the Classroom." In J. Flood, ed. *Promoting Reading Comprehension*. Newark, DE: International Reading Association, 1984.

Meyer, B. J. F., and R. O. Freedle. "Effects of discourse type on recall." *American Educational Research Journal* 21 (Spring 1984): 121–143.

Reading in America: A Perspective on Two Assessments. Denver, CO: National Assessment of Educational Progress, 1981.

Nezworski, T., N. L. Stein, and T. Trabasso. "Story structure versus control effects on children's recall and evaluative inferences." *Journal of Verbal Learning and Verbal Behavior* 21 (1982): 196–206.

Pearson, P. D. "Changing the face of reading comprehension instruction." *The Reading Teacher* 38 (April 1985): 724–738.

Pearson, P. D., and R. J. Spiro. "Toward a theory of reading comprehension instruction." *Topics in Language Disorders* 1 (1981): 71–78.

Pressley, G. M. "Mental imagery helps eight-year-olds remember what they read." *Journal of Educational Psychology* 68 (1976): 355–359.

Raphael, T. E. "Teaching learners about sources of information for answering questions." *Journal of Reading* 27 (January 1984): 303–311.

Rumelhart, D. E. *Toward an Interactive Model of Reading, Report No. 56*. San Diego, CA: Center for Human Information Processing, March 1976.

Sadow, M. "The use of story grammar in the design of questions." *The Reading Teacher* 35 (February 1982): 518–522.

Samuels, S. J. "Automatic decoding and reading comprehension." *Language Arts* 53 (1976): 323–325.

Shantz, M. "Briefs: Readability." *Language Arts* 58 (1981): 943–944.

Singer, H., and D. Donlan. "Active comprehension: Problem solving schema with question generation for comprehension of complex short stories." *Reading Research Quarterly* 17 (1982): 166–186.

Smith, F. *Understanding Reading: A Psycholinguistic Analysis of Reading and Learning to Read*. New York: Holt, Rinehart & Winston, 1982.

Spache, G. D. *Diagnostic Reading Scales*, Revised Ed. Monterey, CA: McGraw–Hill, 1972.

Stefferson, M. S., C. Joag–Dev, and R. D. Anderson. "A cross-cultural perspective on reading comprehension." *Reading Research Quarterly* 15 (1979): 10–29.

Stein, N. L., and C. G. Glenn. "An Analysis of Story Comprehension in Elementary School Children." In R. R. Freedle, ed. *New Directions in Discourse Processing*, Vol. 2. Hillside, NJ: Erlbaum, 1979.

Stevens, K. C. "Chunking material as an aid to reading comprehension." *Journal of Reading* 25 (November 1981): 126–129.

Strange, M. "Instructional implications of a conceptual theory of reading comprehension." *The Reading Teacher* 33 (January 1980): 391–397.

Swaby, B. "Using repeated readings to develop fluency and accuracy." *The Reading Teacher* 36 (December 1982): 317–318.

————. *Teaching and Learning Reading: A Pragmatic Approach.* Boston: Little, Brown, 1984.

Taylor, B. M., and R. W. Beach. "Effects of text structure: Instruction on middle-grade students' comprehension and production of expository text." *Reading Research Quarterly* 19 (1984): 147–161.

Taylor, B. M., and S. J. Samuels. "Children's use of text structure in the recall of expository material." *American Educational Research Journal* 20 (Winter 1983): 517–528.

Thomas, E. L., and H. A. Robinson. *Improving Reading in Every Class: A Source Book for Teachers.* Boston: Allyn and Bacon, 1982.

Weaver, L. *Psycholinguistics and Reading: From Process to Practice.* Cambridge, MA: Winthrop, 1980.

Weber, R. M. "A linguistic analysis of first grade reading errors." *Reading Research Quarterly* 5 (1970): 427–451.

Whaley, J. "Story grammars and reading instruction." *The Reading Teacher* 34 (April 1981): 762–771.

10 Remediating Skills in Phonic Analysis

FOCUS   1. Why do children fail in word attack skills?
QUESTIONS   2. How do inductive and deductive phonic instruction differ?
      3. What is the function of phonematic training, and how is it used to remediate faulty phonic skills?
      4. How does the skill instruction model described in this chapter reflect psycholinguistic thought?
      5. What is the relationship between reading connected discourse and developing phonic skills?

A predictable characteristic of remedial readers is their failure to master phonic elements in reading. Instructing children in the phonic skills is one of the most important yet frustrating tasks in the teaching of reading. A listing of the factors contributing to this frustration follows.

- In many traditional reading programs, skills are presented a specific number of times. No adjustments are made for children who need less or more exposure to certain skills. Many children with slower learning rates or other problems require more time for awareness, instruction, and practice.
- Many reading programs employ one instructional strategy in the introduction, practice, and review phases of skill teaching. Adjustments are seldom made for children who cannot learn with that strategy.
- Instruction in skills often lacks thoroughness. Many children quickly forget information that teachers thought they learned.
- Skills are often introduced and practiced in isolation. Many children can "do" skills on a workbook or skill page, but cannot apply them in real reading situations.
- Several strategies exist for decoding words, including phonic analysis. Many programs overemphasize some decoding strategies and underemphasize others. Consequently, children's options for word recognition and analysis are limited.
- Skill instruction is often provided in contexts that have little or no meaning for some children. As a result, they learn little and forget quickly.

In the skill component of the reading program, more than in any other component, success depends on the teacher's willingness and ability to respond to children's needs and characteristics and to modify instruction accordingly.

PRINCIPLES OF SKILL INSTRUCTION

Certain pedagogical principles are fundamental to the successful teaching of skills. These principles help to ensure maximum learning, comprehension, retention, and use of skills. Skills should be presented in the most meaningful contexts. Introducing and demonstrating skills in isolation or in single-sentence contexts is inadequate for providing the concepts necessary for learning. According to DeCecco and Crawford (1974), meaningful material is more rapidly learned than meaningless material and is also remembered for a longer period of time. Although phonic skills might sometimes be isolated, they should be couched in meaningful language. Teachers should assist children in applying skills (Weaver 1988). Vacca, Vacca, and Gove (1987, 219) underscored this point in the following statement:

> Phonic instruction should occur in meaningful language situations. In day-to-day instructional routines, however, phonics has a tendency to get overemphasized in many classrooms. Teachers sometimes find themselves spending an inordinate amount of time on phonics skill sessions that are isolated from continuous, meaningful text. Many lament that they are unable to find the time for their students to practice the application of phonic knowledge to relevant reading material. As a result, youngsters can easily form the wrong message about phonics: reading = phonics or sounding out words.

Skills must be taught thoroughly, particularly to children with learning difficulties or slow learning rates. Children often fail when too many skills are taught too superficially and too rapidly. Cronbach (1977) states that the key to reducing failure in learning is solid, thorough, and meaningful initial learning.

In addition to teaching skills thoroughly, teachers should intentionally give children extra practice in immediately applying newly learned skills in real reading situations. Often, children learn a skill, practice it briefly in a workbook, and days later encounter the skill in actual reading. By then they have probably forgotten the skill or have no idea how it relates to the reading situation. Children must practice a new skill immediately, and the teacher must draw their attention to its application.

Capturing children's attention is essential for skill instruction. Children having the most difficulty in skill learning are often the least attentive. They miss essential information on a daily basis. Simple strategies for getting children's attention include the following:

1. Do not start instruction until you have everyone's full attention. Say "I will know you are ready when your eyes are on me," or "John isn't quite ready. Let's wait until he is."
2. Group the children around an uncluttered table. Make sure they

have nothing in their hands. Distribute pencils, texts, paper, or workbooks only when needed.

3. Separate disruptive children and seat them close to you.

4. Write any needed examples on the chalkboard before calling children to the reading group. If you spend time writing on the chalkboard during the session, the most disruptive child will set the tone.

5. As much as possible, involve the children kinesthetically in learning. For example, have them point to, circle, underline, trace in the air or on the table, or mark information. Try to involve all children simultaneously. For example, provide each child with a pair of "yes/no" cards. As you teach letter-sound relations (i.e., words that begin with the sound /t/), have children respond by holding up the appropriate card.

The three basic phases of skill development are the cognitive awareness phase (children become conceptually aware of the task), the accuracy phase (children practice the task until they achieve mastery or minimize error), and the automatic phase (children overlearn the skill and perform it without conscious effort or overt attention). Researchers often cite the importance of reaching the automatic level in learning. In fact, fluent reading depends on readers' abilities to perform decoding skills automatically (Samuels 1976, Chapman and Hoffman 1977, Calfee and Pointkowski 1981, Chall 1983a). Teachers should move children through each phase of skill development with the aim of helping them to achieve automatic skill performance in reading.

PHONIC CLUES

Readers use a variety of clues to recognize words during reading. An outline of these clues follows.

1. Sight vocabulary clues
   a. Structure words
   b. Content words
2. Meaning clues
   a. Anticipatory
   b. Contextual
   c. Illustrative
3. Visual clues
   a. Configurations
   b. Salient features
4. Structural clues
   a. Affixes
   b. Compounds

5. Phonic clues
    a. Initial single consonants
    b. Final single consonants
    c. Short vowels
    d. Long vowels
    e. Vowel teams
    f. Initial and final consonant combinations
    g. Blending
6. Dictionary clues
    a. Pronunciation
    b. Meaning

This chapter focuses on phonic clues, which provide information about the relationships between letters and the sounds they represent. Readers use phonic clues to match sounds with specific written symbols. Readers can use phonic clues when they learn symbol-sound relationships through direct instruction or by abstraction from direct experience with print. Phonic clues provide vital information in the decoding of print. They also give readers significant independence in the decoding of unknown words (Beck 1981, Chall 1983a, Johnson and Baumann 1984).

The importance of effective phonic instruction was underscored by the report of the Commission on Reading, *Becoming a Nation of Readers* (Anderson et al. 1985). The commission was established in 1983 by the National Academy of Education. It was charged with the task of summarizing the knowledge gained from two decades of research on reading and determining its implications for reading instruction. The report concludes that an early phonic emphasis facilitates word identification, and strongly recommends that children receive intensive, clear phonic instruction from the very start of reading. The report also suggests that from the start of instruction, children should be given all of the elements necessary for constructing meaning.

Phonic instruction centers on teaching children the rules governing letter-sound relationships (Durkin 1987). Major emphasis is placed on the following content:

1. Initial single consonants and the sounds they represent (emphasized in Grade 1): *b, d, f, h, j, k, l, m, n, p, r, s, t, v, w, x, y,* and *z.*
2. Final single consonants and the sounds they represent (emphasized in Grade 1): *b, d, f, l, m, n, p, s,* and *t.*
3. Consonant digraphs and the sounds they represent. Digraphs are two letters representing a single phoneme, or sound (emphasized in Grade 1): *sh, ch, ck, ph, th,* and sometimes *qu.*
4. Consonant blends and the sounds they represent. Blends are two or three letters representing two or three consonant sounds. Each letter in the blend is a distinguishable consonant sound (emphasized in Grade 2): initial blends such as *st, gr, cl, sp, pl, tr,*

br, dr, fr, fl, and *str,* and final blends such as *nd, nk, lk, rt, rd, mp, ft, lt,* and *rn.*

5. Single vowels and the "short" sounds they represent (emphasized in Grades 1 and 2): *a* as in apple, *e* as in egg, *i* as in igloo, *o* as in octopus, and *u* as in up.

6. Vowels and the "long" sounds they represent (emphasized in Grades 2 and 3): *a* as in pane, *e* as in Pete, *i* as in ice, *o* as in home, and *u* as in fume.

7. Vowel combinations and the sounds they represent, including digraphs, dipthongs, and vowel clusters (emphasized in Grades 2 and 3). Digraphs are two letters representing one vowel phoneme, or sound, such as *ea* as in bead, *oa* as in toad, *ai* as in paid, and *ee* as in seed. Dipthongs are two vowels blended to form an elided sound unassociated with either vowel, such as *oi* as in oil, *oy* as in boy, and *au* as in taught. Vowel clusters are irregular vowel combinations that are neither digraphs nor dipthongs, including *ei* as in weight, *ou* as in tough, and *ou* as in cough.

8. R-controlled vowels. A vowel followed by the letter *r* has a unique sound (emphasized in Grades 2 and 3): *ar* as in car, *ur* as in fur, *ir* as in stir, *or* as in for, and *er* as in her.

9. Silent letters or consonant digraphs (emphasized in Grade 3): *kn* as in knife, *gh* as in ghost, *gh* as in cough, *lk* as in talk, *rh* as in rheumatic, *gn* as in gnaw, *pn* as in pneumonia, and *wr* as in wren.

TEACHING PHONIC SKILLS

The purpose of phonic instruction is to provide readers with tools for analyzing unknown words on the basis of their letter-sound relationships. Teachers usually present phonic information to children through two major strategies—synthetic instruction and analytic instruction (Anderson et al. 1985, Vacca et al. 1987).

Synthetic phonic instruction focuses on breaking down the reading task into individual, isolated skill segments, and teaching them in a sequence from smaller to larger segments. For example, children first learn the names of letters and then the sound or sounds each letter represents. When children can perform these two skills automatically, blending is taught. For example, children learn the letter names *p, m, a, n,* and *t.* Next they learn the sound each letter represents ($p = /p/$, $m = /m/$, $a = /a/$, $n = /n/$, and $t = /t/$). Finally, they learn to blend letters to form words ($/m/, /a/, /t/ = mat$ and $/m/, /a/, /p/ = map$). The children then use the words *mat* and *map* in a sentence. In synthetic instruction, teachers often instruct children explicitly in the rules governing various letter-sound relationships.

Analytic phonics, on the other hand, teaches children the larger skill units and then helps children to infer letter-sound relationships. For example, a teacher whose goal is to teach children that m = /m/ first presents sight words such as *man*, *mother*, and *mat* and has children use them in sentences. Next the teacher takes the words out of sentence context, has children see and hear the words, and asks them to identify similarities, abstracting rules about letter-sound relationships. Appropriate rules in this case:

> All three words begin with the same sound, /m/.
> All three words begin with the same letter, m.
> The sound /m/ is represented by the letter m.
> Words that begin with the sound /m/ also begin with the letter m.

The teacher then encourages children to generate other words that begin with m. Finally, the rule m = /m/ is presented.

Both the analytic and the synthetic approaches present the rules of phonics. Both present the isolated sounds of letters and use the phonic segments in whole words. The major difference is the sequencing of instruction. Synthetic instruction begins with the parts and moves to the whole, while analytic instruction begins with the whole and moves to the parts. Controversy surrounds the question of which instructional method is better (Chall 1983a, 1983b). The Commission on Reading (Anderson et al. 1985, 57) reported:

> [R]esearch provides insufficient justification for strict adherence to either overall philosophy. Probably, the best strategy would draw from both approaches. . . . Useful phonics strategies include teaching children the sounds of letters in isolation and in words, and teaching them to blend the sounds of letters together to produce approximate pronunciations of words. Another strategy that may be useful is encouraging children to identify words by thinking of other words with similar spellings. Phonic instruction should go hand in hand with opportunities to identify words in meaningful sentences and stories. Phonics should be taught early and kept simple.

The suggestion of early intensive instruction in phonics does not go unchallenged, however. Many professionals in the field of reading believe that phonic instruction should be moderated, especially in the early grades (Smith 1986, Hirsch 1987, Larrick 1987). Their arguments against early intensive phonic instruction follow.

1. A rule-based approach to English spelling is counterproductive because there are too many rules to learn. Researchers have repeatedly attempted to enumerate rules for English spelling. Berdiansky et al.

(1969) analyzed more than 6000 one- and two-syllable words in the meaning vocabularies of average six- to nine-year-old children. The words were taken from commonly used reading books. They discovered 69 graphemic units in the 6000 words. A graphemic unit is a group of two or more letters whose sound cannot be accounted for by single-letter rules (e.g., *ch*, *th*, *ea*, *oc*, *bb*, *ll*). The 69 graphemic units were related to 38 different sounds. There were 166 rules to account for the letter-sound relationships, with 45 exceptions to the rules. Sixty rules related to the pronunciation of 21 consonants, and 106 rules to the pronunciation of 7 vowels (*a*, *e*, *i*, *o*, *u*, *y*, and *w*). These findings do not account for the hundreds of other words children meet in the first three years of reading.

2. Few phonic rules are sufficiently consistent to warrant direct instruction. Research shows that most phonic rules have so many inconsistencies and exceptions that teaching them might be unjustified (Burmeister 1968, Moskowitz 1973, Vaughn–Cook 1977). May and Eliot (1978) claim that only seven rules are consistent enough to be taught directly. These rules follow.

- When the letter g comes at the end of a word or immediately before the letters *a*, *o*, or *u*, it usually represents the hard sound, as in *nag*, *gave*, *go*, and *gun*. Otherwise, it has the soft sound, as in *gem*. (Exceptions: *get*, *girl*, *begin*, or *give*)
- When the letter *c* comes immediately before the letters *a*, *o*, or *u*, it usually represents the hard sound, as in *cap*, *code*, and *cut*. Otherwise, it represents the soft sound, as in *cell*, *city*, and *ceiling*.
- When a single vowel is followed by a consonant or consonant combination in a word or syllable, the vowel represents the short sound, as in *if*, *on*, *candy*, and *dinner*.
- When a vowel digraph is included in a word or syllable, usually the first letter in the digraph represents the long sound and the second letter is silent. This rule holds consistently for the digraphs *ee* (as in *see*), *oa* (as in *boat*), and *ay* (as in *may*). It holds less consistently for the digraphs *ea* (as in *each*) and *ai* (as in *paid*), and holds least consistently for the digraphs *ei* (as in *rein*), *ie* (as in *piece*), and *oo* (as in *boot*) (Clymer 1963).
- In one-syllable words containing two vowels, one of which is a final *e*, the first vowel usually represents the long sound and the final *e* is silent, as in *file*, *made*, and *cute*.
- When the letter *r* immediately follows a vowel, it modifies the sound of the vowel, producing a sound that cannot be classified as either long or short, as in *her*, *far*, and *girl*.
- When a word or syllable ends with only one vowel, the vowel usually represents the long sound, as in *go*, *we*, *so*, *hotel*, and *motor*.

3. Rather than teaching children isolated sounds, teachers might be better advised to teach patterns of words, such as *at*, *mat*, *sat*, *fat*, *cat*,

or *ate, mate, date, hate, state*. Such instruction will assist children in the subconscious formulation of personal "rules" for similarly patterned words.

The real issue is not whether children should receive direct, intensive phonic instruction, but what phonic instruction should be provided, when, by which strategies, and to which children. The remainder of this section considers these questions:

- What phonics should be taught?
- When should phonics be stressed?
- How should phonics be taught?
- Which children need which kind of phonic instruction?

How Words Convey Meaning

Phonics is one strategy readers use to pronounce unknown words. To do this efficiently, however, readers must learn that they do not need all the phonic clues in a word to decode it. Only a few clues are essential—those parts of a word that carry the most information. In the following example, the words in a story selection are reduced to smaller segments. As you read each paragraph, decide which parts of the words provide the most essential information for decoding. The complete story appears intact at the end of the exercise.

CLASSROOM APPLICATION

Intact Paragraph

It was a snowy Christmas Eve and I was seven years old. Papa
was gone. He'd been gone for a while.
Mama said that maybe he'd come back this Christmas . . . maybe.
I didn't believe her though, but I would smile and say,
"Sure he will, Mama."
I just didn't want her to know that I didn't believe.
It would hurt her so.

Ends Deleted

Mam_ wa_ gett____ read__ fo_ wor_ on Christm__ Ev_.
Sh_ sai_ th__ sh_ wou__ ge_ of_ at thr__
an_ the_ we'_ get_ ou_ Christm__ tr__
an_ decora__ it wi__ popco__ hangi__ on thre__
an_ cranber___, cherri__ an_ brea_ c__ int_ al_ th_ shap__
tha_ we cou__ thi__ of.

Beginnings Deleted

__ma __ed to _ay __at __ere _as so __ch __od on _ur __ee
__at if we __dn't __ke __e _____mas __er

we ___ld ___ays _at __e __ee –
_nd __en __'d _ll __ugh.
___ing __e __ee ___ld be _un _or __ma _nd my _ig
___er _ed.

Middles Deleted

T_d w_s tw_ve, a_d he ne__r l_t me fo__et th_t he w_s so
m_ch ol_er th_n me.
I li_ed h_m w_ll en__gh,
al___ugh we we_re al__ys fu__ing o_er st__f.
St__f l_ke w_o g_t to r_de in t_e fr_nt s__t w_th M__a . . .
or wh_t TV sh_w to w__ch . . .
or w_o th__ght of t_e b_st i_ea f__st . . .
or w_o g_t to __e a sh__e l_st . . .

Vowels Deleted

_r wh_ l_ft th_ br_nd n_w b_s_b_ll m_tt _n th_ fl__r s_ th_t
F_ng, __r B_lld_g, c__ld ch_w _t _p _nd l__v_ _nly _ l_ttl_
sp_t _n__t_n . . . th_ p_rt th_t s__d "R_wl_ns" _nd h_d D_l_
M_rphy's n_m_ wr_tt_n _n _t.
M_m_w_s _lw_ys s_y_ng, "_'d l_k_ t_ h_v_ j_st _ne h_r wh_n
y__ tw_ w_r_n't f_ss_ng _t _n_ _n_th_r. F_ss, f_ss, f_ss. _r_n't
y__ t_r_r_d _f f_ss_ng?" T_d _nd m_ w__ld gl_r_ _t __ch _th_r
_nd s_y n_t _n_
w_rd, b_t w_ w__ld b_th b_ th_nk_ng, "N_!"

Consonants Deleted

_a_a _a_ _i_i_ _u___ _o_ u_. __e a__a_ _e__ u_ _u___
__e_ __e _a_ _o _o__. Ea__ o_ u_ _a_ a _a__ _i_ ou_ _a_e
__i__e_ o_ i_, _u__
_i_e __e_ _e _e__ _o ___oo_.

Complete Intact Text

It was a snowy Christmas Eve and I was seven years old. Papa
was gone. He'd been gone for a while.
Mama said that maybe he'd come back this Christmas . . . maybe.
I didn't believe her though, but I would smile and say
"Sure he will, Mama."
I just didn't want her to know that I didn't believe.
It would hurt her so.

Mama was getting ready for work on Christmas Eve.
She said that she would get off at three
and then we'd get our Christmas tree
and decorate it with popcorn hanging on thread
and cranberries, cherries, and bread cut into all the shapes
that we could think of.

Mama used to say that there was so much food on our tree
that if we didn't like the Christmas dinner
we could always eat the tree –
and then we'd all laugh.
Fixing the tree would be fun for Mama and my big
brother Ted.

Ted was twelve, and he never let me forget that he was so
much older than me.
I liked him well enough,
although we were always fussing over stuff.
Stuff like who got to ride in the front seat with Mama . . .
or what TV show to watch . . .
or who thought of the best idea first . . .
or who got to take a shower last . . .

or who left the brand new baseball mitt on the floor so that
Fang, our Bulldog, could chew it up and leave only a little
spot uneaten . . . the part that said "Rawlins" and had Dale
Murphy's name written on it.
Mama was always saying, "I'd like to have just one hour when
you two weren't fussing at one another.
Fuss, fuss, fuss. Aren't you tired of fussing?"
Ted and me would glare at each other and say not one
word, but we would both be thinking, "No!"

Mama was fixing lunch for us.
She always left us lunch when she had to work.
Each of us had a sack with our name written on it, just
like when we went to school.

In attempting to decode the story, you probably made the following observations.

- Reading is most successful when both phonic clues and context clues are used together.
- The more you read and comprehended the material, the easier it became to decode subsequent segments. Because you better understood the semantic context, you could predict the information that should logically follow. Familiarity with the content enhances efficiency in using phonic clues.
- Consonants and the beginnings of words provide the most important clues to word recognition.
- Vowels and the middles of words are the least useful in word recognition.
- A combination of the beginnings and endings of words (deleting the middles) provides almost all the information necessary for decoding print (Weaver 1980).

These findings should guide decisions about which phonic skills to emphasize and how to teach them.

The following list itemizes factors to consider in planning phonic instruction.

- Phonic instruction emphasizes relationships between letters or combinations of letters and their sounds.
- Phonic instruction may be presented through analytic, synthetic, or combination strategies.
- Letter-sound relationships have a large number of often inconsistent rules.
- Rules governing consonants are more consistent than those governing vowels.
- There are seven rules consistent enough to warrant direct, intensive instruction to children.
- Phonic knowledge is indispensable to efficient reading.
- Parts of words differ in the amount of useful information they carry.
- Consonants are more useful than vowels in reading.
- Beginnings and ends of words are more useful than middles in decoding.
- Reading is most efficient when phonic clues are used in conjunction with context clues.

Phonic Skills That Should Be Taught

Since initial and final consonants and consonant combinations are important in decoding, children must learn and use those letter-sound relationships. Few phonic rules are consistent enough to be taught directly. However, children should learn the seven rules that are reliable. The spelling of vowel sounds, particularly of long vowel sounds, varies considerably. While it is important to teach children both short and long vowel sounds, it is counterproductive to directly teach rules governing the many relationships between individual letters and the sounds they represent. Teach children to be flexible in the application of vowel sounds. If they try a short sound for a vowel and it does not suggest a word they know or does not make sense in the sentence, they should try a long sound. For example, a child reading the sentence, "I like to give my cat hugs," might read, give with a long i. The teacher might say, "Let's look at this word again. Did what you read make sense? You know two sounds for the letter i. Why don't you try the other sound! Good job. Now reread the sentence." The teacher reinforces the fact that the word now makes sense.

This suggestion in no way implies that children should not learn reliable generalizations about vowel sounds. It simply means that children must learn strategies enabling them to make quick and appropriate decisions in decoding. This strategy also gives children a workable approach before learning all the complex associations. Once children have been taught the long and short vowel sounds, urge them to use that knowledge in combination with context to decode new words. Rather than directly teaching many unreliable rules, expose children to patterns, or sets, of words (e.g., *ride, hide, side, wide, tide*) and help them to discover the consistent spelling of sound patterns.

When Phonic Instruction Should Be Provided

Phonic information is valuable in the process of reading. Instruction in phonics should begin very early in school (Chall 1983a). Remember, however, that some children lack the constitutional prerequisites for learning explicitly presented phonic information. Prerequisites include skills such as auditory discrimination, auditory segmentation, auditory memory, and auditory blending. Unless children possess these prerequisites, direct phonic instruction will be unsuccessful and frustrating for both teachers and children (Carbo 1987). If children lacking these prerequisite skills must learn phonics, then give direct instruction in the specific skills.

Auditory skills do improve with practice. Some researchers suggest that prerequisite auditory skills are learned skills as well as innate perceptual abilities (Gillet and Temple 1986; Wallach and Wallach 1982). Provide instruction in auditory skills concurrently with reading instruction. As the prerequisites develop, phonic learning progresses more quickly, easily, and successfully.

1. Auditory Discrimination. Auditory discrimination is the ability to hear similarities and differences in sounds. Be cautious in labeling a child deficient in auditory discrimination. Some children seem to have discrimination problems when, in fact, they cannot understand the teacher's dialect or have acuity problems as a result of hearing loss. Children with actual problems in discrimination might benefit from the following practices.

- Show children two or three pictures representing words that are similar in sound (e.g., *bag, bug, big*). Say one of the words and have children select the appropriate picture.
- Repeat pairs of words to children (e.g., *pet* and *pit*) and ask children to tell if the words are the same or different. Vary the words at the beginning (*bit* and *fit, nine* and *mine*), at the end (*beg* and *bet, price* and *prize*), and in the middle (*big* and *beg, rod* and *rid*). The progression (beginning, end, and middle) is presented in order of difficulty.

- Repeat pairs of sounds (e.g., /b/ and /p/) to children and ask them to tell if the sounds are the same or different.
- Present pairs of words and have students tell whether or not they rhyme.
- Have students complete rhyming couplets, such as "The little cat chased the ____." Provide choices initially, such as *dog*, *rat*, and *toy* and have children select the correct rhyming word. Then have children generate words on their own.
- Use nursery rhymes or children's songs with the rhyming words deleted. Have children fill in the rhymes, e.g.,

One *two*
Buckle my ____.
Three, *four*
Shut the ____.

2. Auditory Segmentation. Auditory segmentation is the ability to divide words into their individual parts.

- Begin with compound words (e.g., *doghouse*, *mailman*). Have children identify the individual words within the compound word.
- Present words that have affixes (e.g., *slow–ly* and *re–do*). Have children identify the syllables. They might clap their hands or tap their feet to help themselves "hear" the parts.
- Separate the beginning sound of a word from the remainder (e.g., /r/–/at/). Have the children identify the first sound.
- Say a whole word and then segment the word. Have the children imitate you (e.g., *man*–/m/–/a/–/n/).

3. Auditory Memory. Auditory memory is the ability to hold auditory material in memory. It is an important skill in phonic learning because students must be able to hold segmented sounds in memory long enough to blend them into words. Try the following exercises.

- Present orally a series of unrelated numbers, letters, syllables, or words. Ask children to repeat them. Begin with a few and gradually increase the number.
- Encourage children to memorize verses, poems, or songs.
- Present sentences orally and have students repeat them. Begin with shorter sentences and increase the length as the children gain accuracy and confidence.

4. Auditory Blending. Auditory blending is the ability to blend individual sounds into single words. This ability is crucial in learning phonics. Many children can produce the individual sounds in words but

cannot blend the sounds appropriately (e.g., /st/, /o/, /p/ is read as *start*, *sop*, or *pat*). Strategies for training blending skills follow.

- Pronounce segmented compound words (e.g., *book/shelf*) and have children produce the whole word.
- Pronounce two-syllable words with the syllables detached (e.g., *hun–ter*). Have the children blend the parts to form the word.
- Pronounce one-syllable words with the last syllable separated (e.g., *ra–t*). Have students blend the sounds to produce the word.
- Pronounce one-syllable words with the first sound separated (e.g., *r–at*), and have students blend the sounds.
- Produce the individual sounds of one-syllable words (e.g., /r/–/a/ –/t/) and have students produce the words. Extend the practice to four and five sounds.
- Transfer the auditory stimulus to a visual one. Show children letter cards. Have them sound out the letters and blend them into a word.

Children lacking auditory skills need consistent training. Training in the phonemes or sounds—called phonematic training—can be effective as the following case study shows.

CASE STUDY

David S., an eight-year-old boy, repeated second grade because of his poor performance in reading. After two and one-half years in school, he was still making little progress. Testing showed that all his auditory skills were significantly underdeveloped. Consequently, he found phonics extremely difficult and suffered increasing frustration in school. Although David received daily phonics instruction in school, he seemed unable to learn, remember, and use the skills. David entered an eight-week phonematic training program, conducted three times a week for thirty minutes at a time. The program included the following elements:

1. *Letter/sound training (10 minutes).* David was taught the letter/sound correspondences neurolinguistically. First he saw the letter. Next, he associated a picture with the letter, and last, he heard the isolated sound (e.g., letter card *b*, picture of a boat, sound /b/).

2. Auditory discrimination (5 minutes). David was given pairs of words and sounds and asked to make same-different decisions. He also practiced producing rhyming words.

3. Auditory segmentation (5 minutes). David was given compounds, words with affixes, and one- to three-syllable words and was asked to segment them. Sounds were modeled for David (e.g., "Listen: *pat* = /p/–/a/–/t/. Now you say the parts").

4. *Auditory blending (5 minutes).*   David was presented with segmented words and asked to blend the parts into words.

5. Auditory-visual integration (5 minutes).   David was provided
with letter cards and asked to sound each letter and then to blend the
sounds into words.

To assess the effectiveness of the training, the teacher gave David
a short selection to read before training began. The teacher provided
no instruction or help with unknown words. His reading was taped and
recorded. After training began, David was given the same passage to
read without assistance or feedback after each two-week segment. The
assumption was that the effectiveness of the training would be revealed
through changes in David's ability to decode words using phonic analysis. The reading selection and accounts of David's five readings follow.

The Bluebird's New Adventure

Baby bluebird popped his tiny feathered head out of his
nest, and looked at the world about him.
"Go," said mother bluebird gently.
"Fly around and take a look at your world."
"I'm too afraid to fly," said baby bluebird quietly, trying
hard not to show how much his tiny body was trembling.
"Too afraid to fly!" said mother bluebird in surprise.
"But you are a bird, and birds fly."
"Well . . . I'm too small to fly," said baby bluebird,
pulling his tiny, shaking body deep into his nest.
"Too small to fly!" said his mother.
"You are big enough. You'll see. You are a bird, and birds fly."

David's first reading, before training:

Baby blue put his tin . . . he out of his not, and lived at the
. . . at him. "Go." said mother blue, go. "For away and
take a look at you. . . ."
"I to off to fly," said baby blue, for try had not to she
how much his tin . . . was. . . .
"To a . . . af . . . after to fly!" said mother blue. . . .
"But you are a b . . . b . . . , and b . . . b . . . fly."
"We . . . I to sad to fly," said babby boy, put his tin, . . .
boy down in his n . . . n . . . net.
"To sad to fly," said his mother.
"You are a big. . . . You see. You are a big boy and boys fly."

Notice that David made little effort to apply phonics. He used initial
consonants consistently, but rarely went beyond that point. He also

ignored meanings and failed to self-correct. Notice the inappropriate word blending.

Second reading after two weeks of training:

Baby blue b . . . r, bluber p . . . o . . . p, pop his tin f . . . e . . . t, feet hed, heed out of his n . . . e . . . t, net and l . . . o . . . k, look, looked at the w . . . w . . . window a . . . b . . . t, ab, ab, him.
"Go," said mother bluber g . . . e . . . n, gen, going.
"Fly a . . . r, ar, around and a look at your w . . .
w . . . o . . . r . . . , d, word."
"I am too af, afr, afraid to fly," said baby bluber q . . . qu . . . quickly, tr, tr . . . h . . . a . . . r . . . d, hard not to sh . . . sh . . . o
. . . w, show qu, qu . . . how much his tin, b . . . o . . . , d, bod was tr, tr, trying.
"Too af . . . afr, afraid to fly!" said mother bluber in s . . . s . . . sad.
"But you are a b . . . i . . . r . . . d, bird, bird, and birds fly."
"Well . . . I am too sm . . . all small to fly," said baby blueber, p . . . u,ll pulls his tin, sh, sha, sha, b . . . o . . . d, bod dip into his net.
"To sm . . . all, small to fly," said his mother.
"You are big e, even. You see. You are a b . . . i . . . rd, bird, and birds fly."

Notice that David attempted self-correction. He also tried to sound out words. In the first reading, David tried to sound out six words. In the second reading, he made twenty-nine attempts, eight of which were correct.

Third reading after four weeks of training:

Baby blue b . . . b . . . b . . . i . . . r . . . d, blue, bird, bird, bluebird pop, pop . . . d, popped his tin . . . tin . . . y . . . tiny f . . . e . . . t
. . . fat h . . . he . . . head out of his n . . . e . . . st, nest and looks at the wo . . . wor, l . . . d, wo . . . r . . . ld, world ab . . . ab . . . t, about him.
"Go," said mother blue b . . . i . . . bluebird g . . . gen . . . gen.
"Fly ar . . . ar . . . o . . . nd, arond, around and take a look at your w . . . or . . . ld, world."
"I am too af . . . r . . . d, affered . . . afred . . . I am too afraid to fly," said baby bluebird. qu . . . quickly, tr . . . try . . . trying not to sh
. . . show how much his tin . . . tine, tin . . . y, tin . . . y bod, bod
. . . y, body was tr . . . tr . . . em, treming.
"Too af . . . afr, afraid to fly!" said mother bluebird in s . . . u . . . r, certain.
"But you are a b . . . bird, and birds fly."
"Well . . . I'm, too sm . . . sm . . . all, small to fly," said baby bluebird b . . . lu . . . ll, pull, pulling bluebird his tin . . . y shack bod, body dipping into his n . . . e . . . st . . . nest.

"Too sm . . . small to fly!" said his mother.
"You are big. . . . You'll see. You are a b . . . bird, and birds fly."

Notice David's increasing ability to use phonic skills and to self-correct more automatically.

Fourth reading after six weeks of training:

Baby bluebird pop . . . popped his tin . . . tiny fe . . . feth, feth . . . er . . . his tiny feathers head out of his n . . . nest, and looked at the wor . . . world ab . . . out about him.
"Go," said mother bluebird. gen . . . gent . . . genty.
"Fly ar . . . around and take a look at your wor . . . world."
"I'm too af . . . afraid to fly," said baby bluebird qu . . . quite, quite . . . ly, tr . . . try, trying hard not to sh . . . show how much . . . how much his tin . . . y tiny . . . tiny body was tr . . . em, tremb, trembling.
"Too af . . . afraid to fly!" said mother bluebird in s . . . u . . . r, s . . . u . . . r, sur . . . pr, super.
"But you are a bird, and birds fly."
"Well . . . I'm too sm . . . small to fly," said baby bluebird p . . . u . . . ll, p . . . ll, pull, pulling his tin . . . y . . . tiny, sh . . . sh . . . sh . . . ack . . . shacking, body dep . . . deep into his n . . . e . . . s . . . t . . . nest.
"Too small to fly!" said his mother.
"You are big en, en . . . and you'll see. You are a bird and birds fly."

David gained power in his reading. He used phonic skills more successfully, and he focused on acquiring meaning. His mistakes made more sense ("super" for "surprise") and his overall reading performance became more positive.

Fifth reading after eight weeks of training:

Baby bluebird popped his tiny feathers . . . feathered head out of his nest, and looked at the wor . . . world about him.
"Go," said mother bluebird gen . . . gently . . . gently.
(/g/ as in *gun*)
"Fly around and take a look at your w . . . world."
"I'm too af . . . afraid to fly," said baby bluebird qu . . . qu . . . iet, quietly, tr . . . trying hard not to show how much his tin . . . tiny body was tr . . . em . . . tembling.
"Too afraid to fly!" said mother bluebird in sur-surp-r-surprise.
"But you are a bird, and birds fly."
"Well . . . I'm too sm . . . small to fly," said baby bluebird, p . . . u . . . pulling his tiny sh . . . ake . . . ing, shaking body deep into his nest.

"Too small to fly!" said his mother.
"You are big e . . . enough. You'll see. You are a bird and birds fly."

David used both phonic skills and context to decode the words "surprise" and "shaking" which he read correctly for the first time. Phonematic training enabled David:

- to "sound out" words more successfully
- to blend more accurately
- to use phonic skills more often
- to self-correct more often
- to gain more confidence in reading

Phonic instruction is necessary in the early stages of reading development. However, children must be able to hear phonemes and to cope with auditory demands. Children might need instruction in the auditory skills in order to fully benefit from phonic instruction.

How Phonics Should Be Taught

Teachers spend a major part of their daily instructional time teaching children phonic skills. However, this means that children spend significantly less time having firsthand experiences with print (Goodman 1986). For many children, isolated skill learning does not get transferred to the actual reading of print. Despite skill instruction, many children fail to learn and to use the skills, particularly children with noninductive learning styles and with slow learning rates. Failure to learn skills can often be traced to the following reasons.

- Instructional modifications are not provided for children.
- Children do not possess the prerequisite skills for skill learning.
- Teachers follow basal suggestions too closely, presenting too many skills too quickly and too superficially, particularly for remedial readers.
- Teachers provide insufficient conceptual preparation for skills. As a result, many slower learners memorize skills but do not understand how they work and cannot apply them with consistent success.
- Skills are not immediately transferred to actual reading. In a typical basal reading lesson, children learn a phonic skill in sentence isolation and complete a workbook page that often fails to reinforce the skill. When children finally read a selection, no effort is made to incorporate examples of the new skill into the text (Osborn 1984). In addition, teachers often forget to remind children of newly learned skills as they read. Average or inductive readers

can cope with these realities because (1) they conceptually understand the skills, (2) they read enough on their own to practice skills themselves, or (3) they already knew the skill. Many poor readers are at a clear disadvantage on all three counts.

Children with reading difficulties require different strategies in order to learn and apply phonic skills. Teachers should practice the six instructional principles discussed earlier in this chapter:

1. Skills should be presented in the most meaningful contexts.
2. Skills must be taught thoroughly, particularly to slow or poor readers.
3. Children's attention must be secured prior to instruction.
4. Teachers must intentionally help children apply newly gained skills immediately in real reading situations.
5. Fast learners need less exposure to skills; slow learners need more as well as a greater variety.
6. Skills should be learned to an automatic level and automatically applied.

To provide more effective instruction in phonic skills, teach skills more thoroughly and in a more meaningful manner.

Figure 10.1 presents a skill instruction model for effective instruction of skills. The purpose of this model is to move children through the four levels of learning—awareness, instruction, practice, and independence. This is accomplished by moving through the four pedagogical levels. Explanations of the four instructional levels follow. The phonic skill *ch* = /*ch*/ is used as an example to show the model at work.

Level A: Awareness. The purpose of this level is to prepare children conceptually for instruction by heightening to the level of comprehension their awareness of the skill to be taught. Find a meaningful, short passage with many examples of the skill to be taught. Sources for such material are whole language series such as Sounds of Language Series by Martin and Brogan (1974), published by Holt, Rinehart & Winston, or the Consonant Capers Series by Ribisl and Ribisl (1975), published by the Houghton Mifflin Company. Although such sources provide appropriate material, the most effective awareness material is written by teachers themselves, such as the following passage for teaching the skill "*ch*."

> *Charlie Chan* lives in a big house. He has a secret hideout at the top of his *cherry* tree. *Charlie* has a table and *chair* in his hideout. He keeps pieces of *chalk* to write secret messages to his friends. *Charlie* quickly climbs down a strong *chain* when he smells something good coming from his mother's kitchen. Today she is baking *chocolate chip* cookies.*

*Brenda Vogt, Colorado Springs (CO) Public Schools, 1980.

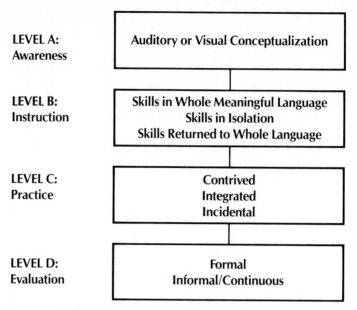

LEVEL A: Awareness	Auditory or Visual Conceptualization
LEVEL B: Instruction	Skills in Whole Meaningful Language Skills in Isolation Skills Returned to Whole Language
LEVEL C: Practice	Contrived Integrated Incidental
LEVEL D: Evaluation	Formal Informal/Continuous

FIGURE 10.1   The Skill Instruction Model

At the awareness level, read such a passage to children to establish a conceptual basis for the skill. Notice the consistent use of the skill element *ch* and the meaningful level of the material. You might need to read the selection twice.

Level B: Instruction. This level goes beyond the awareness level to the actual teaching stage. Instruction includes three important steps:

Step 1. Introduce the skill in whole language. Reread the skill selection, but ask questions that force children to focus on the words containing the specific skill element. Write children's responses on the chalkboard or on a sheet of paper. Your line of questions might include the following:

- What is the name of the boy in the story? (Charlie Chan) Extend the question: Have you ever heard that name before? Where? What kind of name do you think it is?
- Where is Charlie's secret hideout? (cherry tree) Extend the question: What is a secret hideout? Do you have one at home? Why would someone have a secret hideout?
- Charlie has a table in his hideout. What other furniture does he have there? (chair) Extend the question: What other furniture would you have?
- What does Charlie have to write with? (chalk) Extend the question: What material does Charlie Chan write on? How do you know? Could he have used regular school paper? Why or why not?

- How does Charlie get down from the tree house? (chain) Extend the question: What other ways could he have used to get down from the tree?
- What kind of cookies is his mother baking? (chocolate chip) Extend the question: What is your favorite cookie?

The main purpose of the questioning is to elicit from the children the words containing the skill element to be learned. Include extension questions to expose children to interpretive and evaluative thought. After all questions have been asked and discussed and the answers written down, review the skill questions again, pointing to the words as the children respond. In this way children can center their attention on the skill.

Step 2. Teach the words in isolation. Draw children's attention to the specific phonic element by asking questions like What do you hear that is the same in all these words? What do you see that is the same in all these words? What letters make the sound you hear at the beginning of these words? Isolate the letters *ch*. Engage the children in the following activities.

- Have children generate words that begin with *ch*. List the words on the chalkboard and encourage children to read the words with you.
- Choose a few key words, place them in sentences, and have children read the sentences.
- Say individual words and have children point to the correct words.
- Say a number of words including both *ch* and non-*ch* words. Have children tap or clap when they recognize words that begin with *ch*.

Step 3. Return the words to whole language. Do this by giving the children the original passage to read with you. They will then apply their newly learned skills to actual print. If the original passage is too difficult for them, write or find another using the skill.

Level C: Practice. Three types of practice are contrived, integrated, and incidental practice. Contrived practice is the use of preconstructed or original skill material directly related to specific skills. The traditional workbook may be used. Remember, however, that the workbook is an instructional tool and should be completed under the instruction or guidance of the teacher. Suggestions for other activities to use for contrived practice follow.

- Use tachistoscopes to provide practice in words containing the specific phonic element. The tachistoscopes may show the whole words, as in Figure 10.2. A tachistoscope might also present words in such a way that the initial digraph *ch* is separated from

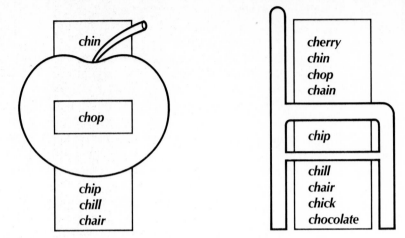

FIGURE 10.2   Examples of Tachistoscopes

the phonograms, as in Figure 10.3. This version allows children to practice their blending skills as well.

- Use flip charts, shown in Figure 10.4. An alternative to constructing flip charts is to make sets of note cards for initial consonants and blends, for vowels, and for final consonants and blends. Change the cards to create new words for practice.
- Construct a cardboard circle and write words around the circle. Attach a pointer, or spinner. Have children spin the pointer and read the word to which it points. Figure 10.5 shows a *ch* skill practice wheel.
- Construct games to reinforce skills. Make game boards from 2 × 3 sheets of cardboard and illustrate them or decorate with pictures

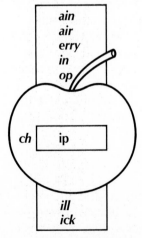

FIGURE 10.3   A Tachistoscope with a Digraph and Phonogram

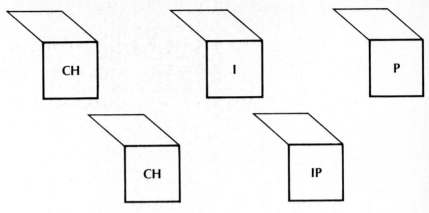

FIGURE 10.4   Flip Charts

FIGURE 10.5   A Skill Practice Wheel

cut from magazines. Laminate the board for durability. Figure 10.6 presents an example. Avoid writing the words on the spaces; use word cards so that you can use the same board for many skill practices. The game may be played with a die. The children choose a word card to read. If they read correctly, they roll the die and they move the number of spaces indicated.

- Use appropriate segments from published phonic skill programs. Many publishers provide practice kits including books, skill pages, games, workbooks, and activity pads for reinforcing a variety of phonic skills. A listing of some of the programs follows.

Phonics and Word Power (Xerox Educational Publishing)
Phonics We Use (Lyons and Carnahan Educational Publishers)

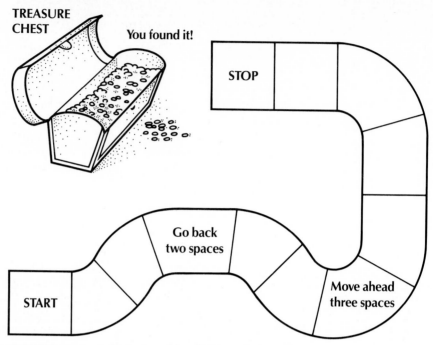

FIGURE 10.6 A Game Board for Skill Reinforcement

Phonovisual Phonics Program (Phonovisual Products)
New Phonics Skill Text Series (Charles E. Merrill)
Speech-to-Print Phonics and *Speech-to-Print Phonics*, 2nd ed.
  (Harcourt Brace Jovanovich)

- Provide listening exercises in which children listen to a series of words (e.g., words beginning with *ch* and *sh*) and distinguish those beginning with a given sound (e.g., /ch/).

One mistake teachers make is going directly to the practice phase (the workbook) for skill instruction. It is important to observe the awareness and instructional phases. If children encounter noticeable difficulty in the practice stage, return to the previous instructional phase. Remember to let as little time as possible lapse between the instruction and practice phases.

Integrated practice combines skill practice with reading. As children read material during the day, those who need more practice in the skill (e.g., *ch*) should read selections containing that skill. Remedial readers need all the reading practice and reinforcement they can get.

Incidental practice informally involves children in practicing skills. During free reading or sustained silent reading periods each day, the teacher can make available materials containing the specific skill. Certain children might be directed to choose from specific material so that skills can be reinforced in an informal, incidental manner.

Level D: Evaluation. Formal evaluation involves the use of assessment tests, standardized or non-standardized testing instruments. Test results should be used to assist children, to assess their strengths and weaknesses, and to determine the need for reteaching. Formal evaluation is rarely done during the normal classroom instructional period, unlike informal evaluation. As children read in the course of the school day, the teacher should make informal assessments of children's use of the skill taught. When children apply the skill, give recognition and praise ("Good for you for remembering the sound of *ch*"). When children omit the skill, remind them of it. When they consistently ignore or mispronounce it, reteach the skill.

Decoding Multisyllabic Words

As reading material becomes more complex, students encounter longer words. Students need productive strategies for decoding these words. Syllabication instruction has been criticized by many professionals in the field of reading research and instruction (Cunningham 1976). Research gives no evidence that syllabication training affects reading comprehension. The most-taught syllabication rules seldom work with words of three or more syllables as there are more exceptions to the rule than examples. Critics point out that many workbooks use words students can already pronounce, canceling any need for syllabication rules. Despite the criticisms, syllabication rules can give children helpful guidelines for decoding multisyllabic words. As always, however, children should be encouraged to use the rules in addition to context clues.

Syllabication has both an auditory and a visual dimension. Children should be exposed to the auditory component first, which focuses on hearing the syllabic divisions of words. Aulls (1982) recommends the following procedures for teaching children auditory syllabication.

1. Syllables are parts of words. Teach children that if they say a word with one part, they will move their mouths once (e.g., *cow*). If they say a word with two parts, they will move their mouths twice (e.g., *sandwich*). Present a number of words of one, two, and three syllables, and ask children to say the words, noting how many times they moved their mouths.
2. You can hear the numbers of syllables in words. Assist children in tapping, clapping, or patting the syllabic patterns of words. Use words of varying numbers of syllables and provide a lot of practice.

The visual dimension of syllabication focuses on training children to segment words visually into units. Aulls proposes five principles for teaching children visual syllabic units. The principles are stated as syllabication rules to teach to children as generalizations:

1. A visual (written) syllable must contain either a single vowel (e.g., *man*) or a vowel combination (e.g., *main*).
2. The vowel or vowel combination is preceded or followed by a single consonant or a consonant combination (e.g., *stop*, *throw*, and *other*).
3. Counting the number of vowel units in a word usually identifies the number of syllables in the word.
4. Knowing the expected number of syllables (by counting the vowel units) is a way to check accuracy in pronunciation.
5. Knowing which consonant letters are normally not divided is helpful in syllabication. Useful guidelines follow.

- Consonant digraphs (*ph, th, ch, wh, ng, gp, nd*) are never divided.
- Consonant blends (*pl, fl, gl, br, cr, fr, gr, pr, tr, sc, sl, sm, scr, sp, st, sw*) are usually not divided.
- Suffixes (*ness, ly, ing, tion, ward, ful*) and prefixes (*un, pre, bi, re*) are usually separate syllables.
- Two consonants (that are not consonant digraphs or blends) occurring side by side are usually divided (*dag/ger, cir/cus, un/til, sin/gle, pret/zel*).

As in all skill instruction, the most important aspect is use. As you read with children, encourage them to use their skills to decode unknown words. Also encourage children to use context in addition to syllabication generalizations. Context is invaluable because syllabication rules provide only approximations to correct pronunciation in most cases. Rules should be used in conjunction with other decoding tools. Encourage children to be flexible in their quest for meaning.

Selecting the Appropriate Kind of Phonic Instruction

Phonic knowledge is extremely important in learning to read. However, different children have different needs. Phonic instruction as the major decoding strategy is most appropriate for children with the necessary prerequisites. For these children, phonic learning should proceed at an expected pace and with expected ease using either synthetic or analytic instruction. A combination of both strategies, as presented in the skill instruction model, seems best.

For children who lack the prerequisites, phonic instruction might center primarily on readiness activities. As these children learn phonic concepts, simultaneously give strong sight-word instruction to compensate for their inadequacies in phonics. The skill instruction model is again recommended, because it presents skills meaningfully and provides immediate practice in transferring skills to whole language. The method also provides as much synthetic practice and drill as the children need.

SUMMARY   Graphic language contains several resources for finding clues to word recognition. One major resource is phonics. Phonic instruction is one of the teacher's most challenging responsibilities in giving children clear, appropriate, and successful skill instruction. In order to do this, teachers must teach skills in the most meaningful contexts and apply them in real contexts. They must teach skills thoroughly after winning children's full attention. Skill instruction should take into account the three phases of skill development—awareness, accuracy, and automaticity.

Strategies of phonic instruction include synthetic phonics, which begins with the parts and builds to the whole, and analytic phonics, which begins with the whole and progresses to the parts. Whatever strategies are used, a strong emphasis on phonic instruction is recommended. The Commission on Reading (1985) concluded that children should receive early and intensive instruction in phonics. Critics of early intensive phonic instruction argue for a strong meaning component.

This chapter asked which phonic skills should be taught, when, how, and to whom. The most consistent rules should be taught immediately as generalizations. These rules include (1) most consonant rules, (2) rules for initial and final consonant combinations, (3) the seven most stable phonic generalizations, (4) both sounds for vowels with instruction to try one and then, if that doesn't work, to try the other. Phonic instruction should be provided as early as possible so long as children have the prerequisites. If prerequisites are lacking, teach the skills. Give phonic instruction in four phases: awareness, instruction, practice, and evaluation. The sole purpose of reading instruction is to further reading performance in children. If children are not learning to read through phonic instruction, try using another strategy.

R • E • F • E • R • E • N • C • E • S

Anderson, R. C., E. H. Heibert, J. A. Scott, and I. A. Wilkinson. *Becoming a Nation of Readers: The Report of the Commission on Reading.* Washington, D.C.: National Institute of Education, 1985.

Aulls, M. W. *Developing Readers in Today's Elementary School.* Boston: Allyn and Bacon, 1982.

Beck, I. L. "Reading Problems and Instructional Practices." In T. S. Waller, and G. E. Mackinnon, eds. *Reading Research: Advances in Theory and Practice*, Vol. 2. New York: Academic Press, 1981.

Berdiansky, B., B. Cronnell, and J. Koehler. *Spelling-Sound Relations and Primary Form—Class Descriptions for Speech—Comprehension Vocabularies of 6–9 Year Olds*. Technical Report No. 15. Inglewood, CA: Southwest Regional Laboratory for Educational Research and Development, 1969.

Burmeister, L. E. "Usefulness of phonic generalizations." *Reading Teacher* 21 (January 1968): 349–356.

Calfee, R. C., and D. C. Pointkowski. "The reading diary: Acquisition of decoding." *Reading Research Quarterly* 16 (1981): 346–373.

Carbo, M. "Deprogramming reading failure: Giving unequal learners an equal chance." *Phi Delta Kappan* 69 (November 1987): 197–202.

Chall, J. S. *Stages of Reading Development*. New York: McGraw–Hill, 1983a.

———. *Learning to Read: The Great Debate*, 2nd ed. New York: McGraw–Hill, 1983b.

Chapman, L. J., and M. Hoffman. *Developing Fluent Reading*. Milton Keynes, England: Open University Press, 1977.

Clymer, T. "The utility of phonic generalizations in the primary grades." *The Reading Teacher* 16 (January 1963): 252–258.

Cronbach, L. J. *Educational Psychology*, 3rd ed. New York: Harcourt Brace Jovanovich, 1977.

Cunningham, P. M. "Investigating a synthesized theory of mediated word identification." *Reading Research Quarterly* 11 (1976): 127–143.

DeCecco, J. P., and W. R. Crawford. *The Psychology of Learning and Instruction*. Englewood Cliffs, NJ: Prentice–Hall, 1974.

Durkin, D. *Teaching Young Children to Read*, 4th ed. Boston: Allyn and Bacon, 1987.

Gillet, J. W., and C. Temple. *Understanding Reading Problems—Assessment and Instruction*. Little, Brown, 1986.

Goodman, K. S. *What's Whole in Whole Language?* Ottawa, ONT: Scholastic, 1986.

Hirsch, E. D. *Cultural Literacy*. Boston: Houghton Mifflin, 1987.

Johnson, D. D., and J. G. Baumann. "Word Identification." In P. D. Pearson, R. Barr, M. Kamil, and P. Mosenthal, eds. *Handbook of Reading Research*. New York: Longman, 1984.

Larrick, N. "Illiteracy starts too soon." *Phi Delta Kappan* 69 (November 1987): 184–189.

Martin, B., and P. Brogan. *Sounds of Language Readers*. New York: Holt, Rinehart & Winston, 1974.

May, F. B., and S. B. Eliot. *To Help Children Read: Mastery Performance Modules for Teachers in Training*. Columbus, OH: Merrill, 1978.

Moskowitz, S. "On the Status of Vowel Shift in English." In T. E. Moore, ed. *Cognitive Development and the Acquisition of Language.* New York: Academic Press, 1973.

Osborn, J. *Evaluating Workbooks, Reading Education Report No. 52.* Urbana, IL: University of Illinois Center for the Study of Reading, 1984.

Samuels, S. J. "Automatic decoding and reading comprehension." *Language Arts* 53 (1976): 323–325.

Smith, F. *Insult to Intelligence: The Bureaucratic Invasion of Our Classrooms.* New York: Arbor House, 1986.

Vacca, J. L., R. T. Vacca, and M. K. Gove. *Reading and Learning to Read.* Boston: Little, Brown, 1987.

Vaughn–Cook, A. F. "Phonological Rules and Reading." In R. Shuy, ed. *Linguistic Theory: What Can It Say About Reading?* Newark, DE: International Reading Association, 1977.

Wallach, L., and M. A. Wallach. "Phonemic Analysis Training in the Teaching of Reading." In W. M. Cruickshank and J. W. Lerner, eds. *Coming of Age: The Best of A.C.L.D.*, Vol. 3. Syracuse, NY: Syracuse University Press, 1982.

Weaver, C. *Psycholinguistics and Reading: From Process to Practice.* Cambridge, MA: Winthrop, 1980.

———. *Reading Process and Practice: From Socio-Psycholinguistics to Whole Language.* Portsmouth, NH: Heinemann, 1988.

11 Remediating Skills in Sight and Meaning Vocabulary

FOCUS
QUESTIONS
1. Why do many children progress from grade to grade with underdeveloped sight vocabularies?
2. How can teachers integrate the McNinch sight word plan into daily reading instruction?
3. How can workbook instruction facilitate the learning and retention of sight vocabulary?
4. What are the six principles of sight word instruction?
5. What are some strategies for the daily development of meaning vocabulary?
6. What are the steps in the Beck, Perfetti, and McKeown vocabulary training program?
7. How does a "full-blown conceptual approach" to the teaching of vocabulary differ from the traditional approach?
8. What are the similarities and differences between the Beck, Perfetti, and McKeown and the Schwartz and Raphael vocabulary strategies?

By the time typical six-year-olds enter school, they use and comprehend language proficiently. They know between 6000 and 8000 word forms in one or more of the following vocabularies.

- The listening vocabulary, which consists of words that children comprehend when they hear them. Children might not use the words, but understand them when they are spoken by others. This vocabulary is usually the largest.
- The speaking vocabulary, which consists of words children recognize, understand, and produce orally. Though continually growing this vocabulary is smaller than the listening vocabulary.
- The reading vocabulary, which consists of words that children can decode and comprehend. The words are decoded by sight recognition, contextual analysis, picture clues use, or by phonic analysis. Most children entering first grade have at least a minimal reading vocabulary. Most recognize their names, signs for restaurants or amusement centers, names of cereals and other food items, and the like. Others recognize much more. The reading vocabulary quickly expands when reading instruction begins.
- The writing vocabulary, which consists of words children understand, produce orally, read, and spell. Because of the multiple demands, this vocabulary is usually the smallest for most children and adults.

This chapter presents instructional strategies for developing all the vocabularies: sight vocabulary (reading) and meaning vocabulary (reading, listening, speaking, and writing). Children with reading difficulties do not automatically recognize a large number of words, nor do they understand many semantic units used in print. Their comprehension suffers as a result. The strategies that are presented in this chapter will assist teachers in appropriately developing both sight and meaning vocabularies.

SIGHT WORD INSTRUCTION

Johnson and Pearson (1984) noted that the term "sight vocabulary" can mean three different things to teachers of reading. First, it means the words readers recognize and identify immediately both in context and in isolation. Second, it means the new vocabulary items taught directly as a part of daily reading or content area instruction. Third, it means the small corpus of words occurring so frequently in print that they are viewed as essential to fluent reading. Most of these high frequency words are structure words that children find uninteresting, unmeaningful and difficult to learn.

Whatever definition of "sight vocabulary" reading teachers use, the instruction of sight words is one of their prime concerns. The following six principles may be used as a guide for sight-word instruction:

1. Sight-word instruction should respect children's learning rates.
2. Poor performance and slow learning rates call for greater thoroughness of instruction.
3. Sight words taught in isolation should be restored to whole language contexts.
4. Sight vocabulary should be learned to an automatic level.
5. Sight vocabulary instruction should focus on the most useful and vital words.
6. Intensive practice must be provided on frequently confused or quickly forgotten sight vocabulary.

Respecting Children's Learning Rates

Sight word instruction should respect children's learning rates. Expect children with average to slow learning rates to learn a reasonable number of words (between five and seven) in one instructional session. If the maximum number of words is approached or exceeded, maintain a balance between easy-to-learn and difficult words. Four factors affect ease of learning:

- Structure versus content words. Structure words (*in, the, through*) are generally more difficult to learn than content words (*table, elephant, house*).
- Low-imagery words (*air, plan, from*) are generally more difficult to learn than high-imagery words (*book, tree, school*).
- Low emotional-content words (*moth, wire, made*) are generally more difficult to learn than words with high emotional content (*mother, love, friend, mad*).
- Words whose sounds are inconsistent with their spelling (*the, enough, said*) are generally more difficult to learn than those with sound spelling consistency (*hat, stop, man, get*).

Slow readers often face the problem of having to cope with too many words at one time and with words that are not chosen for ease or difficulty of learning. As you choose sight words for instruction, identify an appropriate number and include a mix of easy and difficult words.

Thoroughness of Instruction

The thoroughness of sight word instruction should vary with the performance and learning rates of children. The slower the learning rate, the more thorough and intensive instruction must be. Manning (1980) designed a thorough and intensive strategy for sight word instruction, which takes into account the three levels of learning—awareness, instruction, and practice. The procedure consists of seven steps involving three modes of learning, three types of skill development, and the individual differences within each group of children. Manning named the strategy the $3 \times 3 \times I$ procedure.

The first three steps of $3 \times 3 \times I$ procedure tap the three modes of learning—visual, auditory, and kinesthetic. Children receive word instruction through all three modes. First, the teacher places the words on individual flash cards, to control exposure and to facilitate quick recognition throughout the session. The teacher highlights the visual aspects of the words. For example, the teacher might say, "Look at this word. This word is *stand*. Look at the letters in the word. Trace the letters with your eyes: s, t, a, n, d. See the small word *and* in the word. Look at the first two letters in the word." In the visual segment, the teacher might also block parts of the word to direct children's attention to visual patterns.

In the auditory segment, the teacher highlights the heard aspects of the word. For example, the teacher might say, "Listen to the word *stand*. Listen to the first part of the word, /st/. Now listen to the last part, /and/. The word is *stand*."

In the kinesthetic segment, children use movement in learning the word. They might trace the word on their palms or in the air with their fingers, or write the word on paper. Teachers might type the words and ask children to circle, underline, or otherwise identify specific words.

The procedure's second set of three steps taps three types of skill development. These are word meaning, phonic analysis, and word recognition. In the word meaning segment, teachers focus children's attention on the meaning of words. For example, the teacher might say, "The word *stand* is the opposite of *sit*. John, would you stand." In the phonic analysis segment the teacher might say, "Look at the word *stand*. Listen to the first two letters. The letters *s, t* represent the sounds you hear at the beginning of words like *stop, stem, stone,* and *star*. Listen to that sound—/*st*/. Now listen to the next part of the word. The letters *a, n, d* say /*and*/. Listen to the sounds—/*a*/, /*n*/, /*d*/, *and*. Now put the parts together—/*st*/, /*and*/ is *stand*." In the word recognition segment, the teacher flashes the word and asks the children for a quick response.

The "I" in the $3 \times 3 \times I$ procedure refers to individual differences among children in a group. Despite efforts to group children homogeneously, teachers must remember that children always display a range of performance, abilities, and learning rates. To accommodate individual differences, have weaker readers respond more frequently than better readers. This way, rather than each child responding once, the weakest reader receives the most practice. Instead of putting the cards away at the end of the lesson, call on individual children to hand in the cards as they read the words. Give weaker readers more cards to give them more practice. The following example shows how a teacher might use the $3 \times 3 \times I$ procedure in actual vocabulary instruction.

CLASSROOM APPLICATION

"Boys and girls, today we are going to learn five new words (*stand, pony, enough, bring, umbrella*). Look at the words on the cards. Look at them again." (Awareness)

"Look at the first word. The word is *stand*. Look at the letters in the word: *s, t, a, n, d*. Trace the letters with your eyes. Look at the first two letters in the word—*st*. Now look at the small word *and* at the end of the word." (Visual)

"Now listen to the word: *stand*. Listen to the beginning of the word: /*st*/. Listen to the end of the word: /*and*/. The word is *stand*." (Auditory)

"Look at the word again. Listen to the first part: /*st*/. The letters *st* stand for the sound you hear before words like *step, star, stem,* and *start*. Can you think of another word that begins like *stand*? Now look at the next part of the word. It says *and*. If I take the *st* from stand and put a *b* there, I have the word *band*. If I put an *h* there, I have the word *hand*. If I put an *l* there, what word do I have? Now, with the letters *st* I have the word *stand*." (Phonic analysis)

"The word *stand* is the opposite of *sit*. Mary, please stand. Good job." (Meaning)

After all the words have been taught, the practice phase begins. The teacher flashes the words quickly and asks children to respond. The teacher then gives children a slip of paper with the new words, as in Figure 11.1. The teacher gives directions to children that involve kinesthetic learning and also utilize the meaning, phonic analysis, and recognition skills. The teacher might say, for example, "Put the number 1 beside the word *enough* (recognition). Underline the word that is something you use in the rain (meaning). Circle the word that begins like *stone* (phonic analysis). Put the number 2 beside the word that ends like *sing* (phonic analysis). Circle the animal word (meaning). Now read each word quickly (recognition)."

Manning's $3 \times 3 \times I$ procedure provides intensive, thorough, direct instruction of sight vocabulary. It is also an excellent method of reinforcing such skills as phonic analysis and meaning. The Manning procedure emphasizes the rehearsal and review of words and a teacher-directed approach. Research shows that these aspects of vocabulary instruction are extremely important (Groff 1981).

McNinch (1981) created another remediation strategy. The strategy includes the following steps.

1. *Demonstration.* The teacher chooses a word from children's listening and speaking vocabularies. The word is presented in oral language context; for example, "John and Mary like to *stand* in the pouring rain."
2. *Continued demonstration.* The teacher presents the word in a written sentence in which all the other words are in the students' sight vocabulary; for example, "I like to *stand* up."
3. *Interaction.* The teacher isolates the word. Students' attention is drawn to word features, such as beginning and ending letters, number of letters, vowels, endings, prefixes, small words within words, and the like.
4. *Clarification.* Students read the word in a sentence in which all other words are in the students' sight vocabularies.
5. *Application.* The students read meaningful print in which the word appears. The text may be any familiar print, such as portions of a basal text, excerpts from language experience stories,

enough

umbrella

stand

pony

bring

FIGURE 11.1   Practice Sheet

or teacher-created print. The word under study should appear
several times throughout the selection in order to provide meaningful practice.

6. *Practice for mastery.* The teacher selects activities, such as
games, flash cards, work sheets, and word banks, which focus
on the new words and provide practice for mastery.

The McNinch strategy involves intensive teacher-directed instruction,
the monitoring of student behavior, and a variety of practice options.

Restoring Isolated Sight Words to Whole Language Contexts

Sight words instructed in isolation should be restored to whole language
contexts. Researchers have sought the most effective ways to teach sight
vocabulary. Ehri and Wilce (1980) report that teaching sight words in
context may result in slower learning of the words' graphic and phonic
features. Students who learned isolated sight words from flash cards
could more easily identify the phonic features of words than students
who learned words in sentence context. However, those who learned
words in context were more proficient in such language features as syntax and semantics. The research findings suggest that both isolated instruction and context are beneficial. The answer is to teach sight words
in isolation but to place them back immediately into meaningful context.
It is important that children learn individual sight words, but words seldom occur in isolation. When children recognize words in isolation, they
often fail to transfer that recognition to connected discourse. Children
need to learn the word *enough*, for example, but if a sentence in the reading selection reads, "They had enough to eat," readers also need to see the
phrase "enough to eat" or the entire sentence. Introducing phrases and
sentences that incorporate individual words helps children develop contextual expectations of words and gives them incidental exposure to
other words as well. Another benefit is that phrase and sentence instruction increases children's fluency.

Learning Sight Vocabulary to an Automatic Level

Sight vocabulary must be learned to an automatic level. Children must be
able to recognize sight words instantly. Decoding and word recognition
must reach an automatic level before children can focus on comprehension. Direct and thorough instruction helps children achieve mastery
and advance to the automatic level. In addition, children should have extended sight-word practice. Students might practice words in word
banks. They might time themselves on word lists until they beat their pre-

vious times, or work in pairs timing each other on reading sight-word lists. Use games to reinforce sight words, and have students read sight words in phrases, sentences, and connected discourse.

The workbook provides excellent opportunities for sight-word reinforcement. Most teachers restrict their use of workbooks to publishers' guidelines. Any given page presents only the skill that is taught. However, each workbook page can be used to reinforce a variety of skills, including sight vocabulary. Teach each page to the maximum. Use each page as a kinesthetic response page, having children circle given words (circle the word *from*), underline word parts (underline the base word in the word *standing*), point to words or phrases (point to the phrase *under the table*), mark through synonyms or antonyms (mark an X through the word that means *big*), and identify phonic elements within words (circle the word that begins like *stand*). These activities not only give children additional practice in sight vocabulary, but also force children to become involved with learning. Activities allow teachers to observe which children are approaching fluency in skills and which require further practice or reteaching.

Focusing on the Most Useful and Vital Words

Sight vocabulary instruction must focus on the most useful and vital words. It is unrealistic to think that all groups of children can be taught all the sight vocabulary they need prior to each reading selection. Slow readers often encounter more unknown words in a selection than the teacher has time to teach. It is essential, then, that teachers choose from among the unknown words those that are most appropriate and vital to instruction. These words warrant direct instruction. Guidelines for choosing words follow.

1. Teach words that occur most frequently in print. Children who cannot instantly recognize words that occur most frequently in written material are at a clear disadvantage in reading. Teachers of remedial readers should emphasize high frequency words. There are several high frequency word lists available, including The Dolch Basic Sight Word List (Dolch 1942), The New Instant Word List (Fry 1980), and The Johnson Basic Vocabulary of Sight Words (Johnson 1971). Perhaps the most extensive word frequency count is presented in *The American Heritage Word Frequency Book* (Carroll, Davies, and Richman 1971). The count is a computer assembled selection of 5,688,721 words in 500 word samples taken from 1045 published texts written for grades three through nine in the United States. The book provides breakdowns for grade levels in a variety of content areas. The five hundred most frequently used words in print, based on that survey, are presented in Table 11.1. The Johnson list, recommended for grades one and two, appears in Tables 11.2 and 11.3. The Johnson list arranges words alphabetically rather than in rank order.

TABLE 11.1   Most Frequently Used Words in Print

Rank 1–100

the	be	which	into	made
of	this	their	has	over
and	from	said	more	did
a	I	if	her	down
to	have	do	two	only
in	or	will	like	way
is	by	each	him	find
you	one	about	see	use
that	had	how	time	may
it	not	up	could	water
he	but	out	no	long
for	what	them	make	little
was	all	then	than	very
on	were	she	first	after
are	when	many	been	words
as	we	some	its	called
with	there	so	who	just
his	can	these	how	where
they	an	could	people	most
at	your	other	my	know

Rank 101–200

get	also	help	should	sound
through	around	put	Mr.	below
back	another	years	home	saw
much	came	different	big	something
before	come	away	give	thought
go	work	again	air	both
good	three	off	line	few
new	word	went	set	those
write	must	old	own	always
our	because	number	under	looked
used	does	great	read	show
me	part	tell	last	large
man	even	men	never	often
too	place	say	us	together
any	well	small	left	asked
day	such	every	end	house
same	here	found	along	don't
right	take	still	while	world
look	why	between	might	going
think	things	name	next	want

Rank 201–300

school	I	keep	land	boy
important	form	children	side	once
until	food	feet	without	animals

TABLE 11.1   (Continued)

life	high	times	however	change
enough	year	story	sure	answer
took	mother	boys	means	room
sometimes	light	since	knew	sea
four	parts	white	it's	against
head	country	days	try	top
above	father	ever	told	turned
kind	let	paper	young	3
began	night	hard	miles	learn
almost	following	near	sun	point
live	2	sentence	ways	city
page	picture	better	thing	play
got	being	best	whole	toward
earth	study	across	hear	five
need	second	during	example	using
far	eyes	today	heard	himself
hand	soon	others	several	usually

Rank 301–400

money	half	really	though	letter
seen	sentences	table	started	among
didn't	red	remember	idea	4
car	fish	tree	call	A
morning	plants	000	lived	letters
given	living	course	makes	comes
trees	wanted	front	became	able
I'm	black	known	looking	dog
body	eat	American	add	shown
upon	short	space	become	mean
family	United States	inside	grow	English
later	run	ago	draw	rest
turn	kinds	making	yet	perhaps
move	book	Mrs.	hands	certain
face	gave	early	less	six
door	order	I'll	John	feel
cut	open	learned	wind	fire
done	ground	brought	places	ready
group	lines	close	behind	green
true	cold	nothing	cannot	yes

Rank 401–500

built	oh	list	seemed	strong
special	person	stood	felt	voice
ran	hot	hundred	kept	probably
full	anything	shows	America	needed
town	hold	ten	notice	birds
complete	state	fast	can't	area

TABLE 11.1 (Continued)

Rank 401–500 (Cont.)

horse	common	tired	finally	mountains
Indians	stop	road	summer	heavy
sounds	am	questions	understand	carefully
matter	talk	blue	moon	follow
stand	quickly	meaning	animal	beautiful
box	whether	coming	mind	beginning
start	fine	instead	outside	moved
that's	5	either	power	everyone
class	round	held	says	leave
piece	dark	friends	problem	everything
slowly	girls	already	longer	game
surface	past	warm	winter	system
river	ball	taken	Indian	bring
numbers	girl	gone	deep	watch

Source: Used by permission from *The American Heritage Word Frequency Book,* copyright 1971 by American Heritage.

TABLE 11.2 Johnson's First-Grade Words

a	children	got	kind	off
above	come	had	let	old
across	could	hand	like	one
after	day	hard	little	open
again	days	has	look	or
air	did	have	love	out
all	didn't	he	make	over
am	do	help	making	past
American	don't	her	man	play
and	door	here	may	point
are	down	high	me	put
art	end	him	men	really
as	feet	his	miss	red
ask	find	home	money	right
at	first	house	more	room
back	five	how	most	run
be	for	I	mother	said
before	four	if	Mr.	saw
behind	gave	I'm	must	school
big	get	in	my	see
black	girl	into	name	seen
book	give	is	never	she
boy	go	it	new	short
but	God	its	night	six
came	going	it's	no	so
can	gone	just	not	some
car	good	keep	now	something

TABLE 11.2   (Continued)

soon	they	took	way	why
still	think	top	we	will
table	this	two	well	with
than	those	under	went	work
that	three	up	what	year
the	time	very	when	years
then	to	want	where	yet
there	today	wanted	which	you
these	too	was	who	your

Source: Excerpts from *Teaching Reading Vocabulary*, Second Edition, by Dale O. Johnson and P. David Pearson, copyright © 1984 by Holt, Rinehart and Winston, Inc., reprinted by permission of the publisher.

TABLE 11.3   Johnson's Second-Grade Words

able	close	idea	outside	thing
about	company	knew	own	things
almost	cut	know	part	thought
alone	different	last	party	through
already	does	leave	people	together
always	done	left	place	told
America	each	light	plan	town
an	early	long	present	turn
another	enough	made	real	until
any	even	many	road	us
around	ever	mean	same	use
away	every	might	say	used
because	eyes	morning	says	water
been	face	Mrs.	set	were
believe	far	much	should	west
best	feel	music	show	while
better	found	need	small	whole
between	from	next	sometimes	whose
board	front	nothing	sound	wife
both	full	number	started	women
brought	great	of	street	world
by	group	office	sure	would
called	hands	on	take	
change	having	only	tell	
church	head	other	their	
city	heard	our	them	

Source: Excerpts from *Teaching Reading Vocabulary*, Second Edition, by Dale O. Johnson and P. David Pearson, copyright © 1984 by Holt, Rinehart and Winston, Inc., reprinted by permission of the publisher.

Analysis of such lists demonstrates that the most frequently occurring words are structure words, which are most difficult to learn. It is important, then, to teach these words with other words that are easier to learn, and to place words within the context of whole language.

2. Teach words most essential for understanding of selections. Apart from high-frequency words, selections have key words that are vital to comprehension. These words should be taught directly. For example, if the selection is about glaciers, *glacier* is an essential word.

3. Teach words that have common structures that are easily generalized. To maximize instruction in teaching poor readers, teach them words that have common structures and emphasize those structures during instruction. The word *slide*, for example, is not only a high frequency word, but also a word with the *sl* blend and with final *e* construction, which occur frequently in print and are vital structures to learn. Highlight and discuss these generalizable structures during vocabulary instruction.

4. Spend little time directly instructing words unique to a selection and rarely met in print. Present and discuss such words prior to reading the selection or explain them during reading. Instructional time for children with slower learning rates is better spent on more useful items.

5. Do not spend direct instructional time teaching person or place names. Present these during the preparation time for content and concepts before children read the selection.

Providing Children with Intensive Practice

Intensive practice must be provided in sight vocabulary that is frequently confused or quickly forgotten. Many children confuse words that are structurally similar (e.g., *them* and *then*, *through* and *though*, *make* and *made*). This confusion is at times the result of inappropriate instruction. When children learn isolated vocabulary, they often choose the easiest or least important clues for recognition. For example, if the words *them*, *little*, *yellow*, and *dog* were taught together, children might recognize the word *them* solely because it is the only word beginning with the letters *th*. They might recognize the word *yellow* on the basis of its clear configuration. Consequently, when they encounter a new word—*that*—the children might respond *them* because they overgeneralized the *th* clue. Samuels (1976) suggests that when single-letter clues fail to distinguish one word from another, children resort to attending to all the letters in a word.

When children frequently confuse structurally similar words, help them to make distinctions by focusing their attention on the similarities and differences among the whole words. Manning (1980) presents an intensive structure-word practice effective in helping children to learn structure words automatically and to avoid confusion among similar word forms. The strategy, called Small Word Practice, proceeds as follows:

- Choose four to six key words that children need to practice (e.g., *even*, *enough*, *through*, and *then*).
- For each key word, choose as distractors three or four structurally similar words or words that are often confused with the key word (e.g., *even* / *ever*, *every*, *envy*; *then* / *thin*, *than*, *when*).
- Divide a sheet of paper into four parts. Label the sections *A*, *B*, *C*, and *D*.
- In each section, place all the key words and their distractors, varying the order and position of words in each section, as shown in Figure 11.2. Make copies of this sheet for the students.
- Write each key word on a flash card, and use the flash cards to present the words. Point out each word's distinctive features, use it in a sentence, and spell it.
- Fold the word sheets so that only one section is visible, and pass out the sheets. Begin with section *A*. Show the flash card with the first word, *even*. Say, "Look in line 1. Find the word *even*. Put a box around the word *even*." Discuss the distractors. Have the children note the differences and similarities between the key word and its distractors. For example, ask children how they know that *ever* is not *even*. Discuss the clues. Move on to line two. Show the word *enough*. Say, "Look in line 2. Find the word *enough*. Underline the word *enough*." Discuss the differences and similarities and point out the distinctive features. Continue through all the words in section *A*.

A 1. even, every, ever, envy 2. ever, enough, though, away 3. when, than, thin, then 4. though, thing, through, throw	**B** 1. through, though, throw, thing 2. ever, even, envy, every 3. away, though, enough, ever 4. then, when, than, thin
C 1. then, than, when, thin 2. though, through, thing, throw 3. envy, every, even, ever 4. though, away, ever, enough	**D** 1. enough, away, ever, though 2. ever, every, envy, even 3. when, then, thin, than 4. though, throw, through, thing

FIGURE 11.2   Small Word Practice

Source: Adapted from J. D. Manning, *Reading: Learning and Instructional Processes* (Geneva, IL: Paladin, 1980), 191–196.

- Refold the papers to expose section *B*. Proceed more quickly, giving students fewer directions, discussing less, and moving at a faster pace. For example, show the card that says *through*, and say, "Line 1. Circle the word *through*." Show the card that says *ever*, and say, "Line 2. Underline the word *ever*." Continue in this way through section *B* to force quick recognition of the words.
- Expose section *C*. Give still fewer clues and go faster. This time give directions before children begin the task. You might say, "I am going to show you a word quickly and tell you what to do on the page. Listen carefully and do just as I say." Show the first word for approximately one second and then remove the card. Say, "Circle." You might ask individual children to say the word ("John, what is that word?"). Continue through section *C*.
- Expose section *D*. Without exposing the card, say each word and have the children mark the word. For example, you might say, "Line 1, circle *enough*. Line 2, underline *even*."

The Small Word Practice is an excellent strategy for giving children intensive practice and for helping them to discriminate quickly among easily confused words. The strategy may be modified to help children attend to specific parts of words. For example, if children tend to ignore the beginnings of words, use displays such as *say*, *stay*, *stray*, *slay*. If the middles of words are confused, use *ride*, *rude*, *rode*. If children confuse endings of words, use, for example, *them*, *then*, *this*, *these*, or *play*, *playing*, *played*, *plays*. The discussion step is vital in this procedure because it highlights the distinctive features and clarifies the confusions. Remember also to have children practice these words in whole connected print.

Another intensive strategy is recommended by Johnson and Pearson (1984). They suggest a five step multimodal instructional procedure, as follows.

Step 1: Seeing. Write the word on a flash card, a piece of paper, or on the chalkboard. Try to illustrate the word either by labeling classroom objects (e.g., *desk*, *chair*, *window*) or by using pictures. Some words are difficult to illustrate (e.g., *air*, *then*, *so*), but use illustrations as much as possible.

Step 2: Discussing. After writing the word, read the word to the children. Discuss the word, drawing on children's experiences and interests. Some words, especially structure words, are difficult to discuss, in which case move on to Step 3.

Step 3: Using. Ask children to use the word in sentences. Generate synonyms and antonyms. Write the sentences on the board and discuss their functions. Have students compare and contrast the words with words they already know and use.

Step 4: Defining. Provide a definition for the word. The definitions should be in children's own words and not from a dictionary. Ask children what the words mean to them.

Step 5: Writing. Finally, encourage children to practice writing the words both in isolation and in context. Children might write the words in their personal dictionaries, word books, or word banks. Have children read and reread these written segments to encourage transfer into actual print. Remember to continually expose children to actual reading. There is no substitute for exposure to real reading. The more children practice vocabulary in contextual reading, the more automatic and useful their word recognition will be.

MEANING-VOCABULARY DEVELOPMENT

The importance of meaning-vocabulary development is undisputed in the literature on reading instruction. Reading teachers would agree that vocabulary development should be a priority and that vocabulary knowledge clearly affects performance in reading comprehension (Graves and Prenn 1986, Johnson and Von Hoff Johnson 1986, Ruddell 1986, Thelen 1986). The relationship between vocabulary and comprehension is expected because vocabulary represents words, words represent concepts, and concepts are the basis of comprehension. The relationship has been discussed by many researchers in the field of reading (Crist and Petrone 1981, Beck et al. 1982, Kameenui et al. 1982, Johnson and Pearson 1984, Johnson 1971, 1983). As Pearson (1985, 729) states, "A reader's knowledge about a topic, particularly key vocabulary, is a better predictor of comprehension of a text than is any measure of reading ability or achievement."

The clear importance of vocabulary instruction might lead you to expect commercial reading series to pay significant attention to the direct teaching of vocabulary. Analysis indicates, however, that series offer little more than peripheral experiences with vocabulary, especially the shallow preinstruction of words (Beck et al. 1979). Clearly, this aspect of language development, written and oral, must receive significantly more attention.

Vocabulary research has focused on discovering instructional designs resulting in maximum vocabulary growth, and the relationships between vocabulary instruction and comprehension growth (Pany and Jenkins 1978, Anderson and Freebody 1981, Beck et al. 1980, Kameenui et al. 1982, Johnson 1983, Anders and Bos 1986, Johnson and Von Hoff Johnson 1986). Although researchers do not all agree on the best format or design for vocabulary training or on the exact nature of the relationship between vocabulary and comprehension, they each contribute valuable information. Their research suggests seven guidelines for vocabulary development:

1. Create a word-aware environment.
2. Make direct instruction in vocabulary a priority.
3. Provide long-term, indepth experiences with the words taught.

4. Stress the semantic fit.
5. Involve students intensively in their learning of words.
6. Stress the most usable words.
7. Create opportunities for students to use newly learned vocabulary.

Creating a Word-Aware Environment

One of the most important factors in the development of meaning vocabulary is a learning environment that clearly values words. For many children, vocabulary instruction means receiving a list of words, looking them up in the dictionary, and writing definitions in sentence format. Children leave the experience as ignorant of the real meanings of the words as they were before. They do not have a true appreciation of language, do not view words as interesting, and do not enjoy the feeling of empowerment that an ever-expanding vocabulary can provide (Hirsch 1987). One of the most valuable experiences you can provide for children is a word-aware context. Make an effort throughout each school day to share with children your value of words. Use any opportunity to draw children's attention to words. Some useful strategies include the following.

- As you read to children, take the time to comment on a few interesting words. Discuss these words with children, write them on the chalkboard, and mention them during the day. The same strategy may be used as children are reading to you.
- Prior to reading instruction or to instruction in content areas (social studies, science, civics, math), take the time to isolate a few key vocabulary items that carry important conceptual weight, and preteach those items. During discussion relate the words to children's experiences.
- Reward children's efforts to use varied vocabulary. When children use an interesting word, compliment them and call attention to the words. Be as creative as possible in your attention. For example, raise a "word wizard" flag, ring a "word champ" bell, place a name on the "word crackerjack" ladder, or add to a "word demon" track.
- Take opportunities during experiences with print to have children focus on words. For example, as you read ask children to give you synonyms or antonyms of words. Ask them to find words that have special meaning or to identify multiple meanings of words.
- Use word play. Designate "word opposites" mornings in which statements are made with opposite meanings. For example, "It is a beautiful and sunny day" becomes "It is an ugly and gloomy

night." Children can use their detective skills to decipher sentences.

- Take five minutes during the day for a "word sharing" period. During this time, encourage children to bring in words they like and to share them with the class. Share your new or interesting words with children as well.
- Encourage children to keep a "favorite word" notebook. Each day they may enter any word of interest encountered that day.

These activities make children aware of vocabulary and demonstrate to them your value of words. Perhaps the most valuable gift you can give the children in your classroom is an environment that continuously reinforces vocabulary and that stresses the importance and enjoyment of learning.

Making Direct Instruction in Vocabulary a Priority

Significant research supports the direct instruction of vocabulary (Crist and Petrone 1981, Beck et al. 1982, Kameenui et al. 1982, Johnson 1983). In direct vocabulary instruction teachers (at times, in conjunction with students) choose words for study. Teachers build a conceptual base for the learning of the words. They do this by linking words to children's prior knowledge and by stressing the richest and most meaningful semantic relationships. Teachers then involve students in the discussion and elaboration of words and meanings. Finally, teachers provide follow-up opportunities for the reinforcement, practice, and use of new words.

This direct instruction in vocabulary contrasts with the traditional approach. Pearson (1985, 728) described a situation in which a young teacher was remarking on the excellent vocabulary lesson he had created. He explained that he had the children look up new words in their pocket dictionaries and then write each word in a sentence. The teacher showed some of the students' responses, one of which read:

> Word: Exasperated
> Definition: Vexed
> Sentence: He was exasperated.*

Pearson commented that the teacher knew only that (1) the child could find the word in the dictionary, (2) the child could copy the first available definition, and (3) the child recognized that a word ending in *ed* could serve in the past participle slot in a sentence. The teacher did not know if the child knew the meaning of the word or experienced the word in its fullest sense. Another example of a "passive" vocabulary experience concerns a teacher who provided her class with ten new words each week.

*P. D. Pearson, "Changing the Face of Reading Comprehension Instruction," *The Reading Teacher* 38 (April 1985), 728. Used with permission of the International Reading Association.

Children were responsible for writing the words in a notebook, finding dictionary definitions and using the words not in a sentence but in a paragraph. One student's entry read:

Word: Frugal
Definition: To save
Paragraph: Last week Mary and I were walking by the lake. Mary fell in the lake. "Frugal me, frugal me," cried Mary, so I jumped into the lake and frugaled Mary.

The child clearly understood one meaning of the word *save*, but not the word *frugal*, nor the relationship between the words *frugal* and *save*. Young children require direct instruction to help them focus on the most salient meaning clues and relate words to meaningful experiences.

Emphasis on direct vocabulary instruction does not diminish the importance of self-direction in learning vocabulary. Children should become responsible for their own learning. Remember, however, that children must attain the awareness, instructional, and practice stages before they can be expected to cope with independence. The early learning stages also permit the development of the word-aware environment, which is critical to appropriate vocabulary growth.

Providing Long-Term, Indepth Experiences with Words Taught

Research on vocabulary instruction reveals that long-term programs have the most positive effect on vocabulary growth and reading comprehension (Draper and Moeller 1971, Beck et al. 1982, Stahl 1986). Blachowicz (1985) suggested several reasons long-term vocabulary programs are more effective than the typical "one shot" instructional approaches. First, students have the necessary time for developing target content and skills. Second, students receive repeated exposure to words, which is important to learning and retention. Third, long-term programs give children the opportunity to encounter words in a variety of situations. Finally, children are allowed to practice the words in real reading contexts.

Teachers often fail to appreciate the vocabulary load with which children cope. Consider a typical day, for example. During the reading period, there might be four or five unknown words. The math lesson might present one or two new terms. The social studies period may include another four or five new items, and the science lesson may contribute an additional three or four words. In one day, therefore, children might be faced with at least twelve to fifteen unknown words. Children cannot be expected to learn this number of new items each day. This overload of unknown or superficially mentioned words contributes to children's lack of interest in words and in language.

Engaging children in a short-term, one-shot discussion of new vocabulary items does little to promote the quality and quantity of vocabulary growth they need to cope with the ever-increasing demands of school. Children need a context in which they receive instruction and practice with the same words over an extended period of time.

An effective long-term vocabulary training program was presented by Beck, Perfetti, and McKeown (1982). The purpose of the program is to give students thorough, extended instruction in words and to develop "deep and fluent" word knowledge. The instructional activities include definition, sentence generation, classification, oral and written production, and gaming tasks. Tasks take place under both timed and untimed conditions, and focus on forming strong connections between new vocabulary items and prior knowledge. The program takes place over a twelve-week period. Each week consists of a five-day cycle in which children receive instruction in eight or nine words. Children focus on the same words for twenty to thirty minutes per day for five days. Each week's eight or nine words are chosen from one of several semantic categories. Some of the semantic categories and words used in the original study follow.

Vocabulary Training Program

Semantic Category	Words Selected
Week 1: People	*accomplice, virtuoso, rival, miser, novice, philanthropist, hermit, tyrant*
Week 2: What you can do with your arms	*beckon, embrace, knead, flex, hurl, seize, nudge, filch, thrust*
Week 3: Eating	*obese, glutton, devour, appetite, fast, wholesome, nutrition, famished, edible*
Week 4: Eyes	*gape, spectator, binoculars, squint, focus, scrutinize, glimpse, inspector*
Week 5: Moods	*cautious, jovial, glum, placid, indignant, enthusiastic, diligent, envious, impatient*
Week 6: How we move our legs	*stalk, galumph, vault, trudge, patrol, meander, strut, lunge, dash*
Week 7: Speaking	*wail, chorus, proclaim, mention, banter, commend, berate, urge, retort**

*I. L. Beck, C. Perfetti, and M. G. McKeown, "The Effects of Long-Term Vocabulary Instruction on Lexical Access and Reading Comprehension," *Journal of Educational Psychology* 74:510. © Copyright 1982 by the American Psychological Association. Adapted by permission of the publisher and author.

Instructional activities for learning each set of words follow the same five-day cycle:

Day One: On the first day of each cycle, students are given log-sheets with the words to be learned and their definitions. The teacher reads each word and definition. Students repeat this exercise and then write the word on their sheets.

Next, for each word the teacher provides an associated word, and asks students to explain why the words fit together. For example, for the word *accomplice*, the teacher might choose the associated word *crook*.

Finally, the group plays an affective association game called "Yeas and Boos." The teacher says a word (e.g., *miser*). Each child responds "yea" if the word elicits a positive response, or "boo" if it elicits a negative response. Children are asked to share their reasons for responding negatively or positively to each word. Their rationales, and not their original response, are what is important. In this phase, children form emotional associations essential to comprehension and recall.

Day Two: On the second day of each cycle, children are introduced to a sentence completion activity. The activity helps the children demonstrate their conceptual understanding of the words, as in the following examples from the original study.

- The *accomplice* swore he would never break the law again because _____.
- The audience asked the *virtuoso* to play another piece of music because _____.*

Notice that appropriate sentence completion requires a clear conceptual understanding.

The second activity on day two is a definition matching task. The group is divided into teams. Each team is presented with a matching activity requiring them to match words with appropriate definitions. Teams compete on the basis of accuracy and speed of matching.

Day Three: On the third day, students are required to generate new contexts for each word and to identify expected associations. For example, the original items include the following.

- Which of these things would an accomplice be likely to do?
  a. squeal to the police in return for not having to go to jail.
  b. rob a bank by himself.
  c. enjoy babysitting.
  Write one more thing here that an accomplice might do.
- Which one of these things would a *virtuoso* be likely to do?
  a. forget the notes to the music she is playing.
  b. play so well that the audience bursts into applause.

*Beck et al. (1982), 510. Adapted by permission.

c. wear clothes that don't match.
Write one more thing here that a virtuoso might do.*

Day Four: On the fourth day, students participate in a timed matching activity called "Ready, Set, Go." Students draw lines to connect words to their appropriate definitions. As they do so, a partner times them. Students have four tries or "laps" to achieve a set time or to better their previous time.

Next, students complete a creative thinking activity in which they must think of words in different ways and explore possible semantic overlaps among the words. For example, consider the following activity from the original study.

People Pairing Worksheet

1. Could an accomplice be a novice?
2. Would a hermit likely be an accomplice?†

This activity sometimes produces unexpected responses from children, as in a recent application of the original program to a group of gifted third grade students. In response to the question, "Could a philanthropist be a miser?" one young girl said, "Yes. Some people can give away a lot of money and things to charity and people. This is what a philanthropist does. They might, though, not want to be kind and thoughtful to people they know. This is what a miser does. People can be philanthropists with money and misers with themselves." Activities like the People Pairing Worksheet encourage such quality of thought.

Day Five: On the fifth day, students take a multiple choice test. An additional feature is the "Word Wizard" component in which children earn "Word Wizard" points by providing evidence that they have seen, heard, or used the words outside of class.

You modify this vocabulary training procedure to meet your instructional needs. For example, you might wish to try a four-week or a two-week program. You might use the procedure as vocabulary preparation for a future instructional unit. For example, if you know that in two weeks you will be introducing a new unit on Economics, you might identify six to ten words pertaining to the new unit and provide experience with those words (e.g., *population, goods, services, exchange, price, competition, wage, partnership, labor,* and *supply*). This intensive vocabulary experience provides children with full-blown conceptual knowledge of key words, and also serves as content preparation for the upcoming instructional unit.

Whatever instructional strategies you choose, remember that children need more than a cursory introduction to new vocabulary. They

---

*Beck et al. (1982), 510. Adapted by permission.
†Ibid.

need long-term exposure to and interaction with new words. The central goal of vocabulary instruction is to have children "own" words in the most complete sense possible. Your time and personal involvement are essential to this goal.

Stressing Semantic Fit

Traditionally, vocabulary instruction has tried to make children aware of what words mean in terms of their definition and of how those words are used in language (Vacca et al. 1987). Pearson (1985) suggested that teachers make a clear instructional shift, emphasizing not the definition of words, but the "fit" of words in children's semantic repertoires—the "semantic fit" of the word.

Pearson noted that new concepts are learned only in connection with pre-existing concepts. Teachers should change the question asked prior to vocabulary instruction from "What is it children *do not* know and how can I get that into their heads?" to "What is it children *do* know that is similar to the new concepts and how can I use it as an anchor point?" Pearson pointed out that adults tend to explain new concepts or words to other adults by using the logic, "Well it is sort of like ____, but. . . ." Such statements establish a link between the new concept and prior knowledge, and then explain how the new concept is different. For example, you might say, "A *hovel* is sort of like a *shed*, but it is more *dilapidated* and *miserable*." This strategy not only gives you a meaning of the word, but also tells you where it fits in your semantic knowledge bank. Vocabulary instruction should focus on "semantic elaboration and semantic fit rather than definition and usage" (Pearson 1985, 729).

Two well-accepted strategies emphasizing semantic fit are semantic feature analysis and semantic mapping. Semantic feature analysis is a "procedure for helping pupils to see how words within a given category are alike and different and to relate the meanings of new words to prior knowledge" (McNeil 1984, 104). Technically, identical synonyms do not exist in that no two words have exactly the same meanings. Semantic feature analysis clarifies the unique properties of words and shows how unknown words relate to known ones.

Semantic feature analysis consists of the following steps.

1. Select a topic or category (e.g., modes of travel, forms of shelter, shapes, emotions, etc.).
2. List in a vertical column some words related to the topic (e.g., for "forms of shelter" list *cabin, barn, tent, castle*).
3. List in a horizontal row some features characteristic of the words (e.g., *large, small, elaborate, simple, dilapidated, scary*).
4. Place pluses (+) and minuses (−) in the matrix boxes to indicate the presence or absence of features for each word in the column.

5. Add additional words and features (e.g., *shed*, *villa*, *palace*).
6. Discuss each word in terms of its shared and unique properties.

Figure 11.3 presents a semantic feature analysis for the concept of "shelters."

For more precision of meaning, use a numerical system. For example, 0 = none, 1 = little, 2 = some, 3 = a lot. Figure 11.4 shows this modification. Another option is a scale, such as A = definitely, B = definitely not, and C = possibly. Compared to other concepts of shelters, the word *castle* might receive an A for the features *large*, *elaborate*, and *expensive*, a B for the features *small* and *simple*, and a C for the features *highly decorated*, *sparse*, *dilapidated*, and *scary*.

In addition to showing the unique properties of a concept, semantic feature analysis can also be used to categorize concepts (e.g., both palaces and castles are large shelters; sheds, cottages, and hovels are small shelters), and to rank concepts in terms of a given feature (e.g., a shed is very simple; a cottage is kind of simple; a palace isn't simple at all).

Semantic mapping uses graphic representations to illustrate concepts and their interrelationships. Categories link known concepts with

Kinds of Shelters	Large	Small	Elaborate	Simple	Highly Decorated	Sparse	Dilapidated	Scary	Expensive
Palace	+	−	+	−	+				+
Shed		+		+		+			
Hovel	−	+	−	+	−	+	+		−
Cottage				+					
Castle	+	−	+	−			−	+	+
Barn			−	+	−				
House				+					
Bungalow			−	−					
Mansion	+	−	+		+	−			+
Shack	−	+	−	+	−	+	+	+	−
Hut			−		−	+			−

FIGURE 11.3   Semantic Feature Analysis of "Shelters"
Source: Adapted from Dale D. Johnson, Susan Toms-Bronowski, and Susan D. Pittelman, *An Investigation of the Trends in Vocabulary Research and the Effects of Prior Knowledge on Instructional Strategies for Vocabulary Acquisition* (Madison, WI: University of Wisconsin, Center for Education Research, 1981), 40.

Kinds of Shelters	Large	Small	Elaborate	Simple	Highly Decorated	Sparse	Dilapidated	Scary	Expensive
Palace	3	0	3	0	3	0	0	0	3
Shed	0	3	0	3	0	1	1	1	0
Hovel	0	3	0	3	0	3	3	1	0
Cottage	0	2	0	2	0	1	0	0	0
Castle	3	0	3	0	3	1	0	1	3

FIGURE 11.4   Modified Semantic Figure Analysis
Source: Johnson et al. 1981, 40.

new concepts. A complete semantic map generally includes four basic categories: class, property, related concepts, and example. The word class is the superordinate category of which the word is an example (e.g., an orange is a *fruit*). The properties of a concept are its characteristics, traits, or qualities (e.g., an orange has *juice* inside and is *sweet*). Related concepts are those concepts with similar features (e.g., an orange is somewhat like a *grapefruit*, a *tangerine*, a *lemon*). An example is a representative of a concept or class of concepts (e.g., a *Valencia* is an example of a kind of orange). Figure 11.5 presents a semantic map of the word *orange*. Figure 11.6 presents a semantic map of *dog*.

A semantic map may also be used to discover words with text-specific meanings. Johnson et al. (1981) introduced refocused semantic maps, which explore the specialized meanings of words. The teacher initiates refocusing by finding a word in a selection that has a specific usage other than the common meanings. Teacher and students first construct a semantic map of common meaning, as in Figure 11.7. After reading the selection, they discuss the new meaning of the word and revise the map to incorporate the new meaning, as in Figure 11.8. Semantic feature analysis and semantic mapping are useful strategies for helping children create a "semantic fit" for vocabulary. Semantic fit increases their depth of understanding and retention of vocabulary items.

Involving Students in the Learning of Words

There is no doubt that vocabulary development relates directly to language development. Language development is an active process demanding involvement, emotional investment, and purposeful action. Vocabulary instruction should involve students in learning (Carr and Wixson 1986). Notice that all the strategies in this chapter include a stu-

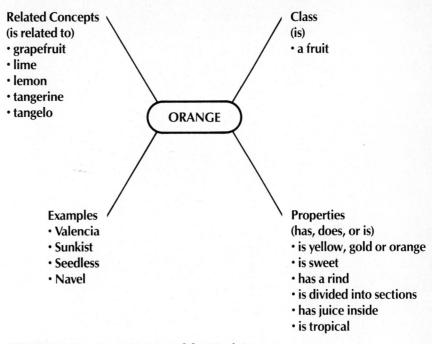

Related Concepts
(is related to)
• grapefruit
• lime
• lemon
• tangerine
• tangelo

Class
(is)
• a fruit

ORANGE

Examples
• Valencia
• Sunkist
• Seedless
• Navel

Properties
(has, does, or is)
• is yellow, gold or orange
• is sweet
• has a rind
• is divided into sections
• has juice inside
• is tropical

FIGURE 11.5   Semantic Map of the Word *Orange*

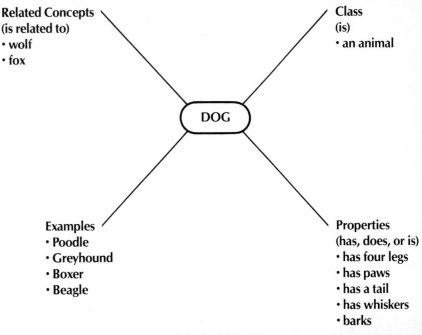

Related Concepts
(is related to)
• wolf
• fox

Class
(is)
• an animal

DOG

Examples
• Poodle
• Greyhound
• Boxer
• Beagle

Properties
(has, does, or is)
• has four legs
• has paws
• has a tail
• has whiskers
• barks

FIGURE 11.6   Semantic Map of the Word *Dog*

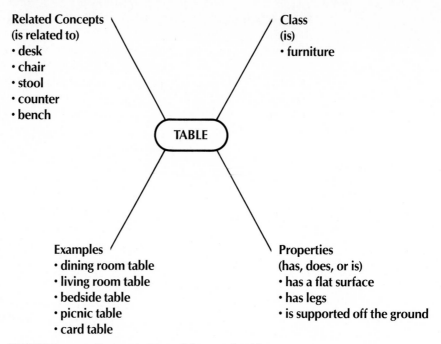

FIGURE 11.7 Semantic Map of the Word *Table*

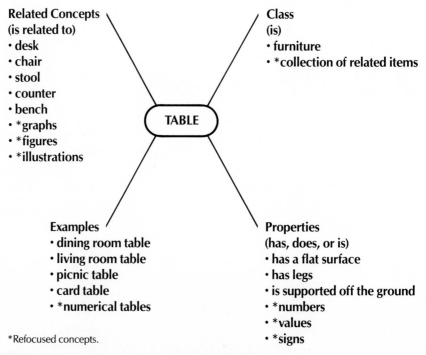

*Refocused concepts.

FIGURE 11.8 Refocused Semantic Map of *Table*

dent participation segment. Participation not only helps students to better grasp the concepts, but also gives them foundation strategies that will allow them to become independent in vocabulary acquisition.

Schwartz and Raphael (1985) stress learning independence in their "concept of definition" strategy. This strategy emphasizes the role of students in figuring out for themselves the meanings of new words. The researchers commend direct instruction of vocabulary, but believe strongly in instruction that gives students control over their own learning.

The "concept of definition" procedure teaches children strategies for expanding their vocabulary and mastering unfamiliar concepts. Students select and evaluate various sources of information for determining word meanings, and combine the new information with their prior knowledge to form complete word definitions.

A schematic word map is used to teach the concept of definition. The word map includes the class, properties, and examples of a concept by asking three questions: What is it? (class), What is it like? (properties), and What are some examples? (examples). Figure 11.9 shows this type of word map.

Schwartz and Raphael created a four-day instructional cycle for teaching children the concept of definition. On the first day, tell children

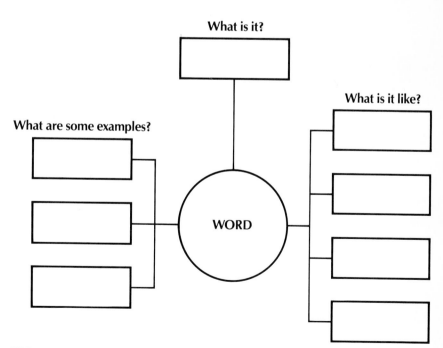

FIGURE 11.9   Word Map

Source: From R. M. Schwatz and T. E. Raphael, "Concept of Definition: A Key to Improving Students' Vocabulary," *The Reading Teacher* 39 (November 1985): 201. Reprinted with permission of R. M. Schwartz and the International Reading Association.

that the new strategy will help them gain more control of their comprehension of text. Introduce the word map structure. Tell children that the three things they need to really understand a new word are the class, properties, and examples of the word. Show them where these fit on the word map. Children work with familiar words and generate class, properties, and examples. The teacher helps them organize words and phrases into the three map categories. For example, the following list might be arranged as in the word map in Figure 11.10.

Soup

chicken noodle
served with sandwiches
tastes good
is a liquid
eat it with a spoon
served before the main dish
served in a bowl
food*

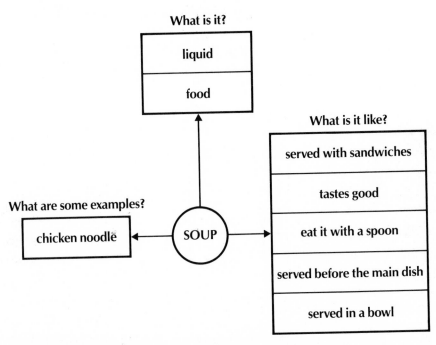

FIGURE 11.10   Word Map for the Word *Soup*

Source: From R. M. Schwartz and T. E. Raphael, "Concept of Definition: A Key to Improving Students' Vocabulary," *The Reading Teacher* 39 (November 1985): 202. Reprinted with permission of Robert M. Schwartz and the International Reading Association.

*Schwartz and Raphael (1985), 202. Reprinted with permission of Robert M. Schwartz and the International Reading Association.

The second lesson involves identifying the components of a definition from a complete context. The contexts are contrived in that they include at least one class, three properties, and three examples of the concepts, as in the following passage.

Crops

Have you ever been to a farm? Have you ever seen a farmer at work with his crops? Crops come from seeds planted by the farmer early in the Spring. The farmer takes care of his seeds all Spring and Summer long. Early in the Fall, crops are harvested and taken to market. At the market they are sold to people like you and me. Farmers can plant different kinds of crops. Some plant potatoes. Some plant onions. Some plant corn and tomatoes. Fresh crops taste good.*

The passage is discussed to identify the three components of the definition, which are mapped, as in Figure 11.11. Encourage students to add their own ideas and knowledge of the concept to the map.

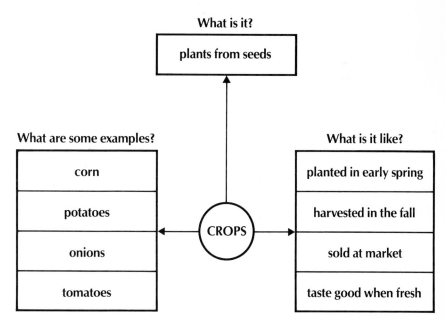

FIGURE 11.11   Map of the Passage "Crops"
Source: From Schwartz and Raphael (1985), 202. Reprinted with permission of Robert M. Schwartz and the International Reading Association.

*Source: Schwartz and Raphael (1985) 202. Reprinted with permission.

The third lesson provides incomplete contexts with some categories deleted. For example, a passage might read:

Environment

You hear a lot these days about our environment, but what exactly is it? We hear a lot of talk about a clean environment. Many parts of our environment need cleaning. The better our environment, the happier we can be.*

Students identify segments that are deleted (class and properties), and use dictionaries, textbooks, encyclopedias, or other sources to fill in the map.

In the fourth and final lesson, students practice writing definitions including all components, without actually mapping the word. They think about each category, gather all necessary information, and write the definitions. Students receive complete and incomplete definitions, identify each, and add any components needed to construct complete definitions. Finally, students are asked, "What do you do to figure out the meaning of a new word?" Assist students in verbalizing the fact that a complete definition includes what the word is (class), what the word is like (properties), and examples of the word (examples).

The "concept of definition" technique involves students intensively in the learning of new vocabulary. It also gives them tools for moving toward greater independence and self-monitoring in learning.

Stressing the Most Usable Words

Teachers often complain that remedial readers know so few words in any given selection that it is difficult to decide which words to give instructional attention. This is a legitimate complaint. Choosing vocabulary is challenging and must be done selectively. A few guidelines for choosing instructional vocabulary follow.

1. Choose words that are most frequently used. Focus on words found most often in print and in spoken language. Include some unusual and interesting words. Sometimes extremely unusual words capture children's attention, making it easier for them to learn and retain those words. However, concentrate most intensively on words they will encounter often in language.

2. Emphasize words containing structural elements that will help children to figure out new words. Graphic language contains many structural clues that are invaluable in both decoding and comprehension. Among the most useful of structural clues are affixes and compounds.

*Schwartz and Raphael (1985), 202. Reprinted with permission of Robert M. Schwartz and the International Reading Association.

Affixes are one or more letters or sounds attached to the beginnings (prefixes) or ends (suffixes) of words. They give added meaning to words and cannot stand on their own. They must be attached to base words to have meaning. Affixes, therefore, give readers at least two important clues: decoding and meaning. Children must learn to recognize and understand common prefixes and suffixes, as well as the base words on which affixes depend. Table 11.4 lists some of the more common affixes, along with their meaning and an example.

TABLE 11.4   Affixes

Affix	Meaning	Example
Prefix		
ambi	both	ambidextrous
anti	against	antitoxin
auto	self-propelling	automobile
	or self	autobiography
bene	good	benefit
bi	two	bilingual
centi	one hundred	centrigrade
circum	around	circumscribe
contra	against	contradict
dis	not	disbelief
extra	beyond	extracurricular
hyper	over	hyperactive
hypo	under	hypotension
in	not	invulnerable
inter	between	interval
im	not	improper
micro	small	microscopic
multi	many	multimillionaire
over	too much	overabundance
pan	all	Pan-American
poly	many	polygamy
post	after	postmortem
pre	before	prepay
pseudo	false	pseudonym
re	again	redo
retro	backward	retrospect
semi	half	semicircle
sub	under	submerge
super	above	superimpose
tele	far off	television
trans	across	transport
tri	three	triangle
un	not	unplug
uni	one	unicycle

(continues)

TABLE 11.4   (Continued)

Affix	Meaning	Example
Suffix		
able	can be done	readable
ana	a collection of	Americana
ancy	the state of	truancy
er	person who	teacher
esque	in the style of	statuesque
ette	little	dinette
ful	full of	joyful
fy	to become	purify
gram	something written	telegram
ie	little	doggie
ism	a belief	Communism
ist	one who	artist
ize	to make	civilize
less	without	motherless
ling	young	duckling
ment	the state of	puzzlement
ness	the state of	darkness
or	one who	doctor
ward	toward	homeward

Do not expect children to memorize a list of affixes. As in all vocabulary instruction, teach affixes directly and thoroughly and provide frequent practice. Make sure children can recognize and identify root words within longer words. Early in their reading experiences, orally present familiar, meaningful words and ask children to detect smaller (base) words within them (e.g., *unhappy, helpful, kingdom, jewelry, violinist,* and *disagree*). When children can do this orally, introduce them to the visual forms. Then provide instruction in affixes.

Other meaningful word parts are inflectional endings such as *s* (*beds*), *es* (*horses*), *ed* (*wanted*), *ing* (*talking*), *er* (*bigger*), and *est* (*slowest*). Inflectional endings differ from suffixes in that the addition of a suffix usually changes the word's class or part of speech, while the addition of an inflection does not.

Word expansion is a valuable strategy for helping children to develop their skills in using affixes and inflectional endings. In expanding a word, children build as many related words as they can from a common base word, as in Figure 11.12. Children might also start with a complex word and identify as many smaller words as they can. For example, begin with a word like *unfaithfulness* and help children identify the words *unfaithful, faithfulness, faithful,* and *faith.*

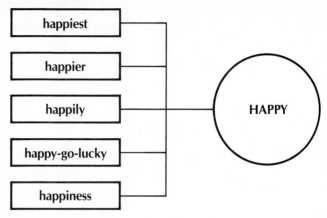

FIGURE 11.12   Word Expansions

Compound words are single word units formed from the combination of two morphemes that can each stand independently as base words, e.g., *mailbox* and *steamboat*. The recognition of compound words requires children to use visual analysis skills to visually segment the compound into two words (*saw / dust* rather than *sawd / ust*), and meaning skills to recognize that the meaning of the compound word is similar to the combination of its parts (*sawdust*) = dust from a saw.

Johnson and Pearson (1984) identify six specific types of compounds:

- Root two is "of" root one, e.g., *nightfall* = fall of night, *riverbank* = bank of the river.
- Root two is "from" root one, e.g., *sawdust* = dust from a saw, *moonlight* = light from the moon.
- Root two is "for" root one, e.g., *bathroom* = room for a bath, *wallpaper* = paper for a wall.
- Root two is "like" root one, e.g., *cottontail* = tail like cotton, *frogman* = man like a frog.
- Root two "is" root one, e.g., *bluebird* = bird is blue, *pipeline* = the line is a pipe.
- Root two "does" root one, e.g., *towtruck* = a truck does towing, *scrubwoman* = a woman does scrubbing.*

The structures of the six types of compounds need not be overemphasized or formally taught. Instead, try the following activities, practicing one type of compound at a time.

*Excerpts from *Teaching Reading Vocabulary*, Second Edition, by Dale O. Johnson and P. David Pearson, copyright © 1984 by Holt, Rinehart and Winston, Inc., reprinted by permission of the publisher.

- Ask children questions such as, "What would you call a woman who scrubs? A truck that tows?"
- Reverse the process and ask, "If a scrubwoman is a woman who scrubs, what is a towtruck?"
- Have children use compounds in sentences, select compounds to fit cloze passages, and the like.

3. Choose words essential to understanding the selection. Some words are central to the meaning of reading selections. For example, if the selection is about a glacier, teach words such as *glacier*, *iceberg*, and *snow*. Distinguish between teaching vocabulary for long-term retention and teaching vocabulary for immediate understanding of content. Directly transferable and frequently used words require and deserve intensive instruction. They should be taught thoroughly and practiced often. Words critical to the selection at hand might be less important in general language because they seldom appear in print and in oral language. Many person and place names fall into this category. Teach these words less thoroughly or without aiming for automaticity.

Blachowicz (1985) suggested that the following three questions can help teachers choose the most usable words: Is it important for students to know this word five years from now? Will knowing this word help them figure out other words related to it? Is the word's meaning essential to understanding this selection? If the answer to the first two questions is "yes," then teach the word for retention. If the answer to only the third question is "yes," then teach the word for immediate use in selection comprehension.

Creating Opportunities for Students to Use Newly Learned Vocabulary

The only goal of vocabulary development is use. If words are not used, children forget their meanings and teachers waste the time spent in initial instruction. Place emphasis on providing many opportunities for children to interact directly with words. Experiences with oral and graphic language should be the classroom's central focus. Children should daily listen to and read print. As you read, identify and enjoy interesting words. As they read, highlight, analyze, and discuss words. Make vocabulary development an ongoing practice.

Other than immersing children in written and oral language, try instructional strategies for fostering vocabulary use. The "Word of the Week" strategy focuses on one word per week, which is chosen by the teacher, by the children, or by both. The word is discussed, defined, elaborated on, and used. It is then placed on a card and displayed in a prominent spot. Children are encouraged to use "their" word all week long. They might receive points for using the word—one point for speaking it and five points for using it in writing. Use one word for the entire class, or a different word for each reading group.

Another strategy is the "Word Outlaw," which forces children to vary their vocabulary. There are words that children tend to overuse in both oral and written language (e.g., *nice, fine, pretty, happy, sad*). Identify one overused word per week and outlaw that word. No one in the classroom should use the word in speech or in writing during that week. Provide alternatives for the outlawed word on a "word ladder" displaying substitute words. Teacher and children generate synonyms to add to the list throughout the week. Children quickly make a game of this strategy. They enjoy monitoring other students and the teacher to "catch" them using the outlawed word. Figure 11.13 presents a Word Outlaw chart.

The "Favorite Word" strategy encourages each child to choose a favorite word each week. Children enter this word in a Favorite Word notebook or file box and make an effort to use "their" word daily in oral or written language. They also use the word in a creative activity, such as writing a paragraph or story about the word, illustrating the word in a drawing or painting, writing a poem relating to the word, making a word collage, or composing a song about their word. At the end of the week children share results with the class.

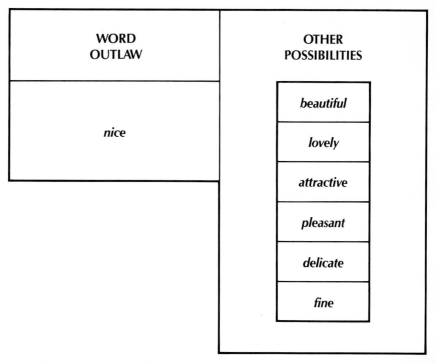

FIGURE 11.13   Word Outlaw Chart

Remember that words taught each day must be practiced and reinforced. Teacher-made worksheets, teacher-made games, and published materials help provide ongoing practice in vocabulary. Word meanings must be repeated often enough for children to move through the awareness, instructional, and practice phases to the independent phase.

SUMMARY   Vocabulary development must be a priority in reading instruction. Sight vocabulary and meaning vocabulary are both vital to appropriate reading growth. Six principles guide sight vocabulary instruction. Instruction should respect children's learning rates. Poor readers and children with slow learning rates need more thorough instruction. Sight words taught in isolation should be restored to whole language contexts. Children should learn sight vocabulary to an automatic level. Instruction should focus on the most useful and vital words. Intensive practice must be provided in sight vocabulary that is frequently confused or quickly forgotten.

Seven principles guide meaning vocabulary instruction. Teachers should create a word-aware environment, give priority to direct instruction, provide long-term and indepth experiences with taught words, and stress semantic fit. Teachers should also involve students intensively in learning words, stress the most usable words, and create opportunities for students to use newly learned vocabulary.

Children with reading difficulties need a great deal of attention in the area of vocabulary. Teachers should make vocabulary a priority in reading instruction. Guidelines call for substantive instruction, frequent use, and intensive practice.

R · E · F · E · R · E · N · C · E · S

Anders, P. L., and C. S. Bos. "Semantic feature analysis: An interactive strategy for vocabulary development and text comprehension." *Journal of Reading* 29 (April 1986): 610–616.

Anderson, R. C., and P. Freebody. "Vocabulary Knowledge." In J. T. Guthrie, ed. *Comprehension and Teaching: Research Reviews.* Newark, DE: International Reading Association, 1981.

Beck, I. L., E. S. McCaslin, and M. G. McKeown. *The Rationale and Design of a Program to Teach Vocabulary to Fourth-Grade Students.* Pittsburgh, PA: University of Pittsburgh, Learning Research and Development Center, 1980.

Beck, I. L., M. G. McKeown, E. S. McCaslin, and A. M. Burkes. *Instructional Dimensions That May Affect Reading Comprehension: Exam-*

ples from Two Commercial Reading Programs. Pittsburgh, PA: University of Pittsburgh, Learning Research and Development Center, 1979.

Beck, I. L., C. Perfetti, and M. G. McKeown. "The effects of long-term vocabulary instruction of lexical access and reading comprehension." *Journal of Educational Psychology* 74 (1982): 506–521.

Blachowicz, C. L. Z. "Vocabulary development and reading: From research to instruction." *The Reading Teacher* 38 (May 1985): 876–881.

Carr, E., and K. K. Wixson. "Guidelines for evaluating vocabulary instruction." *Journal of Reading* 29 (April 1986): 588–595.

Carroll, J. B., P. Davies, and B. Richman. *The American Heritage Word Frequency Book.* New York: American Heritage, 1971.

Crist, R., and J. Petrone. "Learning concepts from contexts and definitions." *Journal of Reading Behavior* 9 (1981): 271–277.

Dolch, E. W. *The Basic Sight Word Tests,* Parts 1 and 2. Champaign, IL: Garrard, 1942.

Draper, A. G., and Moeller, G. "We think with words (therefore, to improve thinking, teach vocabulary)." *Phi Delta Kappan* 52 (1971): 482–484.

Ehri, L. C., and L. S. Wilce. "Do beginners learn to read function words better in context or in lists?" *Reading Research Quarterly* 15 (1980): 275–285.

Fry, E. B. "The new instant word list." *The Reading Teacher* 34 (December 1980): 284–289.

Graves, M. F., and M. C. Prenn. "Costs and benefits of various methods of teaching vocabulary." *Journal of Reading* 29 (April 1986): 596–602.

Groff, P. "Directed instruction versus incidental learning of reading vocabulary." *Reading Horizons* 21 (Summer 1981): 262–265.

Hirsch, E. D. *Cultural Literacy: What Every American Needs to Know.* Boston, MA: Houghton Mifflin, 1987.

Johnson, D. D. "A basic vocabulary for beginning readers." *Elementary School Journal* 72 (October 1971): 29–34.

———. *Three Sound Strategies for Vocabulary Development, Occasional Paper No. 3.* Columbus, OH: Ginn, 1983.

Johnson, D. D., and P. D. Pearson. *Teaching Reading Vocabulary.* New York: Holt, Rinehart & Winston, 1984.

Johnson, D. D., S. Toms–Bronowski, and S. D. Pittleman. *An Investigation of the Trends in Vocabulary Research and the Effects of Prior Knowledge on Instructional Strategies for Vocabulary Acquisition.* Madison, WI: University of Wisconsin, Wisconsin Center of Educational Research, November 1981.

———. "An Investigation of the Effectiveness of Semantic Mapping and Semantic Feature Analysis with Intermediate Grade Level Children." Program Report No. 83–3. Madison, WI: Wisconsin Center for Education Research, 1982.

Johnson, D. D., and Von Hoff B. Johnson. "Highlighting vocabulary in inferential comprehension instruction." *Journal of Reading* 29 (April 1986): 622–625.

Kameenui, E. J., D. W. Carnine, and R. Freschi. "Effects of text construction and instructional procedures for teaching word meanings on comprehension and recall." *Reading Research Quarterly* 17 (1982): 367–388.

McNeil, J. D. *Reading Comprehension: New Directions for Classroom Practice.* Glenview, IL: Scott, Foresman, 1984.

McNinch, G. H. "A method for teaching sight words to disabled readers." *The Reading Teacher* 35 (December 1981): 269–272.

Manning, J. D. *Reading: Learning and Instructional Processes.* Geneva, IL: Paladin House, 1980.

Pany, D., and J. Jenkins. "Learning word meanings: A comparison of instructional procedures and effects of measures of reading comprehension with learning disabled students." *Learning Disability Quarterly* 1 (1978): 21–32.

Pearson, P. D. "Changing the face of reading comprehension instruction." *The Reading Teacher* 38 (April 1985): 724–738.

Ruddell, R. B. "Vocabulary learning: A process model and criteria for evaluating instructional strategies." *Journal of Reading* 29 (April 1986): 581–587.

Samuels, S. J. "Modes of Word Recognition." In H. Singer and R. Ruddell, eds. *Theoretical Models and Processes of Reading*, 2nd ed. Newark, DE: International Reading Association, 1976.

Schwartz, R. M., and T. E. Raphael. "Concept of definition: A key to improving students' vocabulary." *The Reading Teacher* 39 (November 1985): 198–205.

Stahl, S. A. "Three principles of effective vocabulary instruction." *Journal of Reading* 29 (April 1986): 662–668.

Thelen, J. N. "Vocabulary Instruction and Meaningful Learning." *Journal of Reading* 29 (April 1986): 603–609.

Vacca, J. L., R. T. Vacca, and M. K. Gove. *Reading and Learning to Read.* Boston: Little, Brown, 1987.

12 Remediating Skills in Language

1. What is the relationship between reading and oral language development?
2. What are some reasons for underdeveloped receptive and expressive language?
3. What strategies can be used to develop receptive language skills?
4. How can teachers use reading instruction to facilitate expressive language skills?
5. How can teachers foster oral language development during reading instruction?

Children's oral language development affects their reading performance. Reading is a language process and therefore shares some basic features with oral language. Oral and written language forms have common elements: syntax (word order), semantics (word meaning), and phonology (sound). Because of these shared elements, both reading and oral language have similar predictability. In both forms, sounds occur in a particular order and meanings cluster around predictable semantic contexts. The oral language that children have been developing and practicing since birth operates on the same fundamental principles as reading. Oral language thus potentially provides the ideal transition into print.

This clear relationship between oral and written language might suggest that the rules governing oral language development and learning apply directly to the learning and development of reading. The relationships, however, are not identical. There are some important differences between the two language forms (Smith 1982).

1. Reading requires some specific skills that are not required in oral language. Reading includes a graphic component consisting of letters and the sounds they represent. Learning this component requires specific skills, such as visual acuity and discrimination, and auditory discrimination, segmentation, and blending. These specific skills make reading in school a "taught" craft. Oral language, on the other hand, is learned naturally and quite intuitively.

2. Children acquire oral language in a primarily tension-free environment. They have considerable freedom to learn language at their own pace, using their own techniques. This is not often true of reading acquisition, especially in school settings.

3. Language learning is a gradual process beginning at birth and continuing through life. Children entering first grade are expected to have underdeveloped linguistic skills. Reading, on the other hand, usually begins abruptly in kindergarten or first grade. By grade three, children are expected to master the fundamental decoding component.

4. Most children have significantly stronger natural reinforcement and motivation toward oral language learning than toward graphic language learning. This is particularly true of children with a history of reading failure from their first exposure to print.

These differences remind us that although oral and graphic language are clearly and unquestionably related, they are not the same thing. This chapter investigates the nature of oral language development, discusses reasons for underdeveloped language skills, and presents strategies for remediating inadequate language skills and for facilitating language growth.

THE NATURE OF ORAL LANGUAGE DEVELOPMENT

Language is one of the most complex human behaviors. It is learned so naturally that most adults take the magnitude of the task for granted. Adults remember and consider the process of linguistic growth only when they observe that something has gone wrong in an individual's language development.

The initial learning of language has fascinated scholars for centuries. However, most of the research on language acquisition and development has been done in the past twenty years. This research adds to our understanding of the language learning process. Several consistent findings emerge based on analysis of this research.

Language Acquisition: An Active Process

From birth, children actively process information. They are constantly affected by and responsive to their linguistic environment (Duchan 1986). They react to language and produce its sounds. Long before they speak with any clarity, they understand intuitively that language is used for specific purposes, such as communicating and meeting one's needs. As they begin to build their language, they do so through active involvement in the language experience. Children constantly act on and react to language in an effort to solve the problem of speech (Lindfors 1985). Language learning is not a passive process.

Linguistic Stages of Language Development

Children progress gradually through specific linguistic stages. According to Hoskisson and Tompkins (1987, 18), "Young children acquire oral language in a fairly regular and systematic way. All children pass through the same stages, but they do so at widely different ages." Descriptions of some of the better-defined stages follow.

1. Babbling (birth to approximately one year) represents the first sounds the infant makes. During the first few months of life, the sounds produced in babbling are the same in all languages and reflect the entire range of sounds. After approximately three months, however, the children stop producing sounds that are not present in their linguistic environment, and replicate only the sounds they hear (Norton 1980).

2. In the holophrastic stage (approximately one to two years), children begin to use single words—called holophrases—to communicate the meaning of entire sentences. A child might say *wa–wa* to mean "I want some water," or *jacket* to mean "Put on my jacket and take me outside." Holophrastic speech allows children to begin to use language for social reasons. During this time, children's naming vocabulary develops rapidly.

3. During the telegraphic stage (approximately two to three years), children develop syntax, or grammar, as they begin to use combinations of two or more words. Language at this stage often sounds like the language adults use when they send a telegram. Function words are omitted. Children might say sentences like, "All gone milk," "Mary dress," "Gimme juice," or "No want night–night." As children mature linguistically, telegraphic language develops into more complete sentence structure. Late in the telegraphic stage children develop grammatical structures such as subject, verb, and object word order (e.g., The cat ran up the tree); plural suffixes (e.g., The boys ran down the street); possessives (e.g., It is John's toy); affirmatives and negatives (e.g., John is here; John is not here); and noun modifiers (e.g., The little dog has a big bone).

By the time children enter first grade, the following linguistic structures should be stabilized in their speech:

- *Complete sentence structure.* Children should use the subject-verb-object construction.
- *Possessives.* Children should understand the concept of possession and be able to form possessives of most nouns they know.
- *Plurals.* They should understand that plural signifies more than one and be able to form plurals of most nouns. Children might overgeneralize the *es* marker (e.g., "oxes" instead of *oxen*).
- *Negatives.* They should discriminate between affirmative and negative and know the significance of the word *not.*
- *Singular and plural verbs.* Children should know that the verb signals subject number (e.g., The dog sits; the dogs sit).
- *Conditional clauses.* Children should recognize that clauses beginning with *if* have significance.
- *Negative affix un.* They should understand the significance of *un*, as in *locked* versus *unlocked.*

- *Self-embedded* sentences. They should understand sentences such as "The girl that owned the dog went into the store."
- *Reflexive pronouns.* Children should understand pronoun referents, as in "Mary pushed her" or "Mary washed herself."

Although children have learned most syntactic structures by the age of six, they have not yet mastered some forms. Some syntactic rules remain largely unmastered even by age ten. These forms include the following.

- Appositives. (John, *the sailor*, returned home today.)
- Relative clauses. (Susan, *who is wearing a red dress*, is on the swing.)
- Complement constructions. (*The fact that* John is late angers mother; *John's being late* angers mother.)
- Delayed reference. (Mother promised Henry to go; Susan asked Michael where to put the bike.)
- Delayed time-sequence. (Get me the glass, *but first* close the door.)
- Passive constructions. (Susan was stared at by the little dog.)

These constructions must be taught directly to children and practiced orally for extended periods if teachers expect children to understand and use them. Table 12.1 shows the development of language through more complex stages.

TABLE 12.1   General Language Characteristics: Birth to 12 Years

Birth to 3 months	Young children start with all possible language sounds and gradually eliminate sounds that are not used around them.
1 year	Many children speak single words (e.g., *ma–ma*). Infants use single words to express entire sentences. Complex meanings might underlie single words.
1½ years	Many children use two- and three-word phrases ("See baby"). Children begin to develop their own language rule systems. Vocabularies are about 300 words.
2 to 3 years	Children use such grammatical morphemes as plural /s/, auxiliary verb *is*, and irregular past tense. They use simple and compound sentences and understand tense and such numerical concepts as *many, few,* and *some.* Vocabularies are about 900 words. Structures such as subject-verb-object order, possessives, affirmatives, negatives, and modifiers develop.
3 to 4 years	The past tense appears but children often overgeneralize the *ed* and *s* markers. Negative transformation stabilizes. Children understand numerical concepts such as *one, two, three.* Speech becomes more complex with more adjectives, adverbs, pronouns, and prepositions. Vocabulary is about 1500 words.

(continues)

TABLE 12.1 (Continued)

4 to 5 years	Language is more abstract, and more basic rules of language are mastered. Children produce grammatically correct sentences most of the time. Vocabulary includes approximately 2500 words.
5 to 6 years	Most children frequently use complex sentences. They use correct pronouns and verbs in the present tense. The average number of words per oral sentence is 6.8. It has been estimated that the children understand approximately 6000 words. Structures such as the negative affix *un*, reflexive pronouns, complex verbs, and passive sentences develop.
6 to 7 years	Children speak in complex sentences using adjectival clauses. Conditional clauses beginning with *if* appear. Language becomes more symbolic. Children understand concepts relating to time and the seasons. Average sentence length is 7.5 words.
7 to 8 years	Children use relative pronouns as objects in subordinate adjectival clauses ("I have a cat that I feed every day"). Subordinate clauses beginning with *when*, *if*, and *because* appear frequently. Embedded sentences are commonplace. The average number of words per oral sentence is 7.6.
8 to 10 years	Children begin to relate concepts to general ideas through the use of such connectors as *meanwhile* and *unless*. The subordinate connector *although* is used correctly by 50 percent of children. The active present participle and perfect participle appear. The average number of words in an oral sentence is 9.0.
10 to 12 years	Children use complex sentences with subordinate clauses of concession introduced by *nevertheless* and *in spite of*. The auxiliary verbs *might*, *could*, and *should* appear frequently. Children have difficulties distinguishing among past, past perfect, and present perfect tenses. The average number of words in an oral sentence is 9.5.

Source: From D. Norton, The Effective Teaching of Language Arts (Merrill, 1980).

Learning from Immersion in Language

From birth, most children are surrounded by language. They hear language, see people responding to language, hear the different tones of language, and experience the variety of emotions expressed by language. Through this immersion in language, they begin to abstract certain consistencies or regularities (rules) and to gradually solve the problem of how to understand and use language. Immersion is perhaps the most important variable in language learning (Chapman 1981). This concept of immersion is a key variable in language remediation and facilitation.

Language Models

As children develop their language, they use it in a variety of ways and for a variety of purposes. Researchers suggest that children learn to use language for specific purposes. They practice the functions of language in their experiences. Halliday (1975) suggests that children learn seven different "models" or functions of language, and develop them according to children's need for each model in their environments. The seven models of language are:

1. *The instrumental model.* Language is used to communicate one's needs to others and to get those needs met, e.g., "I want a cup of juice" or "Give me my ball." It takes the form of requests or persuasion.
2. *The regulatory model.* Language is used as a means of control over the behavior of others, e.g., "Don't!" or "Stop it!" It might take the form of giving orders, manipulating, or controlling.
3. *The interactional model.* Language in this model is used to interact with others on an interpersonal level. It is also used to establish and define social relationships, e.g., "How are you?" or "Are you okay?" It may include forms such as negotiation, encouragement, or expression of friendship.
4. *The heuristic model.* Language is used to gain information and knowledge. Questions are asked, answers are received, and other questions are formulated, e.g., "What is that? What is it used for? Why?"
5. *The personal model.* Language is used to share feelings, opinions, and personal reactions. Language expresses one's own individuality and personality, e.g., "I feel happy," "I think this is just awful."
6. *The imaginative model.* Language is used imaginatively for amusement, fun, and entertainment. Children express their creativity through play, drama, poetry, and creative literature, e.g., Peter Piper picked a peck of pickled peppers.
7. *The representational model.* Language is used to share information and to represent reality, e.g., "It is so dark!" "Isn't this a large apple!"

Halliday's scheme of language functions provides us with a very useful tool for analyzing linguistic development and interaction in social contexts such as families and classrooms. In some contexts adults overuse and reward certain functions of language and underuse or directly discourage others. For example, they may react to children predominantly in the instrumental mode ("Get me the newspaper," "Fetch me a cup," "Find me a pen") and the regulatory mode ("Don't do that," "Stop that," "Quit," "Go to bed," "Be quiet"). Families might ignore other interactions, such as asking and answering a wide variety of questions (heuristic model), interacting on a personal level (interactional model), sharing and investigating feelings (personal model), enjoying and playing with language (imaginative model), and expressing and checking reality (representational model). The result is that children who develop in such environments use more restricted language than children who receive broader linguistic experiences. Unfortunately, when children growing up in linguistically sparse settings come to school, they are often placed in classrooms in which language variety is not a direct goal. These children do not have an opportunity to extend their language, and all the language arts (speaking, listening, reading, and writing) suffer. Print expresses all seven models of language. Children with limited experience in linguistic variety often find it difficult to understand the more elaborate language of texts.

The importance of language as an agent of personal and environmental adaptation is underscored by Hirsch in his book *Cultural Literacy* (1987, 26). He defines cultural literacy as "a vocabulary that we are able to use throughout the land because we share associations with others in our society." Language is the basis for the development of cultural literacy. It is a vehicle for learning the wide range of information demanded by a complex society.

Halliday's language models help teachers make a clearer distinction between dialect use and underdeveloped language. Do not assume that children who speak dialects (for example, local or ethnic dialects) do not understand or use expanded vocabulary or syntactic forms. Dialect use does not preclude linguistic variety and elaboration. Halliday's models provide a clear, simple, and helpful guide for evaluating language use.

Some sociolinguists attempt to relate language production to social class variables. For example, Bernstein (1961, 1966) classifies language speakers as using an "elaborated code" or a "restricted code." Elaborated-code speakers use language for a wide variety of purposes, such as communication, problem-solving, analysis, synthesis, information gathering, play, and meeting personal needs. Restricted-code speakers, on the other hand, demonstrate a narrow range of grammatical forms, use simple sentences, use few abstract words and subordinate clauses, and have limited vocabularies. They use language primarily to get things done and to react minimally to the linguistic efforts of others.

Bernstein suggests that elaborated-code speakers usually come from the higher socioeconomic classes, in which play, discussion, interaction, sharing, and open conversation are encouraged. Problem-solving and linguistic elaboration are also expected. Children are continually "spoken with" and "read to," and experience a wealth of linguistic variability in written language. Restricted-code speakers, according to Bernstein, usually come from lower socioeconomic classes. Their linguistic environments tend to discourage exploration (often due to limited play space), to emphasize controlling and disapproving language, and to stress "the correct way," thus blocking exploration of alternatives. Such children seldom engage in discussion with adults, and are more accustomed to linguistically passive activities, such as watching television, than to linguistically active ones, such as discussing and reading. Bernstein points out that restricted-code speakers use language appropriate to their linguistic environment, but lack experience with elaborate codes. This often makes school difficult, particularly the language component of the school environment. Bernstein emphasizes that the use of restricted code does not indicate linguistic deficiency or inability, but merely a different language experience. Children hear restricted-code speakers in their social environments and model that code. To modify restricted-code use, teachers need to continually expose children to elaborated-code language through multiple experiences with extended speech, indepth discussion, flexible linguistic contexts, and wide reading experiences.

Learning the Vocabulary and Conventions of Language

Children learn that words carry meaning and that certain words fit into specific language slots and serve specific purposes. For example, they learn that words represent things (*table, fork, friend*), actions (*run, love, bring*), descriptions (*big, green, beautiful*), explanations (*slowly, angrily, loudly*), and connections (*and, plus, in addition*). They learn that language conventions must be observed. For example, specific words are used to open and close conversations ("Hello," "Hi," "How are you?" "Goodbye," "See you later"). Individuals should keep their turn in conversations, and should request and acknowledge information in expected ways ("Please," "Thank you"). Children learn these language conventions through observation of role models in the linguistic environment.

LINGUISTIC VARIATION IN THE CLASSROOM

Teachers are increasingly faced with linguistically and culturally different children in their classrooms. Some teachers believe that linguistic (and other cultural) interference is to blame for children's difficulty in learning language arts. The linguistic interference hypothesis has been repeatedly applied to speakers of black dialect. The hypothesis has been strongly challenged in research and professional literature, however. For example, Harber and Bryen (1976) reported a review of research on the relationship between black dialect and reading performance. They came to the following conclusions:

1. There is no clear-cut evidence that black English interferes with the reading process.
2. No conclusive empirical evidence supports the use of dialect-based texts in place of standard English material.
3. Not enough is currently known about black English phonology to identify the degree of difference between the dialect and the language of textbooks.
4. There is a lack of information concerning other variables affecting reading development in relation to black dialect use. Such variables might include intelligence, social experiences, and cultural background.
5. Many educators have adopted the attitude that black English is inappropriate and that users of that dialect are intellectually inferior. No effective ways have been found to teach teachers that black dialect is an acceptable form of speech that adequately meets users' communication needs.

Dialect Users

Linguists and psycholinguists have made numerous pleas to the educational community to place the issue of dialect use in appropriate perspective (Labov 1970, Dale 1972, Cazden et al. 1972, Lindfors 1980, Phillips 1982). They point out that English dialects share a common language base. Teachers should be careful to react to children's speech on the basis of its semantic quality rather than its phonology. Dialect users must not be viewed as cognitively deficient nor as speakers of a defective language. According to Dale (1972, 258):

> With the decline of the melting-pot theory of American society, social scientists have begun to explore and appreciate the diversity of culture and dialect in the country. Recognition of black English as an autonomous dialect has been delayed by strongly negative attitudes toward its speakers. The language of many black children has been seriously underestimated. An educational system should capitalize on these capacities the children bring to school rather than penalize them.

To give dialect speakers the linguistic credit they deserve, teachers should be sensitive to the predictable differences between most black English dialects and standard English. Understanding these differences assists teachers in making distinctions between children who are dialectically different and those who have difficulty reading and understanding print. Dialect speakers might experience valid difficulties in reading. However, children who pronounce words differently or translate print into their own grammatical structures, but who comprehend and interact with print appropriately, should not be considered to have reading problems. Teachers should refrain from labeling such children as culturally or linguistically deprived or disadvantaged, linguistically deficient, or language delayed. Make efforts to capitalize on children's differences and to extend the language base they bring to school. At all costs, a clear distinction must be made between dialect difference and reading deficiency. This important distinction should be kept in focus continually during instruction and evaluation.

Bilingual Students

Another group of linguistically different children, bilingual students, requires some attention. This group includes children whose families have recently immigrated and children whose families have lived in this country for a long time, but have retained their native language.

The linguistic performance of bilingual students varies greatly. Some children come to school very competent in their native language but lacking basic experiences with English. These children require exposure to and interaction with English. With practice and immersion, they quickly gain facility with English. Other children come to school with underdeveloped linguistic structures (phonology, syntax, and vocabulary/semantics) in their primary language. They also are unfamiliar with English. These children need basic language experiences. They require continuous exposure to language, direct instruction in pronunciation, grammar, and vocabulary meaning, and discussion and verbal communication. Because some of these children have specific language deficits, learning language arts might progress more slowly and require more in-depth instruction. Some children arrive at school well developed both in their native language and in English. These children cope well with regular instruction in classrooms and perform at expected levels. They might differ to varying degrees in their pronunciation (phonology) and complex grammar (complex syntax); however, their comprehension and general communication are strong.

At present, there are three approaches to teaching English to bilingual speakers: (1) the bilingual approach, (2) Teaching English as a Second Language (T.E.S.L.), and (3) the immersion method. The bilingual approach instructs children in the new language for one-half of the school day and in their native language for the remainder of the day. It is believed that instruction in the native language expands and enriches the initial language base and reinforces the foundation for the learning of a new language. Generally, the content areas (reading, math, social studies, science, etc.) are presented in the native language, and the arts, sports, general discussion periods, and the like are done in the new language.

The Teaching English as a Second Language approach trains children in selected syntactic language patterns. Children practice the patterns through repetition until they achieve memorization. They use whole sentences (e.g., How are you? I am well. This is a pen. This is a dog). This is a language pattern drill approach. One criticism of this approach is that structure is overemphasized, and meaning and discussion are not given appropriate attention.

The immersion method provides holistic and continuous exposure to new language. Children are immersed in the new language and receive little formal instruction. Children interact with fluent speakers and learn through repeated practice.

Some bilingual children enter school as fluent readers of their native language. These children must learn English in its oral form and transfer the skill of reading to the new language. This task, though significant, is often not difficult. Other bilingual children have not yet learned to read their native language. For them, the task is considerably more demanding and complex. They must first learn oral English, then learn to read English print. This task is further complicated when children have tried and failed to read their own language.

The issue of how best to teach reading to bilingual children is currently under debate. Some educators suggest that children should first receive reading instruction in their native language. They feel that the primary language provides the strongest linguistic base, which would facilitate ease of learning. After children have learned to read in their own language, they could transfer the acquired skills to the learning of English print. This method is believed to result in more effective long-term retention and learning in both languages.

Other educators believe that children should be taught English print immediately. Since they cannot read what they cannot understand, English is usually spoken orally for at least one year before reading instruction begins. The language experience approach is used. Research on the best instructional approach is inconclusive. Oral discussion, concept elaboration, and vocabulary development are consistently recommended (Hornby 1980, Perez 1981, Hough et al. 1986).

Gillet and Temple (1986) present some helpful guidelines for teaching reading to bilingual children. For those children who do not read in any language:

- Make sure that bilingual children's fluency in oral English matches the level of language in texts. Children should be able to discuss concepts fluently prior to reading texts.
- Provide oral language practice in English until oral English matches that of the textbooks used. Practice should include discussion, listening to material, experiencing concrete activities, manipulating sentence patterns, and dictating stories based on experiences with content.
- Help bilingual children associate spoken and written forms of

words by using labels. Label objects in the environment. Children might practice naming, matching, and discussing the objects.

For children who can read their native language but not English, Gillet and Temple recommend the following:

- Help them with oral English fluency. Their listening comprehension in English should approximate the level of language in the books they have to read.
- Use the written form as an aid to learning the spoken forms of English. Aids might include labeling objects, using picture dictionaries, and illustrating language experience stories.
- Be careful not to confuse oral pronunciation with comprehension. Emphasis should be placed on silent reading of English followed by discussion to check comprehension.

For both groups of children, Gillet and Temple offer the following suggestions:

- Be aware that language is intimately connected with the children's culture and with the things that are familiar and important in their lives.
- Be prepared to make an asset of the language diversity that non-English speakers bring to the classroom. Take the opportunity to learn some of the speakers' language, customs, food, history, literature, and holidays. These activities show respect for the cultures and experiences of the children (Gillet and Temple 1982: 28–29).

Teachers should respect the differences among all students and provide them with experiences that foster optimum growth and development.

REASONS FOR UNDERDEVELOPED LANGUAGE SKILLS

Most children enter first grade with appropriately developed oral language skills acquired through constant interaction with others in their linguistic environment. They have been exposed to a variety of models and have learned slightly different forms from each. They have heard language from adult family members, peers, adult neighbors and friends, television characters, and book characters. They have developed language in contexts predominantly free from stress or tension. For the most part, language learning has been motivating and reinforcing.

Some children, however, come to school with underdeveloped language skills. They demonstrate difficulty in one or both of two major areas: receptive language and expressive language.

Receptive Language Difficulties

Receptive language refers to incoming language. If children have underdeveloped receptive language skills, they do not appropriately comprehend oral (and often written) language. Difficulty in receptive language might be demonstrated in the following ways:

1. Children might not understand many commonly used words. They often have particular difficulty understanding and responding appropriately to abstract words. Many children have lacked a sufficient variety of adult models of oral language. They might not have had adequate conversations with adults, or might not have benefited from being read to regularly. These children need more direct vocabulary discussion and instruction.

2. Children might not understand common sentence forms. Some children have difficulty processing comparatively familiar sentences, particularly when they are asked to draw inferences from what they hear. Such children tend to perform very poorly on reading comprehension tasks.

3. Children might have difficulty following directions because of underdeveloped auditory skills, or because of a lack of attention. Since much school experience involves following directions, they find school tedious.

4. Children might have difficulty listening critically and making judgments. This might be the result of inappropriate listening, weak critical thinking, or both. Many children have not been exposed to purposeful listening in their home environments. They have not been questioned on levels that develop critical thought. In addition, many have not been listened to enough to develop good listening skills from adult models. Listening skills are vital to the development of appropriate comprehension.

Expressive Language Difficulties

Expressive language is language produced by individuals. Children who have underdeveloped expressive language skills have difficulty communicating effectively with oral (and often written) language. Some of the more common areas of difficulty are the following.

1. Children might have difficulty formulating expressive sentences. Such children often speak in sentence fragments and use

few words. They seem hesitant to communicate orally or to participate in discussions.

2. Children might have inadequate speaking vocabularies. Many children use a few words repeatedly and do not introduce new words into their conversations.

3. Children might not display appropriate language skills in school because they perceive school as a threatening environment. Some children feel rejection, hostility, or fear in school, and these feelings cause them to withhold their language. They simply choose not to share their language more than is mandatory. In school, therefore, they do not practice their language normally and it does not develop appropriately.

4. Children might speak with a restricted set of language functions. A few sets might be overused (e.g., instrumental and regulatory), while others might be underused (e.g., interactional, personal, imaginative, heuristic, representational).

REMEDIATING LANGUAGE PROBLEMS AND FOSTERING LANGUAGE DEVELOPMENT

The following strategies are recommended for remediating receptive language skills.

Vocabulary Deficits.   Children who have difficulty with vocabulary development have specific needs in classroom instruction, both individually and in reading groups. The following are some strategies for extending vocabulary:

- Provide vocabulary instruction prior to reading instruction (see Chapter 11).
- Provide experiences, both real and vicarious, for all vocabulary instruction. Relate vocabulary directly to children's experiences.
- Expose children to a variety of interesting words through activities such as Word of the Week and Favorite Word (see Chapter 11).
- Have children match words to pictures or to actual objects.
- Classify words into categories, such as people, food, animals, sports, and emotions. Choose one category per week and have children collect as many appropriate words as possible. Discuss these words and categories thoroughly.
- Show pictures and have children use a variety of words to describe them.
- Focus on synonyms and antonyms. This should be done both formally in planned lessons and informally throughout the day.
- Develop special long-term vocabulary programs to focus directly on vocabulary growth (see Chapter 11).

- Spend time on learning vocabulary automatically.
- Talk about words in every content area. Create a word conscious environment.
- Encourage and praise children for using interesting words. Use charts, graphs, posters, or word ladders to encourage word use.
- Read to children daily and discuss the material with them. Focus on interesting and new words.
- Focus on vocabulary during workbook or text reading. Manipulate the print by asking children to give words beginning with particular letters or sounds, to give synonyms or antonyms for words, to identify why words are different or alike, to state locations where words would be found (e.g., *fish/ocean; lion/jungle*), to state where action words would be done (e.g., *swim/pool; skate/ rink*), and to provide rhyming words.

Failure to Understand Common Language Structure.   To help children extend their language base, the following strategies are suggested:

- Provide children with simple sentences and help them draw inferences. For example, present the sentences, "Up in the mountains the wild flowers were in full bloom. The sun was shining and the air was fresh and very warm." Ask "What season might it be? What makes you think that?"
- Read sentences and have children identify common information such as "who," "when," "where," "why," and "how."
- Read sentences with words or phrases deleted. Have children complete sentences appropriately.
- Play the "I am thinking of a word" game. Have a word in mind, and give clues until the word is guessed.
- Ask questions that develop thinking skills, including divergent and evaluative questions (see Chapter 9). Such questions include "How are a turtle and a fish alike?" "How would a blind person know when food on a stove is burning?"
- Provide much practice in analogies, e.g., "Ring is to finger as bracelet is to ____."

Difficulty in Following Directions.   To develop these skills, try the following strategies:

- Pass out a number of objects and direct students to respond if they have a specific object, for example, "Stand if you have a blue plastic circle," "Put your hand up if you have something you can use for cutting."
- Call children to order or dismiss them using specific directions, for example, "Boys with blond hair may go," "Girls who have on sneakers may go."

- Provide children with blank pieces of paper and pencils. Give directions that result in a specific design, for example, "Draw a circle in the top right-hand corner; draw a triangle in the bottom left-hand corner; write a number seven in the circle."
- Read directions that will result in a usable product, such as a kite, and have children complete the project.
- Have children respond to directions while working in their workbooks. For example, "Circle the word *through*; put an X on the word that begins like *play*; underline the word that means *little*; put a number one beside the word that rhymes with *pin*."

Difficulty in Critical Listening and Responding.   Some examples of activities for developing listening skills follow.

- Model good listening skills for children. Be an active listener by maintaining eye contact with children who speak to you, responding fully to their comments and questions, asking appropriate questions, and encouraging discussion.
- Read daily to children. Read a wide variety of print (stories, factual material, poems, letters, biographies, newspaper articles, children's writings, content-area material, journals, encyclopedias).
- Read to children and have them listen for specific reasons, such as listening for synonyms of a given word, for antonyms, for specific facts, for descriptions, for rhyming words, for reasons for behavior or emotions, for facts or opinions, and for discrepant information.
- Expand the use of questions that develop critical thinking skills. Such questions ask children to predict, to identify facts or opinions, to identify factual or fictional information, to respond to truth or falsehood, and the like.

FOSTERING EXPRESSIVE LANGUAGE

Reading is one of the four language arts. The other three are speaking, listening, and writing. One of the goals of reading instruction is the development and extension of expressive oral language. Some children enter and progress through school with poorly developed expressive language skills. Categories of expressive language disorders and suggestions for their remediation follow.

Difficulty in Formulating Expressive Language.   There are several techniques for extending children's oral language production:

- Model elaborated language for children. Use a wide range of vocabulary. Do not speak down to them.
- Read a variety of literature and provide many opportunities for discussion.
- Expand on "show and tell" by asking questions about objects and having children respond.
- Give children objects to describe in as much detail as possible. Lead them to pay attention to all features, e.g., size, color, texture, use, weight, sound.
- Have children describe pictures in as much detail as possible.
- Use wordless storybooks and have children create texts to go along with the pictures. Help them describe the pictures as fully as possible. A list of the most delightful wordless storybooks follows.

Ah-Choo, by Mercer Mayer
Frog on His Own, by Mercer Mayer
Clementina's Cactus, by Ezra Jack Keats
Noah's Ark, by Peter Spier
Snow, by Isao Sasaki
Elephant Buttons, by Noniko Ueno
Sunshine, by Jan Ormerod
The Silver Pony, by Lynd Ward
Here Comes Alex Pumpernickel, by Fernando Krahn
Deep in the Forest, by Brinton Turkle
Moonlight, by Jan Ormerod
Sing Pierrot, Sing, by Tommie De Paola
The Wild Baby, by Fernando Krahn
Nightdances, by Fernando Krahn
The Happy Dog, by Hieyuki Tanaka

- Help children memorize familiar poems, rhymes, jingles, and songs.
- Provide puppets for role playing.
- Use questions that encourage language, such as "What would happen if . . . ?" "Suppose . . . ?" "How many ways . . . ?" "How do you know that . . . ?" "How do you feel about . . . ?"
- Use sentence expansion techniques. Begin with a simple sentence (e.g., The man ran down the street). Extend on the subject (e.g., What kind of man ran?). Extend on the object (Why did the man run down the street?). The result is an expanded sentence, such as "The man with the broken arm ran with a bound down the street because he was very late for his appointment."
- Use sentence combining techniques:

The butterfly flew gracefully.
The butterfly was large and golden.

It flew to the top of the tree.
The large, golden butterfly flew
gracefully to the top of the tree.

- Provide children with phrases such as "in the house," "over the bridge," and "loud and clear," and have them use the phrases in sentences.
- Make conversation and discussion constant parts of the classroom environment. Expose children daily to a sharing time in which issues of common interest are discussed. This period might at times be loosely structured, thus allowing children to share personal information. At other times, it might be teacher directed for the purpose of discussing class projects and programs, school issues, individual and group progress, and school, community, or national news.
- Have a weekly discussion period designed to develop critical thinking, reasoning, problem solving, and rational thinking skills. During this session, choose a specific topic and set a specific goal. Vary topics and goals weekly. Possible topics might include classroom behavior, playground behavior, helping substitute teachers, reading and discussing a story, discussing a television program, raising money, a possible field trip, putting out a class newspaper, or class responsibility. The overriding goal of these discussion periods should be the use of language and the extension of thinking and problem-solving skills. Direct questions and discussion topics to children who need the language practice. Emphasize modeling and sharing.
- Use a variety of language centers that can be rotated each week or two. Schedule children into these centers according to their individual needs. Centers might include the following activities.

Telephoning. Most telephone companies have kits or materials, including model telephones, for school use. Children can be led to converse about specific issues in the classrooms, about scenes from books, about their reactions to stories, or about topics of their choice.

Interviewing. Children might interview other children or teachers. Their interviews can be tape recorded and later written up for the class. Children might also assume roles based on stories they have read and interview each other.

Storytelling. Children can compose or retell stories. Their stories can be taped and written down later. Older children might work with younger children in transcribing the selections.

Jokes and riddles. These can be read by the teacher on tape and groups of children might work together to compose their own.

Creative dramatics. Assist children in acting out stories or writing their own plays.

Imagining. Children might engage in creative writing and share their stories.

Manipulation. This center would include things to touch, see, feel and do. The objects should be related to content being studied in reading, social studies, science, current affairs, art, or music. Encourage children to experience and discuss the objects.

Brainstorming. In this center, pose particular problems (on tape or in writing). Children work in pairs or in small groups to brainstorm solutions or alternatives and the feasibility or consequence of each solution.

Inadequate Speaking Vocabularies.   The following strategies are recommended:

- Provide incentives for word use. Use the "Word of the Week" in which one word is isolated, taught, and reinforced all week. Teach the word on Monday and have children use the word all week. If they use it correctly in speaking, they earn one point. If they use it correctly in writing, they gain two points. They can earn a maximum of four points per day. Reward them if by the end of the week they earn twelve or more points.
- Have children build words from single root words, such as *man/ postman, mailman, manly, man-of-war, manpower.*
- List and display antonyms and synonyms of words.
- Provide words with multiple meanings (e.g., *run*) and have children use the words in as many ways as possible.
- Provide opportunities for storytelling or retelling of stories that have been read.
- Outlaw "tired" words from the classroom (e.g., *bad, good, big, little, happy, sad*).
- Have children keep personal notebooks of favorite words or new words.
- Have a "Favorite Words" display each week and provide time to discuss new words daily.
- Encourage, recognize, and reinforce the use of new words.
- Focus on long-term, full-blown conceptual vocabulary instruction (see Chapter 11).
- Provide opportunities for planned discussion sessions during which specific topics are discussed.

The Perception of School as a Threatening Environment.   Teachers must take steps to create a classroom environment conducive to the production and development of language. Some suggestions follow.

- Create an open atmosphere in the classroom.
- Provide opportunities for nonverbal activities, such as music, art, dance, and play.
- Enhance children's self-concept and self-image by creating situations for success, praising growth, encouraging success, displaying improved work, and making much of achievements.
- Provide nonthreatening situations in which language can be practiced (e.g., learning centers, story time, and free discussion).
- Be accepting of children's language.
- Praise children when they communicate orally.
- Expose children to literature that deals with a variety of sex roles, and racial, ethnic, and linguistic models.
- Spend time conversing individually with children. Encourage and praise verbal interaction.

Limited Use of Language Functions.   Earlier in this chapter, the seven language functions proposed by Halliday (1975) were identified and discussed. All the functions are vital to the complete development of language. Pinnell (1985) has recommended instructional techniques for the development of each category of language functions. The recommendations follow.

Instrumental Language

- Be accessible and responsive to children's requests, but teach independence by having children state their requests effectively.
- Encourage the use of instrumental language with other children, helping then to expand their own language by providing help and direction to peers.
- Analyze advertising and propaganda, to show children how they can use language to get what they want.

Regulatory Language

- Find instances in which regulatory language is used inappropriately. Teach appropriate regulatory language or the alternative—instrumental language.
- Create situations that let children be "in charge" of small and large groups.
- Try to use less regulatory and more interactive language as a teacher.

Interactional Language

- Create situations that require children to share work areas or materials and to talk about how they will share.
- Find ways of having small groups (especially pairs or trios) discuss a variety of subjects. Through these discussions, students

learn the subject matter more thoroughly as they practice communication.

- Let students work together to plan field trips, social events, and classroom or school projects.
- Whenever possible, mix children of different ages, sexes, and races in work groups or discussion groups.
- Have informal social times. Engage in some talk with students that is not "all business."

Personal Language

- Use personal language to give children permission to share personal thoughts and opinions.
- Be willing to listen and talk personally during transition times, for example, when children are arriving in the morning. Converse with children while on cafeteria or playground duty.
- Provide some comfortable, attractive areas in the classroom where students can talk quietly.
- Encourage parents and family members to visit and participate in classrooms.
- Read stories or books that prompt a very personal response from students. A list of some recommended titles follows.

Where the Sidewalk Ends, by Shel Silverstein
Charlotte's Web, by E. B. White
Tales of a Fourth Grade Nothing, by Judy Blume
Charlie and the Chocolate Factory, by Roald Dahl
The Hundred Penny Box, by Sharon Bell Mathis
Stevie, by John Steptoe
Crow Boy, by Taro Yashima
The Hundred Dresses, by Eleanor Estes
Evan's Corner, by Elizabeth Hill
Sounder, by William Armstrong
Roll of Thunder, Hear My Cry, by Mildred Taylor
Summer of the Swans, by Betsy Byars
Bridge to Terabithia, by Katherine Paterson
Phillip Hall Likes Me, I Reckon Maybe, by Betty Greene

Imaginative Language

- Create situations that naturally elicit spontaneous dramatic play, for example, house corner, dress up, blocks for younger children, and drama and role playing for older children.
- Read stories and books that feed the imagination and serve as a stimulus for art, drama, and discussion.
- Provide time for children to talk in groups or with partners before they begin their writing on imaginative topics.

- Encourage "play" with language—the sounds of words and the images they convey.

Heuristic Language

- Structure classroom experiences so that interest and curiosity are aroused.
- Put children in pairs or work groups for problem-solving activities.
- Create real problems for children to solve.
- Use heuristic language to stimulate such language in children. Saying "I wonder why" often encourages children to do the same. (This question should not be contrived, however; it should be honest.)
- Try projects requiring study on the part of the entire class, including the teacher. Find some questions to which no one knows the answer.

Informative (Representational) Language

- Plan activities requiring children to observe carefully and objectively and then to summarize and draw conclusions from their observations. Field trips are a good opportunity.
- Require children to keep records of events over periods of time and then to look back at their records and draw conclusions, for example, keeping records on classroom pets.
- Use questioning techniques to elicit more complex forms of information giving.
- Instead of having tedious classroom reports, have children give their reports to small groups. Encourage feedback and discussion.

These activities can help teachers use the classroom experience as an opportunity for language stimulation, extension, and remediation.

SUMMARY   The development of language is a fascinating and complex area of study. Most adults acquired language so automatically and effortlessly that they are unaware of the magnitude of the task. By the time most children arrive at school, they have learned a great deal about their language. They have a strong knowledge of vocabulary, and use the language elements of word order (syntax), meaning (semantics), and sound (phonology) to understand and produce language. This knowledge is prerequisite to the acquisition and development of both oral and graphic language.

Some children, however, have underdeveloped language skills. They have difficulty in either or both receptive and expressive language. This inadequacy might negatively affect reading development as well. It is very important to differentiate between children who have legitimate language problems and those who are speakers of dialects. Dialect use does not preclude linguistic inadequacies.

Teachers must help children develop their linguistic abilities, oral and written. Reading instruction should not be divorced from the other language arts. All the language arts are mutually dependent and can be used to extend and enhance one another. The reading period is an ideal time in which to integrate both speaking and reading skills. Ideally, teachers should strive to create within the classroom an environment that is accepting of children's language and committed to linguistic development.

R · E · F · E · R · E · N · C · E · S

Bernstein, B. "Social Class and Linguistic Development: A Theory of Social Learning." In A. H. Halsey, J. Floud, and C. A. Anderson, eds. *Education, Economy, and Society*. New York: Free Press, 1961.

————. "Elaborated and Restricted Codes: Their Social Origins and Some Consequences." In G. Smith, ed. *Communication and Culture*. New York: Holt, Rinehart & Winston, 1966.

Cazden, C. B., V. P. John, and D. Hymes, eds. *Functions of Language in the Classroom*. New York: Teachers College Press, 1972.

Chapman, R. "Mother-Child Interaction in the Second Year of Life: Its Role in Language Development." In R. Schiefelbusch and D. Bricker, eds. *Early Language: Acquisition and Intervention*. Baltimore, MD: University Park Press, 1981.

Dale, P. S. *Language Development: Structure and Function*. Hinsdale, IL: Dryden Press, 1972.

Duchan, J. "Language Intervention Through Sense-Making and Fine Tuning." In R. Schiefelbusch, ed. *Language Competence: Assessment and Intervention*. San Diego, CA: College Hill Press, 1986.

Gillet, J. W., and C. Temple. *Understanding Reading Problems: Assessment and Instruction*. Boston: Little, Brown, 1986.

Halliday, M. A. K. *Learning How to Mean: Explorations in the Development of Language*. London, England: Edward Arnold Ltd., 1975.

————. "Learning How to Mean." In E. Lenneberg and E. Lenneberg, eds. *Foundations of Language Development: A Multidisciplinary Approach, Volume 1*. New York: Academic Press, 1975.

Harber, J. R., and D. N. Bryen. "Black English and the task of reading." *Review of Education Research* 46 (Summer 1976): 387–405.

Hirsch, E. D. *Cultural Literacy*. Boston: Houghton Mifflin, 1987.

Hornby, P. A. "Achieving second language fluency through immersion education." *Foreign Language Annals* 13 (1980): 107–113.

Hoskisson, K., and G. E. Tompkins. *Language Arts: Content and Teaching Strategies.* Columbus, OH: Merrill, 1987.

Hough, R. A., J. R. Nurss, and D. S. Enright. "Story reading with limited English speaking children in the regular classroom." *The Reading Teacher* 39 (1986): 510–514.

Labov, W. *The Study of Nonstandard English.* Urbana, IL: National Council of Teachers of English, 1970.

Lindfors, J. W. *Children's Language and Learning.* Englewood Cliffs, NJ: Prentice–Hall, 1980.

———. "Understanding the Development of Language Structure." In A. Jaggar and M. T. Smith–Burke, eds. *Observing the Language Learner.* Newark, DE: International Reading Association, and Urbana, IL: National Council of Teachers of English, 1985.

Norton, D. *The Effective Teacher of Language Arts.* Columbus, OH: Merrill, 1980.

Perez, E. "Oral language competence improves reading skills of Mexican American third graders." *The Reading Teacher* 35 (1981): 24–27.

Phillips, S. *The Invisible Culture: Communication in the Classroom on the Warm Springs Indian Reservation.* New York: Longman, 1982.

Pinnell, G. S. "Ways to Look at the Function of Children's Language." In A. Jaggar and M. T. Smith–Burke, eds. *Observing the Language Learner.* Urbana, IL: International Reading Association, 1985.

Smith, F. *Understanding Reading: A Psycholinguistic Analysis of Reading and Learning to Read.* New York: Holt, Rinehart & Winston, 1982.

13 Diagnostic and Remedial Instruction Models

FOCUS
QUESTIONS

1. How can the Fernald–Keller technique be adapted for classroom use?
2. How can classroom teachers use the Cooper strategies to remediate reading difficulties?
3. How does the Gillingham method compare to the Fernald–Keller remedial procedure?
4. What are the basic teaching steps in Manning's instructional sequence?
5. What philosophical premises underlie the Manning instructional sequence, and how does the model apply to any subject and to all learners?

This text has emphasized the matching of instructional techniques to student need on the basis of observation and diagnosis. Individual strategies have been recommended in several instructional categories (comprehension, vocabulary, phonic analysis). These strategies can be integrated into reading instruction for a great number of disabled readers.

There are several specialized remedial techniques specifically developed for moderately to severely reading-disabled students. Each technique focuses on students with specific reading disorders and emphasizes individual modalities. This chapter presents a variety of remediation sequences. The intent is not for teachers to adopt one technique for all children or to apply any strategy without modification. The hope is that you will have a wide variety of techniques immediately available for addressing a wide variety of reading problems. You will be able to choose those techniques, in whole or in part, that are appropriate in any given situation. Remember that the goal in remediation is meeting children's needs rather than applying exactly a particular remedial or instructional strategy.

The five remedial models presented in this chapter include the Fernald–Keller V.A.K.T. (Visual, Auditory, Kinesthetic, Tactile) method, the Cooper method, the Gillingham method, the Hegge–Kirk and Kirk method, and the Manning Basic Instructional Sequence. Detailed discussions of these strategies follow.

THE FERNALD–KELLER METHOD

In the early 1940s, Dr. Grace M. Fernald and Helen B. Keller became interested in working with remedial readers. At that time, Fernald was directing the reading clinic at UCLA. The children enrolled in the clinic had average or above average intelligence, but had failed in traditional classroom reading instruction, which tended to focus on auditory-visual strategies. The children were performing more than one year below their grade placement, and were generally very discouraged because of their reading failure. Fernald and Keller (Fernald 1943) devised a multisensory, four-stage program for use on an individual basis. The procedure was very successful and became well publicized as a result. It is still discussed and recommended by several reading experts (Richek et al. 1983, Rupley and Blair 1983, McCormick 1987, Taylor et al. 1988). The method begins by providing motivation. Prior to beginning the techniques, children are placed in a "positive reconditioning" program with the following characteristics:

1. Avoidance of all programs that have been tried unsuccessfully.
2. Avoidance of all situations that might cause embarrassment or frustration.
3. Use of reading and language activities that children can perform well and in which they feel confident.
4. Use of praise and encouragement when children perform successfully.
5. Children are told they are going to experience a new method of learning to read that works.

Positive reconditioning precedes actual remediation because of the belief that reading failure damages children's confidence to the extent that their learning is blocked. The block must be removed before learning can succeed. Children remain in this phase until they seem ready to cope with new instruction. This can last from one week to one month. When children achieve readiness, the first stage begins.

Stage 1: Tracing.   Each child is encouraged to choose one word that she or he has always wanted to use but cannot yet read and write. The child alone must choose the word. After the word has been identified, the following steps are taken.

1. The teacher writes the word with crayon on a large piece of paper. Either cursive or manuscript is used, depending on the child's practice. The teacher says the word while writing it.
2. Children trace the word with a finger until they can write it from memory. Finger contact is essential in this step. As they trace the word, children repeat its syllables. The child gets as many trials as necessary to trace the word from memory.
3. The child writes the word from memory on a piece of paper. If an error is made, the entire word is retraced and then rewritten. No erasures are permitted.
4. The child is encouraged to use the word in context. During the first few sessions, this context might be a single sentence. After the child has learned a number of words, however, the context

might be a short paragraph or story. The story, paragraph, or sentence is typed immediately by the teacher. The child then reads the selection. The teacher provides assistance on any word except the newly learned word.

5. The word is typed on an index card. The child then reads it and files the word in correct alphabetical order in a word file box.
6. Words, sentences, paragraphs, or stories are frequently reviewed.

The tracing stage has these essential components:

- The word must be chosen by the child, not by the teacher.
- The child must trace the word, saying the word while tracing it.
- The child must see and feel the word as a complete unit; therefore no erasures are permitted.
- All modalities must be emphasized.

   auditory (hearing the work spoken and the parts pronounced)
   visual (seeing the word in isolation and in print)
   kinesthetic ("feeling" the word based on its emotional context and on saying the word)
   tactile (writing or tracing the word)

- The teacher provides no direct assistance in phonic analysis. The emphasis is on visual analysis of structural units.
- The word must be used in context.

The length of time a child spends in Stage 1 varies from one to several weeks. When new words are learned quickly and confidently, the child may move to Stage 2. This might happen after as few as ten or as many as a hundred words have been learned.

Stage 2: Writing without Tracing.   In Stage 2, the tracing step is eliminated. The procedure follows.

1. The child chooses a word.
2. The teacher writes the word on a small (3 × 5) index card, saying the word while writing it.
3. The child looks at the word and says it.
4. The child writes the word from memory, saying each part as it is written. If an error is made, the child starts over. No erasures are permitted. Again, structure is stressed.
5. The word is used in a paragraph or short story.
6. The teacher types the copy immediately.
7. The child reads the selection silently, then orally. Again, assistance is provided for any word except the newly learned word.
8. The word is filed in the file box. Words, paragraphs, and stories are reviewed often.

The most significant difference in this stage is the elimination of the tracing step. Children might learn more quickly in this stage than they did in Stage 1.

Stage 3: *Transition to Traditional Print.*   After the child can write new words quickly and accurately after seeing the words and hearing the pronunciations, Stage 3 is begun. In Stage 3, the child begins to read from books. The teacher does not need to write new words for the child. Rather, the child learns words directly from texts. The procedure follows.

1. The child begins to read from simple texts. First, the child scans the page for unknown words, and attempts to decode the words by relating them to known words. Next the child reads the page silently and identifies words that are still unknown.
2. The unknown words are taught as follows:
   a. The teacher pronounces each word for the child.
   b. The child looks at the word in the text and says the word silently.
   c. The child writes the word from memory. If the child is unable to write the word from memory after a number of trials, the teacher writes the word on an index card and the child repeats the process. The child then identifies the word in print.
3. The child practices words by reviewing flashcards and by rereading the material in which the words were found. Students are encouraged to read print often.

Stage 4: *Experiences with Print.*   In this stage, the child no longer needs to write new words. Many experiences with print are provided. The child is encouraged to figure out unknown words either by associating them with already learned words or by using context. Only words that cannot be deciphered by these means are written down and visually analyzed. Fernald suggested in the interest of comprehension that words not taught previously be provided for the child.

The Fernald–Keller method is intensive, individual, and multisensory. Initially, it builds on the interests and motivations of children through individual choice of words and through language experience in the construction of paragraphs and stories. The incorporation of all modalities throughout the steps is clearly a strength.

Although the approach is specifically individual, aspects of it are applicable to group instruction. For example, the tracing step can be incorporated into any instructional setting, as can the multisensory emphasis. During vocabulary instruction, care can be taken to provide experiences with words that are auditory (hearing the word), visual (seeing the word), kinesthetic (reacting emotionally to and saying the word), and tactile (tracing the word or writing the word on rough surfaces such as sandpaper or sand). In addition, the complete procedure can be practiced on one day each week, and parents or older students can be trained to carry out the steps with specific children on a regular basis.

Rupley and Blair (1983) adapted the Fernald method for clinical use. The adaptation retains the essential multisensory thrust of the original approach but simplifies the steps. Their modification results in the following process.

1. The child identifies a word she or he wishes to learn. The teacher prints the word on a 5 x 8 sandpaper card as the child watches.
2. The teacher pronounces the word while the child examines it closely.
3. The child and teacher pronounce the word in unison five or six times.
4. The child takes the card, and as both teacher and child say the word, the child prints the word in a tray filled with moist sand. (Rupley and Blair suggest that the tray can be made from a gift box lid lined with aluminum foil.)
5. The child retraces the word several times, saying the word.
6. The card is shown again and the child pronounces the word. During free time, the child is encouraged to see, say, and trace the word. The child keeps the card and brings it to the next instructional session.
7. Each word is reviewed daily until it is recognized in isolation, in a short list with other words, and in a phrase or sentence. The words are placed in a "Words I Know" envelope. The child reviews these words periodically and uses them to construct sentences and stories. The focus at this point is on comprehension.

THE COOPER METHOD

The Cooper method (1947, 1964) is a modification of the Fernald–Keller approach. The method is geared toward severely disabled students whose reading skills are below the primer level. Like the Fernald method, the Cooper method is an individual approach. It differs in two significant ways from the Fernald V.A.K.T. It places children in a text immediately, and stresses phonic analysis. An outline of the Cooper method follows.

1. The teacher selects a basal reading series and uses an informal reading inventory to assess the child's instructional level. The child is placed in an appropriate book. Ideally, the child has not used the series before.
2. The teacher makes a list of all the words used in the book. The

child is asked to identify the words on the list, and unknown words are isolated.

3. The new words are taught individually using the Fernald method (Tracing and Writing Without Tracing). After children learn each word, they read the words in the context of the text.

4. Words are practiced both in isolation and in context.

5. The child receives ongoing training in visual and auditory discrimination.

6. As reading skills develop, a systematic phonic and structural analysis program begins.

The Cooper method retains the emphasis on multisensory learning, but omits the individual choice of words. Because the new words are taken directly from the texts, they often hold little interest for children. They are usually high frequency words that carry little meaning by themselves and are difficult to learn. The Cooper method, then, does not capitalize on the motivational aspects of the Fernald–Keller approach. Because of this, it is therefore recommended that the Cooper method be used as a bridge from the Fernald approach to traditional classroom instruction.

THE GILLINGHAM METHOD

The Gillingham method is a highly structured, synthetic phonic approach designed for individuals with visual processing problems and with auditory strengths (Gillingham and Stillman 1970). These individuals have severe reading disabilities and have failed in traditional instructional and in remedial settings. The method demands a long-term commitment, as it requires systematic instruction five times a week for a minimum of two years.

The Gillingham method utilizes six basic sensory associations in remediation:

1. *Visual to Auditory* (V–A). Written letters and words (V) are associated with the sounds they represent (A). Students do not vocalize these sounds. They simply see and listen (e.g., the teacher shows a card, *B*, and says b, /b/).

2. *Auditory to Visual* (A–V). In this association, the sounds of letters and words (A) are associated with the visual stimulus (V). This step resembles a spelling task (e.g., the teacher says /b/ and shows the card *B*). The students do not respond, but listen and look.

3. *Auditory to Kinesthetic* (A–K). Here the sounds of the letters and words are associated with muscular action through speech and

writing (e.g., the teacher says /b/, the child repeats the sound and traces the visual stimulus).

4. *Kinesthetic to Auditory* (K–A). The child's hand is guided as the letter or word is traced. At the same time, the name and sound of the letter or word is repeated by the teacher (e.g., child traces *B* as the teacher says *b, /b/*).

5. *Visual to Kinesthetic* (V–K). The graphic forms of letters and words are associated with speech and writing (e.g., the child sees *B*, says *b*, and writes the letter).

6. *Kinesthetic to Visual* (K–V). The acts of speech and writing are associated with the visual forms of letters and words. (The child says a letter and identifies the letter from a display.)

Initial instruction is divided into three segments: learning letters and their sounds, learning words, and applying words in simple sentences. In the first segment, learning letters and their sounds, three fundamental associations are taught. First, the V–A (Visual to Auditory) association is made. The teacher shows the child a card on which a letter has been written (V). The name of the letter is said (A). The student then repeats the name. In listening to and saying the name, the Auditory to Kinesthetic (A–K) association is made. When all the letter names have been mastered, the sounds are highlighted. The teacher shows the letter card (V) and says the sound of the letter (A). The student repeats this (K) and again reinforces the Visual to Auditory and Auditory to Kinesthetic associations (V–A, A–K). Accurate and immediate responses are stressed; therefore the child moves from segment to segment only after previous tasks have been learned automatically.

Second, the student learns to associate automatically the sounds of letters with the letter names. Without showing the card, the teacher makes the letter sound (e.g., /m/ [A]) and the student produces the appropriate letter (m [K]). Third, the teacher prints each letter. The student traces over the original, copies the original, and writes the letter from memory (V–K and K–V associations). Next the teacher says a sound (e.g., /m/) and the student must write the appropriate letter (e.g., m). This is the A–K association. All the letters of the alphabet and the sounds they represent are taught in this manner.

In the second instructional segment, reading words, blending is taught. The initial instruction focuses on the consonants *b, g, j, k, h, m, p,* and *t* and on the vowels *a* and *i*. The consonant–vowel–consonant (CVC) pattern is initially taught. The first consonant and the vowel are grouped together (e.g., *pa*) and the final consonant is added (e.g., *t*), resulting in a blended whole word (e.g., *pa–t* = *pat*). This strategy is practiced repeatedly until children achieve fluency in blending. The other consonants and vowels are then added.

In the third segment, applying words in simple sentences, the focus shifts to reading words in context. After children have mastered basic blending, and can recognize a large number of words, they learn a limited number of sight words. This allows words to be placed in short sentences, paragraphs, and stories, which are read and practiced for fluency. Finally, more complex reading skills are taught (e.g., final *e*, double vowels, and consonant blends), by means of a synthetic phonic method emphasizing the fundamental associations. The Gillingham method was modified by Traub and Bloom (1970) and by Slingerland (1974). The modified approaches include complete sets of remedial materials and a wide range of supplementary materials.

A clear disadvantage of the Gillingham approach is the delay of meaningful print and the resulting de-emphasis on comprehension. The program's length makes the lack of meaningful print and comprehension more serious. The approach is really only an intensive phonic skills program, and should be used in this way. It certainly includes a comprehensive strategy for phonic instruction. Some children would benefit from intensive phonic instruction, but this approach cannot be viewed as a balanced program in reading. It must be modified by a strong language component involving interaction with meaningful print and by the use of oral language knowledge in the learning of graphic language.

THE HEGGE–KIRK–KIRK GRAPHO-VOCAL METHOD

Another synthetic phonic approach is the "Grapho-Vocal" method presented by Hegge, Kirk, and Kirk (1970). This is a systematic, highly structured, programmed approach based on repetition, review, and immediate feedback. The Grapho-Vocal technique is based on four psychological principles.

1. *Reproductive inhibition.* Children will forget all the associations if too many of them are taught at the same time. Because of this, only one sound of a letter is presented and practiced at any given time.
2. *Multiple exposure leads to learning.* Learning is dependent on repetitions; therefore, phoneme-grapheme relationships are presented through drills and repetitions.
3. *Motivation accelerates learning.* Success is a motivating force. Therefore, content is presented in a series of small, easily achieved steps.
4. *Articulation is an aid to learning and retention.* On the basis of this principle, children perform all drills orally.

The approach is created for students with the following characteristics:

- They have failed at normal instructional and remedial efforts.
- They know the letters of the alphabet and the initial consonant sounds.
- They are reading at a primer level.
- They need practice in word structure and auditory discrimination.

The Grapho-Vocal program consists of a series of drills divided into four segments. Segment one presents basic decoding skills. These include short vowels, long vowels, double vowels, vowel combinations, vowel-consonant combinations (phonograms), and some word endings. Drill in these phonic elements is presented in the following steps.

1. Sound words letter by letter (e.g., /m/ /a/ /p/).
2. Blend the sounds (e.g., /m/ /a/ /p/ = /map/).
3. Pronounce the word as a single unit (e.g., /map/).
4. Write the word.

Basic sentences (e.g., A fat cat sat on a big mat) are integrated into these drills. All sentences include only phonetically decodable words.

Segment two presents a variety of vowel-consonant combinations (e.g., *ack, est*). Children begin to read from easy, phonic-controlled texts. All nonphonetic words should be pronounced for students.

Segments three presents complex vowel combinations (diphthongs and digraphs), prefixes, suffixes, and variants. Emphasis is placed on comprehension and vocabulary development.

Segment four consists of supplementary exercises and irregularly pronounced combinations, such as *ought* and *alk*.

The Hegge et al. method provides intensive drill in phonic analysis. Some remedial readers require such extreme skill practice. Remember, however, that a balanced experience with print must involve meaningful material and attention to comprehension. Intensive skills programs must be interpreted and applied within the context of comprehension-centered reading instruction.

THE MANNING BASIC INSTRUCTIONAL SEQUENCE

The Basic Instructional Sequence was created by John Manning (1980). The sequence is designed to provide thorough instruction for children who need remediation in reading. Unlike the approaches presented earlier in this chapter, the sequence is meant to be used with small groups of children. However, it can be used easily with individuals as well (Swaby 1984).

The Manning instructional sequence is based on the concept that certain specific components are essential in effective remediation. Essential components include the following:

1. Preparation for reading, which includes vocabulary preinstruction, concept preparation, and content preparation.
2. Reading and interacting, including oral and silent reading and emphasis on varied questioning and on teaching comprehension.
3. Skill instruction, which should be reflective of the individual needs of children, be based on children's actual reading errors, and be transferred as soon as possible to real reading situations.
4. Extension of reading, which may take the form of vocabulary extension, plot and character analysis, critical thinking and problem solving, the merging of the language arts, or the use of related literature.

While these components are important in all reading instruction, they are essential in the remediation of slow readers. The Manning instructional sequence uses the four components as a foundation for reading remediation. It consists of eight sequentially organized instructional steps that can be applied to any self-contained print, such as a story, an expository selection, or an article. The eight steps include review; introduction to new vocabulary; introduction to new phrases; preparation for reading; oral reading for diagnosis, for instruction, and for practice; silent reading with an emphasis on comprehension; skill instruction; and enrichment. The rationale and a description of each step follow.

Step 1: Review.   Children forget rapidly. They require repeated review to ensure learning and retention. In addition, because learning to read is an accumulation of skills, insights, vocabulary, and knowledge, information taught on one day will be important on the next. This information should be reviewed to aid comprehension and retention.

Before beginning a new lesson, children are reminded of previously learned information that might be important in the new lesson. This information might be in the form of vocabulary items, phrases, skills, concepts, or a combination. A review gives children a frame of reference for new learning. It also orients children's attention to the learning of a new task. A review therefore precedes any instruction.

Step 2: Introduction to New Vocabulary.   The teacher can assume that children being taught on their instructional level will not know certain vocabulary items in the text. Instructional success depends to a large degree on teaching new vocabulary before reading begins.

Before presenting a lesson, then, the teacher reads the selection and identifies the vocabulary items that should be pretaught. The teacher carefully chooses the most useful and essential vocabulary and identifies an appropriate number of items (between five and seven) so as to complement children's learning rates. Vocabulary is presented trimodally—

orally, visually, and kinesthetically. Children should be able to identify each word automatically before proceeding to the next step in the sequence. A detailed explanation of Manning's vocabulary presentation $(3 \times 3 \times I)$ appears in Chapter 11. This procedure is used to teach vocabulary thoroughly. The new vocabulary phase ends in a kinesthetic step in which all the words that have been taught are listed on a sheet of paper, as in Figure 13.1. The teacher provides each child with a vocabulary sheet and a pencil. Children are directed to identify words based on phonic elements, meaning, and quick recognition. For example, the teacher might say, "Circle the word that means shy" (meaning); "put a number 1 beside the word that begins like *frog*" (phonic analysis); "underline the word *especially*" (recognition). The teacher observes to identify children who are confident of the words and those who might require reteaching. The kinesthetic step is therefore used diagnostically.

Step 3: Introduction to New Phrases.   One predictable reading pattern of poor readers is word-by-word reading. Teachers often teach children, particularly poorer readers, word by word, or worse, word part by word part. Furthermore, teachers often accept children's word-by-word reading, making no effort to correct their reading style or to help them read more fluently. Phrase instruction fulfills many purposes. It builds fluency, provides additional practice in vocabulary, contributes to incidental learning, provides language from which to build predictions from print, and gives children confidence as they meet prelearned phrases in the text.

The teacher identifies in the text the phrases that include the vocabulary items to be taught in Step 2. For example, if the word *basement* is chosen for instruction in Step 2, the teacher finds the sentence in the text in which the word *basement* occurs. The sentence might read, "John and Martin ran to the basement door." The phrase chosen for instruction is "to the basement door." Phrases, like words, are taught thoroughly. Students are required to identify the phrases quickly before moving on to the next step. The final phase is the kinesthetic step, as in Step 2.

| basement |
| timid |
| especially |
| frightened |
| listened |
| standing |
| brightly |

FIGURE 13.1   Kinesthetic Step of the Manning Sequence

Step 4: Preparation for Reading.   Reading is interaction between the reader and the print. It is dependent on the reader's interest in the text and prior knowledge about the concepts and content of the text. The importance of preparation for reading is discussed at length in Chapter 9.

Before reading begins, the teacher prepares children conceptually for reading the text, and encourages them to predict and anticipate meaning from the text. The title, pictures, subheadings, and phrases can all be used to help children predict the content. In addition, a wide variety of strategies (e.g., advance organizers, overviews, listing, reading to them, filmstrips, films, models, and experiences) are available for preparing children conceptually, depending on textual demands and children's prior knowledge (see Chapter 9).

Step 5: Oral Reading.   Oral reading, particularly in the early stages, is essential for identifying children's reading strengths and weaknesses, and for assessing the skills children are or are not using in their reading. Oral reading is often grossly misused, resulting in the reinforcement of bad habits and patterns of reading failure.

Manning suggests that oral reading should have three purposes: diagnosis, instruction, and practice. Oral reading for diagnosis involves assessment. As children read, the teacher daily records and analyzes their oral reading errors. The teacher keeps a small notebook for each group of children, as in Figure 13.2. This tool is indispensable for diagnosing and identifying children's skill needs. If oral reading is used daily for diagnosis, the teacher can identify patterns of errors for individual children and provide skill instruction specific to their needs. For this purpose have children read orally only for short periods of time because this strategy reinforces bad reading habits by allowing them to read poorly without assistance. Figure 13.3 presents an oral reading diagnostic report form. This form may be used to record and analyze oral reading errors. After diagnostic reading is completed, instructional reading begins.

Oral reading for instruction involves providing for children a model of appropriate oral reading. The teacher reads a short section of print fluently and with appropriate expression. The students listen, follow along in the text, and reread the section appropriately. Instructional reading (echoic reading) gives children a model of good oral reading, allowing them to improve their reading skills.

Children who are poor readers need much practice in reading, but the practice must reinforce good reading habits. Oral reading for practice assumes that children are reading well and developing their skills appropriately. If this is not the case, then oral reading for practice is discontinued and oral reading for instruction is reinstated.

Step 6. Silent Reading.   The goal of all reading instruction is to develop independent reading skills. Silent reading development is vital from the earliest stages of reading instruction. For remedial readers,

Date _____			
Child	Word	Child Said	Analysis
John	*in*	*on*	sight vocabulary
	them	*then*	sight, endings
	stop	*sop*	*st* combination
	ride	*rid*	silent *e*
	drive	*div*	*dr* – silent *e*
Mary	*them*	*the*	sight vocabulary
	enough	–	sight vocabulary
	even	–	sight vocabulary
	though	*the*	sight vocabulary
	great	*gret*	*ea* combination

FIGURE 13.2 Oral Reading Error Record

however, silent reading should begin with short segments of one or two sentences and should be followed by questions requiring all levels of interaction with print. As silent reading performance and comprehension develop, passage length should increase. The teacher directs children to read segments of print silently. A variety of questions are used to assess comprehension. The focus is on teaching comprehension through strategies such as modeling (see Chapter 9).

Step 7: Skill Instruction.   As children read, their skill deficits will become clear. Skill knowledge is important in reading, but skill use is even more important. Direct skill instruction should be a priority. As children grow older, their skill deficits increase until more skills are lacking than there is time to teach. It is vital, then, that teachers identify the most indispensable skills and focus instructional attention on those skills.

Teachers listen carefully to children, identify the skills that are missing, and teach the skills that are most important. A helpful question to ask in prioritizing skill instruction is, "What are the skills, which, if learned, would result in the most immediate, significant improvement in reading performance?" The answer to this question allows the emphasis to fall on the use and transfer of skills to actual reading. If the diagnostic segment identifies skills needed by an entire group of children, then group skill instruction is justified. Otherwise, individual children are instructed on the skills they need most. Chapter 10 provided an extensive discussion of skill instruction.

Step 8: Enrichment.   Reading involves interaction and communication. After children read a selection, various strategies should be used

Name			Pages Read
Date	Word	Child Said	Reading Behavior

Error Analysis Record

Phonic Needs						Structural Analysis		
Sight Vocabulary	Initial Consonants	Final Consonants	Consonant Clusters	Vowels	Base Words	Compounds	Affixes	Contractions

FIGURE 13.3 Oral Reading Diagnostic Report

to extend their comprehension, appreciation, and enjoyment of reading. Strategies such as vocabulary extension, writing, creative drama based on the text, art, character analysis, problem solving, reading related literature, or role playing are appropriate for enrichment.

The Basic Instructional Sequence provides an excellent structure for effective remediation at all levels. The sequence is flexible enough to incorporate many philosophical positions (e.g., phonics, linguistics, language immersion, basal). It can also be applied to any content material (e.g., social studies, literature, science, and civics). If the reading selection is too long to be completed in one instructional session, the sequence can be divided over two or three class periods. The sequence can be stopped after Steps 3, 4, 6, or 7. The only rule about breaking the sequence is that each class period must begin with a review phase.

No one remedial program will meet the needs of all remedial readers. All programs offer techniques and strategies that might be effective with a wide range of learners. Whichever program or programs you choose, you should remember that the most essential ingredients are your observations and analyses of the learners and your discovery of their strengths, weaknesses, needs, and learning styles. According to Taylor, Harris, and Pearson (1988, 388), "An effective remedial reading program does not conform to one pattern—different teachers have success with different approaches." They also state that the most effective programs demonstrate the following ten characteristics.

1. Pupils are selected for remedial instruction on the basis of their potential to benefit from such help. Stated another way, low rank in reading achievement is not the sole basis for selection.
2. Pupil progress is documented in a number of ways and shared with the child. Emphasis is placed on showing gains that are realized on a day-by-day basis. Comparisons with other learners are avoided in favor of self-comparisons.
3. Instructional approaches and materials are built on the child's personal interests and are adjusted to the child's reading level.
4. Remedial instruction is approached differently from ways previously used with the learner. The novelty inherent in the change of methods is used to full advantage by giving the child a fresh start in new materials and with new techniques.
5. The learner is introduced to remedial instruction in a way that guarantees success. Tasks are pitched at a level and in such a manner as to break the cycle of failure all remedial readers experience daily. The language experience approach is an example of a method that can be employed to ensure success.
6. Instruction is based on the individual strengths and needs of the learner. Lock-step programs that ignore the child's uniqueness are avoided.

7. Instruction is related to actual reading as much as possible, with minimal drill on isolated skills. Predictable books of high interest are used to ensure success and keep motivation high.
8. The learner is encouraged to select appealing materials from among those the teacher believes are written at a level the child can handle easily.
9. The reading specialist communicates regularly with the classroom teacher about the nature of the remedial instruction being provided, progress made, and ways regular classroom instructions can be adjusted to accommodate the child's needs.
10. The child is excused from the remedial program as soon as possible. The reading specialist then follows up with the classroom teacher to determine if adjustment is progressing normally.*

These valuable and important characteristics should be remembered in any remedial endeavor.

SUMMARY   Effective remediation depends on the availability of a wide range of instructional techniques that can be used with a variety of reading problems. Many children have severe deficits in reading and require intensive remedial strategies. Five models of remedial instruction are the Fernald–Keller V.A.K.T., the Cooper method, the Gillingham phonic method, the Hegge–Kirk–Kirk Grapho-Vocal method, and the Basic Instructional Sequence. Teachers are urged not to focus on the accurate application of any one method, but to become familiar with all strategies, to evaluate the specific needs of children, and to choose the appropriate approach or combination of methods to meet children's needs.

R·E·F·E·R·E·N·C·E·S

Cooper, J. L. "A procedure for teaching non-readers." *Education* 67 (1947): 494–499.

———. "An adaptation of the Fernald–Keller approach to teaching an initial reading vocabulary to children with severe reading disabilities." *The Australian Journal on the Education of Backward Children* 10 (March 1964): 131–145.

*From B. Taylor, L. A. Harris, and P. D. Pearson, *Reading Difficulties: Instruction and Assessment* (New York: Random House, 1984), 388–389. Reprinted by permission.

Fernald, G. M. *Remedial Techniques in Basic School Subjects.* New York: McGraw–Hill, 1943.

Gillingham, A., and B. W. Stillman. *Remedial Training for Children with Specific Difficulty in Reading, Spelling, and Penmanship,* 7th ed. Cambridge, MA: Educators Publishing Service, 1970.

Hegge, T. G., S. A. Kirk, and W. D. Kirk. *Remedial Reading Drills.* Ann Arbor, MI: George Wahr Publishers, 1970.

Manning, J. C. *Reading: Learning and Instructional Processes.* Geneva, IL: Paladin House, 1980.

McCormick, S. *Remedial and Clinical Reading Instruction.* Columbus, OH: Merrill, 1987.

Richek, M. A., L. K. List, and J. W. Lerner. *Reading Problems: Diagnosis and Remediation.* Englewood Cliffs, NJ: Prentice–Hall, 1983.

Rupley, W. H., and T. R. Blair. *Reading Diagnosis and Remediation Classroom and Clinic,* 2nd ed. Boston: Houghton Mifflin, 1983.

Slingerland, B. *A Multisensory Approach to Language Arts for Specific Learning Disability Children.* Cambridge, MA: Educators Publishing Service, 1974.

Swaby, B. *Teaching and Learning Reading.* Boston: Little, Brown, 1984.

Taylor, B., L. A. Harris, and P. D. Pearson. *Reading Difficulties: Instruction and Assessment.* New York: Random House, 1988.

Traub, N., and F. Bloom. *Recipe for Reading.* Cambridge, MA: Educators Publishing Service, 1970.

14 Motivating Children to Read

FOCUS
QUESTIONS

1. How do lack of interest in and motivation toward reading relate to failure in reading?
2. What elements in the home environment contribute to motivation toward reading?
3. How can teachers work with parents to motivate children to read?
4. What role do computers play in the remediation of reading skills?
5. How can computers be used to motivate children to read?

Few teachers would deny the importance of motivation in learning to read. Neither instruction nor remediation should neglect attention to motivation. Many children find reading so difficult and unrewarding that they are completely unmotivated toward reading:

> I once asked one of these children who happened to be in second grade whether or not he liked to read. "Sure," he lied casually. "Do you read for fun at home?" I asked naively. "Are you kidding me!" he responded, looking at me as though I had lost my sense of reason. Then he remembered for a second the ideal nature of the student-teacher relationship, one which had been temporarily abandoned throughout most of the interaction and said, "Well, I read sometimes when I go to the doctor and my mother makes me read one of the books there." I was grateful that at least twice per year this youngster "read for fun," by his interpretation.

Other children possess the skills of reading but never learn to read because they are not motivated to pick up an unassigned book and read. Therefore, they do not get enough practice in reading to learn to read well.

One of the most important and basic goals of reading instruction must be the development and fostering of motivation toward reading. Teachers have the responsibility of providing motivation in the instructional and remedial environments. However, the most effective way to achieve this goal is for both teachers and parents to combine their efforts and expose children to the pleasure of reading in the total home-school environment.

MOTIVATION FOR READING

Several decades ago, the need to motivate children toward reading was less important than it is today. Reading was one of the two main ways of finding out about the world. People listened to the radio or read newspapers and magazines. Forms of family entertainment were extremely limited, and reading to and with the family, conversing and discussing, and interacting were established parts of growing up. Adults recognized the importance of reading and encouraging children to read. Children saw adult models reading and sharing print, and they developed a value for print.

Today our society has changed drastically. The family structure is significantly more flexible. Entertainment options are diverse. Most homes have not only radios but one or more televisions. Many have video recorders, which bring the facilities of movie theaters within their own walls. Video game machines also provide entertainment for children both inside and outside of the home. People are much more mobile. Print occupies a different position in society. People can find out a great deal about their neighborhood, town, state, or country without ever reading print. The classics are available without print as many books in complete and abridged forms become available in cassettes. People may listen to Shakespeare, Twain, Brontë, and Longfellow as they drive through town. Television has been used to pacify children from a young age. Before they reach the first grade, many children have been exposed to thousands of hours of television.

The basic structure of the family is changing drastically as well. In most cases, both parents or the single parent in the home work, and time with children is limited. There is little time to sit down with, read to, discuss with, and interact with children—even in homes with the most well-intentioned parents. In most American homes, adults seldom read for pleasure, and children are not accustomed to owning and enjoying books. Children's lifestyles minimize the actual time during which they are exposed to the pleasure and the power of print. The report of the Commission on Reading, *Becoming a Nation of Readers* (Anderson et al. 1985, 77), supports the fact that reading plays an insignificant part in the lives of most children. The report states that "for the majority of children, reading from books occupied one per cent of their free time, or less. In contrast, the children averaged 130 minutes per day watching TV, or about one third of the time between the end of school and going to sleep."

Consequently, educators must realize that attention to motivation is especially imperative today. Educators must also understand that while some children will successfully learn to read without any overt efforts on the part of teachers to motivate them, some children will learn only if teachers first create the desire to read and an interest in print.

Factors Affecting Motivation

There are several factors at home and at school that affect children's motivation toward reading. Teachers must be able to identify motivational factors in order to create an appropriate environment within the classroom and to make appropriate recommendations to parents.

The Home Environment

Children begin very early to form impressions about the value of reading. The behavior of parents, of other adults, or of older siblings contributes to the values children develop toward learning and toward learning to read. The home clearly has the greatest single influence on the learning of young children (Durkin 1966, Snow 1983, Goldfield and Snow 1984, Finn 1986, France and Meeks 1987, Resnick et al. 1987). This significant influence is to be expected, since young children spend approximately five hours at home for every hour spent at school. Many factors in the home environment contribute to children's motivation toward learning and learning to read (Neuman 1986). A listing of these factors follows.

- The home contains a variety of printed material. Children are exposed early to newspapers, magazines, picture books, story books, books of poetry and rhymes, and the like. Printed material is available and familiar to children.
- Adults read often to gather information and for pleasure. Children see the adults in their family reading print, sharing what they read, enjoying print, and discussing print. Parents might not read all the time, but print is a consistent part of their lives. They read to become informed, to perform tasks such as cooking and home repairs, to relax, and to entertain themselves and others.
- Parents take children to the public library on a regular basis, and choose books for them and with them.
- Parents encourage children to participate in reading. They encourage children to read the pictures and to join in reading familiar words, phrases, and passages.
- Children have available to them printed material that interests them. Parents respond to and encourage their interests.
- Children have personal collections of books. They have favorite books and are encouraged to use them.
- Children are read to at home. From early years, parents have read and reread children's favorite stories and poems. They have discussed the stories, talked about feelings, outcomes, events, and characters. Reading to children is a stable part of the home environment (Vukelich 1978, Anderson et al. 1985).
- Reading is seen as a tool for gathering information. When children ask questions, parents often go to books to find the answers. Thus, children see that print can give them information they need.
- Print is often used as a reward. As a treat, children may hear "just one more story." When children do something well, they are read to as a reward.
- As children grow up, they are encouraged to write, to learn words, and to read on their own. Their successes are encouraged, praised, reinforced, and rewarded.

- Parents take time to answer children's questions about print. They expose children to books that emphasize the alphabet sounds, rhymes, words, and letters.
- Parents show an interest in children's school activities and work. They discuss school with children and support school assignments.
- Parents take time to discuss problems and issues with children, and to provide them with assistance and guidance.
- Reading is never used as a punishment.

The importance of the home environment in children's learning is underscored by the Commission on Reading (Anderson et al. 1985), which made the following recommendations.

1. Parents play roles of inestimable importance in laying the foundation for learning to read. Parents should informally teach preschool children about reading and writing by reading aloud to them, discussing stories and events, encouraging them to learn letters and words, and teaching them about the world around them. These practices help prepare children for success in reading.

2. Parents have an obligation to support their children's continued growth as readers. In addition to laying a foundation, parents need to facilitate the growth of older children's reading by taking them to libraries, encouraging reading as a free time activity, and supporting homework.

3. Parents should read to preschool children and informally teach them about reading and writing. Reading to children, discussing stories and experiences with them, and—with a light touch—helping them learn letters and words are practices that lead to eventual success in reading.

4. Parents should support school-aged children's continued growth as readers. Parents of children who become successful readers monitor their children's progress in school, become involved in school programs, support homework, buy their children books or take them to the libraries, encourage reading as a free time activity, and place limits on such activities as TV viewing (Anderson et al. 1985: 57, 117).

Children who grow up in such environments come to school not only with a great deal of usable information about reading but also with natural curiosity and motivation toward further learning.

The School Environment

When children come to school, factors within the school environment add to their motivation toward reading and toward learning to read. This motivation is imperative in the learning process. To the extent that children come to school without motivation from home environments, motivation in the school environment becomes extremely more important. Several factors contribute to motivation within the school environment.

- Teachers expose children frequently to interesting literature. Children are reminded continually of the importance of reading, because teachers read to them daily.
- The school recognizes, reinforces, and encourages reading. Reading is an obvious school priority. Reading clubs, contests, classroom competitions, and the like are sponsored by the school.
- Time is provided for children to read books they like. All children get an opportunity during the school day to read or to look at books that interest them.
- Teachers know the interests of children and take the time to suggest and present books or magazines that will be motivating to them.
- Teachers constantly modify the instruction of reading so that children's needs are met. The focus is on teaching children, on providing successful experiences with learning, rather than on teaching a particular program exactly as prescribed.
- Time is provided for children to share what they have read with teachers and with each other.
- Children are publicly recognized and rewarded for progress in reading.
- Children are encouraged to write and to read books on their own.
- The materials that children are asked to read are interesting to them and appropriate to their developmental needs. Some educators blame the reading failure of many children on the fact that the materials they are asked to read insult their language abilities and fail to interest them (Bettelheim and Zelan 1982). Content should interest children and motivate them toward learning to read.
- A variety of print is provided for and actively used with children. This includes newspapers; magazines; encyclopedias; easy reading books; high interest–low vocabulary books; wordless, predictable pattern books; poems; rhymes; plays; picture books; and comic books.
- Reading lessons are taught in an interesting, varied manner. The pace of the sessions does not foster boredom.
- Children are constantly made to interact with print. Questions and tasks focus on helping children respond to, identify with, become involved in, learn from, and enjoy print. Ideally, parents and teachers should work together to motivate children toward learning, especially reading.

Teachers of all children, but of remedial students especially, must have a goal of implementing strategies that motivate children to read. Many strategies are relatively simple to institute and can be easily integrated into traditional instructional formats. The strategies fall into two categories: working with the home environment, and improving the school environment.

DEVELOPING AND MAINTAINING MOTIVATION AT HOME

Teachers have the potential for affecting children's motivation toward reading by creating open, frequent, healthy communication between the home and the school. If children are to learn to read, then the efforts of the school must be reinforced at home (France and Meeks 1987). This is true for all children, but especially for children who are experiencing difficulty in learning to read.

Teachers often criticize parents for not becoming more involved in their children's education. Indeed, some parents do not accept any responsibility for their children's learning. However, parents might not respond appropriately because they do not know specifically what to do with their children; they do not understand the extent to which they should become involved in school nor do they realize the importance of that involvement. Some parents do not feel welcome in classrooms. They feel that they would be intruding. Many more parents would become involved if teachers instituted frequent and specific communication between school and home. Such communication would add significantly to the motivation children feel toward learning and reading.

Teachers can use the following strategies to communicate with the home. Teachers can give specific suggestions to parents so they can help their children to read (Swaby 1984).

1. At the start of the school year, send home a "Reading and Your Child" sheet that provides parents with general ideas about reading with their children. This sheet can include such suggestions as the following.

- Read to your child at least ten minutes a day.
- Provide a quiet time free from television and radio to read to and with your child.
- Position the book so that your child can see the print.
- As you come to special words, repeated phrases, and the like, point them out to your child.
- Encourage your child to read familiar segments with you.
- Discuss the story with your child.

- Read something interesting yourself within sight of your child each week.

Be careful not to include too many suggestions at one time.

2. Periodically throughout the school year, provide parents with "How To" sheets addressing specific topics, such as "How to Question Your Child," "How to Help Your Child with Phonics," "How to Build a Sight Vocabulary," "How to Increase Reading Rate," "How to Develop Your Child's Speaking Vocabulary," and "How to Choose Books for Your Child." Each sheet should contain a few clear, simple suggestions. Figures 14.1 and 14.2 are samples of "How To" pages. Limit these sheets to one page with clear, useful, and practical ideas. It is important to give ideas and guidelines about helping children with phonics. Otherwise, parents might resort to needless, inappropriate, and harmful drill that has the potential of threatening the parent-child relationship and of causing children to avoid reading. Providing parents with alternatives to meaningless drills can greatly foster phonic learning.

3. Send home monthly progress charts with children. The charts should present areas of growth, areas that need practice, and specific suggestions to parents for helping children at home. The information should not be elaborate, but must be very specific. An example is presented in Figure 14.3.

How to Help Your Child with Phonics

When you have some free time with your child, before or after meals, before bedtime, after reading, setting the table, etc., play the following games.

1. "Starts Like" game: Give me a word that starts like *step* or *boy*, etc., or find a word in this line that starts like *Mom*.

2. "Ends Like" game: Give me a word that ends like *man*, or find a word on this line that ends like *map*.

3. "Rhymes With" game: Give me a word that rhymes with *bed*, or finish this poem with a word that rhymes.

4. "Thinking Of" game: I am thinking of a word that begins with *m*. (Child guesses.) It ends with *n*. (Child guesses.) It shines at night. Give clues until the correct word is guessed.

5. "Provide the Missing Word" game: Give the child a sentence or read a sentence, and delete or cover the last word, e.g., "I'd better open the _____."

Have your child guess any word that fits. Then give letter clues as in item 4 until the child guesses the word. Go back and say or read the entire sentence.

FIGURE 14.1 "How To" Page—Sample A

How To Help Your Child to Develop Auditory Skills

During the next two months, focus on these skills. Use free time daily to engage in the following activities.

1. "Same-Different" game: Are these words the same or are they different? Begin with beginning sounds, e.g., *bat* and *fat*. Move to ending sounds, e.g., *bat* and *bag*. Finally, use middle sounds, e.g., *bit* and *bet*. If children are not able to identify similarities and differences appropriately, tell them the correct answers, e.g., "Listen; *bat* and *hat* are different." Exaggerate the target sound.

2. "Put-It-Together" game: Break words apart and have children identify the whole word. Begin with easy words like compounds (e.g., *milk–man*; *fast–ball*). Move to roots and endings (e.g., *slow–ly*, *bright–er*), two syllable words (e.g., *bro–ther*, *i–ron*), three letter words (e.g., *m–a–n*, *s–i–t*), and more complex words (e.g., *fl–ow–er–s*, *f–ire–tr–u–ck*).

3. "Memory" game: Provide children with sequences of words or numbers and have them repeat. Begin with two items and increase to five or six (e.g., 1, 9; 8, 3, 5; *horse*, *give*; *pin*, *hand*, *run*).

FIGURE 14.2 "How To" Page—Sample B

Reading Progress Chart

Name: _____

Areas of Growth:

1. Recognizing the words *them, in, through, school,* and *is*.
2. Using beginning sounds *bl, pr, pl,* and *st*.
3. Attitude toward reading.

Areas of Need:

1. Recognizing the words *enough, some, then, said* and *late*.
2. Pronouncing beginning sounds *sl, sp, th* and *gr*.
3. Predicting what might happen next.

Comments:

Parents, as you read with Michael this month, please:

1. point out words beginning with *sl, sp, th,* and *gr,* and discuss them with him.
2. make flash cards of the words *enough, some, then, said,* and *late*.
3. stop frequently as you read stories and have Michael predict what might happen next.

Thank you for working with Michael. I am very pleased with his progress.

FIGURE 14.3 Monthly Progress Chart

4. With poorer readers, send home weekly practice sheets and ask parents to practice with children. Time the words, phrases, sentences, or short paragraphs, and ask parents to encourage children to practice until they cut their time in half. Weekly word practice sheets may be simple, like the one in Figure 14.4.

5. Before beginning each unit, send a "Unit Information Sheet" home with children. Let parents know about the unit to be presented and suggest library books that would be helpful to read to children. This is particularly important for children who lack basic concepts, or who have difficulty in comprehension. An example of an information sheet is shown in Figure 14.5.

6. Invite parents to be "parent helpers." Give them opportunities to volunteer their services for regularly scheduled, short segments of time, so they do not see the time commitment as too overwhelming.

7. Institute a "Parent Helpers at Home" program for parents who work all day outside of the home and cannot help in the classroom. Rather than coming into classrooms and working with individuals or small groups, these parents would agree to perform certain tasks at home with their children and to send a completed checklist back to school each week. The checklist would include specific, reading-related tasks. An example is shown in Figure 14.6.

8. Make parent-teacher conferences as positive, specific, and helpful as possible. Inform parents of specific areas of growth and need. Give them specific suggestions for helping their children. Acknowledge evidence of parents' work with children and encourage further involvement.

9. Provide parents with a recommended book list. You might also include educational toys and games that reinforce needed skills. Book lists are particularly helpful around major holidays because they make good gift suggestions.

Word Practice Sheet

Name: _____

Words	Phrases
in	we went to school
the	I went home
went	the big man
school	in the house
mouse	a little mouse
we	go to school
Time: 30 seconds	Time: 1 minute 15 seconds
Goal: 10 seconds	Goal: 40 seconds

FIGURE 14.4   Weekly Word Practice Sheet

Unit Information Sheet

Dear Parents,

     Next month we will be beginning our Social Studies unit on Human Emotions. The unit will last for two weeks. Prior to and during this time, please read at least four of the following books to Michelle and discuss with her the specific emotions involved. All the books are in our school library and at the public library.

    Crow Boy, by Taro Yashima
    The Hundred Dresses, by Eleanor Estes
    The Hundred Penny Box, by Sharon Bell–Mathis
    All Together, One At a Time, by E. L. Konigsburg
    Amos Fortune: Free Man, by Elizabeth Yates
    Don't Feel Sorry for Paul, by Bernard Wolf

    Also, on February 8, PBS is presenting Marge Blaine's *The Terrible Thing That Happened at Our House*. It deals with the topic of feelings of children. It would be helpful if you watched the program with Michelle and discussed it with her. Thank you.

FIGURE 14.5 Unit Information Sheet

    10. Create a monthly calendar for parents. Each day suggests an activity related to learning to read. The activities might include visual and auditory discrimination tasks, auditory and visual memory activities, sight word review, reading assignments, games, visits to the library, rewards for something well done, writing projects, observations and discussions about nature, worksheet assignments, and story writing and reading.

    11. Provide parents with weekly activity packets that reinforce skills. Packets should contain supplementary or teacher-made materials, not just more workbook pages. The packets should be done by children with the assistance of parents, and should include skills that require practice and reinforcement, not new skills.

    12. Provide parents with a variety of purposes for reading to children. Most parents do not realize that reading to children can focus on different goals. Parents can and should read for different purposes. You might designate one month for a specific form of reading. Send home the purpose along with specific suggestions for fulfilling that purpose, as in the following example.

CLASSROOM ACTIVITY

Month One
Purpose: Reading to develop children's listening and speaking vocabularies.

Parent Helpers in the Home: Reading Checklist

Name _____

Dear Parents:

     During this week, please take the time to complete the following tasks with your child. As you do so, please check off the task and return this checklist on Monday morning _____ (date).

TASKS   COMPLETED

1. Help your child review the following sight words: *through, enough, strange, breakfast, parade, beautiful*.
2. Read and discuss the following books.
   Life in The Sea, by Eileen Curran
   Look Again, by Tana Hoban
   Life in The Pond, by Eileen Curran
   The Amazing Seeds, by Ross Hutchins
3. Help your child practice the following relationships:
   pr = /*pr*/, *gr* = /*gr*/, *sp* = /*sp*/. Have your child see favorite pictures beginning with each. For example, *gr* = picture of Gremlin, and *sp* = picture of a spear. Other ideas are on the "How to Help Your Child with Phonics" sheet sent home last month.

Thank you for being a "Parent Helper at Home."

FIGURE 14.6 Reading Checklist for Parents

    Method: As you read to your children this month, focus on discussing interesting words. For example:

- Name objects in pictures or words in print.
  ("Do you remember the name of this animal?")
- Discuss words that mean the same as words in the text.
  ("Can you tell me another word for *big*?")
- Discuss words that mean the opposite of words in the text.
  ("If the girl was not tall, she would be ____.")
- Encourage children to act out words.
  ("How would your face look if you were depressed?")
- Have your child choose a favorite word in the selection. Write that word on a note card. Your child might illustrate the word. Put the word in a conspicuous place, and draw attention to and use the word as often as possible.

    Suggested Literature: Any book may be used for vocabulary development, including picture dictionaries, alphabet books, and workbooks. Some fine books are:

- *The ABC Bunny*, by Wanda Gag
- *Richard Scarry's Lowly Worm Book*, by Richard Scarry
- *My First Book of Words*, by Tadasu Izawa
- *The Cat in the Hat Beginners Book Dictionary*, by P. D. Eastman
- *ABC, An Alphabet Book*, by Thomas Matthiesen
- *The King Who Rained*, by Fred Gwynne

Other examples of reading purposes, focus areas, and recommended literature are presented in Figure 14.7. A different specific purpose might be emphasized each month.

---

1.   Purpose: To expose children to the pleasure of print.

     Method: Concentrate on the story line. Read with expression. Discuss characters and settings. Discuss pictures. Point out shapes, colors. Have your child react to selections.

     Suggested
     Books: *The Snowy Day*, by Ezra Jack Keats
               May I Bring a Friend, by Beatrice DeRegniers
               Sylvester and the Magic Pebble, by William Steig
               Why Mosquitoes Buzz in People's Ears, by Verna Aardema
               Fables, by Arnold Lobel
               Strega Nona, by Tomie DePaola
               Millions of Cats, by Wanda Gag
               Peter's Chair, by Ezra Jack Keats
               Make Way For Ducklings, by Robert McCloskey
               Where the Wild Things Are, by Maurice Sendak
               Gregory, the Terrible Eater, by Marjorie Sharmat
               There's a Nightmare in My Closet, by Mercer Mayer

2.   Purpose: To develop children's sensitivity to feelings.

     Method: Focus questions on feelings, e.g.,
               How do you feel about this?
               How would you feel if this happened to you?
               How is the character feeling now?
               I would feel awful if this happened to me.
               How would you feel?
               How does that make you feel?

     Suggested
     Books: *Ira Sleeps Over*, by Bernard Waber
               The Tenth Good Thing About Barney, by Judith Viorst
               Alexander and the Terrible, Horrible, No Good, Very Bad Day, by Judith Viorst
               The Giving Tree, by Shel Silverstein
               Crow Boy, by Taro Yashima

FIGURE 14.7   Purposes for Reading to Children, Methods, and Suggested Literature for Each Purpose

The Hundred Dresses, by Eleanor Estes
Nobody Listens to Andrew, by Elizabeth Guilfoile
Swimmy, by Leo Leonni
Nobody Asked Me If I Wanted a Baby Sister, by Martha Alexander
Benjie On His Own, by Joan Lexau
Evan's Corner, by Elizabeth Hill
Everett Anderson's Goodbye, by Lucille Clifton
Tuck Everlasting, by Natalie Babbitt
Bridge to Terabithia, by Katherine Paterson
Roll of Thunder, Hear My Cry, by Mildred Taylor
The Summer of the Swans, by Betsy Byars
Sounder, by William Armstrong
The Slave Dancer, by Paula Foy
A Wrinkle in Time, by Madeleine L'Engle
Up a Road Slowly, by Irene Hunt
Witch of Blackbird Pond, by Elizabeth George Speare

3. Purpose: To stimulate children's sense of humor.

    Method: Focus on humor. Laugh and enjoy with your child.

    Suggested
      Books: *Stoo Hample's Silly Joke Book*, by Stoo Hample
               Silly Questions and Funny Answers, by William Wiesner
               Ballpoint Bananas and Other Jokes for Kids, by Charles Keller
               Rain Makes Applesauce, by Julian Sheer
               Are You My Mother? by J. D. Eastman
               No Kiss for Mother, by Tomi Ungerer
               Crictor, by Tomi Ungerer
               Horton Hatches An Egg, by Dr. Seuss
               Curious George, by Hans Rey
               Once a Mouse, by Marcia Brown
               The Best Christmas Pageant Ever, by Barbara Robinson

4. Purpose: To expose children to new concepts.

    Method: Spend much time expanding specific concepts that may be unfamiliar to children. Discuss the concepts. Read the books over and over to children.

    Suggested
      Books: *Symbols*, by Rolf Muller
               Hailstones and Halibut Bones, by Mary O'Neill
               Big Ones Little Ones, by Tana Hoban
               Opposites, by Sandra Boynton
               In and Out, Up and Down (Sesame Street Books)
               Soil, by Richard Cromer
               Prehistoric Monsters Did the Strangest Things, by Leonora and Arthur Hornblow
               A House Is a House for Me, by Mary Ann Hoberman
               Tyrannosaurus Wrecks, by Noelle Sterne

FIGURE 14.7   (Continued)

Anno's Mysterious Multiplying; Anno's Counting House; Anno's Alphabet; Anno's Animals; Anno's Italy; Anno's Britain; Anno's USA; Anno's Counting Book, by Mitsumasa Anno
The Cloud Book, by Tomi DePaola

5. Purpose: To develop children's reading ability.

    Method:
    - Provide a quiet time and place for reading.
    - Have the book clearly visible to children.
    - Run your fingers slowly under the words as you read.
    - Use books with clear and easy language patterns (predictable print).
    - Repeat the selections frequently.
    - Involve children in the process. Have them read along with you after they have heard the selections a few times.

    Suggested Predictable Print Books:
    Brown Bear, Brown Bear, What Do You See? by William Martin Jr.
    The Very Hungry Caterpillar, by Eric Carle
    Fortunately, by Remy Charlip
    Ten Little Animals, by Carl Memling
    Chicken Soup with Rice, by Maurice Sendak
    But Not the Hippopotamus, by Sandra Boynton
    Don't Forget the Bacon, by Pat Hutchins
    How Joe the Bear and Sam the Mouse Got Together, by Beatrice De Regniers
    The Napping House, by Audrey Wood
    The Very Busy Spider, by Eric Carle
    Hush Little Baby, by Margot Zemach
    One Monday Morning, by Uri Shulevitz
    The Little Red Hen, by Paul Galdone
    The Runaway Bunny, by Margaret Wise–Brown
    If I Had, by Mercer Mayer
    One Fine Day, by Nonny Hogrogian
    Goodnight Moon, by Margaret Wise–Brown
    My Five Senses, by Aliki
    The Very Hungry Caterpillar, by Eric Carle

FIGURE 14.7   (Continued)

DEVELOPING AND MAINTAINING MOTIVATION AT SCHOOL

One of the most important factors in the development of motivation toward reading is the classroom environment. Motivation and interest are not likely to occur in an environment that does not foster and encourage open communication, language stimulation, and a wide variety of print opportunities. Although specific suggestions can be made to help teachers interest children in reading, motivation depends to a large extent on the teacher's attitude, behavior, and personal reaction to print. Teachers who love to read, enjoy books, and value reading for the sheer joy of it tend to transmit to children an interest in and a curiosity about reading and learning to read. Delight in reading is often contagious, and many children who are exposed to this delight "catch" the joy of reading.

Among the most important ingredients in a motivating reading environment are delight in and sharing of print. Certain principles are basic to creating a motivating, stimulating, and interesting classroom reading environment. A discussion of these principles follows.

Principle 1: Read Aloud to Children Every Day.   Part of every school day should be devoted to the reading of interesting, high-quality, varied material to children. Children need to hear the sound of print read by a capable, interested adult model. The selections read should not be limited to narrative material, but should include factual material. Emphasize a variety of literature. Children should be exposed to print that makes them think, respond, laugh, cry, learn, change, and grow. Reading to children not only exposes them to fine printed material, but also makes them realize that reading is important enough for the teacher to routinely take the time to do so. Teachers should include books they love and in which they have a personal investment.

There are several categories of books that are too good for children to miss. These include the Caldecott Award books, presented yearly for the most outstanding picture book; the Newbery Award books, presented yearly for the most outstanding book (literature) for children; the International Reading Association Children's Book Award; the American Book Awards; and the Coretta Scott King Award books (see Appendix A).

There are so many excellent books for children that it is often difficult for teachers to keep up with the titles. Fortunately, there are several helpful professional books and periodicals that provide current reviews of children's and adolescents' literature. These publications are immensely valuable to teachers in choosing appropriate literature. Some of the most useful sources follow.

Books

This Way to Books, by Caroline Bauer (H. W. Wilson, 1983).
Books Kids Will Sit Still For, by Judy Freeman (Alleyside Press, 1984).

For Reading Out Loud!, by Margaret Kimmel and Elizabeth Segel (Delacorte Press, 1983).

A Parent's Guide to Children's Reading, by Nancy Larrick (Bantam Books, 1983).

Sharing Books with Young Children, by James Thomas and Marilyn Vaughn (T. S. Denison, 1982).

Adventuring with Books: A Booklist for Pre-K to Grade 6, by Mary Lou White (National Council of Teachers of English, 1981).

The Read-Aloud Handbook, by Jim Trelease (Penguin Books, 1985).

Periodicals

Book Review Digest (monthly)
        H. W. Wilson and Company
        950 University Avenue
        Bronx, NY 10452

The Booklist (bimonthly)
        American Library Association
        50 E. Huron Street
        Chicago, IL 60611

The Bulletin of the Center for Children's Books (monthly)
        University of Chicago Press
        5801 Ellis Avenue
        Chicago, IL 60637

The Horn Book Magazine (six times per year)
        Horn Book Inc.
        585 Boylston Street
        Boston, MA 02116

Cricket Magazine (monthly)
        Open Court Publishing Company
        1058 Eighth Street
        LaSalle, IL 61301

School Library Journal (monthly)
        R. R. Bowker & Co.
        1180 Avenue of the Americas
        New York, NY 10036

In addition, *The Reading Teacher* annually publishes in the October issue the "Children's Choices" in literature—a valuable guide for teachers.

Principle 2: Provide Time for All Children to Read and to Share Books. It is important that children are given daily opportunities to read for pleasure. While free reading need not take long periods of time, at least fifteen to thirty minutes per day should be provided. Many classrooms across the country have instituted "sustained silent reading" periods in which all individuals in a classroom read print of their choice for a set period of time, usually between ten and thirty minutes per day (McCracken and McCracken 1978, Aulls 1982). Children are not held accountable for their reading. They simply read for their own purposes material of their own choice. In some cases, reluctant readers experience difficulty choosing material to read. Teachers need to be aware of this situation and be willing to suggest possible books. A wide variety of print should be available. A type of book that is essential in classrooms with remedial readers is the high interest–low vocabulary book. As the name suggests, these books utilize easily decodable words, but appeal to older readers. These books are indispensable in classrooms as it is important that remedial readers have access to books they can read. A list of popular high interest–low vocabulary series is presented in Appendix B.

In addition to sustained silent reading, teachers can provide a "browse with books" period during which children read, look at pictures, skim through books, read together, read with older children, and so on. A time is provided each week for children and teachers to share with the class their favorite books they have read during free reading time. This sharing period can also be used as an advertisement session in which children present commercials to promote their favorite books.

Principle 3: Provide a Mini-Library in Your Classroom.   Part of developing an interest in books is having available a variety of interesting books. Classrooms should contain several categories of books, including picture books, wordless story books, predictable pattern books, easy reading books, high interest–low vocabulary books, comic books, magazines, trade books, newspapers, content-area books, encyclopedias, poetry anthologies, plays, and children's original writings. These books can be obtained from several sources. Books may be borrowed weekly from the library. Teachers and children might bring in their favorite books. Parents might be asked to donate one piece of print each semester. Parent-teacher organizations might be asked to donate books. Books can be bought inexpensively from rummage or garage sales, discount stores, and charitable organizations. Public libraries often donate old or damaged books, and local businesses might be asked to donate books. Teachers also can suggest titles of books and magazines to be added to school libraries. Numerous fine titles have been suggested in this chapter. Teachers are encouraged to use a variety of other print sources as well. Appendix C presents a list of popular magazines for children. Many contain material that can be used for instruction and also for the extension of concepts in literature and in the content areas.

Principle 4: Identify Children's Interests.   Many children become "turned off" to reading because the material they are asked to read holds no interest for them. They have never found in the pages of a book any content that captured their attention. If teachers are aware of children's interests, they can choose instructional material that might be motivating to them. In addition, teachers can guide children's reading into areas of interest. One way to identify interests is to administer an interest inventory to each child at the start of the school year. This inventory can then be used as a guide for selecting material. Questions appropriate for an interest inventory follow.

Interest Inventory Questions

Do you have a library card?
How often do you go to the library?
Do you like to be read to?
What books do you like to have read to you?
Does someone read to you often at home? Who?
Do you have favorite books or stories? What are they?
How many books do you own? Where do you keep them?
What kinds of stories do you like most?
Can you read any books all by yourself? Which ones?
What is the last book you read?
What is your favorite TV show? Why do you like it?
Do you have any collections? What do you collect?
Do you have any hobbies? What are they?
What sports do you like most?
What is your favorite part of the school day? Why?
What is your least favorite part of the school day? Why?
Would you like to learn to read well? Why or why not?
If you could read anything you wanted to, what would you read?
What do you dislike reading or having read to you?
What do you usually do in your spare time?
What do you most enjoy doing at home?
What games do you most like to play?
Do you have a pet? What is it?
If you could take any type of lessons, what would you like to learn
    to do?
What are you afraid of?
Have you taken any trips? Where did you go? What was your favor-
    ite trip?
Have you ever been to the zoo? a concert? camp? a museum? a park?
    a farm? a picnic?
Do you have any favorite movies?

Another format for an interest inventory contains statements to be completed. In this format, children are presented with the beginning of sentences and are asked to finish the sentences, as in the following example.

I like _____.
My favorite friend is _____.
I am very happy when _____.
I am very unhappy when _____.
School makes me feel _____.
I am best at _____.
I feel good when _____.
I can't _____.
Reading makes me _____.

I wish that I could _____.
I worry about _____.
If I could read, I'd read about _____.
I hate _____.
I do really well at _____.
People make me feel _____.
I like it when my friends _____.
My best friend is _____.
My mother _____.
My father _____.
The thing I like best about myself is _____.
I get angry when _____.
Sometimes I wish I could _____.
My favorite subject is _____.
At school, I really like _____.
School is _____.
I am very _____.

Sentence completion exercises allow teachers to observe children's emotions concerning reading and learning tasks, as well as to identify children's specific interests.

Principle 5: *Provide Incentives for Children to Read.* Some children become initially motivated toward reading when they are rewarded for reading. Some teachers feel that children should be intrinsically motivated to learn, and that external motivation is inappropriate. Remember, however, that for most reluctant or remedial readers, learning to read is not only a difficult task, but one that has resulted in continual failure. It is unlikely, then, that these children have experienced the joy, success, and satisfaction of print that intrinsically motivates children to read. Incentives are often necessary to provide initial motivation.

Several motivational strategies can provide a stimulus for reading. Reading competitions can be instituted, in which children earn points for reading and responding to books. By accumulating a set number of points, they earn certain privileges. It is important not to set limits too high. Requiring ten books before providing a reward might immediately defeat children who have never read a book from cover to cover.

Teachers can also involve children in "Book Karate," in which children read a certain number of books and complete specific tasks related to each book. On the basis of the number of books read, they earn "karate belts" of different colors. Children might strive to achieve a "black belt" by the end of the school year. To increase incentive and to prevent frustration, "qualifying stripes" might be awarded between achievements of belts. Table 14.1 presents a possible organizational structure for Book Karate. Emphasis is placed on advancement, not on reaching the highest level.

TABLE 14.1   Book Karate Format

Level	Number of Books Required	Number of Activities Per Book
White Belt	5	1
Qualifying Stripe	8	1
Yellow Belt	10	1
Qualifying Stripe	14	1
Orange Belt	16	1
Qualifying Stripe	19	1
Purple Belt	22	2
Qualifying Stripe	26	2
Blue Belt	29	2
Qualifying Stripe	33	2
Green Belt	36	2
Qualifying Stripe	40	2
Brown Belt	44	3
Qualifying Stripe	49	3
Black Belt	55	3

Provide a wide variety of activity options for children. One of the worst things teachers can do is to require a traditional book report for each book read. There are hundreds of interesting activities students can perform to demonstrate their comprehension of books, including the following activities.

- Tell the story to your teacher.
- Draw a picture of your favorite part of the story.
- Make a cassette recording of the story.
- Decorate the classroom door like your favorite scene.
- Make your own book jacket.
- Make a collage of your favorite scenes or character.
- Write a poem about the story.
- Write a commercial about the book.
- Prepare a book display.
- Tell the story to a group of younger children.
- Tell the story to the class.
- Write a letter to the author and discuss your most and least favorite parts.
- Create a tissue paper stained-glass window showing your favorite scene or character.
- Create a wall hanging of a favorite scene.
- Designate one day during which children dress like favorite characters.
- Make feltboard characters and scenes, and use the material to retell the story.

- Create "Who Am I" riddles based on book characters.
- Prepare a two- to five-minute speech about the book.
- Make a bookmark illustrated with a favorite scene or character.
- Make a collection of favorite quotations from the book.
- Make a character line. Identify one character and choose ten words that best describe the character. Justify each word with quotes from the book.
- Give a book report in pantomime.
- Create paper puppets and perform a puppet show based on a favorite scene.
- Create a game based on the story.
- Construct a crossword puzzle based on the book.
- Retell the story on tape for younger children. Create your own sound effects.
- Choose a series of scenes and create original illustrations.
- Make a mobile of characters, objects, or scenes from the story.
- Create a dance routine based on the story.
- Identify ten reasons you liked the book.
- Create a fifteen-item test on the book.
- Create a "Book of the Week" display.
- Make and illustrate an alphabet book with letters representing a character, event, idea, or scene from the story.
- Write a character sketch of a book character.
- Compose a song about the story.
- Draw a picture about the story.
- Decorate a wastebasket, box, or storage bin with scenes from the story.
- Memorize a part of your book and recite it to your teacher.
- Illustrate a paper bag and wear it to advertise the book.
- Write a newspaper advertisement for the book.
- Find out ten facts about the author of the book.
- Make a comic strip about your favorite scene.
- Use an opaque projector to show the book's illustrations to the class. Tell the story from the pictures.
- Construct a flipchart or set of illustrations that tell the story.
- Make a list of ten of your favorite words in the book.
- Compare and contrast two book characters.
- Tell the story to a friend.
- Construct a shadow box showing a favorite scene.
- Paint a poster of a favorite scene.
- Create a set of charades revealing characters and events in the story.
- Find magazine illustrations relating to the book, and make a collage.
- Make a placemat showing a favorite scene, and laminate.
- Write a letter to a character in the book.

- Create a different ending to the story.
- Make a timeline showing the most important sequential events.
- Create a word tree with your favorite words and meanings from the book.
- Make a map illustrating places in your story.

Another idea is to have "Readers of the Week" or "Readers of the Month" presentations. Present two awards—"Reader of the Most Books" and "Most Improved Reader." Children might be given certificates to take home. Teachers should also continually recognize before the class those children who show progress in reading, in terms of both performance and attitude.

Principle 6: *Add Variety to Instructional Sessions.* It is difficult for children to be motivated toward reading when the teaching sessions lack variety, interest, interaction, and appropriate pacing. During reading instruction, teachers should use a variety of strategies to introduce, develop, assess, and reinforce reading material. The matching of instructional strategies to students will result in the variation of teaching that is vital to learning and to motivation toward learning. Lessons should never be allowed to be slow-paced, boring, or completely predictable. Teachers should make an effort to involve all children in the material through appropriate questioning strategies.

Principle 7: *Involve Children in the Writing Process.* Give them opportunities to read their own written work and that of their peers.

THE LINK BETWEEN WRITING AND READING

Throughout this text, reading has been described as one of the language arts—reading, writing, speaking, and listening—which share common language features of sound, word order, and meaning. This means that there is a natural interdependence among these arts. Research has long established that a strong writing program enhances a reading program (Bond and Dyxtra 1967). Leaders in the field of reading education have also consistently called for a more direct link between reading and writing instruction than currently exists (Graves 1982, Froese and Straw 1981, Smith 1982). Children's own writing clearly provides strong motivation toward reading. Suggestions for involving children in writing follow.

1. *Expressive writing.* Expressive writing is defined as "thinking aloud intended for the writer's own use, such as first-person anecdotes, diary entries, personal letters and notes" (Britton et al. 1975, 287). This form of writing focuses on writers' emotions, feelings, and personalities. It is personal writing, relatively free in form. Consequently, this type of writing is naturally motivating. In order to encourage expressive writing, give children notebooks they may keep as private property. They may

decorate them and write in them whenever they wish. Children are given five to ten minutes each day to write in their notebooks. They are encouraged to write letters or notes to each other, parents, friends, siblings, or teachers; holiday or birthday greetings to friends and family; and accounts of experiences. Each day, prior to the writing period, the teacher brainstorms possible topics with children. The discussion is geared toward generating interest. For example, the teacher may ask children to think of and share topics, experiences, or ideas that they might want to write about. The ideas might be listed on the chalkboard. Children are then asked to choose a specific topic on which to write. Some children might finish pieces they had started earlier. Once a week children share one piece of writing with the teacher, who responds to the content rather than to the mechanics. During conferences with the teacher, questions focus on completeness of thought and clarity of expressions. To help children develop their writing, use questions and comments such as "Can you tell me what will happen next?" "Tell me a bit more about this part of your story;" "Will you read me your favorite part?" "Would you like to add anything to this?" "I'm not sure what you are saying here; can you make it clearer to me?" "Is that what you wanted to say?" "Are you pleased with how this part sounds?" At least twice a month, children are asked to choose one piece to share with the class. This piece is edited with the teacher's help, rewritten, and read to the group by the student.

Graves (1982, 1983) provides clear and detailed discussions of this form of writing for teachers who are interested in becoming more knowledgeable about this process.

2. *Writing texts to wordless storybooks.* Some children require more direct, organized, sequential, and structured experiences with writing than expressive writing provides. They need to "see" the process and to engage in specific patterns of writing, such as writing from wordless storybooks. As the name implies, these are books with pictures that tell a definite story, although no words are included. After looking at the pictures, enjoying and discussing them, and discovering the plot, children are encouraged to "tell the story" in their own words. Thus, they construct a text to go along with the pictures. The teacher's task is to generate discussion and to transcribe the children's words. The teacher might respond to the story content by asking questions and making comments that relate to the completeness and clarity of the text. This is a good strategy for getting children into writing. It can be used easily with children as young as pre-kindergarten age. This form of writing not only begins to build children's concept of story, but also provides them with a whole structure in which to create. When the stories are completed, they are reread and edited. Teachers then have a perfect opportunity to discuss such features as capitalization, punctuation, quotation, and word choice. The stories are typed, illustrated by the children, and used for free reading, group reading, instructional reading, or story telling. The following list summarizes the steps involved in wordless storybook writing.

- Choose a wordless text.
- Look through the book and discuss the pictures on each page.
- Go through the book again to identify the plot.
- Start from the beginning. Create the text page by page.
- Edit, type, and illustrate.

Figure 14.8 is an example of a text written to Fernando Krahn's wordless storybook, *The Mystery of the Giant Footprints*. It was written by a five-year-old kindergartner, David. This was one of David's first pieces of writing. David was able, with assistance, to read "his" story. After repeated readings, he proudly read and reread it alone. It was also one of David's first successful, enjoyable, and motivating reading experiences. Writing was David's inroad to reading. Children should have many opportunities to engage in writing and reading of this type. A list of popular and interesting wordless storybooks follows.

The Silver Pony, by Lynd Ward
Elephant Buttons, by Noriko Ueno
Noah's Ark, by Peter Spier
Frog on His Own, by Mercer Mayer
Anno's Journey, by Mitsumasa Anno
Snow, by Isao Sasaki
Clementina's Cactus, by Ezra Jack Keats

　　　Once upon a time there was a huge snow storm. Mother, Dad, and the two kids went to their house in the middle of a forest. It really snowed hard. In the morning, they went to the window and looked out at the snow. There they saw huge footprints like a giant monster.

　　　"I'd better get my gun," said the Father, this monster could be dangerous. The family decided to follow the footprints. They followed them up a high hill. They followed them through a big wood. They followed them through the town but the footprints kept going. Other people became curious. They followed too. Everyone went across a lake, on a tiny ledge and to a dark cave. They went into the cave. They were afraid, but they went. And what did they see? Not one creature, but two. The only thing was that each creature had only one large foot. They looked like twin monsters.

　　　"They are big, but they look so friendly," said the kids.

　　　"Can we have them as pets?" asked the children.

　　　"No!" said Mother.

　　　"Well, if you take care of them and treat them with care," said Father. The children were happy, so they took them home. The friendly creatures hopped on their one foot like kangaroos. The children fed the creature pets. They loved spaghettios.

FIGURE 14.8 Text Written by a Student to a Wordless Storybook

Here Comes Alex Pumpernickel, by Fernando Krahn
The Happy Dog, by Hieyuki Tanaka
Arthur's Adventure in the Abandoned House, by Fernando Krahn
The Wild Baby, by Fernando Krahn
Nightdances, by Fernando Krahn
Sing, Pierrot, Sing, by Tomie de Paola
The Grey Lady and the Strawberry Snatcher, by M. Bang
Paddy Underwater, by John Goodall
Paddy Pork—Odd Jobs, by John Goodall
Deep in the Forest, by Brinton Turkle
Frog, Where Are You? by Mercer Mayer
Ah–Choo, by Mercer Mayer
Moonlight, by Jan Ormerod

3. *Writing stories based on highly predictable pattern books.* Predictable pattern books are texts that have very obvious language patterns such as Bill Martin's *Brown Bear, Brown Bear, What Do You See?* (1983). The text begins:

Brown Bear, Brown Bear
What do you see?
I see a Redbird looking at me.
Redbird, Redbird
What do you see?
I see a Yellow Duck looking at me.
Yellow Duck, Yellow Duck
What do you see?
I see a Green Frog looking at me.*

Predictably, the next stanza begins, "Green Frog, Green Frog what do you see?" The green frog will see another animal of another color "looking at me." The language pattern is obvious and predictable.

In using predictable books for writing, the books are read several times until children can identify and repeat the patterns. At this point, "what if" writing begins. The teacher might ask children, "What if we wanted to write our own Brown Bear story? How could we begin our story? What could we say instead of Brown Bear? Could we say 'Mary, Mary' or 'John, John' or 'Plant, Plant' or 'Table, Table?' How else could we begin our story? Think for a minute, and find your favorite ways to begin our story." With questions and comments such as these, children are led to write their own stories based on the structure of predictable print books. With repeated exposure to this strategy, children will require less prodding and guidance from teachers, as the following case suggests.

*From *Brown Bear, Brown Bear, What Do You See?* by Bill Martin, Jr., pictures by Eric Carle. Copyright © 1967, 1983 by Holt, Rinehart and Winston. Reprinted by permission of Henry Holt and Company, Inc.

CASE STUDY

Recently, I worked with a first grade class on a predictable print writing assignment. The text was the Brown Bear story mentioned before. After reading the story and motivating their own writing with the "what if" strategy, the group constructed the following story:

Puddle, puddle
What do you see?
I see children
splashing in me.
Children, children
What do you see?
I see the rain
coming toward me.
Rain, rain
What do you see?
I see a bumpy frog
looking at me.
Bumpy frog, bumpy frog
What do you see?
I see a brown bear
looking at me.
Brown bear, brown bear,
What do you see?
I see a big tree
looking at me.
Big tree, big tree
What do you see?
I see the blue sky
looking at me.
Blue sky, blue sky
What do you see?
I see a rainbow
looking at me.
And that's just what I see.

All children were excited about their writing, contributed fully, and enjoyed the task. It was interesting to see the children edit their work, question their choices, change words to make the material more logical, and critically analyze their writing. Because of the predictability of the language and the fact that they wrote the text, every child could read the material easily.

The identical procedure may be used for reading instruction. After material has been edited, it may be typed, illustrated by the children, and bound. Gillet and Temple (1982) provide clear and simple directions for binding books. Their directions follow:

Step 1. Cut two pieces of cardboard for the front and back covers of the book. Make sure they are the same size. Lay the pieces side by side. Leave enough space between for the pages to be inserted. The width of a pencil is enough.

Step 2. Place the cardboard on top of the cover material which has been cut (in one piece) one inch larger than the cardboard on all sides. Use any attractive paper, wallpaper, fabric, or contact paper for covers. Bond the cover material to the cardboard with glue or with photographic drymount paper and a warm iron.

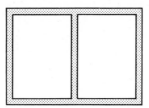

Step 3. Fold down the corners of the cover material over the cardboard. Then fold over the edges and glue the corners and the edges to the cardboard.

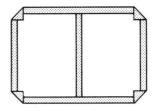

Step 4. While the glue dries, cut sheets of paper for pages. Cut each sheet slightly smaller than the entire opened cover. Don't cut down the middle of the sheet. Instead, fold in half and sew the sheets down the fold, using white thread. Dental floss works well as a substitute for thread. Place stitches about one-quarter inch apart (see diagram on page 372).

Step 5. Place sewn pages into the cover with stitching against the space between the cardboard. Glue the first page to the inside cover, covering up the raw edges of the material. Repeat with the last page and the back cover. This forms end papers and holds the entire book together.*

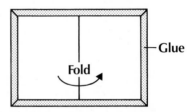

Books are placed in school or classroom libraries. Children are encouraged to read and practice their books and to share them with others. Books can be used for reading instruction as well. Sight words can be isolated, placed on cards, and drilled. Phonic skills can be reinforced using words from the books, and questions can be asked to develop comprehension skills. Books can also be practiced for fluency. Predictable print reading and writing should be a routine part of children's language arts experiences (Bridge et al. 1983, Heald–Taylor 1987). A list of predictable print books is presented in Appendix D.

4. *Writing stories based on specific formats or structures.* Some children need a transition between the writing of wordless or predictable print texts and independent writing. Controlled writing provides such a transition. Controlled writing is writing based on preconstructed, incomplete structures. Story form writing, mentioned in Chapter 9, falls in this category. In story form writing, children finish an incomplete story.

First, general story elements, such as characters, settings, major idea, climax, and sequence of events are discussed with children. Next, the specific story elements of the story form are discussed in detail. For example, in elaborating on the four characters the following questions might be asked: "Who are they?" "What are they like?" "What types of personalities might they have?" "What might they look like?" "How might they interact with each other?" "Given the title, what might each of them do?" The title and the main idea are then analyzed. Students are guided

*From Jean Wallace Gillet and Charles Temple, *Understanding Reading Problems: Assessment and Instruction*, pp. 359–360. Copyright © 1982 by Jean Wallace Gillet and Charles Temple. Reprinted by permission of Scott, Foresman and Company.

to discover the meaning of the main idea, to brainstorm on the question of how the main idea relates to each of the characters, and to relate the main idea to personal experiences. Next, the sequences of events are brainstormed. Children are led to analyze the events and to identify the problem in the story. Finally, the children elaborate on the plot, add as many events to the story as they wish, and complete the story. Children then read and share their stories. Initially, the teacher directs this procedure several times. As children begin to internalize the process, they work in pairs or in small groups to complete stories. As the process becomes more automatic, children may complete stories independently. Finally, they fill out a story form as an outline for independent creative writing of their own.

Another form of structured writing is triad writing. Triad writing uses a triangular structure to relate words at each point to a title in the center of the triangle. An example is provided in Figure 14.9. The triangle is shown to children and the title is discussed. Next, the words are discussed as they relate to each other. For example, the teacher might ask, "How are a boat and a storm related?" "What relationships can you think of between a boat and a shipwreck?" "What might a shipwreck and a storm have to do with each other?" After all relationships have been explored, the information is used to generate the major story elements of (1) characters, (2) settings, (3) problem, (4) solutions, and (5) major ideas. As the story emerges, the concepts of word choice, sequence, and clarity of presentation are discussed. After the story is created orally, it is transcribed, edited, and read by children.

Structured writing provides children with a framework for writing. It gives them a "concept of story," which forms the foundation for future narrative writing. For children who are not natural writers, this form of writing helps them to abstract story elements and to make decisions relating to appropriate writing. Children are encouraged to read and reread their stories. Stories can also be bound and entered in permanent library collections and used for direct instruction.

Shipwreck

Title:
"Stranded"

Boat   Storm

FIGURE 14.9   Triad Writing

My Book about Cats

Cats are animals with claws and whiskers and are very fast and *smart*. A leopard can run up to 70 m.p.h. with its polka-dot coat. It keeps it warm in the winter but cool in the summer. From kittens to tigers, cats are very playful—playful and fierce. A lion tugs on a rope and. . . . oh boy! When a cat pulls in her claws, it means that it won't scratch. However, a cheeta can't pull their claws in.

Siamese cats do *not* speak Siamese. (They don't speak U.S.A. either.) They do speak cat language (MEOW). They talk to each other. I am not saying that a lion talks to a kitten. That would be too dumb. The kitten wouldn't understand anyway.

A black panther will be a good mother and a good father too. But you have to be careful. They are not always gentle.

A Poem

We're almost done with our little book. I'll tell you the name of our author—Her name is Brooke! Now if you liked this book about cats, you will like my *The Little Book About Mammals.* These cats sure do.

FIGURE 14.10   Factual Text Written by a Student

5. *Writing factual information books.* Most children have a great deal of information about at least one topic. They might know about their pets, dinosaurs, football, video games, cars, dolls, and so on. Teachers should encourage children to dictate or write about what they know. As children write, teachers should respond to the content of the material. Questions that help children to more adequately express what they know should be asked. Parent volunteers, advanced students in the classroom, or children in higher grades might assist teachers in transcribing younger children's work. After the stories have been edited, a final draft is made. Finished informational books might be illustrated and shared with the class or group, peers, family members, the principal, special teachers, or other school personnel.

To write factual selections, children must have available to them a variety of factual information. In their daily oral reading to children teachers should include a number of factual, informative selections. The information should be discussed with children and the concepts they contain fully developed. As the material is read, the ways in which the authors present information should be analyzed. This analysis will help children to see how written information is organized. As they write their own factual material, then, they can use the patterns they have heard to organize their selections.

There are many fine books currently available that provide children with valuable factual information. Some of these sources are listed in Appendix E. Exposure to factual material allows children to accumulate information that can be written, read and shared. Figure 14.10 presents a

How to Make a Peanut Butter and Jelly Sandwich

First you take two pieces of bread from the bread bag. You can use white bread, or brown bread or raisin and cinnamon bread which I like a lot. Then you can cut off the crust if you want to eat it faster. Then take peanut butter. I like smooth peanut butter, because the crunchy one gets in my teeth. Take a knife and put lots of peanut butter on the bread. Lots makes it nice and chewy. Then take jelly. I usually have grape or strawberry or raspberry or blueberry, but grape is my favorite. Put lots of jelly. Sometimes when you put lots on, when you bite it some falls out and you can eat it off the plate with your finger. Then I put the two jelly butter sides together for a sandwich, Eat it for lunch or dinner or breakfast. You can eat it with milk or apple juice or soda which my mother doesn't let me drink. You can have another one tomorrow.

FIGURE 14.11   Factual Selection Written by a Student

factual text written by a six-year-old girl, Brooke. Notice the effect of factual content on her writing.

Brooke is an intellectually gifted child. At six years old, her intellectual abilities are clear in her writing. But what of children who are not identified as gifted, but as learning disabled? With practice, these children produce beautiful writing as well. Figure 14.11 presents the factual writing of Herbert, a six-year-old boy who was in a special learning program and who used to say, "I can't read 'cause I'm too dumb." Notice how full and clear writing is when you write about what you know. Herbert wrote his selection and within a week was able to read it fluently. He was so proud that he read it to anyone who would listen. It was the first time that he knew he could learn. Children should have frequent opportunities to write selections like this and to share their material with friends, family, teachers and others.

6. *Writing creative stories.* As children gain experience with writing, they should be encouraged to write creative stories based on familiar experiences or on fantasy. It is important that teachers frequently read a variety of stories to children in order to develop interest and to expose them to several different plots, organizational patterns, and writing styles.

COMPUTERS AND READING REMEDIATION

The 1980s will undoubtedly be remembered as the first decade in which computers became a routine part of society and of the school environment. Though computers have been used for instruction and remediation since the start of the 1970s, their presence has been most visible during the early 1980s. Comptuers hold tremendous promise for providing significant instruction, remediation, and motivation at many levels of learning. They have already had a major impact on education, and many writers predict that they will become primary instructional tools in the majority of classrooms within very few years (Brandt 1983, Dammeyer 1983, Melmed 1983). Blanchard and Mason (1985) state that by the beginning of 1984, only 14 percent of the 15,000 United States public school districts were not using computers for instruction. Since then, that percentage has no doubt dramatically lowered. It is already imperative that all teachers have at least a working knowledge of computers. In the field of reading instruction, the potential for computers is limited only by the knowledge and creativity of those who use them.

Types of Computer Applications

According to the literature on the use of computers in education, there are two broad categories of computer applications in reading: computer-assisted instruction (CAI) and computer-managed instruction (CMI). Computer-assisted instruction is a process in which learners interact directly with the computer and perform lessons that are displayed on the screen. These lessons include drill and practice exercises in reading skills, such as letter identification; sight-word practice; vocabulary; phonics; word, sentence, paragraph, and passage comprehension; and syllabication. Computer-assisted instruction also includes tutorial programs designed for remedial readers and games used for extensions, practice, and reinforcement. As students interact with computers and perform specific tasks, their responses are analyzed, incorrect responses are identified, and students are given opportunities to correct their errors. Many programs provide additional activities at the same level of difficulty as the level at which the errors were made until children demonstrate mastery at that level. Other programs provide a specified number of chances for correction; then, if the child's response is still incorrect, the program automatically gives the correct response. Several programs are designed to foster motivation by using children's names in responding to their input. For example, the computer might print, "That's the right answer, Susan"; "Try again, Peg"; "Good job, Jeff."

Computer-managed instruction refers to the use of the computer not only as an instructional tool as in CAI, but as a record keeper, diagnostic tester, test scorer, and prescriber of what students should study next (O'Donnell 1982). Students are usually given tests to take on the computer. The computer scores the tests, records and analyzes the results, summarizes the analysis, prescribes the level at which the child should receive instruction, and stores that information for the future use of the teachers. CMI proves extremely useful to teachers because it relieves them of a great deal of tedious and time-consuming record keeping.

Computer Applications to Reading Remediation

Computers have major applications to reading management, instruction, and remediation. The remarkable versatility of the computer makes its applications to the field of reading nearly limitless. Thompson (1980), in reviewing the applications of computers to reading instruction, emphasizes this versatility by making the following points:

1. Computers are capable of containing programs based on the entire range of reading theories. Material can reflect phonic, linguistic, or psycholinguistic perspectives.
2. Computers are capable of supporting a variety of reading content. Exercises can be provided in vocabulary development, word recognition, decoding, and comprehension.
3. Computers are capable of being used equally effectively with different kinds of learners. They can provide instruction, practice, remediation, and extension to gifted, average, remedial, or severely handicapped readers.
4. Computers are capable of being used in a variety of settings. They may effectively be used with individuals, pairs, small groups, or large groups.

This versatility makes the computer a most valuable asset to teachers. The speed with which computers are being introduced into schools is making it imperative for all teachers to have at least a working knowledge of computers. This by no means indicates that all teachers must become experts in computers. In fact, this assumption causes some teachers to feel intimidated by the rapidly progressing computer age. That interpretation is inaccurate, however. Teachers must eventually become familiar with computers, but there are varying degrees of knowledge. O'Donnell (1982) defines three levels of computer knowledge: computer awareness, computer use, and computer programming. A discussion of each level follows.

Level 1: Computer Awareness. Individuals gain a basic understanding of computers. This involves an awareness of the role of computers in society and the impact of this technology on society. This awareness might be gained by building a personal knowledge base through discussions with interested individuals and through the reading of journals, periodicals, and books that provide information relevant to computers and their use. A fine collection of articles dealing with issues in computer education can be found in *Run: Computer Education*, 2nd edition, by D. Harper and J. Stewart (Brooks/Cole Publishers, 1986). Articles dealing with learning theory, teaching exceptional children, and several other relevant topics are included. All teachers need to reach the level of awareness as soon as possible. One step in helping teachers reach this level is for school libraries to subscribe to a number of the suggested periodicals.

   Level 2: Computer Use.   Individuals learn to actually use the computer—to view and evaluate instructional programs; to provide instruction, drill, practice, and remediation for children; and to keep records of students' progress and needs. Although school administrators must assume major responsibility for providing adequate inservice experiences and teacher training in the use of computers, teachers must also take independent steps toward educating themselves. All universities and colleges now offer programs in computer use. Teachers might enroll in such classes and learn the basic steps in computer application. In addition, several fine self-help books are available, including the following.

> *Kids and the Apple*
> *Kids and the VIC–20*
> *Kids and the Atari*
> > (Prentice–Hall)
> *Armchair Basic*
> > (McGraw–Hill)
> *Introduction to Basic for the VIC–20*
> > (Commodore Business Machines)
> *The Elementary Apple*
> *Data Most*
> *I Speak Basic*
> > (Hayden Book Company)
> *Introduction to Computers in Education for Elementary and Middle School Teachers*, by D. Moursund
> > (International Council for Computers in Education)
> > Dept. of Computers and Information Science
> > University of Oregon
> > Eugene, Oregon 97403
> *Learning with Logo*, by Daniel Watt
> > (McGraw–Hill 1983)
> *Logo: Lessons in Logo*, by S. Cary and M. Walker
> > (Terrapin Inc. 1985)
> *Introduction to Computer Application*, by A. Luehrmann and H. Peckham
> > (McGraw–Hill 1986)

   When teachers have a basic knowledge of how to use computers, they can begin to critically preview software for classroom use. There are many publishers that provide fine computer programs for the instruction and remediation of reading. All categories of reading skills are available. These include sight vocabulary reinforcement, phonic instruction, comprehension, structural analysis, and reading games. The following companies publish recommended programs for remediation.

- American Microware Corp.
  1264 Deer Trail
  Libertyville, IL 60046
- Developmental Learning Materials
  1 DLM Park
  Allen, TX 75002
- Blyth Valley Software
  Box 1
  Oakhurst, CA 93644
- Comp. Ed.
  8626 N. 48th Dr.
  P.O. Box 35461
  Phoenix, AZ 85069
- Educational Curriculum Software
  127 Dayton Ave.
  Manorville, NY 11946
- EduSoft
  Box 2560
  Berkeley, CA 94702
- Follett Library Book Company
  4506 Northwest Highway
  Crystal Lake, SC 60014
- The Learning Company
  545 Middlefield Road
  Menlo Park, CA 94025
- The Learning Line
  P.O. Box 577
  Palo Alto, CA 94302
- Queue Information Software
  798 North Ave.
  Bridgeport, CT 06604
- Sunburst Educational Computer Courseware
  39 Washington Avenue
  Pleasantville, NY 10570–9971
- Scholastic Inc.
  730 Broadway
  New York, NY 10003
- Troll Associates
  320 Rt. 17
  Mahwah, NJ 07430
- Weekly Reader Family Software
  Xerox Education Publications
  245 Long Hill Road
  Middletown, CT 06457

These are a few of the many publishers of computer software in reading. Publications such as the following are catalogs of the best-selling computer software and reviews of educational computer materials from a wide variety of publishers.

> *Educational Software for the School*
>   Computer Learning Source
>   5746 North Academy Blvd.
>   Colorado Springs, CO 80907
> *The Book of Apple Software*, 6th Ed.,
>   by J. Stanton, M. McCroskey, and M. Mellin, eds.
>   Vans Nuys, CA: Arrays, Inc., 1985.
> *Computer Industry Almanac*
>   by E. Juliassen, P. Isaacson, and L. Kruse, eds.
>   Dallas, TX: Computer Industry Almanac, 1987.
> *Free (And Almost Free) Software for the Macintosh*
>   by R. C. Eckhardt
>   New York: Crown Publishers Inc., 1987
> *Microcomputer Marketplace*
>   New York: R. R. Bowker Company, 1987
> *The 1986 Programmers' Markets*
>   by B. M. McGehee, ed.
>   Cincinnati, OH: Writers Digest Books, 1985

Because of the proliferation of software available for remediation in reading, it is necessary for teachers to have appropriate criteria for evaluating and choosing programs that will meet children's needs. A comprehensive and sensible evaluation guide is found in the *Evaluator's Guide for Microcomputer-Based Instructional Packages* (1982) developed by Project Micro SIFT, Dept. F, Computer and Information Science (Eugene, OR: University of Oregon, Eugene, OR 97403). The criteria include the following.

Content

- The content is accurate, with information that is current and accurate.
- The content has educational value; content is useful and important in the school curriculum.
- The content is free from racial, ethnic, and sex stereotypes.

Instructional Quality

- The purpose of the software is well defined and the package achieves its defined purpose. Objectives are clear and stated in terms of expected student behaviors.
- The presentation of the content is clear and logical. Information is well organized. Definitions and explanations are available when necessary, and there is a smooth transition between concepts.

- The level of difficulty is appropriate for the target audience. The responses (multiple choice, manipulating graphics, single key-stroke, etc.) are age appropriate. Examples and illustrations are age and maturity appropriate. Steps are logical; the program has multiple uses and automatically branches from less to more complex remediation and drill.
- The use of the package is motivational. Students are addressed in personal style, and the overall tenor of interaction is warm, friendly and helpful. The program uses and provides for a variety of responses. Reinforcement is positive; the student has a pleasant experience and desires to use the package again.
- Feedback on student responses is effectively employed. Feedback is relevant to students' responses and therefore credible. Feedback is nonthreatening, yet corrective, and is given with appropriate frequency and immediately after response. Feedback tells why a response was incorrect, and the program adapts to the learner by adjusting the difficulty level of the content.
- The learner controls the rate and sequence of presentation and review. The student has control over time limits, pacing, and the rate of presentation. The program allows the student to begin at an appropriate level.

Technical Quality

- User support materials are comprehensive. Student material includes preinstruction activities, guides to use, and followup material. Teacher material provides suggestions, rationale for use, and activities.
- The user support materials are effective. The user can easily and independently operate the program.

Level 3: Computer Programming.   This is the most complex level and requires the most sophisticated training. There is a great need for classroom teachers to become involved in the actual writing of computer programs for classroom remediation and instruction. Some available programs lack pedagogical credibility because they are written by individuals unfamiliar with how children learn reading and with the problems that result when the learning to read process has been negatively affected. Teachers interested in computer-assisted instruction who acquire skills in computer programming could add significantly to the quality of remedial and instructional reading material designed for the computer. However, a lack of programming skills should not prevent teachers from creating material. Interested teachers can work with expert programmers to jointly develop excellent instructional software for the classroom.

As teachers become progressively more familiar with the use of computers, they will find them to be a highly effective, captivating, and motivating remedial and instructional tool.

SUMMARY   An essential ingredient of any remedial program in reading is the motivation of children to want to read. Although motivation is necessary for all children, it is indispensable for remedial readers, because their history of reading failure often leads them to resist reading instruction in order to preserve their self-respect. Because attitudes toward learning are just as important as skills, motivation must be high on the list of teacher priorities. A well-balanced and effective reading program exposes children to the techniques of reading, while immersing them in the joy of reading. Motivation toward reading is most effectively achieved when home and school work together to maintain interest in reading. This chapter presented several techniques for use at school and at home to generate interest in and motivation toward reading. The most valuable gifts adults can give children are the tools to perform the language arts and the desire to use those tools.

R·E·F·E·R·E·N·C·E·S

Anderson, R. C., E. H. Hiebert, J. A. Scott, and A. G. Wilkinson. *Becoming a Nation of Readers: The Report of the Commission on Reading.* Urbana, IL: Center for the Study of Reading, 1985.

Aulls, M. W. *Developing Readers in Today's Elementary School.* Boston, MA: Allyn and Bacon, 1982.

Bettelheim, B., and K. Zelan. *On Learning to Read: The Child's Fascination with Meaning.* New York: Vintage Books, 1982.

Blanchard, J. S., and G. E. Mason. "Using computers in content area reading instruction." *Journal of Reading* 29 (November 1985): 112–117.

Bond, G., and R. Dyxtra. "The cooperative research program in first-grade reading instruction." *Reading Research Quarterly,* Vol. 2 (Summer 1967): 5–142.

Brandt, R. "Doing better with less." *Educational Leadership* 40 (February 1983): 3.

Bridge, C. A., P. N. Winograd, and D. Haley. "Using predictable materials vs. preprimers to teach beginning sight words." *The Reading Teacher* 36 (May 1983): 884–991.

Britton, J., T. Burgess, N. Martin, A. McLeod, and H. Rosen. *The Development of Writing Abilities.* London, England: Macmillan Education Ltd., 1975.

Dammeyer, J. W. "Computer-assisted learning—or financial disaster." *Educational Leadership* 40 (February 1983): 7–9.

Durkin, D. *Children Who Read Early: Two Longitudinal Studies.* New York: Teachers College Press, 1966.

Finn, C. E. *What Works: Research About Teaching and Learning.* Washington, D.C.: U.S. Department of Education, Office of Educational Research and Improvement, 1986.

France, M. G., and J. W. Meeks. "Parents who can't read: What the schools can do." *Journal of Reading* 31 (December 1987): 222–227.

Froese, V., and S. B. Straw, eds. *Research in the Language Arts.* Baltimore, MD: University Park Press, 1981.

Gillet, J. W., and C. Temple. *Understanding Reading Problems: Assessment and Instruction.* Boston: Little, Brown, 1982.

Goldfield, B. A., and C. E. Snow. "Reading Books with Children: The Mechanics of Parental Influence on Children's Reading Achievement." In J. Flood, ed. *Promoting Reading Comprehension.* Newark, DE: International Reading Association, 1984.

Graves, D. H. *Donald Graves in Australia: "Children Want to Write."* Edited by R. D. Walshe. Exeter, NH: Heinemann Educational Books, 1982.

———. *Writing: Teachers and Children at Work.* Exeter, NH: Heinemann Educational Books, 1983.

Heald–Taylor, G. "Predictable literature selections and activities for language arts instruction." *The Reading Teacher* 41 (1987): 6–12.

McCracken, R. A., and M. J. McCracken. "Modeling is the key to sustained silent reading." *The Reading Teacher* 31 (January 1978): 406–408.

Martin, B. *Brown Bear, Brown Bear, What Do You See?* New York: Holt, Rinehart & Winston, 1983.

Melmed, A. S. "Productivity and technology in education." *Educational Leadership* 40 (February 1982): 4–6.

Neuman, S. B. "The home environment and fifth grade students' leisure reading." *Elementary School Journal* 86 (1986): 335–343.

O'Donnell, H. "Computer literacy, part I: An overview." *The Reading Teacher* 35 (January 1982): 490–494.

———. "Computer literacy, part II: Classroom application." *The Reading Teacher* 35 (February 1982): 614–617.

Resnick, M. B., J. Roth, P. M. Aaron, J. Scott, W. D. Wolking, J. J. Larsen, and A. B. Packer. "Mothers reading to infants: A new observational tool." *The Reading Teacher* 40 (May 1987): 888–894.

Smith, F. *Understanding Reading: A Psycholinguistic Analysis of Reading and Learning to Read.* New York: Holt, Rinehart & Winston, 1982.

Snow, C. E. "Literacy and language: Relationships during the preschool years." *Harvard Educational Review* 53 (May 1983): 165–189.

Swaby, B. *Teaching and Learning Reading* Boston: Little, Brown, 1984.

Thompson, B. J. "Computers in reading: A review of applications and implications." *Educational Technology* 20 (August 1980): 38–41.

Vukelich, C. "Parents are teachers: A beginning reading program." *The Reading Teacher* 31 (February 1978): 524–527.

15 Linking Learning with Instruction

FOCUS 1. What are the six pedagogical steps involved in diagnosis and
QUESTIONS   remediation?
2. What is the significance of planning in the diagnostic/remedial cycle?
3. What is the importance of assessing distance in remediation?
4. What factors should be taken into account when planning
   preinstructional experiences for children?
5. What is the continuous nature of the diagnostic/remedial process?

Throughout this text, the concepts of classroom diagnosis and remediation have been fully discussed. In Chapter 1, a definition of diagnosis was
presented, as follows.

> Diagnosis is an ongoing procedure that involves *continuous analy-
> sis* of students' behavior, *measurement* of samples of their behavior,
> *careful evaluation* of the measurement results, and *change* of in-
> structional strategies that results in positive change of students' be-
> havior.

The four major concepts of continuous analysis, measurement, evaluation, and change have been fundamental issues in each chapter of this
book. The concept of change is elaborated in relation to the definition of
remediation given in Chapter 6. Remediation is defined as:

> The application of intervention instructional strategies designed to
> provide learners with the skills, competencies and behaviors they
> need to improve their performance in a given area.

These definitions of diagnosis and remediation have informed the entire
content of this text. The two concepts express the instructional goals of
teachers with children who experience difficulty in learning to read. All
the information in this text has aimed to help teachers make appropriate
diagnoses, plan suitable programs, and provide instruction that moves
children closer to expected performance in reading. This process can be
divided into the following pedagogical behaviors.

- diagnosis (formal and informal)
- planning
- preinstruction
- instruction
- evaluation
- reinforcement

1. *Diagnosis.* This refers to the use of a combination of measures (observation, teacher-made tests, informal inventories, formal tests) to determine the performance levels and needs of children. Needs are prioritized in that skills are identified that, if learned, would result in the greatest improvement in performance. These skills become the targets of remediation.

2. *Planning.* After diagnosis has been made, instruction is planned. Planning involves the setting of instructional goals based on the needs of learners, and the choice of appropriate strategies and material to achieve those goals. The needs of children include not only academic reading skills, but also language, experiential, conceptual and emotional skills. Planning should take into account all identified needs that might affect reading performance.

3. *Preinstruction.* Planning is followed by preinstruction, the purpose of which is to lessen the distance between what children bring to a learning task and what the task demands. Preinstruction might be necessary in one or more of the following areas: vocabulary, phrases, language, concepts, content, skills. Depending on the distance between the task and the learners, the teacher chooses preinstructional strategies that will adequately prepare children for learning (Pearson 1985, Collins et al. 1980, Smith 1982).

4. *Instruction.* The preinstruction phase is followed by actual instruction, which is guided by factors that have been proven in research to affect learning positively. For example, sufficient time is provided for instruction; children are prepared for learning; direct instruction is provided; appropriate and meaningful activities are used; children's performance is continually monitored; and immediate, appropriate feedback is provided (Gage and Giaconia 1981, Rosenshine 1979). These factors are discussed at length in Chapter 6.

5. *Evaluation.* Throughout the lesson and upon completion of instruction, the pedagogical strategies and the students' responses to those strategies are evaluated. Evaluation involves the analysis of the effectiveness of the lesson. Skills that have been learned and that are lacking are identified. Instructional strategies are also analyzed. Those that are successful are noted, and those that are not are slated for modification. Plans for future instruction are made based on children's performance and needs.

6. *Reinforcement.* Finally, skills that require further practice are identified, and reinforcement is provided through worksheets, games, reading practice, repeated readings, or drills. Continual instruction and exposure to actual reading of print is provided in order to ensure the maintenance of skills.

These six instructional behaviors complete the diagnostic/remedial cycle. Implementation of all the steps allows teachers to provide appropriate learning environments for children, to teach so that children will learn or to link learning with instruction. These are not merely theoretical behaviors; they are practical factors that make teaching and learning more productive. The following application shows how the six factors related to the successful diagnosis and remediation of a third grade student, Robert H.

DIAGNOSIS

Robert H. is a nine-year-old third grader who is currently repeating the third grade. Observation shows Robert to be appropriately mature for his age. Physically, he is well developed. Actually, Robert is the leader of his class in athletic activities. He is a sociable child, and is very well liked and respected.

After four years of school, Robert's reading level is approximately 1.8 overall. Phonic skills are extremely weak. He has significant difficulty responding appropriately to long vowels, consonant combinations, and multisyllabic words. Many sight words are not known automatically. In addition, Robert's comprehension skills, both literal and inferential, are weak and underdeveloped. Recently, Robert has been very unmotivated toward reading, and continually makes efforts to avoid the task. His self-confidence is clearly undermined when he is involved in reading activities. Robert's parents are interested in his academic growth. However, print does not seem to play an important part in the home. Robert is rarely read to. He cannot identify his favorite story, book, or poem.

In order to gain specific information about Robert's intellectual performance and ability, formal tests were administered. The results follow:

- I.Q. (WISC): 98 (slightly below average I.Q.)
- Overall Reading (Durrell Analysis): 2.1
- Oral Reading (Durrell Analysis): 1.6
- Silent Reading (Durrell Analysis): 1.2 (comprehension very weak at 20 percent)
- Letter Names and Sounds (Durrell Analysis): 100% (above grade 1)
- Consonant Combinations (Durrell Analysis): Below first grade
- Short Vowels (Durrell Analysis): 100% (above grade 1)
- Long Vowels (Durrell Analysis): 1.8
- Oral Vocabulary (Durrell Analysis): 2.8
- Sight Vocabulary (Durrell Analysis): 1.6

Based on the results of both formal and informal diagnosis, Robert's teacher makes the following summary observations.

1. Robert's strengths are oral vocabulary and letter-sound relationships.

2. Robert's weaknesses are oral and silent reading, comprehension, sight vocabulary, long vowels, and consonant combinations.

These observations allow Robert's teacher to begin the second step, planning.

PLANNING

The teacher will use Robert's strengths and weaknesses to plan an instructional program. The long-term goals of instruction are identified as follows:

1. To improve Robert's literal and inferential comprehension skills.
2. To teach Robert the long sounds represented by the vowels.
3. To teach Robert a minimum of fifteen new sight words per week.
4. To teach Robert the sounds represented by the two-letter consonant blends.
5. To increase Robert's oral and silent reading levels by at least six months in each school year.
6. To build on Robert's already strong oral vocabulary.

Instructional sessions are planned around these general goals. Each reading period includes vocabulary development (sight and meaning), an oral and silent reading segment, specific skill instruction, and comprehension development.

Today, the reading selection that is being planned for Robert is "At Home on the Ranch" by Harrison Hawkins. The selection is found in *Kick Up Your Heels*, the Scott, Foresman Reading Series (1981) First Grade Primer.

[Page 1] What do you think a ranch is like today? It is not very much like the ranches in the old cowboy shows on TV. There are cowboys on the ranch of today. There are cowgirls too. Cowboys and cowgirls are called ranch hands. Many ranch hands have horses today. But they use trucks just as much as they use horses. The main work of the old-time ranch hand was looking after the cattle. Cattle need hay and good water. The old-time ranch hand let the cattle move across the ranch to find these things. Today ranch hands look after cattle. But they don't do it in the same way. They let the cattle stay where they are. They carry hay to the cattle in trucks.

[Page 2] The old-time cowboy let the cattle run all across the ranch. Today there are many trucks on the roads. The cattle could get hurt. So today ranch hands make their cattle stay behind fences. They must make sure all the fences and roads are in good shape.

[Page 3] On many days, ranch hands start work before breakfast. They ride out across the ranch. One of them will make a fire. He makes breakfast while the others work with the cattle. "Come and get it," he calls. The ranch hands are happy to stop working and have breakfast. They think eating outside is great.

[Page 4] Ranch people do not like cold, stormy weather. Old-time ranch hands just had to sit out the stormy weather. They could not get to their cattle. The cattle did not have enough to eat. Today ranch hands can use planes to get hay to their cattle. They can move across the ranch even if the roads are washed out.

[Page 5] The best time on the ranch is roundup time. The old-time cowboys would ride across the ranch looking for cattle. It took days and days for the roundup. Some cattle would always get away. The cowboys would ride after them. They would lasso the ones that ran off. Today ranch people know how to lasso too. But not many cattle get away. They stay all together behind the fences.

[Page 6] Old-time ranch hands would move the cattle down the trail after the roundup. One would call, "Move them out." The cattle would start down the road. The ranch hands would ride their horses. But it was a long walk for cattle. Today ranch people carry their cattle on trucks or trains. The cattle don't walk the long trail.

[Page 7] A ranch is not all work and no play. Work comes first. But the people on a ranch have good times after their work is over. They like to sit around a fire at night. They eat and show off with the lasso. They sing and think about the old-time cowboys.*

The selection is specifically chosen because it contains several skills that Robert needs. The factual content lends itself to the development of literal comprehension. In addition, the passage has a clear compare-contrast organization that may be used to develop convergent and divergent thought. The selection contains several vocabulary items that can be used for sight and meaning vocabulary extension. Finally, several phonic skills are reinforced in the passage. These include long vowels (e.g., *main, need, roads, eat, trail, shape, fire, use, plane ride*), and consonant combinations (e.g., *breakfast, great, stop, train, ranch*).

After the selection has been identified, the teacher assesses the distance between the content demands and what Robert can bring to the task in the areas of content, concepts, vocabulary, and skills. The results of the assessment follow.

Content: Medium to high.

Robert was born in the inner city. He has never been out of the city. When asked if he knew what a ranch was, he replied, "No." He knew who cowboys were; however, he said that cowboys lived long ago and that

---

*From Harrison Hawkins, "At Home on the Range," in *Kick Up Your Heels*, Scott, Foresman Reading Series, First Grade Reading, © Scott, Foresman and Company (1981), 147–154.

there were no real cowboys living today. His information relevant to ranches and cowboys is clearly very sparse.

Concepts: Medium to high.

Robert lacks many concepts that are important in the selection. These include the concepts of *ranch*, *roundup*, *trails*, *ranch hand*, and *lasso*. In addition, the comparison between "old-time" and "today" is not clear to him.

Vocabulary: Medium.

There are both sight and meaning vocabulary items that might be unknown. For example, words such as *ranch*, *behind*, *shape*, *fire*, *lasso*, *trail*, and *roundup* might not be understood or known by sight.

Skills: Medium.

Robert has difficulty with words containing long vowels and consonant combinations. In this passage, there are several words that require both of these skills. In addition, comprehension skills of factual recall and comparison/contast will be challenging for Robert.

In general, the passage will be of medium to great difficulty for Robert. This means that the teacher will instruct the selection directly, preteach significant content, concepts, and vocabulary, and emphasize appropriate skills for reinforcement and maintenance. Questioning will be used throughout in order to develop literal and inferential thinking. Modeling will be used as the need for it becomes evident. The teacher is now ready to move on to step three, preinstruction.

PREINSTRUCTION

Based on the analysis of distance, it is clear that Robert requires preinstruction—preparation in content, concepts, and vocabulary. First, content and concepts are provided. The teacher chooses two books: *Cowboys: What Do They Do?* by Carla Greene (Harper 1972) and *Cowboys*, by Marie and Douglas Gorsline (Random 1980). She reads sections from the books to Robert and discusses the pictures and illustrations. The discussion gives Robert necessary information that adds to his prior knowledge and provides a stronger base for comprehension.

Next, the teacher preinstructs seven vocabulary items and phrases chosen from the selection.

> *ranch:* meaning is vital to the passage; *ch* combination.
> *trails:* meaning important; *tr* consonant combination; *ai* vowel combination
> *shape:* *sh* consonant combination; final *e* construction
> *lasso:* meaning important
> *breakfast:* *br* consonant combination; *st* consonant combination
> *across:* high frequency word
> *while:* high frequency word; final *e* construction

All words are taught through the Manning (1980) 3 × 3 × I design. Phonic analysis and meaning are stressed. The following phrases are also taught.

ranch hands
down the *trail*
in good *shape*
with the *lasso*
start work before *breakfast*
across the ranch
while the others walk

The phrases, the title of the passage, and the illustrations on the first two pages are used to predict the content of the passage. Predictions are written by the teacher, and reading begins in order to check predictions.

INSTRUCTION

The teacher explains to Robert that the selection tells how ranches and cowboys of today compare to those of a long time ago. Robert is asked to share his own ideas. Robert is then shown the form in Figure 15.1. The teacher tells Robert that as he reads, he should look for ways in which ranches of long ago and today are the same and ways in which they are different. As he reads he will look for information to complete the chart.

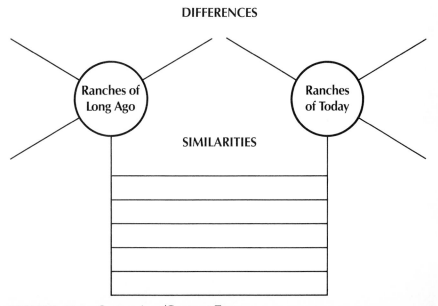

FIGURE 15.1   Comparison/Contrast Form

Robert is directed to read the first page orally. He is reminded to build clear pictures as he reads. As Robert reads, the teacher keeps a record of his errors, as in Figure 15.2. The teacher notes that besides failing to use phonic information, Robert also does not spontaneously correct himself even though his errors completely distort meaning. Each time Robert makes an error, the teacher asks, "Does that make sense?" Robert either corrects his errors independently or is shown how to do so by the teacher. The teacher makes self-monitoring and self-correction major long-term goals for Robert. These skills will be stressed in this and in future lessons.

The teacher monitors Robert's reading and uses echoic reading when he reads nonfluently. The following questions are asked after the page is read.

- Have you ever seen an old cowboy show on TV? Which one? What were ranches like on those shows? How do you think today's ranches might be different?
- Who are ranch hands? Why do you think cowboys and cowgirls are called ranch hands?
- What might trucks be used for today? How might trucks make life on today's ranches easier?

The next page is read orally in order to answer the last question. Again, an oral reading error record is kept, and questions such as the following are asked:

- What was the main job of the old-time ranch hand?
- How did the old-time ranch hands get cattle to water and food?
- How do today's ranch hands get cattle to the water and food they need?
- What things do both ranch hands do? What things are done differently?

○ WORD WAS	CHILD SAID
shows	sows (© with help)
there	they (© with help)
many	may (© with help)

○

© means "corrected."

FIGURE 15.2   Error Record Sheet

The similarities and differences are written down by the teacher. Self-monitoring is encouraged and any spontaneous attempt at self-correction is recognized and praised.

The following page is read silently. Robert is reminded to make clear pictures of each sentence. He is asked to read to find out another difference between today's ranches and old-time ranches. Robert does so and responds appropriately. His teacher is careful to commend him for his correct responses, to praise him for his accurate pictures, and to encourage him to continue his good performance. Because Robert reads the page at an appropriate rate and answers the questions freely, the teacher instructs him to read the following two pages silently. The teacher gives the following directions: "Read to find (1) one good thing that happens to ranch hands, (2) one big problem faced by old-time ranch hands, and (3) how today's ranch hands solve the problem." Robert reads the two pages. He is able to answer the first question, but misses the problem and solution. The teacher asks him to reread the last page, make clear pictures, and find a problem and a solution. Robert does so and answers the question correctly. The teacher notes that two full pages of silent reading without teacher intervention might be too much for Robert at this time.

The similarities and differences are noted and written down. Robert is asked to read the next page orally. Again, errors are noted, self-correction is encouraged, and echoic reading is used when necessary. Robert is asked to read the next page silently. Again, he is reminded to make clear pictures. When he is finished reading, the teacher presents him with two statements:

> Old-time ranch hands had to know how to lasso cattle. Knowing how to lasso is not as important to today's ranch hands.

Robert is asked to respond true or false to each statement and to support his answer by reading appropriate segments from the text. Robert likes this task and completes it well. Similarities and differences are once again noted. The next page is read silently to find another point of difference. He responds correctly. The teacher asks Robert to read the phrase "Move them out" in the same way as ranch hands would say it. The last page is read orally. The teacher discusses with Robert the things that ranch hands do for entertainment. At the end of the passage, the teacher asks Robert the following questions:

- Why do you think the author wrote the passage?
- Which type of life do you like best—the life of old-time ranch hands or the life of today's ranch hands? Why?
- Would you like to live on a ranch? Why or why not?

The comparison/contrast chart is now completed. It looks like the chart in Figure 15.3.

Skill instruction focuses on long vowels. Final *e* and double vowel constructions are reviewed. Robert is then presented with a sentence completion task that highlights long vowels, as follows:

1. Ranch hands must make sure that fences and roads are in good _____.
2. Ranch hands cook breakfast over the _____.
3. In the winter, cattle on old-time ranches might not have enough to _____.
4. Today ranch hands can use _____ to get food to cattle.
5. Ranch hands _____horses.
6. On old-time ranches, cattle moved down the _____ after the roundup.

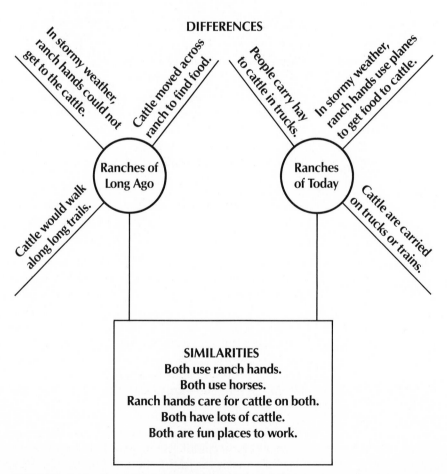

FIGURE 15.3   Completed Comparison/Contrast Form

7. Sometimes in the winter _____ are washed out.
8. In the evenings, ranch hands have a good _____ around the fire.

PLANES   RIDE   TRAIL
ROADS   TIME   SHAPE
FIRE   EAT

First, the teacher asks Robert to read each of the words. They discuss why each has the long vowel sound. He then completes each sentence with an appropriate word. Continual self-monitoring and self-correction are stressed.

Throughout the instruction, the skills of prediction, self-monitoring, visualization, fluency, and critical thinking are stressed. These are continuous processing skills—skills that are essential to appropriate understanding of language, both oral and written. At the end of the instructional segment, the teacher takes time to share with Robert her perceptions of his performance. She tells him those things he did well, those that showed improvement, and those that need work. After the discussion, she gives him the following note to take home.

Robert,
You did well today:

- reading a difficult passage
- predicting what might happen next
- reading closely for details.

You are improving in:

- reading smoothly
- making clear pictures as you read
- reading words with short vowel sounds
- reading words with beginning consonant combinations.

We will work hard to:

- read words ending with final *e*
- read words with double vowels
- recognize sight words quickly
- draw inferences.

Good job, Robert!

Notice how specific the comments are. Recognizing the importance of self-concepts to learning, the teacher uses this strategy to build Robert's self-confidence and self-esteem and to share his accomplishments with his family (Beane et al. 1980).

EVALUATION

After the session, the teacher evaluates the lesson. Both instructional strategies and student responses are assessed. The following conclusions are made based on the instruction.

- The material was challenging but of appropriate difficulty.
- Preinstruction is essential to Robert's success in reading. This is particularly true for challenging content.
- Vocabulary preinstruction was extremely beneficial.
- Visualization helps Robert to recall details during reading.
- Robert needs more practice reading factual material.
- Self-monitoring and self-correcting need to be ongoing areas of emphasis for Robert.
- Long vowels and consonant combinations still pose a problem for Robert. These skills require continual reteaching and reinforcement.
- Robert must be exposed to a variety of higher level questions in order to help him develop critical thought.
- The sight words *their, even, they,* and *were* need to be practiced to an automatic level.

The teacher uses the evaluation to activate step six, reinforcement.

REINFORCEMENT

In order to reinforce needed skills, the teacher uses the following activities.

1. Robert is given a list of twelve sight words. The words are taken from the passage he just read; however, they are sight words common to most written material. The words chosen are:

after	*while*
same	*they*
where	*enough*
across	*would*
could	*behind*
sure	*their*

He is timed on the reading of the words, and his time is recorded. He is told to practice reading the words until he can decrease his time by one half.

2. The teacher constructs the following passage.

It is fun to work on a ranch. Ranch hands do many *neat* things. They *ride* horses and take *care* of cattle. They *make* sure that cattle get enough to *eat*. They also keep *roads* and fences in good *shape*. Sometimes they *ride* along *trails*. When there is too much *rain* and *snow* to get through, they *use planes* to *take feed* to the cattle. They work *real* hard. At night, they sit around the *fire*, and sing, talk, and have lots of fun.

The passage includes several words with long vowels and sight words that Robert needs to practice. Robert is timed on his first reading of the passage. His time is recorded, and he is told to practice reading the passage until he can decrease his time by at least one third.

All the information in the evaluation section is used to plan further lessons. In this way, the diagnostic/remedial process begins again. Notice how the steps interlock and form a continuous cycle. The same cycle is applied to small group instruction. The strengths and needs of each student in the group are diagnosed. It is important to realize that all grouping is a compromise, and that no group is truly homogeneous. Strengths and needs are unique, although there are often overlapping categories. Children's reading performance is analyzed and a pattern of strengths and needs is identified for each child. If teachers practice keeping oral reading records on children for diagnosis, children's error trends become more evident. The strengths and weaknesses will help teachers to focus intense instruction on the appropriate children. To see how the process would apply to a group of students, consider the hypothetical reading group to which Robert H. might belong.

CLASSROOM APPLICATION

Number of children in group: 6

Grade: 3

Reading level: 1.6–2.4

Text used: *Kick Up Your Heels* (Scott, Foresman).

Strengths and Weaknesses of Children:

Child 1.   Strengths: Letter names and sounds, vocabulary (oral), short vowels.

              Needs: Consonant combinations, vowel combinations, long vowels, sight vocabulary, literal and inferential comprehension, motivation.

Child 2.   Strengths: Letter names and sounds, meaning vocabulary, literal and inferential comprehension, atttitude and motivation.

              Needs: Short and long vowels, consonant combinations, sight vocabulary, fluency.

Child 3.   Strengths: Fluency, sight vocabulary, short and long vowels, consonant combinations, decoding through
phonic analysis.

Needs: Literal comprehension, most forms of higher
level thinking (prediction, inferential thinking,
etc.), attitude, self-correction.

Child 4.   Strengths: Higher level thinking, automatic priming, drawing inferences and predicting, using picture
clues, self-correcting based on meaning, initial
single consonants, some short vowels (a, o, e),
meaning vocabulary, attitude.

Needs: Short vowels, long vowels, consonant combinations, sight vocabulary, fluency.

Child 5.   Strengths: Attitude, self-confidence, sight vocabulary,
phonic analysis, fluency, literal comprehension.

Needs: Inferential thinking, predicting, meaning vocabulary.

Child 6.   Strengths: Motivation, self-concept, letter names and
sounds, oral vocabulary, literal comprehension.

Needs: Fluency, self-monitoring and self-correction, automatic sight vocabulary, consonant and vowel
combinations, inferential comprehension, single vowels.

Group diagnosis leads to the following conclusions.

- All six children know letter-sound correspondences.
- Children 1, 3, 4, and 5 have mastered short vowels.
- Children 3 and 4 have mastered phonic analysis.
- Children 2, 4, and 6 have literal comprehension strengths.
- Children 2 and 4 have general comprehension strengths.
- Children 1, 2, 4, and 5 have complex phonic needs.
- Children 2 and 4 need to focus on phonic analysis, particularly vowel and consonant combinations, and on sight vocabulary.
- Children 3 and 5 need to focus on comprehension development, both literal and inferential.
- Children 1 and 6 need to focus on decoding and on comprehension.

A needs profile of the six children is presented in Figure 15.4. This diagnosis is valuable in planning because it provides teachers with specific diagnostic information and allows them to direct specific forms, amounts, and intensities of instruction to appropriate individuals.

During the planning phase, the instructional material is chosen. Distance is measured. The needs of the children are diverse. Some require preinstruction in concepts, content, and vocabulary. All students receive all preinstruction; however, content and concept information is

	Consonant Combinations	Vowel Combinations/Long Vowels	Sight Vocabulary	Literal Comprehension	Inferential Comprehension	Motivation	Short Vowels	Fluency	Higher Level Thinking	Attitude	Self-Correction	Prediction	Meaning Vocabulary
Child 1	✓	✓	✓	✓	✓	✓							
Child 2	✓	✓	✓			✓	✓						
Child 3				✓	✓			✓	✓	✓	✓		
Child 4	✓	✓	✓			✓	✓						
Child 5				✓							✓	✓	
Child 6	✓	✓	✓		✓	✓	✓		✓				

FIGURE 15.4   Needs Profile of Six Children

focused on children 1, 3, 5, and 6, because they require more comprehension activation. During vocabulary preinstruction phonic clues are focused on children 1, 2, 4, and 6. All children are urged to visualize the words. Intensive instruction is provided for all.

During instruction, literal and inferential questions are focused on students who need the specific skills. Modeling is used as it becomes necessary. Based on students' needs, each is encouraged to read smoothly, to make clear pictures, to predict, to self-correct, to focus on details, or to reread for clearer understanding. There is a reason for each question or direction provided for children, and that reason is based on individual student need. Skill instruction is differentiated in that skills that are beneficial to all children and are seldom overlearned are taught to the entire group. Most higher level comprehension skills fit into this category. Skills that are clearly known or not known are taught only to those who need them. Most phonic and structural skills fall in this category. At the end of the lesson, each child is told what was done well, what showed improvement, and what needed further work. Evaluation of the lesson and of student performance takes place in the same manner as was described for Robert H.

Children receive practice and reinforcement based upon their needs. Some might be practicing sight vocabulary, others working on timed readings, and others doing skill exercises or completing skill sheets. Reinforcement is individualized based on specific needs. The process ends and begins again. Supporting the entire instructional program is a strong recreational reading program that includes daily free reading, daily reading to children, reading of student composed books, and frequent motivation and competitions.

SUMMARY   This chapter has attempted to synthesize the content of this text into a manageable, meaningful, and practical whole. It demonstrates how actual instruction of individuals and groups can be affected by the principles of diagnostic/remedial teaching. These principles include diagnosis, planning, preinstruction, instruction, evaluation, and reinforcement.

Teaching reading can be one of the most difficult, time-consuming, and challenging tasks. It can also be one of the most rewarding and meaningful ones. As a teacher of reading, you have the opportunity to make a significant difference in the lives of children. Children can learn to read. It is a psychological imperative that you believe this. You, as a teacher, can help children learn to read. Your chances of success will increase if you focus on teaching children – on understanding their strengths, their needs, their interests, and their motivations. Best wishes to you in this endeavor.

R · E · F · E · R · E · N · C · E · S

Beane, J. A., R. P. Lipka, and J. W. Ludewig. "Synthesis of research on self-concept." *Educational Leadership* 38 (October 1980): 84–89.

Collins, A., J. S. Brown, and K. M. Larkin. "Inferences in Text Understanding." In R. J. Spiro, B. C. Bruce, and W. F. Brewer, eds. *Theoretical Issues in Reading Comprehension.* Hillsdale, NJ: Laurence Erlbaum, 1980.

Durrell, D. *Durrell Analysis of Reading Difficulty.* New York: The Psychological Corporation, 1980.

Gage, N. L., and R. Gianconia. "Teaching practices and student achievement: Causal connections." *New York University Education Quarterly* 12 (Spring 1981): 2–9.

Gorsline, M., and D. Gorsline. *Cowboys.* New York: Random House, 1980.

Greene, C. *Cowboys: What Do They Do?* New York: Harper & Row, 1972.

Manning, J. C. *Reading: Learning and Instructional Processes.* Geneva, IL: Paladin House, 1980.

Pearson, P. D. "Changing the face of reading comprehension instruction." *The Reading Teacher* 38 (April 1985): 724–738.

Rosenshine, B. "Content, Time, and Direct Instruction." In P. Paterson and H. Walberg, eds. *Research on Teaching, Concepts, Findings and Implications.* Berkeley, CA: McCutchan Publishing, 1979.

Smith, F. *Understanding Reading: A Psycholinguistic Analysis of Reading and Learning to Read.* New York: Holt, Rinehart & Winston, 1982.

Wechsler Intelligence Scale for Children—Revised. New York: The Psychological Corporation, 1974.

Appendix A

Award Winning Books

CALDECOTT AWARD WINNERS (1950–1988)

1950   *Song of the Swallows*, by Leo Poloti (Scribner)
1951   *The Egg Tree*, by Katherine Milhous (Scribner)
1952   *Finders Keepers*, by William Lipkind (Harcourt Brace Jovanovich)
1953   *The Biggest Bear*, by Lynd Ward (Houghton Mifflin)
1954   *Madeleine's Rescue*, by Ludwig Bemelmans (Viking)
1955   *Cinderella, or the Little Glass Slipper*, by Charles Perrault, translated by Marcia Brown (Scribner)
1956   *Frog Went A–Courtin*, by John Langstaff (Harcourt Brace Jovanovich)
1957   *A Tree Is Nice*, by Janice May Udry (Harper & Row)
1958   *Time of Wonder*, by Robert McCloskey (Viking)
1959   *Chanticleer and the Fox*, by Barbara Cooney (Crowell)
1960   *Nine Days to Christmas*, by Marie Hall Ets (Viking)
1961   *Baboushka and the Three Kings*, by Ruth Robbins (Parnassus)
1962   *Once a Mouse*, by Marcia Brown (Scribner)
1963   *The Snowy Day*, by Ezra Jack Keats (Viking)
1964   *Where the Wild Things Are*, by Maurice Sendak (Harper & Row)
1965   *May I Bring a Friend?* by Beatrice Schenk de Regniers (Atheneum)
1966   *Always Room for One More*, by Sorche McLeodhas (Holt, Rinehart & Winston)
1967   *Sam, Bangs & Moonshine*, by Evaline Ness (Holt, Rinehart & Winston)
1968   *Drummer Hoff*, by Barbara Emberley (Prentice-Hall)
1969   *The Fool of the World and the Flying Ship*, by Arthur Ransome (Farrar, Strauss & Giroux)
1970   *Sylvester and the Magic Pebble*, by William Steig (Windmill)
1971   *A Story—A Story*, by Gail Haley (Atheneum)
1972   *One Fine Day*, by Nonny Hogrogian (Macmillan)
1973   *The Funny Little Women*, by Arlene Mosel (Dutton)
1974   *Duffy and the Devil*, by Harve Zemach (Farrar, Straus & Giroux)
1975   *Arrow to the Sun*, by Gerald McDermott (Viking)
1976   *Why Mosquitoes Buzz in People's Ears*, by Verna Aardema (Dillon)
1977   *Ashanti to Zulu: African Traditions*, by Margaret Musgrove (Dial, 1977)
1978   *Noah's Ark*, by Peter Spier (Doubleday)
1979   *The Girl Who Loved Wild Horses*, by Paul Goble (Bradbury)
1980   *Ox-Cart Man*, by Donald Hall (Viking)
1981   *Fables*, by Arnold Lobel (Harper & Row)
1982   *Jumanji*, by Chris Van Allsburg (Houghton Mifflin)

1983   *Shadow*, translated by Blais Cendrars (Scribner)
1984   *The Glorious Flight*, by Marsha Brown (Scribner)
1985   *St. George and the Dragon*, by Margaret Hodges (Little, Brown)
1986   *The Polar Express*, by Chris Van Allsburg (Houghton Mifflin)
1987   *Hey, Al*, by Richard Egielski (Farrar, Straus & Giroux)
1988   *Owl Moon*, by Jane Yolen (Philomel)

CALDECOTT HONOR BOOKS

1982   *On Market Street*, by Arnold Lobel (Greenwillow)
1982   *Outside Over There*, by Maurice Sendak (Harper & Row)
1982   *A Visit to William Blake's Inn*, by Nancy Willard (Harcourt Brace Jovanovich)
1982   *Where the Buffaloes Begin*, by Olaf Baker (Warner)
1983   *A Chair for My Mother*, by Vera Williams (Greenwillow)
1983   *When I Was Young and in the Mountain*, by Cynthia Rylant (Dutton)
1984   *Little Red Riding Hood*, by Trina Schart (Holiday)
1984   *Ten, Nine, Eight*, by Molly Bang (Greenwillow)
1985   *Hansel and Gretel*, by Rika Lesser (Dodd, Mead)
1985   *Have You Seen My Duckling?* by Nancy Tafuri (Greenwillow)
1985   *The Story of Jumping Mouse*, by John Steptoe (Lothrop)

NEWBERY AWARD WINNERS (1950–1988)

1950   *The Door in the Wall*, by Marguerite de Angeli (Doubleday)
1951   *Amos Fortune, Free Man*, by Elizabeth Yates (Aladdin)
1952   *Ginger Pye*, by Eleanor Estes (Harcourt Brace Jovanovich)
1953   *Secret of the Andes*, by Ann Nolan Clark (Viking)
1954   *And Now Miguel*, by Joseph Krumgold (Crowell)
1955   *The Wheel on the School*, by Meindert DeJong (Harper & Row)
1956   *Carry On Mr. Bowditch*, by Jean Lee Latham (Houghton Mifflin)
1957   *Miracles on Maple Hill*, by Virginia Sorensen (Harcourt Brace Jovanovich)
1958   *Rifles for Watie*, by Harold Keith (Crowell)
1959   *The Witch of Blackbird Pond*, by Elizabeth George Speare (Houghton Mifflin)
1960   *Onion John*, by Joseph Krumgold (Crowell)
1961   *Island of the Blue Dolphins*, by Scott O'Dell (Houghton Mifflin)
1962   *The Bronze Bow*, by Elizabeth George Speare (Houghton Mifflin)
1963   *A Wrinkle in Time*, by Madeleine L'Engle (Farrar, Straus & Giroux)

1964 *It's Like This, Cat*, by Emily Cheney Neville (Harper & Row)
1965 *Shadow of a Bull*, by Maia Wojciechowska (Atheneum)
1966 *I, Juan de Pareja*, by Elizabeth Borten de Trevino (Farrar, Straus & Giroux)
1967 *Up a Road Slowly*, by Irene Hunt (Follett)
1968 *From the Mixed-Up Files of Mrs. Basil E. Frankweiler*, by E. L. Konigsburg (Atheneum)
1969 *The High King*, by Lloyd Alexander (Holt, Rinehart & Winston)
1970 *Sounder*, by William Armstrong (Harper & Row)
1971 *Summer of the Swans*, by Betsy Byars (Viking)
1972 *Mrs. Frisby and the Rats of NIMH*, by Robert O'Brien (Atheneum)
1973 *Julie of the Wolves*, by Jean George (Harper & Row)
1974 *The Slave Dancer*, by Paula Fox (Bradbury)
1975 *M. C. Higgins the Great*, by Virginia Hamilton (Macmillan)
1976 *The Grey King*, by Susan Cooper (Atheneum)
1977 *Roll of Thunder, Hear My Cry*, by Mildred Taylor (Dial)
1978 *Bridge to Terabithia*, by Katherine Paterson (Crowell)
1979 *The Westing Game*, by Ellen Raskin (Dutton)
1980 *A Gathering of Days*, by Joan Blos (Scribner)
1981 *Jacob Have I Loved*, by Katherine Paterson (Crowell)
1982 *A Visit to William Blake's Inn: Poems for Innocent and Experienced Travelers*, by Nancy Willard (Harcourt Brace Jovanovich)
1983 *Dicey's Song*, by Cynthia Voight (Atheneum)
1984 *Dear Mr. Henshaw*, by Beverly Cleary (Dell)
1985 *The Hero and the Crown*, by Robin McKinley (Greenwillow)
1986 *Sarah, Plain and Tall*, by Patricia Mac Lachlan (Harper & Row)
1987 *The Whipping Boy*, by Sid Flieschman (Greenwillow)
1988 *Lincoln: A Photo Biography*, by Russell Freedman (Clarion)

INTERNATIONAL READING ASSOCIATION CHILDREN'S BOOK AWARDS

1975 *Transport 7–14–R*, by T. Degens (Viking)
1976 *Dragon Wings*, by Laurence Yep (Harper & Row)
1977 *A String in the Harp*, by Nancy Bond (Atheneum)
1978 *A Summer to Die*, by Lois Lowry (Houghton Mifflin)
1979 *Reserved for Mark Anthony Crowder*, by Alison Smith (Dutton)
1980 *Words by Heart*, by Ouida Sebestyen (Little, Brown, 1980)
1981 *My Own Private Sky*, by Delores Beckman (Dutton)
1982 *Goodnight Mister Tom*, by Michelle Magorian (Harper & Row)
1983 *The Dark Angel*, by Meredith Ann Pierce (Little, Brown)
1984 *Ratha's Creature*, by Claire Bell (Atheneum)
1984 *Badger on the Barge*, by Janni Howker (Greenwillow, 1985)

AMERICAN BOOK AWARDS

1969 *Journey from Peppermint Street*, by Meindert De Jong (Harper & Row)
1970 *A Day of Pleasure: Stories of a Boy Growing Up in Warsaw*, by Isaac Bashevis Singer (Farrar, Straus & Giroux)
1971 *The Marvelous Misadventures Of Sebastian*, by Lloyd Alexander (Dutton)
1972 *The Slightly Irregular Fire Engine*, by Donald Barthelme (Farrar, Straus & Giroux)
1973 *The Farthest Shore*, by Ursula Le Guin (Atheneum)
1974 *The Court of Stone Children*, by Eleanor Cameron (Dutton)
1975 *M. C. Higgins, the Great*, by Virginia Hamilton (Macmillan)
1976 *Bert Breen's Barn*, by Walter D. Edmonds (Little, Brown)
1977 *The Master Puppeteer*, by Katherine Paterson (Crowell)
1978 *The View from the Oak*, by Judith and Herbert Kohl (Scribner)
1979 *The Great Gilly Hopkins*, by Katherine Paterson (Crowell)
1980 *A Gathering of Days*, by Joan Blos (Scribner)
1980 *A Swiftly Tilting Planet*, by Madeleine L'Eengle (Dell)
1981 *The Night Swimmers*, by Betsy Byars (Delacorte)
1981 *Oh, Boy! Babies*, by Alison Cragin Herzig and Jane Lawrence Mali (Little, Brown)
1982 *Westmark*, by Lloyd Alexander (Dutton)
1982 *Words by Heart*, by Ouida Sebestyen (Bantam, 1987)
1982 *A Penguin Year*, by Susan Bonners (Delacorte)
1982 *Outside Over There*, by Maurice Sendak (Harper & Row)
1982 *Noah's Ark*, by Peter Spier (Doubleday)
1983 *Homesick: My Own Story*, by Jean Fritz (Putnam)
1983 *Marked by Fire*, by Joyce Carol Thomas (Avon)
1983 *Chimney Sweeps*, by James Cross Giblin (Crowell)
1983 *Dr. De Soto*, by William Steig (Farrar, Straus & Giroux)
1983 *Miss Rumphius*, by Barbara Cooney (Viking)
1983 *A House Is a House for Me*, by Mary Ann Hoberman (Puffin)

CORETTA SCOTT KING AWARDS

1970 *Martin Luther King, Jr.: A Man of Peace*, by Lillie Patterson (Garrard)
1971 *Black Troubador: Langston Hughes*, by Charlemae Rollins (Rand McNally)
1972 *17 Black Artists*, by Elton C. Fax (Dodd, Mead)
1973 *I Never Had It Made*, by Jackie Robinson as told to Alfred Duckett (Putnam)
1974 *Ray Charles*, by Sharon Bell Mathis (Crowell)
1975 *The Legend of Africana*, by Dorothy Robinson (Johnson)
1976 *Duey's Tale*, by Pearl Bailey (Harcourt Brace Jovanovich)
1977 *The Story of Stevie Wonder*, by James Haskins (Lothrop)

1978   *Africa Dream*, by Eloise Greenfield (Crowell)
1979   *Escape to Freedom*, by Ossie Davis (Viking)
1979   *Something on My Mind*, by Nikki Grimes (Dial)
1980   *The Young Landlord*, by Walter Dean Myers (Viking)
1980   *Cornrows*, by Camille Yarbrough (Coward, McCann & Geohegan)
1981   *This Life*, by Sidney Poitier (Knopf)
1981   *Beat the Story Drum, Pum—Pum*, by Ashley Bryan (Atheneum)
1982   *Let the Circle Be Unbroken*, by Mildred Taylor (Dial)
1983   *Mother Crocodile: An Uncle Amadou Tale from Senegal*, by Rose Guy (Delacorte)
1983   *Sweet Whispers, Brother Rush*, by Virginia Hamilton (Philomel)
1983   *Black Child*, by Peter Mugabane (Knopf)
1984   *Everett Anderson's Goodbye*, by Lucille Clifton (Holt, Rinehart & Winston)
1984   *My Mama Needs Me*, by Mildred Pitts Walker (Lothrop)
1985   *Motown and Didi*, by Walter Dean Myers (Viking)

Appendix B

High Interest–Low Vocabulary Materials

Series (by publisher)	Grade Level	Interest Level
Bantam Books (New York)		
Choose Your Own Adventure (53 books: Fantasy adventures)	4	Intermediate to Junior High
Time Machine (8 books: Time-travel adventures)	4	Intermediate to Junior High
Bowmar/Nobel Publishers (Oklahoma City, OK)		
Starting Line (4 programs: cats, racing, wheels, kickoff)	Pre-K–2	Intermediate to Junior High
The Monster Series (10 books in 2 series)	1–3	Series 1: K–1 Series 2: 2–4
Gold Dust Books (3 copies of six different titles)	2.0–2.9	Intermediate
Reading Incentive Program (Titles on horses, motorcycles, slot car racing, dune buggies)	3–5	Intermediate through secondary
Children's Press (Chicago, IL)		
The Mania Books (13 books on cowboys, dogs, volcanoes, etc.)	1	K–5
Ready, Set, Go (18 books)	1.1–3.0	1–6
New True Books (147 content-area readers)	2.0–3.4	K–4
Curriculum Associates, Inc. (North Billerica, MA)		
Fable Plays for Oral Reading (Aesop's Fables)	1–3	1–5
Fairy Tale Plays for Oral Reading	1–3	2–5
Primary Plays for Oral Reading	2	2–4
Dale Seymour Publications (Palo Alto, CA)		
Giant First Start Readers (8 stories)	1	Primary
Troll First–Start Easy Readers (10 titles)	1	Primary
I Can Read and Write Books (6 titles)	1–2	2–5
Stamp–A–Story Minibooks (30 story poems on reproducible pages)	1–3	1–5
Thunder the Dinosaur Books (10 books)	2	K–4
Easy–To–Read Mysteries (10 books)	3	2–4
The Mr. Books and Little Miss Books	4	3–6

Series (by publisher)	Grade Level	Interest Level
E.M.C. Publishing (St. Paul, MN)		
Science Readers (3 high-interest kits)	2–3	2–9
Fiction Readers	3	4–9
(4 sets on ghosts, danger, courage, science fiction, etc.)		
Biography content:		
Superstars	3	3–9
Headliners 1 & 2	4	4–12
Center Stage	4	4–12
Black American Athletes	5	4–12
Man Behind the Bright Lights	5	4–12
Easy–To–Read Classics	3–6	7–12
Monsters and Mysteries	5–6	4–12
Fearon Education (Belmont, CA)		
Jim Hunter Books	1.0–3.0	6–12
(16 spy adventures)		
Galaxy 5	1.8–3.0	6–12
(6 titles: fantasy adventures)		
Specter	1.9–2.8	7–12
(mystery, weird events, psychic phenomena)		
Pacemaker Classics	2.0–2.9	5–12
(12 titles: adaptations of classic novels)		
Quicksilver Books	3.0–4.5	4–8
(10 books on crime fighters, fads, dogs, cars, horses, etc.)		
Fastback Books	4.5–5.0	7–12
(6 sets: mystery, crime, sports, horror, romance)		
Garrard Publishing Co. (Champaign, IL)		
Begin to Read with Duck and Pig (4 books)	1	K–4
Old Witch Books (15 readers)	1–2	K–4
Dolch Series:		
First Reading Books	1	1–4
(17 titles: Use the Dolch Basic Sight Words)		
Basic Vocabulary Books (17 titles)	2	1–6
Folklore of the World Books	3	2–8
Pleasure Reading Books	4	3–6
(Rewritten classics)		
Globe Book Company (New York)		
Journeys to Fame (22 biographies)	2–3	7–12

Series (by publisher)	Grade Level	Interest Level
Legends for Everyone (24 titles: "Rip Van Winkle," "Paul Bunyon," "Calamity Jane," etc.)	3	6–8
Holt, Rinehart & Winston (New York)		
Accent on Reading Skills	2–8	4–8
Modern Curriculum Press (Cleveland, OH)		
Double Scoop Readers (12 books about trolls and cows)	Pre-K–1.5	1–3
Primary Sight-Word Readers (28 books: animals, friendship, and adventure)	Pre-K–1	1–2
Beginning to Read Books (More than 100 titles)	Pre-K–2	1–3
Bright Idea Books (16 books: at the zoo, flying to the moon, in the air, etc.)	1–2	1–3
See How I Can Read Books (6 books)	1–2	2–3
The High Action Treasure Chest	2.1–3.5	4–Adult
Traditional Tales Books (6 Classic folk tales)	3.0–4.9	4–6
Scholastic, Inc. (Jefferson City, MD)		
Sprint Libraries (More than 50 titles)	1–5	4–6
Science Research Associates, Inc. (Chicago, IL)		
Development Reading Laboratory Kit 1 (6 levels of books)	1.2–2.2	2–6
Super A, Super AA, Super BB Kits. (Comic book readers: comedy, mystery, spy stories, science fiction)	2–5	4–8
Pilot Library Series (Excerpts from children's literature: 72 titles)	3–8	2–12

Appendix C

Magazines for Children

Animals
(Ages 8–16; articles about animals throughout the world)
Massachusetts Society for the Prevention of Cruelty to Animals
350 S. Huntington Ave., Boston, MA 02130

Boys Life
(Ages 8–18; fiction and nonfiction; focus on outdoor skills and hobbies)
Boy Scouts of America
1325 Walnut Hill Lane, Irving, TX 75038

Chickadee
(Ages 4–8; nature magazine)
The Young Naturalist Foundation
59 Front St. E., Toronto, ON M5E 1B3

Child Life
(Ages 6–12; stories, articles, puzzles; focus on good health habits)
P.O. Box 10681, Des Moines, IA 10681

Children's Digest
(Ages 8–10; suspense and humor; articles on health, sports, nutrition)
P.O. Box 10681, Des Moines, IA 50381

Children's Playmate Magazine
(Ages 8–10; stories and poems; focus on good health, exercise, safety)
P.O. Box 1068, Des Moines, IA 50381

Cobblestone
(Ages 8–14; fiction and nonfiction; focus on American history)
20 Grove Street, Peterborough, NH 03458

Cricket
(Ages 6–12; excellent children's fiction, folklore, nonfiction, poetry)
P.O. Box 2670, Boulder, CO 80322

Current Science
(Ages 12–16; recent developments in science and health)
Xerox Education Publications
4343 Equity Dr., Columbus, OH 43228

Ebony JR
(Ages 6–12; stories and articles that focus on black experiences)
Johnson Publishing Company, Inc.
820 S. Michigan Ave., Chicago, IL 60605

The Electric Company Magazine
(Ages 6–10; educational puzzles, games, jokes)
200 Watt Street, P.O. Box 2924, Boulder, CO 80322

Highlights for Children
(Ages 2–12; stories, word games, puzzles, craft activities)
2300 West Fifth Ave., P.O. Box 269, Columbus, OH 43272

Humpty Dumpty's Magazine
(Ages 4–6; simple puzzles, crafts, stories)
P.O. Box 10681, Des Moines, IA 50381

Jack and Jill
(Ages 6–8; stories about health, exercises, safety, nutrition)
P.O. Box 10681, Des Moines, IA 50381

Junior Scholastic
(Ages 12–16; current information on U.S. and world affairs)
P.O. Box 644, Lyndhurst, NJ 07071–9985

Muppet Magazine
(Ages 8–14; games, jokes, cartoons, articles, interviews with celebrities)
P.O. Box 300, Patterson, NJ 12563

National Geographic World
(Ages 8–13; articles and pictures about wild animals, pets, hobbies)
17th and M Streets N.W., Washington, D.C. 20036

National Wildlife
(Ages 10–16; wild animals, conservation, ecology)
National Wildlife Federation
1412 16th Street N.W., Washington, D.C. 20036

Odyssey
(Ages 8–14; astronomy and outer space)
P.O. Box 92788, Milwaukee, WI 53202

Penny Power
(Ages 8–14; consumer information)
P.O. Box 2878, Boulder, CO 80322

Plays
(Ages 3–12; one-act plays and programs)
120 Boylston St., Boston, MA 02116

Ranger Rick
(Ages 5–12; science, conservation, nature study)
National Wildlife Federation
1412 16th Street N.W., Washington, D.C. 20036

Scienceland
(Ages 5–8; science and nature topics)
501 Fifth Ave., New York, NY 10017–6165

Stone Soup: A Magazine by Children
(Ages 5–12; stories, book reviews, poems, and art by children)
Children's Art Foundation
915 Cedar Street, Santa Cruz, CA 95060

Appendix D

Predictable Print Books

Adams, Pam. *This Old Man* (Grossett and Dunlap, 1974)

Aliki. *Go Tell Aunt Rody* (Macmillan, 1974)

———. *Hush Little Baby* (Prentice–Hall, 1968)

Bailian, Lorna. *Where in the World Is Henry?* (Bradbury, 1972)

Barohas, Sarah. *I Was Walking Down the Road* (Scholastic, 1975)

Bauer, Caroline. *My Mom Travels a Lot* (Frederick Warne, 1981)

Bayer, Jane. *My Name Is Alice* (Dutton, 1984)

Boynton, Sandra. *But Not the Hippopotamus* (Simon & Schuster, 1982)

Brett, Jan. *Annie and the Wild Animals* (Houghton Mifflin, 1985)

Brown, Margaret Wise. *Four Fur Feet* (William R. Scott, 1961)

———. *Goodnight Moon* (Harper & Row, 1947)

———. *Home for a Bunny* (Golden Press, 1956)

———. *Where Have You Been?* (Scholastic, 1952)

Carle, Eric. *The Grouchy Ladybug* (Crowell, 1975)

———. *The Mixed Up Chameleon* (Crowell, 1975)

———. *The Very Hungry Caterpillar* (Collins World, 1969)

———. *Papa, Please Get the Moon for Me* (Picture Book Studio, 1986)

———. *What's For Lunch?* (Putnam, 1982)

Charlip, Remy. *Fortunately* (Parents' Magazine Press, 1964)

———. *What Good Luck! What Bad Luck!* (Scholastic, 1969)

de Regniers, Beatrice. *How Joe the Bear and Sam the Mouse Got Together* (Parents' Magazine Press, 1965)

———. *The Little Book* (Henry Z. Walck, 1961)

———. *May I Bring a Friend?* (Atheneum, 1972)

Duff, Maggie. *Rum Pum Pum* (Henry Z. Walck, 1972)

Duke, Kate. *Guinea Pig A–B–C* (Dutton, 1983)

———. *Guinea Pigs Far and Near* (Dutton, 1984)

Emberly, Ed. *Klippity Klop* (Little, Brown, 1974)

Ets, Marie Hall. *Elephant in a Well* (Viking, 1972)

Galdone, Paul. *Henny Penny* (Scholastic, 1968)

———. *The Little Red Hen* (Scholastic, 1973)

————. *The Three Bears* (Scholastic, 1972)

————. *The Three Billy Goats Gruff* (Seabury Press, 1973)

————. *The Three Little Pigs* (Seabury Press, 1970)

Ginsburg, Mirra. *Across the Stream* (Puffin Books, 1985)

Goss, Janet and Jerome Harste. *It Didn't Frighten Me* (Willowwisp, 1985)

Howard, Jane. *When I'm Sleepy* (Dutton, 1985)

Hutchins, Pat. *Good Night Owl* (Macmillan, 1972)

————. *Rosie's Walk* (Macmillan, 1968)

Keats, Ezra Jack. *Over in the Meadow* (Scholastic, 1971)

Kraus, Robert. *Whose Mouse Are You?* (Collier Books, 1970)

Langstaff, John. *Over in the Meadow* (Harcourt Brace Jovanovich, 1957)

Lobel, Arnold. *A Treeful of Pigs* (Greenwillow, 1979)

————. *On Market Street* (Scholastic, 1981)

————. *The Rose in My Garden* (Greenwillow, 1984)

Martin, Bill. *Brown Bear, Brown Bear* (Holt, Rinehart & Winston, 1970)

————. *Fire! Fire! Said Mrs. McGuire* (Holt, Rinehart & Winston, 1970)

Mayer, Mercer. *If I Had . . .* (Dial Press, 1968)

————. *Just For You* (Golden Press, 1975)

————. *Just Grandma and Me* (Golden Books, 1983)

McGovern, Ann. *Too Much Noise* (Scholastic, 1967)

Ormerod, Jan. *Young Joe* (Lothrop, 1986)

Polushkin, Maria. *Mother, Mother, I Want Another* (Crown, 1978)

Preston, Edna. *Where Did My Mother Go?* (Four Winds Press, 1978)

Sarnoff, Jane. *That's Not Fair* (Scribner, 1980)

Seeger, Paul. *Abiyoyo* (Macmillan, 1986)

Sendak, Maurice. *Pierre* (Harper & Row, 1962)

————. *Where the Wild Things Are* (Harper & Row, 1963)

Seuss, Dr. *Oh, The Thinks You Can Think* (Random House, 1975)

————. *The Cat in the Hat* (Random, 1957)

Spier, Peter. *The Fox Went Out on a Chilly Night* (Doubleday, 1961)

Tolstoy, Alexei. *The Great Big, Enormous Turnip* (Franklin Watts, 1968)

Welber, Robert. *Goodbye, Hello* (Pantheon, 1974)

Wildsmith, Brian. *Cat on the Mat* (Toronto: Oxford Press, 1982)

————. *Toot Toot* (London: Oxford Press, 1984)

Williams, Barbara. *Never Hit a Porcupine* (Dutton, 1977)

Appendix E

Nonfiction Books and Series

NONFICTION BOOKS

Adler, David A. *All Kinds of Money* (Watts, 1984) (Primary)

———. *Base Five* (Harper & Row, 1975) (Primary)

Aliki. *Corn Is Maize: The Gift of the Indians* (Harper & Row, 1976) (Primary)

———. *Digging Up Dinosaurs* (Harper & Row, 1981) (Primary)

———. *Feelings* (Greenwillow, 1984) (Primary)

———. *Fossils Tell of Long Ago* (Harper & Row, 1983) (Primary)

———. *Mummies Made in Egypt* (Harper & Row, 1979) Primary–Intermediate)

———. *My Five Senses* (Harper & Row, 1972) (Primary)

———. *My Visit to the Dinosaurs* (Harper & Row, 1969) (Primary)

Anderson, Norman, and W. R. Brown. *Ferris Wheels* (Pantheon, 1983) (Intermediate)

———. *Fireworks: Pyrotechnics on Display* (Dodd, Mead, 1983) (Intermediate)

———. *Halley's Comet* (Dodd, Mead, 1981) (Intermediate)

———. *Lemurs* (Dodd, Mead, 1984) (Primary–Intermediate)

Bealer, Alex W. *Only the Names Remain: The Cherokees and the Trail of Tears* (Harper & Row, 1972) (Intermediate)

Berger, Gilda. *Apes in Fact and Fiction* (Watts, 1980) (Intermediate)

———. *Aviation* (Watts, 1980) (Intermediate)

———. *Easter and Other Spring Holidays* (Watts, 1983) (Intermediate)

———. *Mountain Worlds: What Lives There* (Putnam, 1978) (Intermediate)

Bernstein, Joanne, and S. V. Gullo. *When People Die* (Dutton, 1977) (Primary)

Bertoldi, Joyce. *Cherry Berry: Cherry Growing, Harvesting and Processing* (Colorado: Observation Research Pub., 1983) (Primary–Intermediate)

Blumberg, Rhoda. *The First Travel Guide to the Bottom of the Sea* (Lothrop, 1983) (Intermediate)

———. *The First Travel Guide to the Moon* (Scholastic, 1984) (Intermediate)

————. *The First Travel Guide to the Moon: What to Pack, How to Go and What to See When You Get There* (Scholastic, 1980) (Primary–Intermediate)

————. *Sharks* (Watts, 1976) (Intermediate)

————. *The Truth About Dragons* (Scholastic, 1980) (Intermediate)

Branley, Franklyn. *Air Is All Around You* (Harper & Row, 1984) (Primary)

————. *Comets* (Harper & Row, 1984) (Primary)

————. *Dinosaurs, Asteroids and Superstars* (Harper & Row, 1982) (Intermediate)

————. *Feast or Famine: The Energy Future* (Harper & Row, 1980) (Intermediate)

————. *Halley: Comet* (Lodestar Books, 1983) (Upper Intermediate)

————. *Jupiter: King of the Gods, Giant of the Planets* (Lodestar Books, 1981) (Upper Intermediate)

————. *Mysteries of Outer Space* (Lodestar Books, 1984) (Intermediate)

————. *The Planets in Our Solar System* (Harper & Row, 1983) (Primary)

Charlip, Remy, and M. Beth. *Handtalk: An ABC of Finger Spelling and Sign Language* (Scholastic, 1980) (Primary)

Cobb, Vicki. *The Secret Life of Hardware: A Science Experiment Book* (Harper & Row, 1982) (Intermediate)

————. *The Secret Life of School Supplies* (Harper & Row, 1981) (Intermediate)

Cole, Joanna. *A Bird's Body* (Morrow, 1982) (Primary)

————. *Cars and How They Go* (Harper & Row, 1983) (Primary)

————. *A Cat's Body* (Morrow, 1982) (Primary)

————. *A Chick Hatches* (Morrow, 1976) (Primary)

————. *A Dog's Body* (Morrow, 1985) (Primary)

————. *A Frog's Body* (Morrow, 1980) (Primary)

————. *How You Were Born* (Morrow, 1984) (Intermediate)

————. *A Snake's Body* (Morrow, 1981) (Primary)

Crosby, Alexander. *Tarantulas* (Walker, 1981) (Primary–Intermediate)

Dowden, Ann. *Look at a Flower* (Harper & Row, 1963) (Intermediate)

————. *From Flower to Fruit* (Harper & Row, 1984) (Upper Intermediate)

————. *State Flowers* (Harper & Row, 1978) (Intermediate)

Facklam, Margery and Howard. *The Brain: Magnificent Mind Machine* (Harcourt Brace Jovanovich, 1982) (Intermediate)

Fenner, Carol. *Gorilla, Gorilla* (Random House, 1973) (Primary)

Gans, Roma. *Rock Collecting* (Harper & Row, 1984) (Primary)

————. *When Birds Change Their Feathers* (Harper & Row, 1980) (Primary)

Gustafson, Anita. *Burrowing Birds* (Lothrop, 1981) (Intermediate)

————. *Some Feet Have Noses* (Lothrop, 1983) (Intermediate)

Hodgman, Ann, and R. Djabbaroff. *Skystars: The History of Women in Aviation* (Atheneum, 1981) (Intermediate)

Kurelek, William. *A Prairie Boy's Summer* (Houghton Mifflin, 1975) (Intermediate)

————. *A Prairie Boy's Winter* (Houghton Mifflin, 1984) (Primary)

Lasky, Kathryn. *Dollmaker* (Scribner, 1981) (Intermediate)

Lauber, Patricia. *Journey to the Planets* (Crown, 1982) (Intermediate)

————. *Life on a Giant Cactus* (Garrard, 1974) (Primary–Secondary)

————. *Too Much Garbage* (Garrard, 1974) (Primary–Intermediate)

————. *Seeds: Pop Stick Glide* (Crown, 1981) (Primary)

Lerner, Carol. *Flowers of a Woodland Spring* (Morrow, 1979) (Primary)

————. *On the Forest Edge* (Morrow, 1978) (Primary)

————. *Pitcher Plants: The Elegant Insect Traps* (Morrow, 1983) (Primary–Intermediate)

————. *Seasons of the Tallgrass Prairie* (Morrow, 1980) (Primary)

Meltzer, Milton. *All Times, All Peoples: A World History of Slavery* (Harper & Row, 1980) (Intermediate)

————. *The Chinese Americans* (Harper & Row, 1980) (Intermediate)

————. *The Human Rights Book* (Farrar, Straus & Giroux, 1979) (Intermediate)

————. *The Jewish Americans: A History in Their Own Words* (Harper & Row, 1982) (Intermediate)

Moche, Dinah L. *The Astronauts* (Random House, 1979) (Primary)

Morrison, Velma. *Going on a Dig* (Dodd, Mead, 1981) (Intermediate)

Rockwell, Anne. *Boats* (Dutton, 1982) (Early Primary)

————. *Cars* (Dutton, 1984) (Early Primary)

Scott, Jack D. *Alligator* (Putnam, 1984) (Intermediate)

————. *Discovering the American Stork* (Harcourt Brace Jovanovich, 1976) (Primary)

————. *Discovering the Mysterious Egret* (Harcourt Brace Jovanovich, 1978) (Primary)

————. *The Fur Seals of Pribilof* (Putnam, 1983) (Intermediate)

————. *Moose* (Putnam, 1980) (Intermediate)

————. *Orphans from the Sea* (Putnam, 1982) (Intermediate)

Selsam, Millicent, and Joyce Hunt. *A First Look at Animals with Backbones* (Walker, 1978) (Primary)

————. *A First Look at Cats* (Walker, 1981) (Primary)

————. *A First Look at Dinosaurs* (Walker, 1982) (Primary)

————. *A First Look at Rocks* (Walker, 1984) (Primary)

————. *A First Look at Spiders* (Walker, 1983) (Primary)

————. *A First Look at Whales* (Walker, 1980) (Primary)

Simon, Seymour. *Computer Sense, Computer Nonsense* (Harper & Row, 1984) (Primary–Intermediate)

————. *How to Be a Space Scientist in Your Own Home* (Harper & Row, 1982) (Intermediate)

————. *Look at the Night Sky: An Introduction to Star Watching* (Penguin, 1979) (Intermediate)

————. *The Moon* (Scholastic, 1984) (Primary)

————. *Poisonous Snakes* (Scholastic, 1981) (Primary–Intermediate)

————. *Secret Clocks: The Time Senses of Living Things* (Penguin, 1981) (Primary–Intermediate)

————. *Tropical Saltwater Aquariums: How to Set Them Up and Keep Them Going* (Viking, 1976) (Intermediate)

Watson, Jane. *Alternate Energy Sources* (Watts, 1979) (Intermediate)

NONFICTION SERIES

The Let's–Read–and–Find–Out Series (Primary), by Paul Showers (Thomas Crowell, 1968)
  Hear Your Heart
  How Many Teeth
  Your Skin and Mine
  A Drop of Blood
  Look At Your Eyes

The Five Senses Series (Primary), by M. Rius, J. M. Parramon, and J. J. Puig (Barron's, 1985)
  Smell
  Sight
  Hearing
  Taste
  Touch

Art Series (Primary), by Ibi Lepscky (Barron's, 1984)
  Pablo Picasso
  Leonardo da Vinci

Art Series: Art Start—Very First Books for Children (Primary), by Ernest Raboff (Doubleday, 1982)
  Pablo Picasso
  Paul Klee
  Marc Chagall

Animal Lives Series (Primary) (Children's Press International, 1982)
  Life of a Rabbit
  Life of a Dog
  Life of a Cat
  Life of a Hamster

Usborne Introductions (Intermediate), by Chisholm and Beeson (London: Usborne Publishing/Oklahoma: E. D. C. Publishing, 1984)
  Introduction to Biology
  Introduction to Physics
  Introduction to Chemistry

Mysteries and Marvels Series (Primary–Intermediate) (London: Usborne Publishing/Oklahoma: E. D. C. Publishing)
  Animal World
  Ocean Life
  Plant Life
  Insect Life
  Reptile World
  Bird Life

Science Experiments You Can Eat (1972) (Primary–Intermediate) and *More Science Experiments You Can Eat* (1979) (Primary–Intermediate), by Vicki Cobb (Harper & Row)

Women of Our Time Series (Upper Primary–Intermediate) (Viking Penguin/Puffin Books)
  Dorothea Lange: Life Through the Camera, by Milton Meltzer (1986)
  Babe Didrikson: Athlete of the Century, by R. R. Knudson (1986)
  Eleanor Roosevelt: First Lady of the World, by Doris Faber (1986)
  Diana Ross: Star Supreme, by James Haskins (1985)
  Betty Friedan: A Voice for Women's Rights, by Milton Meltzer (1986)
  Martina Navratilova: Tennis Power, by R. R. Knudson (1986)

The Brown Paper School Book Series (Little, Brown)
  Only Human, by Neill Bell (1983)
  Make Mine Music! by Tom Waltner (1981)
  The Book of Where, by Neill Bell (1982)
  Everybody's A Winner, by Tom Schneider (1976)
  Word Words, by Cathryn Kaye (1985)
  The Book of Think, by Marilyn Burns (1976)
  Beastly Neighbors, by Mollie Rights (1981)
  Math for Smarty Pants, by Marilyn Burns (1982)

      Good for Me, by Marilyn Burns (1978)
      This Book Is About Time, by Marilyn Burns (1976)

Childhood of Famous Americans (Macmillan, Aladdin Books)
      Susan B. Anthony, by Helen Monsell (1960)
      Henry Ford, by Hazel Aird and Catherine Ruddiman (1960)
      Benjamin Franklin, by Augusta Stevenson (1983)
      Thomas A. Edison, by Sue Guthridge (1959)
      Daniel Boone, by Augusta Stevenson (1961)
      John Fitzgerald Kennedy, by Lucy Post Frisbee (1964)
      Betsy Ross, by Ann Weil (1983)
      Molly Pitcher, by Augusta Stevenson (1983)
      Clara Barton, by Augusta Stevenson (1962)

Random House All–About Books
      Animal Journeys, by Theodore Rowland–Entwistle (1987)
      War and Weapons, by Brian Williams (1987)
      The Age of Steam, by Jonathan Rutland (1987)
      Built to Speed, by Jonathan Rutland (1987)
      Knights and Castles, by Jonathan Rutland (1987)

Biography

Adler, David. *Our Golda: The Story of Golda Meir* (Watts, 1982) (Primary)

Adoff, Arnold. *Malcolm X* (Harper & Row, 1972) (Primary–Intermediate)

Bacon, Margaret. *I Speak for My Slave Sister: The Life of Abby Kelley Foster* (Harper & Row, 1974) (Intermediate)

Cross, Helen. *The Real Tom Thumb* (Scholastic, 1980) (Primary–Intermediate)

Davis, Ossie. *Escape to Freedom: The Story of Young Fredrick Douglass* (Viking, 1978) (Upper Intermediate)

De Kay, James T. *Meet Martin Luther King Jr.* (Random House, 1969) (Upper Primary–Intermediate)

Fox, Mary. *Jane Goodall: Living Chimp Style* (Dillon, 1981) (Upper Primary–Intermediate)

Franchere, Ruth. *Cesar Chavez* (Harper & Row, 1973) (Primary–Intermediate)

———. *The Wright Brothers* (Harper & Row, 1972) (Primary–Intermediate)

Fritz, Jean. *The Double Life of Pocahontas* (Putnam, 1983) (Intermediate)

———. *George Washington's Breakfast* (Putnam, 1969) (Primary–Intermediate)

———. *Homesick: My Own Story* (Putnam, 1982) (Primary–Intermediate)

————. *The Man Who Loved Books* (Putnam, 1981) (Upper Intermediate)

Glickman, William. *Winners on the Tennis Court* (Avon, 1979) (Upper Intermediate)

Greenfield, Eloise. *Mary McLeod Bethune* (Harper & Row, 1974) (Primary–Intermediate)

————. *Paul Robeson* (Harper & Row, 1975) (Primary–Intermediate)

————. *Rosa Parks* (Harper & Row, 1973) (Primary–Intermediate)

Hamilton, Virginia. *W. E. B. DuBois: A Biography* (Harper & Row, 1972) (Intermediate)

Harris, Janet. *The Woman Who Created Frankenstein: A Portrait of Mary Shelley* (Harper & Row, 1979) (Upper Intermediate)

Haskins, James. *From Lew Alcindor to Kareem Abdul–Jabbar* (Lothrop, 1979) (Upper Intermediate)

————. *George McGinnis: Basketball Superstar* (Hastings, 1978) (Upper Intermediate)

————. *I'm Gonna Make You Love Me: The Story of Diana Ross* (Dell, 1982) (Upper Intermediate)

————. *Leaders of the Middle East* (Enslow, 1984) (Intermediate)

————. *Lena Horne* (Putnam, 1983) (Upper Intermediate)

————. *The Life and Death of Martin Luther King* (Lothrop, 1977) (Intermediate)

————. *Magic: A Biography of Earvin Johnson* (Enslow, 1982) (Intermediate)

————. *Scott Joplin: The Man Who Made Ragtime* (Stein and Day, 1980) (Upper Intermediate)

Jackson, Jessie. *Make a Joyful Noise Unto The Lord: The Life of Mahalia Jackson, Queen of Gospel Singers* (Harper & Row, 1974) (Intermediate)

Krementz, Jill. *A Very Young Circus Flyer* (Knopf, 1979) (Intermediate)

————. *A Very Young Dancer* (Knopf, 1976) (Intermediate)

————. *A Very Young Gymnast* (Knopf, 1978) (Intermediate)

————. *A Very Young Rider* (Knopf, 1977) (Intermediate)

————. *A Very Young Skater* (Knopf, 1979) (Intermediate)

Latham, Jean L. *Anchor's Aweigh: The Story of David Glasgow Farragut* (Harper & Row, 1968) (Intermediate)

————. *Elizabeth Blackwell: Pioneer Woman Doctor* (Garrard, 1975) (Primary–Intermediate)

————. *Rachel Carson: Who Loved the Sea* (Garrard, 1973) (Primary)

Lee, Betsy. *Judy Blume's Story* (Dillon, 1981) (Intermediate)

Levinson, Nancy. *Contributions of Women: Business* (Dillon, 1981) (Upper Intermediate)

Litsky, Frank. *Winners in Gymnastics* (Avon, 1979) (Intermediate)

Richardson, Nigel. *Martin Luther King* (David and Charles Pub, 1983) (Intermediate)

Author Index

Subject Index